THE WUHAN LOCKDOWN

THE WUHAN LOCKDOWN

GUOBIN YANG

Columbia University Press

New York

Columbia University Press
Publishers Since 1893
New York   Chichester, West Sussex
cup.columbia.edu

Library of Congress Cataloging-in-Publication Data
Names: Yang, Guobin, author.
Title: The Wuhan lockdown / Guobin Yang.
Description: New York : Columbia University Press, 2022. |
Includes bibliographical references and index.
Identifiers: LCCN 2021027456 (print) | LCCN 2021027457 (ebook) |
ISBN 9780231200462 (hardback) | ISBN 9780231200479 (trade paperback) |
ISBN 9780231553636 (ebook)
Subjects: LCSH: Quarantine—China—Wuhan—History—21st century. |
COVID-19 (Disease)—China—Wuhan.
Classification: LCC RA655 .Y36 2022 (print) | LCC RA655 (ebook) |
DDC 362.1962/4140951212—dc23
LC record available at https://lccn.loc.gov/2021027456
LC ebook record available at https://lccn.loc.gov/2021027457

Cover image: © Gan Junchao. Wuhan People's Hospital, March 5, 2020.
Cover design: Lisa Hamm

To Lan, Jeff, and our families in China

CONTENTS

PREFACE

The novel coronavirus (COVID-19) outbreak in the city of Wuhan hit China at a time of political and cultural complacency.[1] The national propaganda machine had already been gearing up to celebrate the "full establishment of a moderately wealthy society." Back in the early 2000s, President Xi Jinping's predecessors had set 2020 as the year of achieving this goal. Xi had also made it his priority. Establishing a "moderately wealthy society" is linked to Xi's grandiose political agenda of achieving "the rejuvenation of the great Chinese nation."[2] In the service of this agenda, Chinese official media had created a facade of harmony and prosperity.

Wuhan is the crossroads of China. A metropolis with a population of about 11 million, it lies at the center of China's most important railway and highway lines. China's longest and busiest river, the mighty Yangzi, meanders through Wuhan, where it is joined by the Han River. In the busiest travel season of the year, the week before the Lunar New Year's Day, about 15 million travelers pass through Wuhan, mostly by train. Imagine the shock of cutting off all transportation in and out of Wuhan with a notice of only half a day. This was what happened when the Wuhan municipal government announced on the night of January 22 that beginning at 10:00 a.m. the following day, the city would be strictly locked down.

It was only two days before the most important festival of the year, and the city was already full of festivities. The lockdown changed everything. What transpired in the first few days of the lockdown was like scenes taken straight from Hollywood apocalypse movies. Streets with no signs of people or traffic. Homeless cats scavenging in abandoned construction sites. Crowds panic-shopping in grocery stores. Self-quarantined residents peeping out from behind their apartment windows. Gated communities with their gates sealed to block people from leaving or entering. Death, sorrow, and anger filling the air and social media.

Wuhan's lockdown would eventually last for seventy-six days and turn out to be an event of world-historical proportions. For better or worse, it lives up to Wuhan's prominent place in modern Chinese history. The 1911 Revolution, which overthrew China's last imperial dynasty and established the Republic of China, started in Wuchang, which is part of Wuhan.[3] In the Asian Pacific theater in World War II, after Nanjing fell to Japanese invaders in 1937, the republican government relocated temporarily to Wuhan. Although Wuhan eventually fell to the Japanese, the Battle of Wuhan from June 11 to October 27, 1938, became a critical turning point in China's War of Resistance against Japan by inflicting the heaviest casualties on Japanese troops in the first period of the war.[4]

Wuhan was also a center of political action in Mao Zedong's Cultural Revolution (1966–1976). In the early days of the Cultural Revolution, on July 16, 1966, the seventy-two-year-old Mao made a public performance of his revolutionary (and physical) vigor by joining Wuhan's eleventh annual swimming competition across the Yangzi River. Photographs of his swim, printed in national newspapers, became icons of the Cultural Revolution. A year later, in the famous Wuhan Incident in July 1967, two leading members of Mao's Cultural Revolution group who were visiting Wuhan from Beijing were beaten up and abducted by Wuhan's conservative Red Guards. Mao, who was making a secret visit to Wuhan, was forced to fly to Shanghai at 2:00 a.m. on July 21, escorted by air force fighters. As the China historians Roderick MacFarquhar and Michael Schoenhals write, Mao's lieutenants back in Beijing, who urged him to leave Wuhan, "may well have had in mind not only the Wuhan incident of October 11, 1911, which led to the unravelling and finally the collapse of the Qing dynasty, but also the arrest of Chiang Kai-shek in Xi'an in 1936 by one of his generals."[5]

What happened in Wuhan in 2020? Why? How did the state and citizens manage the crisis? How did they interact? How did residents cope with daily life and work?

* * *

I followed the lockdown in Wuhan and the COVID-19 pandemic in China from my home in Philadelphia. I have relatives and friends in China. Although they were mostly not in Wuhan, they voluntarily confined themselves to their homes and experienced many of the same fears and hardships as residents in Wuhan. While American media reports spotlighted China's draconian approach to containing the coronavirus,[6] often noting that such measures could happen only in an authoritarian regime, what moved me most was the resilience and grit of hundreds of millions of ordinary Chinese amid all the hardships. COVID-19 was an unprecedented catastrophe. It upset the lives of a nation overnight. The certainty of everyday life dissolved into quicksand. Little was known about this virus in January 2020. No one knew how long the lockdown would last.

Yet as the lockdown passed from days to weeks, the city endured. Medical workers made great sacrifices, working to exhaustion even though they initially did not have adequate protective gear. Volunteers across the nation mobilized to provide assistance to Wuhan. Ordinary residents, including my eighty-year-old-plus parents, "fought" the virus by strictly following stay-at-home orders. They lived through COVID-19 and the lockdown with a silent courage that filled me with awe. They suffered more than many others physically and psychologically because they were among the first to be exposed to this novel virus. They had no other people to learn from and no time to prepare for it. Yet they accepted the new routine of home quarantine with resignation and grace. Deep down in their hearts, they harbored a sense of humility toward life. For them, life is the most precious thing one can have in this world, and one must do everything possible to preserve it. It is precious not only, not even primarily, to the self. If one's life is just one's own, that would be simple, but, no, it is also part of one's family. As one diarist wrote,

> In the days of the lockdown, I have particularly strong feelings about the following:
>
> My body does not belong to me alone, but to the whole family.
>
> No one in the family has a body that belongs only to the individual person. It all belongs to the whole family. May the whole family be safe and happy![7]

In later months, when I witnessed the indifference of some of my American compatriots toward mask wearing and stay-at-home orders and, indeed, the arrogance of those who denied the existence of the virus when tens of thousands were dying from it, I could not help pondering why. Don't Americans conventionally and proudly talk about placing a higher value on human life than other countries, especially China? If that's the case, why did so many people put up with the astronomical number of COVID fatalities? Was it because Americans value small individual freedoms (such as the freedom not to wear a face mask) more than human life? Or was it just that terrible political leadership caused so many Americans to doubt public-health guidelines?[8]

In the face of the sacrifices made by so many ordinary people, mere attempts to theorize look rather pale. Their extraordinary experiences cannot be distilled into a few propositions without losing their sheer wealth and human touch. Their concreteness defies abstraction. My primary goal in this book is to tell the human stories in Wuhan against the background of their complex historical and social contexts.

* * *

Recent Chinese history has seen several national disasters. The Sichuan earthquakes in 2008 caused more than 87,000 deaths and tens of thousands of injuries. The SARS (severe acute respiratory syndrome) outbreak in 2003 caused 349 deaths on the mainland and 299 deaths in Hong Kong. These disasters devastated cities and towns, wreaking havoc in the lives of millions. None of them, however, left the wealth of personal and social records that we have seen emerge from the COVID-19 pandemic. It was nothing less than a miracle that so many people in Wuhan and other parts of China (and later the world) took it upon themselves to write about their daily lives and the lives of others. Some chronicled their experiences with audio recordings, videos, photographs, and other artistic forms. Many wrote diaries. Often shared on China's popular social media platforms, these personal writings reached publics at home and abroad. Sociologists call these social records "personal documents," "life records," and "documents of life."[9] They are unparalleled primary sources for capturing the visceral and emotional dimensions of ordinary people and their daily lives. The voices in these records have a special power of their own, and I try here to tell these people's stories in their own voices as much as I can. Only in this way is it possible to convey the grace and resilience of humanity under duress.

I started my research in late January 2020, as soon as Wuhan was shut down. For hours every day, I would be glued to the web, browsing social media sites and reading the numerous accounts online. As I read them, I archived what I believe were the most valuable records of the human experiences of the Wuhan lockdown—the personal documents and life records produced by ordinary people and published and shared on social media. They came in the following varieties:

- Lockdown diaries
- Published interviews, oral histories, and other stories of individuals who joined volunteer networks to provide support to residents in Wuhan
- Text, image, video, and audio files about everyday life and volunteerism
- Postings and reader comments on WeChat, Sina Weibo, and several video-streaming sites
- Poems, cartoons, and paintings about the pandemic
- Media reports from both state-affiliated and commercial media
- Policy documents and speeches by party leaders at local and central levels

- Transcripts of daily press conferences held locally and nationally
- COVID-related communication and public announcements produced by communities and government agencies and posted on their WeChat public accounts

These records make up the primary sources for the stories I tell. The most important of these sources are the "lockdown diaries" (*fengcheng riji* 封城日记) posted on WeChat, Sina Weibo, and other social media platforms. I followed a dozen diarists on these platforms, regularly searched for others using the Chinese search engine Sogou, and saved them as I read them.

The term *lockdown diaries* was initially a specific reference to diaries about the Wuhan lockdown. As more cities were shut down in China and residents elsewhere started posting their own online diaries, lockdown diaries also came to be called *pandemic diaries* (*yiqing riji* 疫情日记). I use these two terms interchangeably. From late January to November 2020, I collected more than 6,000 diary entries, including about 500 entries written by seventeen authors from different world cities, such as Sydney, Melbourne, Vancouver, Paris, Milan, London, Philadelphia, and New York.[10] Also posted on WeChat and Weibo, such overseas pandemic diaries enjoyed the same circulation as diaries produced inside China.

Although the vast majority of these writings were called "diaries" by their authors, my collection also includes a sample of diary-like social media posts. These posts were put up as regularly as if the authors were keeping a conventional diary; a few authors explicitly called their social media posts "diaries." In this sense, daily social media posts are the diaries of the social media age.

For practical and methodological reasons, I conducted only a small number of remote interviews with diarists cited in this book, usually to clarify questions I had about their diaries. In practical terms, it was impossible to travel to Wuhan or China during the period I was writing this book. In methodological terms, for the stories I try to tell, diaries are a superior form of data to interviews. Although the public nature of lockdown diaries and the prevalence of internet censorship meant that their authors necessarily wrote with more caution than usual, the diaries were nevertheless products of the moment. They are the ideal documents for understanding the visceral feelings, thoughts, and activities of the diarists caught in their own daily struggles. What they wrote about reflected the contingencies of the day. They wrote today with no idea of what was to come the next day. It is difficult for retrospective interviews to retain that sense of immediacy and urgency. Even more importantly, since COVID-19 became a pandemic and some Western politicians and media began to blame it on China, the Wuhan lockdown became and continues to be a politically touchy topic in China. Chinese official discourse attempts to produce grand narratives of triumph and bravery. Patriotic sentiments are soaring. Under these circumstances, it is hard for human subjects not to be influenced by the dominant official narratives. Their retrospective accounts may be colored by postpandemic politics. The diaries were also likely to be colored by the politics of their moment, but that is precisely the kind of politics that a historical-sociological account of the event ought to capture.

Reading the diaries of Wuhan lockdown was more than a research experience; it was deeply personal. The diaries do more than shed light on the lives of the individuals who produced them. They offer insights into the social environment in which my own and my in-laws' families in China lived. My parents never once complained to me about their stay-at-home daily routines even when the pandemic was at its worst in China. They always made light of it because they did not want me to worry about them—as is true of so many immigrants, our loved ones back in the "home-land" silently bear the emotional burdens of our diasporic living—but from the diaries and the news I read, I know how many hardships they must have been going through. The diaries helped me understand what was happening on the ground. My own stay-at-home experiences in Philadelphia would have been different without these diaries, for the stories of distant others brought me closer to my family and friends in both China and Philadelphia.

Of the fifteen diarists I contacted, eight responded to my queries. Four agreed to let me use their real names in this book. The other four preferred pseudonyms. For other diarists cited in this book, I use real names if they are already well-known public figures, such as Fang Fang. Otherwise, I use pseudonyms to protect their anonymity. Both to protect diarists' anonymity and because many diaries have since disappeared from the web, I do not provide the original web addresses for diaries cited in this book. Instead, I have used the following citation format: So-and-So's Diary, followed by the date of the entry—for instance, "Guo Jing's Diary, February 7, 2020." All translations of the diaries and social media posts quoted in this book are mine. Chinese names mentioned follow the Chinese convention of family name first, given name second. All the original social media texts, diaries, and user comments are saved in my personal archive.

* * *

Chapter 1 documents the events in the twenty days before the lockdown, showing that a bureaucratic preoccupation with the facade of prosperity may have delayed policy responses to the coronavirus outbreak. Chapter 2 traces the structural transformation of Chinese internet culture and civil society and analyzes the longer-term conditions underlying the policy lapses in handling the pandemic. Zooming into the minutiae of a people's war on COVID-19, chapter 3 shows how the state mobilized resources to implement policies, while citizens resorted to moral acts of cooperation and protest.

Chapters 4 to 9 examine the impact of the lockdown on ordinary life and how citizens individually and collectively engaged in action or civic inaction to fight the pandemic and its secondary disasters, such as racism and discrimination. Chapter 4 takes diary writing as a parable of ordinary people's endurance during the lockdown, showing that individuals managed daily life and personal emotions by writing and sharing online diaries. Chapter 5 offers snapshots of the lives of patients and health-care workers in hospitals, where the fire and thunder of everyday struggle came more from mundane humans than from the divine gods after which the hospitals are auspiciously named. Chapter 6 tells stories of voluntary citizen organizing, highlighting the role of women and the ubiquitous use of social media. Through a case study of an anticensorship protest, chapter 7 shows how citizens subverted censorship through the creative remixing of digital forms. If censorship aims to maintain the positive facade of the Chinese web by controlling what can or cannot appear on it, the anticensorship protest discussed in this chapter thwarted the censorship of a story by keeping it "alive" through an online relay. Taking on the difficult topic of nationalism, chapter 8 finds that the global spread of COVID-19 gave nationalism new wrinkles. In the face of racism abroad, old-fashioned patriotism was rekindled at home, and wolf-warrior diplomats learned the style of global populism. Chapter 9 recounts the story of Li Wenliang, a young physician who lost his life to COVID but was turned into a national martyr through virtual memorialization. It examines the narrative contestation over collective memories of the Wuhan lockdown and explores questions of digital ephemerality and permanence.

As I reflect on the many stories recounted in this book, it dawns on me that they amount to a long series of dramatic scenes and characters. In the conclusion, I highlight broader themes underlying these many scenes and discuss why a "scenic" view, so to speak, promises an open, multilayered, and dialogic understanding of the Wuhan lockdown and of politics and society more broadly.

ACKNOWLEDGMENTS

My first thanks go to all the lockdown diarists cited and not cited in this book. Among the cited diarists, Chu Ma 楚马, Guo Jing 郭晶, Li Xiaoyan 李晓燕, Second Uncle 二叔, Tao Tao 桃桃, Wu Shangzhe 吴尚哲 (known online as Ah-Nian 阿念), Xuan Yue 炫悦, and Ye Qing 叶青 responded to my queries about their diaries. Many other diarists could not be reached and are referred to by pseudonyms. Their lockdown diaries were not only the most valuable life documents for this study but also sources of strength for my own year-long stay-at-home life in Philadelphia.

Several friends who are residents in Wuhan provided valuable help as I did my research and wrote: Dr. Wu Shiwen 吴世文 and Dr. Wang Qiong 王琼 of Wuhan University and Dr. Gu Yu 谷羽 of Hubei University.

Professor Gail Hershatter and Professor Elizabeth J. Perry read the entire manuscript and offered insightful and encouraging comments for revision. I am extremely grateful to them for their longtime mentorship and support and for being such radiant models of scholar-teachers. I am indebted to two anonymous reviewers for their detailed and thoughtful comments, which helped me improve the manuscript. I also thank Ruoyun Bai, Thomas Chen, Bingchun Meng, Elaine Yuan, and Mengyang Zhao for sharing their thoughts and feedback on parts of the manuscript.

Preliminary ideas in parts of this book were presented at a virtual talk at Zhejiang University at the invitation of Professor Wu Fei 吴飞, at a virtual roundtable discussion organized by Professor Jack Qiu of the National University of Singapore, and at a symposium organized by Professor Zhongdang Pan of the University of Wisconsin at Madison and Professor Wei Lu 韦路 of Zhejiang University. I am grateful to them for their longtime support and friendship.

Other friends and colleagues in China who provided help and support in one way or another are Cai Xiongshan 蔡雄山, Chen Jingxi 陈静茜, Lei Weizhen 雷蔚真, Li Kun 李堃, Pan Ji 潘霁, Shi Anbin 史安斌, Shi Zengzhi 师曾志, Wang Zhe 王喆, Wu Xinwei 吴欣慰, Xu Jinghong 徐敬宏, Yan Wei 闫薇, Clara Chuan Yu, Zhang Junfang 张军芳, Zhao Yunze 赵云泽, Zhou Baohua 周葆华, Zhou Kui 周逵, and Zou Jun 邹军.

Scholars at the Social Science Research Council, especially Michael Miller, Alondra Nelson, and Jason Rhody, invited me to contribute an essay to its Mediated Crisis series and gave me an opportunity to write about lockdown diaries in Wuhan.

At the University of Pennsylvania, colleagues in the Annenberg School, the Department of Sociology, the Center for the Study of Contemporary China, Penn Global, and Perry World House have been supportive of my work in more ways than I can mention here. I especially thank Dean John Jackson at the Annenberg School, Dean Steven Fluharty of the School of Arts and Sciences, and Associate Dean Emily Hannum of the School of Arts and Sciences for their unwavering support. For intellectual, professional, and moral support, I am grateful to Rosemary Clark-Parsons, Jacques deLisle, Irmo Elo, Jasmine Erdener, Elisabetta Ferrari, Amy Gadsden, Avery Goldstein, Yue Hou, Klaus Krippendorf, Annette Lareau, Neysun Mahboubi, Scott Moore, Emilio Parrado, Monroe Price, Joseph Turow, Barbie Zelizer, and Tukufu Zuberi. In tracking down references, Sharon Black and Min Zhong at the Library of the Annenberg School provided help in the most timely fashion. I am indebted to all the superb staff at the Annenberg School for their help and support but especially to Richard Cardona, Margie Chavez, Elizabeth Cooper, Alison Feather, Altagracia Felix, Kelly Fernandez, Emma Fleming, Marley Goldschmidt, Rose Halligan, Patricia Lindner, Joanne Murray, Deborah Porter, Julie Sloane, Andres Spillari, and Ashton Yount.

My research and writing benefited from conversations with many PhD students at the University of Pennsylvania, especially students in my two doctoral seminars in the 2020–2021 academic year, The Performance Society and Qualitative Ways of Knowing. Special thanks are owed to Pris Stephanie Nasrat for introducing me to the literature on critical aunty studies and to Haolin (Angela) Deng, Victoria Zhang, and Kyle (K. C.) Legacion for their valuable research assistance.

I thank Clare Foster and Ruichen Zhang for inviting me to contribute an article, "Online Lockdown Diaries as Endurance Art," to their guest-edited special issue of AI & Society (https://doi.org/10.1007/s00146-020-01141-5), which gave me the opportunity to explore the meaning of endurance in lockdown diaries. Parts of the article are incorporated into chapter 4 in this book. I am most grateful to Gan Junchao 甘俊超 for permission to use his photograph on the book cover.

I am honored to publish a third book with Columbia University Press. Colleagues there, especially Jennifer Crewe, associate provost and director of the press, have long supported my work. I am deeply indebted to Eric Schwartz and Lowell Frye, who showed enthusiasm for this project early on and shepherded it through the review and publication processes with great skill and good humor. I am most grateful to my copyeditor Annie Barva for her superb editing of the manuscript and to my supervising editor Michael Haskell for helping to keep the production on schedule. Lisa Hamm was most helpful on matters of design and art used in this book.

I alone am responsible for any flaws this book may have.

I owe my deepest gratitude to my families in China and Philadelphia. My parents, siblings, and in-laws in China are exemplars in managing the hardships of the COVID pandemic. They are my heroes. My brother, Xinbin, always a sharp observer of China's media scene, queried me often as I worked on this manuscript. My wife, Lan, has always been the strongest supporter of all my writing projects, but I owe her even more than ever for her love, care, and sacrifice as I worked on this book. She felt more acutely than I the extreme stress of the pandemic—when we were unable to go out as we used to, I could at least devote my time to writing. We were lucky that our son, Jeff, was around much of the time, on the phone when not in person. His good humor brightened our days.

1

FESTIVITIES, INTERRUPTED

APOCALYPSE

Guo Jing 郭晶 is a social worker and feminist activist. In 2017, Guo started a legal-aid hotline for female professionals who were victims of workplace discrimination. She wrote seventy-six diary entries spanning the seventy-six days of the Wuhan lockdown.[1] In one of them, she wrote that she had just moved to Wuhan in November 2019 and did not have many friends there. I first read her diary postings on a WeChat public account run by a friend of hers. The first four days of her diary, January 23–26, 2020, appeared as one long essay under the title "The Diary of a Woman Who Lives Alone in the Locked-Down City of Wuhan." The essay has more than 100,000 views, the sign of a viral posting on WeChat. Her entries from January 27 to 29 were posted under the title "Rediscovering My Place in an Isolated City," and those from January 30 to February 1 were under "Living with a Sense of Helplessness."

Guo Jing's diary postings in the first days of the lockdown convey her reactions to the lockdown and the sense of apocalypse she felt. January 23, 2020: "When I got up this morning and saw news of the lockdown, I was at a loss what to do. I couldn't anticipate what this would all mean, how long the lockdown would last, and what preparations I should make."[2] January 24, 2020:

The world is so quiet it's scary. I live alone. It's only from the occasional sound in the corridor of the building that I can make sure there are still people around.

I have a lot of time to think about how to survive. I have no resources or social networks within the establishment. If I'm ill, I will be as unlikely as many other ordinary people to receive medical treatment. Therefore, one of my goals is not to let myself get sick. I must persevere in doing physical exercise. To survive, I will need the necessary food, and therefore I must find out about the supply situation of daily necessities. . . . Therefore, today, I went out.[3]

January 27, 2020: "Today the weather was a bit clearer, but still cloudy. After walking for only a few steps outside, I saw two cats on a pile of debris. We stared at each other. This scene has such a strong sense of apocalypse. When we stared at each other, it seemed as if there were only me and the two cats left in this world."[4]

As Guo Jing's diary attests, the initial period of the lockdown in Wuhan was full of apocalyptic scenes that were recorded in diaries, videos, photographs, drawings, and social media postings. Guo's friend Xiao Meili 肖美丽, also a feminist activist, documented some of the best-known and most tragic scenes in a series of ink-and-water paintings that she posted on Sina Weibo. On February 12, 2020, she posted a painting of a ninety-year-old woman named Xu Meiwu 徐美武 sitting next to the bed of her sixty-four-year-old son, who was seriously ill with the coronavirus and was on a ventilator in an ICU. Xiao Meili's annotation on this painting used Xu Meiwu's own words: "After I got to the hospital, I found there was no bed vacancy at all. We could only see the doctor. The crowds were like mountains and oceans. People rubbed against one another. I stood in a line for my son's CT test, and our number [in the queue] was 297. I remember this number clearly because it gave me a feeling of despair."[5]

Xiao wrote in her Weibo posting that it must have been extremely painful for the elderly woman to stand in a long line for her son, yet the mainstream media were praising her for her motherly love. Xiao commented: "I feel such praise is very cruel. . . . Instead of praising her struggling in hardships out of great motherly love, what is more important is that we should ask whose responsibility it is to put disadvantaged individuals like her in such difficult situations?"[6]

Descriptions of painful scenes like this one are sometimes mixed with stories of absurdities that could be imaginable only in a time of apocalypse. Long lists of such absurdities circulated online:

"An elderly man wearing a mask was playing [the Russian song] 'Katyusha' on his accordion while taking a night walk in the street."

"'Help! Help!' A woman on a balcony was knocking on a wash basin while crying out for help."

"Unable to say good-bye, a daughter ran after a vehicle that was taking away her dead mother."

"A vehicle drove right up to a warehouse and picked up a box of face masks for some [privileged] leaders. A long line of medical workers had waited there for hours to receive *their* face masks."

"A truck driver [with a Hubei license plate], finding himself blocked wherever he tried to go, had to live on the highway for twenty days."

"My relative died in the afternoon and so opened up a hospital bed. Please contact that hospital to give it a try."

Each of these lines contains a dramatic story—tragic, inspiring, painful. Such scenes of the pandemic in Wuhan kept people such as Xiao Meili wondering: What happened? How did the apocalypse come about?

THE ANONYMOUS EIGHT

The year 2020 opened with a piece of news about eight individuals being punished for spreading "untruthful information." Only in retrospect did this news seem to take on ominous overtones. The Public Security Department in Wuhan posted the news on Sina Weibo at 5:38 p.m. on January 1, 2020. The short message stated that some medical institutions in Wuhan had recently treated multiple cases of pneumonia, about which the Wuhan

Municipal Health Commission had issued a public notice. Yet some *wang-min* 网民, or netizens,[7] published or retweeted information on social media without verifying its truthfulness, for which they had been "dealt with according to the law."[8] One of the eight was Dr. Li Wenliang 李文亮 at Wuhan Central Hospital.

The news was reprinted in local and national newspapers and broadcast on national television. Xinhua News Agency reprinted the story just three hours later, at 8:39 p.m. The Xinhua story also reported that all of the cases of pneumonia had a history of contact with the South China Seafood Market in Wuhan, no human-to-human transmission had been found, and no health-care workers had been infected.[9]

This news sounded a note of warning and reassurance: it warned people about the consequences of transmitting "untruthful information" on the internet; it reassured the public that the novel cases of pneumonia in Wuhan were not contagious. Thus, between January 1 and January 20, life in Wuhan went on as usual. The city of 11 million remained in a festive mood, first celebrating the Gregorian New Year's Day and then preparing for the Lunar New Year's Day—the biggest festival of the year.

On January 3, Mr. Mei, a retired high-school teacher in Wuhan, walked to a restaurant near his home and paid a deposit of RMB 500 (approximately U.S.$80) for his Lunar New Year family dinner. His family had an annual tradition of gathering for dinner on Lunar New Year's Eve, and he had booked two tables more than two months earlier. On January 10, Mr. Mei attended a lunch gathering hosted by the first class of junior-high students he taught. These students had a tradition of holding a social gathering on January 10 every year. On January 17, Mr. Mei visited the city library to return and borrow books. "I recently heard a coronavirus pneumonia is occurring, but people say it is controllable and does not transmit from people to people," he wrote in his diary on January 17.[10]

On January 20, Mr. Mei went to a hospital to see a good friend whose wife was hospitalized. He saw her illness written on her name card—pneumonia. Seeing doctors in white protective gear worried Mr. Mei. That afternoon he sensed a sudden change of atmosphere. Panic and fear were everywhere. In the evening, his relatives called and urged him to cancel the family's dinner plan, which he did reluctantly. It was only later that Mr. Mei learned that the abrupt change in atmosphere on January 20 was caused by Dr. Zhong Nanshan's 钟南山 public acknowledgment that the novel pneumonia could be transmitted from human to human.[11] Dr. Zhong is China's Dr. Fauci and four years older. Already a revered national hero known for his role in fighting the SARS crisis in 2003, he headed the Senior Experts Team of the National Health Commission, which had been dispatched to investigate the virus situation in Wuhan. It was after the investigation that he warned that the novel coronavirus was infectious. Dr. Zhong's public warning sounded the alarm of a public-health crisis and was a critical factor in the decision to shut down Wuhan. Later in 2020, he would be awarded the highest civilian honor in China for his role in fighting COVID: the Order of the Republic.

Ms. Spring started keeping a diary by accident. January 12 was her husband's birthday, but she forgot it. After her husband reminded her of it, she wrote about the episode in a diary. She continued writing after the lockdown started and did not stop until May 17. By that time, she had posted 123 entries on WeChat. According to the short bio at the end of each of her diary entries, Ms. Spring is a Wuhan native, a member of the Hubei Poetry Society, and a writer. On January 13, a friend of hers who worked in a hospital told her that multiple cases of an unknown pneumonia had occurred in the South China Seafood Market. Her friend reminded her to wear a face mask when going outside. On television, she saw Xinhua News Agency reporting that China had shared the genetic sequence of the novel coronavirus with the World Health Organization (WHO) on January 12, but WHO did not at that time recommend imposing travel and trade restrictions on China. On January 14, Ms. Spring was relieved to see that according to the Wuhan Municipal Health Commission's public notice, there were no new cases of coronavirus and no new deaths. "It does look like there is no human-to-human transmission," she wrote. After breakfast, her husband's brother called from Huanggang to tell them that her mother-in-law had passed away. She and her husband packed quickly, and her daughter drove them to her husband's home village in Huanggang. Upon returning to Wuhan on January 20, she sensed a different atmosphere. People were wearing face masks. Her daughter told her to be careful, but Ms. Spring wrote: "I don't think much of it because I heard that only two days ago Baibuting just held its ten-thousand-family meal. Some places are still holding their Spring Festival gala shows. I still do grocery shopping and go out for walks as usual."[12]

TOFU REPRESENTS POVERTY

The ten-thousand-family meal, *wanjia yan* 万家宴, in Baibuting Community has a twenty-year history. It takes place annually, a week before the Lunar New Year. In 2020, it fell on January 18. About 40,000 people reportedly attended the event at nine designated venues of the Baibuting Community. In an anonymous interview with the press, a staff member of a residential community in Baibuting revealed that they had recommended canceling the scheduled event out of concern about the new pneumonia, but community leaders rejected the recommendation.[13] The event was held as scheduled with great fanfare. The extensive coverage it received in local and national news suggests that so much organization and preparation had gone into the planning of the event that canceling it would cost the community a carefully orchestrated media spectacle.

A story in the national newspaper *Guangming Daily* (光明日报) conveys a sense of the spectacle and its political symbolism. The story reports that the event was officially called "Strive in a New Age to Realize the Dream of Moderate Wealth" (奋斗新时代梦圆小康年). This theme was apparently chosen to echo the main national political slogan of this year, which was to achieve the "full establishment of a moderately wealthy society." The article notes that residents of the community contributed 13,986 dishes in its nine venues. One dish was called "The Motherland Is a Garden Full of Spring, People's Life Is Getting Better and Better." It featured tomatoes carved into flowers to symbolize springtime garden flowers and cucumbers carved into bamboolike shapes to symbolize higher and higher living standards.[14]

Another dish was called "Targeted Poverty Alleviation." The tofu in it represented poverty because it is as "white as a sheet of blank paper," a proverbial phrase for utter poverty. Yet the fish and shrimp in the dish symbolized moderate wealth. This dish symbolized the achievement of "moderate wealth" and the overcoming of poverty. As the media scholar Qian Gang points out, "Chinese leaders do not pass the New Year and the Chinese Spring Festival in the way that ordinary people do. For them, these events are a political stage for the coming year." One of President Xi Jinping's priorities for 2020 was to "loudly proclaim China's success in reaching the 'full establishment of a moderately wealthy society.' "[15] Qian's analysis of the editorial pages in the *People's Daily* (人民日报) and in several local Chinese Communist Party (CCP) newspapers shows that the priority of official media coverage in the initial twenty days of January was precisely that. The ten-thousand-family meal was clearly a spectacle with symbolic meaning.

Baibuting, its name literally meaning "One-Hundred-Step Pavilion" (百步亭), is no ordinary community. A national banner of grassroots community governance, it is divided into twenty-seven gated residential communities with a population of about 140,000. Over the years, it has won numerous accolades as a national model of community governance. In the two months leading up to the gigantic community meal on January 18, for example, numerous events took place in Baibuting that attested to its national fame. In mid-November 2019, the Baibuting Community conducted a training program for fifty-seven community workers from Beijing to teach them the "advanced experiences in community governance."[16] On November 23, 2019, a vice minister of the Central United Front and party secretary of the All-China Federation of Industry and Commerce visited Baibuting Community.[17] On December 2, 2019, a thousand people attended a ceremony to celebrate the community police station, which had recently been selected as one of the nation's top-one-hundred police stations.[18] On December 4, 2019, Baibuting Community proudly posted a story about its director, Wang Bo, who had just been featured on prime-time national television as one of the "most beautiful urban and rural community workers" selected nationally. The posting had a link to China Central Television's (CCTV) ten-minute video about Ms. Wang. It seems as if every week Baibuting Community attracted some important visitors or made national news. A ten-thousand-family meal organized by such a famous community would surely make national news again, as indeed it did. The anticipated publicity would be too dear a loss if the event were canceled.

When the spectacle made national news this time, however, it raised alarm. In her diary entry on January 20, Fang Fang commented on the Baibuting Community meal: "I feel that while the 'Wuhan pneumonia' is still spreading, for a community to hold such a large gathering is tantamount to criminal behavior. No matter how they like formalism and enjoy showing off the peace of a prosperous age, the municipal government should forbid such gatherings and parties."[19]

Because of the continued festivities, when news of community contagion came, it caused more anger than surprise. On February 5, 2020, national news reported a high infection rate in Baibuting Community, suggesting that the festive event may have contributed to the spread of the disease. When Fang Fang blamed this behavior on a culture of formalism, she was attacking one of the most insidious problems in Chinese politics. "Formalism" may not be the best English translation of the Chinese term *xingshi zhuyi* 形式主义, which literally means "obsession with form or with the appearance of things." This obsession with appearance often comes at the expense of substance or reality, sometimes with disastrous consequences. The community transmission of COVID-19 was partly the result of this obsession with appearance. The various manifestations of this formalism at different stages of the war on COVID-19 will become clear in later chapters.

THE WUHAN MUNICIPAL HEALTH COMMISSION'S FIRST PUBLIC NOTICE

The Baibuting celebration was only one of many large festive gatherings that took place in January. On January 17, Wuhan's municipal tourism bureau proudly announced a giveaway of 200,000 tickets to major tourist attractions in the city. On January 21, two days before the lockdown, party and government leaders in Hubei province, headed by provincial party boss Jiang Chaoliang, attended a Lunar New Year gala performance. The Lunar New Year is the most important national holiday; universities, government agencies, and business companies celebrate by holding gala performances.

What was surprising about the gala performance for the Hubei provincial leaders was that it was held the day following Dr. Zhong's public warning that the coronavirus was transmissible among humans.

As party leaders were busy celebrating, residents were shopping and preparing for family celebrations. Wuhan is a national transportation hub because of its unique geographical location. Large numbers of travelers were leaving or returning to Wuhan for the long holiday. Millions passed through Wuhan on their way back home for the festival. Wuhan's mayor acknowledged at a press conference later that 5 million people had left Wuhan in the short period before the lockdown. All this hustle and bustle created a festive mood, an appearance of joy and prosperity. *Renao* 热闹, "hot and noisy," are the Chinese words used to describe such atmospheres. No Chinese holiday is worth its name without an atmosphere of *renao*. Wuhan was appropriately *renao* and seemed well prepared to greet the Lunar New Year. When it was announced on the night of January 22 that the city would be locked down starting the following morning, the news shook Wuhan and the world. It was Wuhan's Pearl Harbor moment, only this attack was coming from an invisible virus.

The coronavirus disease had already been known to medical professionals in several hospitals and to public-health authorities in Wuhan in December 2019. But the public was not informed. The Wuhan Municipal Health Commission initially prohibited public dissemination of the information. When it did start issuing public notices on its website, the notices were misleading.

According to an article by Chinese scientists in *The Lancet* on January 24, 2020, the first patient with symptoms of what would later be known as COVID-19 was traced to December 1, 2019, in Wuhan. The person did not have a history of visiting the South China Seafood Market, the alleged source of the spread of the disease. On December 8, 2019, a man was diagnosed with an unidentified form of pneumonia in Wuhan Central Hospital. He was the owner of a fruit stall inside the South China Seafood Market. On December 26, Dr. Zhang Jixian at the Wuhan Xinhua Hospital received four patients with an unknown pneumonia. The next day she reported these cases to hospital administrators, who in turn made a report to the Center for Disease Control and Prevention (CDC) of Jianghan District in Wuhan.[20]

On December 31, 2019, the Wuhan Municipal Health Commission, the top-level government agency in charge of public-health affairs in Wuhan, issued its first public notice about the coronavirus disease on its website. It stated that twenty-seven cases of an unknown pneumonia had been found, all related to the South China Seafood Market. Seven of these twenty-seven patients were in severe condition. The notice also stated that the main symptoms of this pneumonia were fever, breathing difficulties, and invasive lung lesions. It concluded, "It is believed that these are cases of viral pneumonia. The investigations thus far did not find evidence of human-to-human transmission or the infection of medical personnel."[21]

Just the day before, on December 30, however, the Health Commission had issued an urgent internal notice that prohibited anyone in the health system from disclosing any information related to the coronavirus disease without authorization.

THE CENSURING OF PHYSICIANS IN WUHAN HOSPITALS

Insider stories that surfaced after the lockdown suggest that several doctors had treated patients with a novel pneumonia. A diagnosis report leaked online indicated it was a "SARS-like coronavirus." Dr. Ai Fen 艾芬, head of the Emergency Department of Wuhan Central Hospital, saw this diagnosis on December 30 when a colleague in the Department of Respiratory Diseases in her hospital showed it to her. The diagnosis noted that the patient had contracted a "SARS-like coronavirus." Dr. Ai reported this situation to the Public Health Department in her hospital as well as to the head of the Department of Respiratory Diseases. Later that day, she shared the report with a former classmate, having marked the phrase "SARS-like coronavirus" in red. According to an interview with the popular magazine *People* (人物), this was the diagnosis report that Dr. Li Wenliang shared in his WeChat circles. Li Wenliang would later be known as the "whistleblower of COVID-19" and would die of COVID on February 7, 2020.

Li had started his job as an ophthalmologist at Wuhan Central Hospital in 2014. In an interview with the popular business newspaper *Caixin* (财新) on January 31, 2020, Li recalled that at 5:48 p.m. on December 30, 2019, he had posted a message to a WeChat group of about 150 people, all of whom were former medical school classmates. Screenshots of his WeChat message show that his posting contained the following remarks: "The most recent news is that the coronavirus has been confirmed. . . . Please do not communicate this information beyond this group. Let your families and kinsfolk take precautions." He also posted a doctor's diagnosis based on a CT scan (with the patient's name redacted).[22]

Dr. Xie Linka 谢琳卡 worked in Wuhan Union Hospital, another main hospital later designated to treat COVID patients in Wuhan. In her interview with *Caixin*, Xie revealed that at 8:48 p.m. on December 30, 2019, she posted a message in one of her WeChat groups, warning its 443 members about an unidentified pneumonia: "Don't go to the South China Seafood Market nowadays. Multiple people there have come down with an unidentified pneumonia (similar to SARS). Today our hospital treated multiple patients of pneumonia from the South China Seafood Market. Please be careful and wear masks and have adequate ventilation."[23] Screenshots of both Li's and Xie's WeChat messages were circulated on social media.

What happened to the three doctors afterward are stunning instances of the suppression of personal expression. In her interview with *People* published on March 10, 2020, Ai Fen revealed that at 10:20 p.m. on December 30, 2019, she received a message from her hospital about the Wuhan Health Commission's urgent notice prohibiting people from disclosing information about the coronavirus (see more of Ai Fen's story in chapter 7).[24] Then at around midnight on January 1, Ai received a message from the head of the hospital's Department of Supervision requesting a meeting with her the following morning. At the meeting, in Ai's own words,

> I was reprimanded in such a way as never happened before and never as seriously. . . . I was asked to tell the 200-plus staff in my department one by one verbally—not by WeChat or messaging, but only face to face or by phone—not to say anything related to this pneumonia, not even to one's own husband. I completely blanked out. He didn't chastise me

because I didn't work hard enough, but he sounded as if I had singlehand-edly ruined the wonderful situation of Wuhan's development. I had a feeling of utter despair.[25]

Ai was so crushed that she never mentioned the coronavirus disease to any-one again. She was silenced. She did not even tell her husband about this incident until January 20, 2020, when it became public information that the unidentified form of pneumonia was indeed an infectious coronavirus.

Ai's colleague Li Wenliang was also questioned by the hospital's Department of Supervision about his WeChat posts. On January 3, Li was summoned to the Wuchang District Police Station to sign a "letter of warning." The signed letter has since been leaked online. It warned Li about the following "illegal activity": "On December 30, 2019, on WeChat group [redacted] published untruthful information about seven diagnosed cases of SARS related to the South China Seafood Market." Below this were the following words of warning:

> According to law, with respect to your illegal act of publishing untruth-ful information on the internet, this letter serves as a warning and a reprimand. Your behavior has seriously violated social order. Your behav-ior has gone beyond the limit permitted by law. It is a violation of articles as set out in the Public Security Administration Punishments Law of the People's Republic of China. It is an illegal act!
>
> The Public Security Bureau hopes that you will cooperate with our work, heed the warnings of the police and stop any illegal activity. Can you do that?
>
> Answer: Yes.
>
> We hope you will calm down and carefully think it over. We solemnly warn you: If you stubbornly adhere to your own views and continue to engage in illegal activities without repenting and reforming yourself, you will be punished by the law. Do you understand?
>
> Answer: Understood.[26]

Xie Linka was questioned by the Propaganda Department of her own hos-pital and received a phone call from the police. The police officer did not ask her to sign anything but verbally warned her "not to spread unverified information."[27]

The Wuhan Public Security Department's announcement on Weibo on January 1, 2020, about the disciplining of eight individuals for spreading "unverified information" stated: "The internet is not beyond law. Information and speech published online must abide by laws and regulations. The police department will investigate and punish illegal acts of making up, spreading, and disseminating rumors and disrupting social order. It exercises zero tolerance. We hope that all netizens will follow laws and regulations and refuse to make up, believe, or spread rumors and [will] work together to build a harmonious, clear, and bright cyberspace."[28]

When Ai's superior reprimanded her, she was made to feel that she had "singlehandedly ruined the wonderful situation of Wuhan's development." Now the police were calling on all netizens to "work together to build a harmonious, clear, and bright cyberspace." As will become clear in the next chapter, "clear and bright cyberspace" was the key phrase in a comprehensive strategy of internet censorship under the Xi Jinping leadership. With this rhetoric, we can begin to zero in on the deeper causes of the delayed responses to the coronavirus crisis.

THE WUHAN HEALTH COMMISSION'S ERRATIC BEHAVIOR

At first glance, the behavior of the Wuhan Health Commission was erratic. After its first statement on December 31, 2019, it did not issue any new notice until January 3. This new notice stated that a total of forty-four cases of an unidentified pneumonia had been "found," but "preliminary investigations show that there is no clear evidence of human-to-human transmission, nor has any medical personnel been found to be infected."[29] Its next notice, issued on January 5, announced that a total of fifty-nine cases of an unidentified pneumonia had been "reported." Of these, seven were in serious condition. The earliest case of the disease had occurred on December 12. The notice repeated its earlier statement that "preliminary investigations show that there is no clear evidence of human-to-human transmission, nor has any medical personnel been found to be infected."[30]

The Health Commission issued no public announcements from January 6 to January 10. Its next notice was posted on January 11, 2020. For the first time, it acknowledged that the unidentified pneumonia was confirmed to be a novel coronavirus and reported that preliminary diagnoses had confirmed forty-one cases of novel coronavirus (the previous fifty-nine cases had been called an "unidentified pneumonia"), which included one death, seven serious cases, and two patients who had checked out of the hospital. It also stated that there were 739 close contacts, 41 of whom were medical personnel, yet "no medical personnel have been infected, and there is no clear evidence of human-to-human transmission."[31]

After the rather disconcerting report of forty-one confirmed cases of a novel coronavirus and 739 close contacts, the Health Commission's daily press releases from January 12 to 16 reported that no more new cases had been found. Later it would turn out that new cases of coronavirus had in fact appeared in that period. The twenty-nine-year-old doctor Xia Sisi 夏思思, who died of coronavirus on February 23, was infected by a patient who had been diagnosed with coronavirus on January 14.[32] Why was that case not reported? What happened?

It was not until January 18 that the Health Commission reported four new cases and 763 close contacts. The January 18 notice also mentioned that Thailand and Japan each had identified a case of coronavirus and that both cases had originated in Wuhan, but the news release no longer mentioned whether there was human-to-human transmission.[33] Then on January 20, Zhong Nanshan acknowledged at a press conference that the novel coronavirus was indeed contagious and that fifteen medical personnel had already been infected.[34] This was the first public acknowledgment that the novel coronavirus could be transmitted between humans. Yet in the twenty days between December 31, 2019, and January 20, 2020, precious opportunities had been lost to curtail the spread of the disease.[35]

Chinese media interviews with physicians such as Li, Ai, and Xie point to a possible cover-up. It is less clear who was responsible for the cover-up and why. There were two information lacunae in January: a lack of public statements from the Health Commission from January 6 to January 10 and, after a report of forty-one cases of a novel coronavirus on January 11, the reporting of no new cases in the commission's public notices from January 12 to January 16. At a press conference on January 27, 2020, Wuhan's mayor Zhou Xianwang admitted, "We haven't disclosed information in a timely manner and also did not use effective information to improve our work."[36] He did not explain what caused the delay.

THE "TWO CONGRESSES" IN WUHAN AND HUBEI

One possible proximate cause of the delay had to do with timing. It was the season of the Lunar New Year festival, a time for family reunions and celebrations and a time for exchanging New Year greetings. A public announcement about an epidemic outbreak would halt all these festive activities, as it did when the lockdown was finally announced, and could potentially trigger chaos and public panic.

The unfortunate timing of the outbreak had another wrinkle to it in Wuhan. The two weeks before the Lunar New Year were also the time of the so-called two congresses (*lianghui* 两会)—that is, the annual congresses of China's legislative body, the National People's Congress, and of the Chinese People's Political Consultative Conference. The two institutions consist of multiple levels of assemblies, from the national assembly down to the provincial, municipal, and district assemblies. Each municipal assembly elects delegates to the provincial assembly, which then elects delegates to the National Congress. The two congresses at the municipal level in Wuhan took place January 6–10, followed by the two provincial-level congresses January 11–18.

Thus, four major meetings took place in Wuhan January 6–18, coinciding with the gaps in public announcements about the coronavirus from the Wuhan Health Commission. Major local media channels, such as *Changjiang Daily* (长江日报) and *Hubei Daily* (湖北日报), covered these congresses but made no mention of the epidemic. The media scholar Qian Gang finds that fourteen of the twenty front pages of the *Hubei Daily* from January 1 to January 20 were identical reprints of the front pages of the *People's Daily*. Qian's analysis of the *People's Daily* in the first twenty days of January 2020 shows that the priorities of party media dovetailed with Xi Jinping's three priorities for 2020: to proclaim the successful achievement of "a moderately wealthy society"; to highlight Xi Jinping's core foreign-policy program, the Belt and Road Initiative; and to boost's Xi's image as a "people's leader" on a par with Mao by displaying photographs of him among the people.[37]

Fang Fang wrote about the "two congresses" in her diary posting on March 18, 2020. Continuing her call for investigations into the delayed responses to the COVID outbreak, she argued that many different factors must have worked together to cause the delay and that therefore investigations should start when people's memories of the events were still fresh. A friend had reminded her that the transitional period from winter to early spring was always a season for infectious diseases, yet the two congresses were always held in this season. This prompted Fang Fang to share her own experience as a former delegate, noting that it had long been the case for media to shun negative news during the two congresses: "Frankly speaking, in Hubei, I began attending the two congresses in 1993. I attended the provincial People's Congress and then the Political Consultative Conference for twenty-five years. I know too well the state of affairs immediately before and after the two congresses. To ensure that the two congresses can proceed smoothly, the media are prohibited to cover any negative news. And during that period, in all the government departments almost no one was doing any work because their bosses were attending the two congresses."[38]

Fang Fang then remarked that things were the same this time:

The Municipal Health Commission stopped reporting the number of infected cases. The timing was almost exactly aligned with the two congresses. This was not a coincidence. It was not intended as such either. It was just habitual behavior. This habit was not formed in the past few years. It has been there for many years. For many years, the various departments just postpone their business until after the two congresses. For many years, to guarantee that the two congresses proceed smoothly, the media cover only good news, never bad news. Cadres, journalists, leaders, and even citizens have all become used to this.[39]

The implication was that local authorities in Wuhan and Hubei could be directly responsible for covering up the spread of COVID. An internal report prepared by U.S. intelligence agencies supports this view. According to a *New York Times* story in mid-August 2020, "The report adds to a body of evidence that shows how the malfeasance of local Chinese officials appeared to be a decisive factor in the spread of the virus within Wuhan and beyond."[40] The *Times* story implies that local officials withheld information from Beijing for fear of reprisal but offers no further explanation.

Based on her experience with the two congresses, Fang Fang reasoned that the Municipal Health Commission stopped reporting the number of infected cases during the two congresses in Wuhan not necessarily because there was a deliberate cover-up but because the omission of negative news was habitual bureaucratic behavior during the two congresses. The political scientist Yongshun Cai might view this conduct as a form of "irresponsible state behavior," which occurs when state agents make policy decisions "for the self-serving purpose of image enhancement, with little concern for the economic costs or other negative outcomes of their decisions." Although such behavior is not unique to Chinese bureaucracies, Cai argues that the Chinese political system creates incentive and opportunity for it: "Due to a political arrangement that does not establish a clear link between irresponsible decisions and punishment, cadres often do not incur great risk when engaging in irresponsible activities."[41]

Despite the unknown and uncertain elements of a new epidemic, the early signs of it were serious enough to warrant warning the public. The twenty-day delay in informing the public was irresponsible state behavior, to say the least. In this case, however, the reason was less image enhancement than image management. It was more about bureaucrats controlling potential damage to their image at a time when that image was at its apex. One diarist conjectured, for example, that 2019 had been such a good year for Wuhan that the party leaders there were expecting promotions and a boost in their careers.[42] It was a good year because Wuhan had just had a series of celebrations in 2019 to commemorate the seventieth anniversary of the founding of the People's Republic of China (PRC). Its successful hosting of the Military World Games from October 18 to October 27, 2019, had given Wuhan global publicity. Immediately following the Military Games, the fourth plenary of the CCP Nineteenth National Congress convened in Beijing, which issued a communiqué exalting the advantages of China's political and governance system.[43] With all these major events from 2019 in the background, the two congresses in Wuhan in mid-January 2020 were occasions for celebrating a year's accomplishments. It was the worst possible time to report an epidemic outbreak.

After the SARS epidemic in 2003, China established national early-warning systems for reporting infectious diseases. In 2008, the China Infectious Disease Automated-Alert and Response System was established to harness the power of the internet and mobile phones for rapid reporting of and warning about infectious diseases. Billed as the largest such system in the world, it technically allows grassroots medical facilities such as hospitals to enter information into the system for China's national CDC to receive that information in real time.[44] Although it seemed to have worked well for the 2012–2014 period,[45] it failed miserably this time around. According to an investigative report by *China Youth Daily* (中国青年报), cases of the coronavirus were indeed reported to the national CDC in early January. After mid-January, however, the reporting stopped "for unknown reasons." Although the national early-warning system requires direct online reporting of an infectious-disease event, beginning in mid-January hospitals in Wuhan were told *not* to report cases without prior approval from the provincial Health Commission.[46] Exactly why the system was not used remains a mystery. Scholars have argued that the outbreak of the SARS epidemic in 2003 was caused by administrative failures. Besides the lack of transparency, there were incentives for local bureaucrats to underreport SARS cases.[47] Therefore, establishing national early-warning systems but not fixing flaws in the administration of that system means that it probably will not work.

Wuhan was ultimately locked down on January 23. WHO declared the Wuhan coronavirus outbreak a "public health emergency of international concern" on January 30, 2020, named it "COVID-19" on February 11, and declared it a global pandemic on March 11.[48]

2

ROAD TO APOCALYPSE

CHINESE SOCIETY IN 2011

A tightened political environment hostile to free expression was responsible for the silencing of early whistle-blowers of COVID-19 in Wuhan. How did this political environment come about?

Although it had no definite and unambiguous origin, notable changes began to be introduced after Xi Jinping became the CCP's general secretary in November 2012. These changes were so wide ranging that they cumulatively impaired the conditions for open speech. This is not to say that there was no dissent or critical thinking, but the drum of dominant ideological discourses was loud enough to suppress or drown out alternative voices. Nor did Xi's politics represent a complete break with the past. There were many continuities, and some of the new developments were policy responses to a preexisting crisis of governance. But Xi went further than his predecessors in the changes he introduced to politics, society, and media cultures.

Political uncertainties and even dangers loomed for the Chinese regime in 2011, the year before Xi Jinping became the top CCP leader. It was the year of the Arab Spring revolutions. In January 2011, President Zine El Abidine Ben Ali of Tunisia fled his country. On February 19, barely ten days after President Hosni Mubarak of

Egypt was forced from office by revolutionary insurgents, anonymous calls for a jasmine revolution in China appeared on overseas Chinese websites. In response, party authorities acted preemptively by rounding up prominent dissidents and installing heavy police presence.[1] The strong reactions revealed the anxieties of CCP leaders.

Their anxieties had multiple sources. After the scandal of the melamine-tainted milk powder in 2008,[2] the urban middle class had lived in worry about food safety. Many people saw the root cause of food-safety problems as a failure in party governance. Other social concerns included rising food prices, unstoppable housing prices, unemployment, and growing costs for medical care and education. A crisis of trust plagued public institutions.

Barely a year after the melamine milk scandal in 2008, China passed its first food-safety law, and yet just as the new law came into effect, melamine-tainted milk powder resurfaced on the market in early 2010.[3] Clearly, the problem was systemic, and patching up potholes here and there was no longer an option. China's political system was riddled with deep ruts.

Party leaders wanted to tackle these problems. To gauge public sentiments, Premier Wen Jiabao went online three times to interact with netizens, an unprecedented action.[4] New laws and policies were also introduced to tackle the issues. On May 30, 2011, Xi's immediate predecessor, Hu Jintao, chaired a Politburo meeting to discuss how to strengthen social management. Soon afterward, on July 5, the CCP issued a policy document about innovating social management. The message was clear: the party was having trouble handling all of the social problems China was experiencing and must innovate its methods of governance.

There were other uncertainties. With Hu Jintao's term coming to an end, a successor was due to be selected in 2012. Fierce elite negotiations and a power shuffle took place in 2011. On February 6, 2012, the elite power struggle spilled into public view when Wang Lijun, deputy mayor and police chief in the city of Chongqing, shocked the world by entering the U.S. consulate in Chengdu to seek protection (although he was turned back to Chinese authorities the following day). Wang Lijun was the right-hand man of Bo Xilai, the party secretary of Chongqing and Xi Jinping's rival for the top CCP position. Soon afterward, on March 15, 2012, Bo Xilai was removed from office and tried and sentenced to life in prison in 2013 for bribery, graft, and abuse of power.

In this roiling political season, Chinese cyberspace was full of riotous and contentious activities. That was the internet that Xi would set out to tame after 2012. On July 23, 2011, a high-speed train crashed near the city of Wenzhou, causing forty deaths. The Ministry of Railways came under public attack because of the way it handled or, rather, mishandled the disaster. On September 21, 2011, villagers of Wukan in Guangdong province began several months of organized protest against village cadres who had been accused of selling village land for personal gain. In the middle of the protest, a villager died while in police custody, leading to intervention by the provincial government. The protest ended with villagers electing their own head. This event turned out to be one of the biggest social protests in recent decades.[5] On October 13, 2011, in a small town in Guangdong province, a two-year-old girl called Yueyue was run over by two trucks, one after the other, near her home. Eighteen pedestrians walked right past Yueyue and did not stop to help the poor baby. It was the nineteenth person who walked by, a middle-aged woman, who picked her up and took her to the roadside when Yueyue's mother finally appeared. Yueyue died in the hospital the following day, and the incident triggered a national debate online about the awful moral conditions of Chinese society.[6]

The Guo Meimei incident illustrates well the cyber political culture on the eve of Xi Jinping's ascendance. Guo Meimei was barely twenty years old on June 21, 2011. Like others of her age, she was a netizen who spent lots of time online. On Sina Weibo, China's leading social media platform in 2011, she had posted photographs of herself and her Maserati and Lamborghini, dozens of Hermes handbags, and expensive jewelry.

There was nothing wrong about what Guo was doing on social media. In an age of selfies and in a country with 500 million internet users as of 2011, displays of personal wealth and success on social media could not be more common. Internet culture fed endless online reality shows by enticing users to update their online status and share their personal lives. In 2011, Guo Meimei was just one of millions who displayed their glamorous lives on Sina Weibo.

But the hapless Guo made the mistake of identifying herself as the general manager of a Red Cross Commercial Society on her Weibo account. On June 21, 2011, this job title became a headline on Tianya, one of the most popular online communities then: "New Discovery on

Weibo! A 20-Year-Old General Manager of 'Red Cross Commercial Society,' All Sorts of Wealth Show-Off! Hurry Up and Go See!"[7] The posting linked Guo's wealth to the Red Cross Society of China (RCSC) and ended provocatively: "Whoever continues to donate money to the Red Cross must be a moron!"

To the infinitely curious minds of Chinese netizens, Guo's job title was an invitation for investigation. Many suspected that the Red Cross Commercial Society must be related with the RCSC. To them, Guo's story provided an opportunity to expose the RCSC. At a time of declining trust in official institutions, there was nothing more gratifying to them than to discredit a public agency.

The RCSC made a good target. A member of the International Federation of Red Cross, it is a ministerial-level, quasi-governmental agency qua charity organization. It is led by individuals boasting of high-ranking party leadership credentials. In 2011, the RCSC executive vice president and party secretary was Zhao Baige, a former deputy director and vice party secretary of the National Population and Family Planning Commission. As of February 2020, the RCSC executive vice president and party secretary was Liang Huiling, former head of the Commission for Discipline Inspection in Hebei province. For netizens, challenging the RCSC was an indirect challenge against the legitimacy of the CCP. As students of Chinese politics well know, indirection is a safer strategy of protest than direct confrontation.

An unorganized but concerted online hunt for Guo's connections with the Red Cross thus started. Overnight, Guo and the RCSC became the center of a national internet storm.

INTERNET CULTURE IN 2011

By 2011, an online protest culture had long taken shape, characterized by a playful style, crowdsourced search engines, inventive methods to dodge censorship, and the mass participation of emotional publics.[8] One item in this digital culture of protest has the ghastly name *renrou sousuo* 人肉搜索,

"human-flesh search." In a human-flesh search, netizens use their internet search skills to hunt for information aimed to expose the alleged misdemeanors of individuals ranging from animal abusers to party officials suspected of corruption. Smacking of internet vigilantism, human-flesh search resembles a collective quest for truth or social justice. There is usually a mystery, and the goal is to solve the mystery by uncovering information with whatever means available. For example, in a case in 2007 a peasant named Zhou Zhenglong in Shaanxi province posted photographs of a South China tiger that he claimed he had discovered in the mountains near his village. The mystery to be solved was whether the photographs were authentic or forged. A sustained period of online search, which included the widespread sharing of technical analyses of the photographs, proved that the photographs had been forged and that Zhou had made up his story at the behest of local forestry officials in their attempt to obtain more government funding. The exposure of these forged photographs led to the downfall of several local party officials.[9]

Another item in the repertoire of online protest is *weiguan* 围观, or "spectating." *Weiguan* was once associated with the passivity and numbness of a citizenry unable to take action when seeing fellow citizens in trouble. It was an image of the Chinese nation that the famous writer Lu Xun created in his work in the early twentieth century.[10] The playful crowd wisdom of internet culture gave the term a new lease on life. It now refers to online participation by paying attention. To "like" or to retweet a post is to pay attention. It is a form of collective power, and the target of *weiguan* is turned into an object of the public gaze. Imagine the spectators in a packed football stadium loudly cheering the players, then multiply the numbers by a hundred or a thousand, and one will understand the sense of drama that is created through online spectating. Thus, for some time "*weiguan* is power" was a frequently used internet meme.

Weiguan is a form of networked collective action.[11] It connects online personal talk by individuals into a large-scale dramatic event. *Weiguan* can be serious or playful. To attract attention, discussions about even serious social issues often adopt a humorous style. Jokes, cartoons, parodies, and funny emojis are created and shared and become viral memes. The proliferation of these online symbols suggests that online *weiguan* is not all about spectating. It is also a process of the digital coproduction, appropriation, and remixing of online culture. In other words, *weiguan* is a Chinese form of contemporary remix culture. Much studied by media and communication scholars, remix culture is "a global activity consisting of the creative and efficient exchange of information made possible by digital technologies." Essentially a cut, copy, and paste practice, remix is "the activity of taking samples from pre-existing materials to combine them into new forms according to personal taste."[12] The activity of turning preexisting material into something new is as old as human civilization, but digital technologies and the internet have made remix a distinct feature of digital culture in China as much as in other parts of the world.[13]

The Guo Meimei incident was the result of the same style of online spectatorship and participation. Prior to Sina Weibo and WeChat, Tianya was a popular online community and a hotbed of online protest. Not surprisingly, the Guo Meimei incident started there. But the news quickly spread to Sina Weibo, where remixed screenshots of photographs of Guo's luxury possessions were circulated. Many users left comments on Guo Meimei's Weibo account, such as "What a complicated plot in this play!" "How intriguing! I'm going to stay awake and continue to follow [the event]." There was a palpable excitement, as if people were watching a mystery drama.

Particularly important in this drama was the role of the so-called Big-V's, or verified Weibo users with large numbers of followers. Big-V's were China's de facto internet influencers. Often using dramatic language, their postings were designed to provoke. The well-known sports commentator Huang Jianxiang posted the following message on June 27, 2011: "The state of things has come to such that I personally think that Guo Meimei is a really great person! She is more fucking awesome than Yu Zecheng!" In a popular spy television drama series, Yu Zecheng was a Communist mole in the nationalists' powerful spy agency in the 1940s and always managed to outmaneuver his opponents. Comparing Guo Meimei to Yu Zecheng was a playful way of saying that Guo Meimei was a mole planted within the RCSC to bring it down. This remix of two vastly different characters from two historical eras created a surprising analogy that enticed netizens' interest and participation.

Internet platforms thrive on user participation, just as participation can boost users' social media status. Personal status and business success are interdependent. No users, no business. One consequence of this social media logic is the tendency toward sensationalism: participation may become a form of spectatorship. There is a public relish sometimes bordering on the vicious in the scandalizing of private lives and the debunking of a public institution, as is clear from the Guo Meimei case.

At the same time, however, it is undeniable that netizens also join online protest out of genuine feelings of anger at injustice and sympathy for the poor and weak. Chinese online publics are emotional publics. This is as much true now as it was in the past. As many of the stories in this book show, it is also true of online public responses during the Wuhan lockdown. The primary goal of internet censorship, in fact, is not the foreclosure of dissent or criticisms of the party but the management of increasingly emotional online publics. These unruly publics, to use official media language, can quickly stir up "internet mass incidents" (*wangluo qunti xing shijian* 网络群体性事件), thereby causing social chaos. It is also for this reason that since 2013 the management of online speech has emphasized *wenming* 文明, "civility," and *zheng nengliang* 正能量, "positive energy." As discussed later in this chapter, the discourses of civility and positive energy are propagated to counter online protest by attacking its emotional and allegedly irrational character. Negative emotions that are especially powerful in social protests, such as anger and indignation, are attacked in the name of civility and reason.

XI JINPING CENTRALIZES POWER

Xi Jinping started consolidating his power after he became the CCP general secretary in November 2012. By 2019, two years into his second term, he had accumulated more power than any other party leader after Mao. Until Xi came along, no other person since Mao had been addressed in official media as the "great leader" (*lingxiu* 领袖) beloved of the people.[14] Xi is not only head of the party and the military but also head of the state and the police force, positions that even Mao did not hold. In addition, Xi set up and chairs many other offices that have increasingly taken on the power of the state. As the political scientist Susan Shirk describes the situation, "Within the Party, Xi acts as if he is personally in charge of everything. He chairs eight of the leading small groups including the National Security Commission. Xi also handles internal security directly, thereby reducing the chances of a coup." One of the groups chaired by Xi, called the Leading Small Group on Comprehensively Deepening Reform, "has become a more powerful shadow State Council, usually meeting monthly and issuing specific policies on a wide range of issues, including economic ones."[15] In 2014, Xi made himself the head of the Central Cyberspace Affairs Commission, thus showing the importance he attaches to policies concerning cyberspace.

In centralizing political power, Xi ended the institutional convention of collective leadership established by Deng Xiaoping.[16] Deng abhorred the catastrophe inflicted on the country by Mao's dictatorship. He himself was a victim of Mao's Cultural Revolution. He was publicly denounced and later demoted to a remote rural region. His son was disabled under detention by Red Guards.[17] When Deng reemerged to lead the economic reform in the late 1970s, he set down term limits for party leaders and introduced collective leadership as well as an institutionalized mechanism for power transition: when the incumbent leader started his second term, a successor-in-training would be selected. Xi violated the convention by not selecting a successor-in-training and thus sent a signal that he might stay on after his second term. Even more shockingly, in 2018 the National People's Congress abolished the two-term limit for the president of the state that had been added to the Constitution in 1982 under Deng Xiaoping to prevent the appearance of another Mao.

How could Xi have centralized power to such a degree? Reflecting the current global trend of strongman politics riding waves of populism, Xi has mobilized popular support for his agendas. The anticorruption campaign that he launched is a case in point. Corruption has long troubled China's economic reform. At least six major anticorruption campaigns were conducted after 1982.[18] Yet no previous campaign lasted as long as Xi's or brought down as many party officials. According to one study, the number of disciplined cadres at the vice ministerial level and higher had been kept well under one hundred for each general party congress before 2012 (the CCP congress convenes every five years). The number spiked more than fourfold during Xi Jinping's first term in 2012–2017, reaching 440.[19] For the first time in CCP history, Xi's anticorruption campaign put a former member of the Politburo Standing Committee, Zhou Yongkang, on trial. Once one of the nine most powerful men in China, Zhou was convicted and sentenced to life imprisonment for corruption. Xi's campaign also targeted high-ranking military officers. From 2012 to 2017, sixty-three generals were expelled from the party due to corruption and sent to military courts, including two former deputy chairmen of the Central Military Commission (only one rank below Xi Jinping in military ranking order) and two serving members of that commission.[20]

Xi scored victories on two fronts with his anticorruption campaign: he removed his rivals from leadership positions and thus consolidated personal power, and he won popular support for attacking a deep-seated problem. Corruption breeds public anger and resentment. Bringing down party officials on corruption crimes can diffuse anger and resentment. Interestingly, one study based on an analysis of online comments finds that Xi's anticorruption campaign won popular support for himself more than for the agencies implementing the campaign. The campaign reinforced public support for Xi "at the cost of distracting or even undermining support for institution building."[21]

THE RETREAT OF CIVIL SOCIETY

From the mid-1990s on, the language and practices of civil society became gradually acceptable in China. Nongovernmental organizations (NGOs) appeared and even flourished. They were active in environmental protection, poverty alleviation, charity work, rural education, and many other social issues. Party authorities were wary of NGOs, of course, yet by being creative and by cooperating with the state, NGOs carved out a space of their own.

After the "Arab Spring" uprisings in 2010 and 2011, however, the political environment in China became hostile to NGOs. Detractors viewed them as the foot soldiers of "color revolutions" supported by Western democracy assistance programs.[22] A crackdown on civil society and Western values started with the issuance in April 2013 of "A Communiqué on the Current State of the Ideological Sphere" popularly known as Document 9.[23] The directive urged the party leadership to guard against seven political perils, including constitutional democracy, "nihilistic" and critical views of modern Chinese history, "universal values," neoliberalism, and the promotion of Western notions of media and civil society.[24] *Civil society* became almost a taboo word thereafter. Around the same time, several leftist intellectuals in China advanced the notion of a "people's society" (*renmin shehui* 人民社会) as a superior Chinese alternative to Western civil society.[25] Although their views drew immediate criticisms from their more liberal-leaning peers, in official discourse the concept of civil society faded away.

New legislation was introduced to limit the influence of domestic and international NGOs.[26] In 2016, China issued a charity law concerning domestic nonprofit organizations and a law for managing foreign NGOs. Some Chinese commentators see the charity law as a helpful step because it at least clarifies which organizations can or cannot do fund-raising for charity purposes in China.[27] Before the foreign-NGO law existed, international NGOs in China operated in a gray zone and were supervised by the Ministry of Civil Affairs. The new law requires foreign NGOs to register with the Ministry of Public Security or its provincial-level bureaus, a change that shows a higher concern with security issues associated with foreign NGOs. The foreign-NGO law has implications for Chinese local NGOs as well, though: because of the increased surveillance of foreign NGOs, local groups are less reluctant to partner with them or to seek funding from them.[28]

The crackdown on civil society happened in tandem with a campaign to revive the mass-line tradition in CCP history. As a leadership principle of the Chinese Communist Party, the mass line was institutionalized in the Yan'an period during the anti-Japanese war era. It was Mao's theoretical abstraction of the communist movement's guerilla experience.

Mao wrote of the mass line in 1943: "In all practical work of our Party, correct leadership can only be developed on the principle of 'from the masses, to the masses.' The basic method of leadership is to sum up the views of the masses, take the results back to the masses so that the masses can give them their firm support and so work out sound ideas for leading the work on hand."[29]

In theory, the mass line was the CCP's method of gauging public opinion and tackling elitism by encouraging mass participation. The mass line was much touted in the Mao era but receded from CCP rhetoric when the economic reform began to promote individual success and the entrepreneurial spirit. Now revived under Xi Jinping, the tradition is out of sync with reality. Instead of a method for party leaders to learn from citizens, it is used to mobilize mass surveillance through grassroots institutions.

One example of an institution for mass surveillance is popularly called *Chaoyang qunzhun* 朝阳群众, "Chaoyang masses." Chaoyang is a district in Beijing where the Beijing Capital International Airport is located. In 2013, based on clues provided by mass informants in Chaoyang, Beijing police detained Charles Xue, an internet celebrity and social commentator, on charges of soliciting prostitution. Although Charles Xue may seem to be the first victim of Chaoyang masses, according to a story in the *Evening News of the Rule of Law* (法制晚报), a subsidiary legal affairs newspaper under *Beijing Youth Daily* (北京青年报), Chaoyang masses had worked with the police to catch spies as early as in 1974.[30] Today's Chaoyang masses, however, are equipped with mobile phones and other new technologies. Some use surveillance cameras for neighborhood watch. In 2017, a Chaoyang masses app was launched to assist informants in reporting cases. An informant can take a photo of a suspicious stranger in a neighborhood and upload it to the app to alert the local police.[31]

Who are the Chaoyang masses? They are mostly volunteers but may receive a monthly allowance and training from neighborhood police stations to encourage them to serve as informants. According to the same *Evening News* story, as of July 2017 Beijing's Chaoyang district boasted 190,000 such informants, 130,000 of whom were registered with the local administrative offices. That total translated into 277 people for every square kilometer. Of these people, 60,000 were active operatives. They provided 20,000 clues to the police every month. Typically, informants were retirees with time to kill, but they could also be cleaners, elevator operators, shop owners in the neighborhood, bike repairers, fee collectors for the property-management office. They could be anyone, and yet their identity as informants was not known publicly. They would report any unusual activity or behavior to the local police station. In one case, an informant reported a neighbor to the local antidrug team. Seeing that his neighbor always slept in the daytime and went out at night made him suspicious. Based on this clue, the antidrug team kept watch over this neighbor and broke a drug-dealing ring at his home.[32]

Chinese universities are ideological battlegrounds and prime targets of control. A variation of the Chaoyang masses in universities is the system of student information officers (*xuesheng xinxiyuan* 学生信息员). These students are selected by their institutions to collect and report feedback to administrators about various aspects of their educational experiences, especially teacher conduct and teaching content. The system has existed for a while now—administrative regulations about student information officers issued in 2005 and 2006 can still be found on the websites of some institutions—but it did not seem to be widely implemented until after 2013.[33] At a university in Chongqing, for the 2016–2017 academic year awards were given to selected student information officers to commend their work.[34] At a university in the city of Nanjing in the 2015–2016 academic year, student leaders could receive extra credits for leadership by serving as student information officers.[35] A polytechnic college in Hubei published a news release on November 7, 2019, about a college-wide meeting to honor student information officers.[36]

Student information officers may have wide-ranging responsibilities. They collect student feedback about their education and report the information to school administrators. It may be feedback about administrators, peers, and teachers or about facilities and lab and classroom conditions, but the reported information especially concerns teachers' behavior and teaching activities. This is shown in the standard full name of the position: "student information officers about teaching" (*xuesheng jiaoxue xinxiyuan* 学生教学信息员). In the regulations about student information officers posted on

February 22, 2017, by a university in Guangxi province, the first type of information requested concerns teachers and teaching: "Information officers should collect the following types of information about teachers and teaching: pedagogical reforms, teaching attitudes, teaching contents, teaching methods, teaching practice, moral education of students, teacher conduct as student models, and exemplary cases of abiding by socialist core values in the field of education."[37]

A university in Hainan province emphasized the monitoring and surveillance functions of student information officers. A news release posted on its website on April 30, 2019, stated: "A main responsibility [of student information officers] is to supervise classroom teaching. This includes: teachers' moral behavior, sense of responsibility, teaching preparation before class, the structure of teaching contents, calligraphy on the blackboard, expressiveness, manners, teaching methods and skills, office hours and quality of grading student homework."[38]

The system of student information officers has had a chilling effect on open expression and critical thinking on university campuses. In recent years, faculty members in several universities have been suspended from teaching or fired because students reported them to administrators. A *New York Times* story on November 1, 2019, mentions two cases. In one, a professor of Chinese literature at Chongqing Normal University said that the popular phrase "roll up your sleeves and work hard" was vulgar and coarse. A student reported him for making this remark in class because this phrase allegedly originated from Xi Jinping. The teacher was stripped of his teaching position and reassigned to work in the school library. In the other case, a professor of economics at Xiamen University, You Shengdong, was fired in 2018 after being reported by students for his "radical speech."[39] In a subsequent interview with the *New York Times*, when asked why he lost his job, Mr. You replied that he had made the following comments about positive energy: "energy" is a concept in physics; it can be stronger or weaker but not positive or negative, so he prohibited students from using the phrase in their course assignments or exams.[40] By calling out the problematic language of positive energy, You Shengdong touched a sensitive nerve. He undermined one of two key concepts in the ideological lexicon of the Xi

Jinping era, the other being *wenming*, "civility" or "civilization." Each consists of a set of vocabularies, practices, and institutions, and the two concepts work together to guide public speech, shape individual thinking, and suppress criticism and dissent.

THE IDEOLOGICAL DISCOURSES OF CIVILITY AND POSITIVE ENERGY

A key word in modern Chinese history,[41] *wenming* means "being modern," "having culture," and "having good manners and polite behavior."[42] Talk about *wenming* disappeared during the Chinese Cultural Revolution, when revolutionary rudeness was the order of the day.[43] Its return coincided with the beginning of the economic reform, when ideologies of economic development displaced those of revolution and class struggle. In a speech in 1980, Deng Xiaoping introduced the concept of "socialist spiritual civilization" alongside the idea of "material civilization." Whereas material civilization emphasizes economic development, socialist spiritual civilization concerns "not only education, science, culture . . . but also communist ideas, ideals, beliefs, morality, discipline, revolutionary standpoints and principles and the comradelike relations among people."[44] These two civilizations served important political purposes at a time of transition.

While Deng's notion of spiritual civilization "remained largely grounded in the language of Chinese socialist ideology,"[45] the discourses of civilization under Jiang Zemin and Hu Jintao put more emphasis on China's earlier cultural traditions, especially Confucianism.[46] Xi Jinping inherited this discourse of *wenming* but added his own content to it. Some of Xi's key pronouncements, such as "the China dream" and "the great rejuvenation of the Chinese nation," are positioned in the lineage of China's Confucian civilization. Confucian teachings of family harmony, filial piety, and moral cultivation have become slogans in street-side bulletin boards. In November 2013, Xi Jinping paid a personal visit to Confucius's birthplace, Qufu, where he spoke about the importance of studying Confucian classics. It is in this context that the discourse of civilizing the web takes on new

cultural meanings. Linking online civility to Confucian virtues of harmony, propriety, culture, and self-cultivation elevates online civility to the
significance of a great civilizational tradition.

Compared with *wenming*, positive energy is a more recent addition to
the glossary of CCP propaganda. A concept from popular writings on self-
help and positive psychology, it may have been first introduced into PRC
public discourse via entertainment celebrities from Hong Kong.[47] In 2012,
the concept topped a Chinese-language magazine's list of the top-ten "catchphrases" (*liuxing yu* 流行语) of the year. Apparently deeming this achievement worthy national news, a Xinhua Agency story on December 30, 2012,
exclaimed, "'Positive energy' is absolutely one of the most beloved phrases
of the 1.3 billion people. It is used by head of the state all the way down to
ordinary people."[48]

Xi Jinping elevated the concept of positive energy to the level of national
ideological discourse by using it personally. On December 13, 2012, when
he met with former U.S. president Jimmy Carter, Xi said, "Both China and
the United States should fear no hardships, dare to innovate, and accumulate positive energy."[49] In the newspaper database China National Knowledge Infrastructure, operated by Tsinghua University, the term *positive
energy* appeared 2,133 times in 2012 and then catapulted to 21,358 times in
2013 and 26,147 times in 2014.[50]

This new language of positive energy has attracted much academic attention. Some scholars see it as a form of internet control under the broader
agenda of civility, public morality, and *suzhi* 素质 (quality) education.[51] Others view it as part of the CCP's increasingly proactive approach to propaganda.[52] Still others propose that it is a signature neoliberal concept in its
emphasis on the individual's responsibility for achieving happiness by taking positive attitudes to life and work.[53] The truth is that the discourse of
positive energy is made to do all this work, but not all at the same time.
Rather, it works situationally. It can be used together with the language of
civility to cajole citizens into civil subjects who will contribute positive
energy to society. But under different circumstances, it works as a form of
ideological repression to silence speech. In other words, the ideological discourses of civility and positive energy can serve as both carrots and sticks
depending on the circumstances.

They are powerful concepts because they do not have a clear ideological flavor. Concepts such as class struggle and democracy are immediately recognizable as ideological and are clearly linked to political and social systems and values. But civility and positive energy are not. Although the language of civility and positive energy is frequently transmitted by propaganda and media agencies, it is not imposed on citizens in any simple way. In fact, this language articulates well with the desires and aspirations of modern individuals. Who does not want to be a civilized person in a modern society? Or a person who radiates positive energy if that energy enhances one's personal appeal? People *want* to have culture and civilization; they want to embody positive energy. As the British cultural theorist Ian Chambers once wrote, "Ideology has to negotiate a path through the differential social totality in order to win consensus, and it arises *within* social relationships and particular practices."[54] In the same way, the ideological discourses of civility and positive energy derive their power from their enmeshment with individual desires.

CIVILIZING EMOTIONS

The discourses of *wenming* and *zheng nengliang* appear not only in official speeches and media channels but also in slogans posted in public spaces such as street-side bulletin boards and bus or subway stations and become memelike catchphrases on social media. They are like political advertisements, and their omnipresence creates a social atmosphere hostile to critical expression. But because they are crystallized into memorable slogans and catchphrases, they are easily used to suppress or flood out different views and sentiments and to project an appearance of positivity.

The promotion of positive energy can lead to ludicrous results. On June 1, 2015, a cruise ship named *Oriental Star* capsized in the waters of Hubei province. Only 12 of the 454 people on board survived. In the past, such a tragic incident would have triggered online protest and public calls for investigations, but no such online outcry was heard this time. On the contrary, according to a report from *People's Daily Online* (人民网),

"positive" emotions surpassed "negative" emotions in the first few days. Considering this a successful case of managing online opinion, the report attributed the success to effective government responses: using Weibo and WeChat, government departments publicized the names of all passengers within twenty-four hours, and the information was widely reprinted by regional media, thus dispelling any questioning or protests from the public.[55]

The report did not mention, however, that information and news reporting about the tragic incident were tightly controlled. As the *New York Times* indicated, "Images and reporting from the site of the overturned ship were largely limited to state media outlets for the first 24 hours. A propaganda directive ordered domestic news media not to send reporters to the scene and to rely on accounts from 'authoritative media.'"[56] Public responses, however, revealed the ambivalent effects of positive reporting. For one thing, it is not clear whether negative sentiments were absent because they were not expressed or because they had been censored. According to the *New York Times* story, key words such as *Oriental Star* and *shipwreck* "were the most censored search terms on the Sina Weibo microblog platform."[57] Furthermore, netizens mocked official media efforts to project positive emotions. A post entitled "Ten Most Disgusting Headlines in Official Media" was widely retweeted on Sina Weibo, with headlines such as "On Ground Zero, China's Most Handsome Men Are All There!" and "How Fortunate It Is to Be Born a Chinese!"

This case shows that the management of online emotions is two-pronged. While government policies and mainstream discourses attack the emotional and allegedly irrational nature of online expression, official media promote positive emotions and attack negative ones. This approach may backfire, however. When news stories covering a shipwreck involving 454 deaths focused on inflated expressions of gratitude and praise ("How fortunate it is to be born a Chinese!") instead of probing the causes of the tragedy, they revealed the true face of positive energy as an ideology of control and not a measure of popular sentiments.

All of these changes have created a political environment of artificial harmony and prosperity inhospitable to the expression of "negative" emotions and dissenting opinion.

PARTY-SPONSORED PLATFORMIZATION

Ideological discourses for internet and social control work best when they blend into concrete social and technological practices. In recent years, this blending happens in a process called "platformization," or "the penetration of economic, governmental, and infrastructural extensions of digital platforms into the web and app ecosystems."[58] If social media platforms can shape user behavior through technological affordances in ways consistent with ideological norms, aren't they a more effective form of ideological influence? Facebook and other social media platforms generally encourage users to participate and share personal information, which the platforms monetize through datafication. Having a "like" button but not a "dislike" button under a posting is Facebook's way of encouraging rather than discouraging participation. "Trending topics" and notifications on Twitter and Sina Weibo have similar functions.

The process of platformization in China has different problems and challenges than in the United States, the key difference being "the intrusive role of the state."[59] Platformization in China is state sponsored[60] or, perhaps more appropriately, party sponsored, given the central role of the CCP.[61] At the top of this sponsorship sits Xi Jinping. True to his name as head of the Central Cyberspace Affairs Commission, Xi appears to have a direct personal role in shaping China's internet policies. He frequently mentions the internet in his speeches, and an entire section of the website wenming.cn, run by the CCP Department of Propaganda, is devoted to quotations from those speeches, totaling 532 as of October 7, 2020. The first quotation listed is from a speech Xi made on December 29, 2012, about the China dream of "achieving the great rejuvenation of the Chinese nation." A quotation from a Xi speech on January 25, 2019, uses the metaphor of a "clear and bright" (*qinglang* 清朗) cyberspace: "No matter what types of media, whether they are online or offline, whether they have big screens or small screens, there are no places above the law, no special enclaves for public opinion. Supervisory agencies must perform well their duties of supervision and strengthen the management of emerging media according to the law in order to make our internet space clearer and brighter."[62] Recent quotations are from Xi's speeches on the "people's war" against the coronavirus, such as one where he talked about propaganda work related to the "war": "We've strengthened our propaganda and public-opinion work, integrating online and offline, domestic and international, big issues and small matters, in order to create an atmosphere that builds confidence, warms the heart, and unites the people."[63]

Party-sponsored platformization is a process of the party extending its influence into social media platforms and apps. In this process, the party also aspires to turn its own media agencies into platforms by providing downloadable apps and supporting user participation. It is the continuation of an earlier history of Chinese internet politics into the social media age. In this earlier history, the global internet gradually took on Chinese characteristics in the course of its evolution in China, such that it may have become "a separate closed Monopoly board,"[64] or at least an internet so heavily imprinted with Chinese characteristics that it might be called "the PRC internet."[65] Thus, party-sponsored platformization is not entirely new but is part of a longer history of the political and cultural shaping of the internet in China.

Like the market-dominated platformization in the West, party-sponsored platformization has a technological logic—the technological features of social media platforms shape user behavior. For example, whereas a Weibo user can accumulate thousands and even millions of followers, WeChat users can have only a small number of WeChat friends because WeChat's Moment and chat features are designed mainly for personal use. To read my Moments, you will need to have already become my WeChat friend.[66] WeChat users can build "circles" of friends, but the maximum number of friends in any circle is five hundred. Thus, Weibo is a more public platform with the capacity for large numbers of strangers to interact, whereas WeChat is better suited for small-group interactions.

Second, like the market-dominated platformization in the West, party-sponsored platformization in China has its commercial logic. All the major internet platforms in China—WeChat, Weibo, Baidu, Alibaba, Douban, and so forth—are first and foremost private business firms. Like their U.S. counterparts, they hype the values of connectivity, sharing, and community to incite users to participate in social media interaction.[67] But the commercial logic of Chinese social media platforms also has its own culturally specific elements. For example, one way of promoting user participation is to adapt social media to age-old traditions. During the Lunar New Year celebrations in 2014, WeChat introduced the "virtual red envelope" application. As a popular Lunar New Year custom, parents hand out to children cash gifts sealed in red envelopes. Friends and relatives may also exchange red envelopes. When WeChat introduced its virtual red envelope in 2014, it was an instant hit because of its convenience. On WeChat, you could give virtual red envelopes of small amounts of money to anyone in your contact list. You could also give away red envelopes to members of your WeChat "circles." The money was usually in very small amounts, but the use of the virtual envelopes was a game of virtually socializing with friends. It was so popular that it drove up the number of users of WeChat Pay to rival Alibaba's Alipay.

Third, although American platforms such as Facebook and Twitter have their own politics,[68] there is a distinct Chinese political logic to platformization in China. In this logic, the bottom line of internet politics is the party line.[69] But as in media politics, the boundaries of internet politics in China are fluid and porous, and practices on the ground are often about creative means of negotiation and improvisation.[70] The dialectics of party-line domination and bottom-up practices are intricate. For example, whereas some analysts emphasize the authoritarian nature of Chinese internet politics,[71] others stress contestation,[72] censorship,[73] or citizens' activist and playful appropriation.[74] Still others study issues of internet sovereignty, global internet governance, and cybersecurity.[75]

The political dimension of party-sponsored platformization entails not only the usual methods of censorship but also a growing repertoire of new tactics and methods, especially the use of the ideological discourses of civility and positive energy to cleanse the web of negative emotions. Another method is the "occupying" of the web, or party–state efforts to manage and shape internet expression by directly participating in it, which includes operating official accounts on social media platforms.[76]For example, in September 2010 the Ministry of Public Security held a national conference to promote the use of microblogs by public-security agencies. Methods of "occupying" the web also include what one scholar refers to as "the reinvention of official culture that aims at having a stronger voice online," such as the appropriation of fan culture by the Chinese Youth League's Weibo account.[77]

The political logic of party platformization is not necessarily at odds with the logic of market platformization. On the contrary, it often incorporates elements of the market logic to enhance its appeal. For example, to grow followers and gain user attention, accounts run by government agencies post sensational, clickbait headlines in the style typical of commercial accounts. A study by the Chinese communication scholar Peng Lan 彭兰 shows that almost all of the most popular short videos on the platform Douyin, the Chinese version of TikTok, for the period May 1 to November 30, 2018, were released by state-owned media agencies, and most of their titles were no different from the clickbait headlines of commercial social media accounts:

Woman Hears Strange noise in Living Room at Night. When She Checks, She Encounters This. Dog Saves Her Life at Critical Moment.

It Must Be Because of Divine Connection: Guy in Search of Lost Dog Fell Into a Pit Only to See His Dog There Too[78]

These headlines pique readers' curiosity but deliver no news of any social or political significance. In short, by civilizing, occupying, and commercializing the web, party-supported platformization has dampened the contentious landscape of the Chinese internet.[79]

It was in this web sphere, transformed by the party and depoliticized by profit-driven businesses, that the initial warnings about COVID-19 were snubbed and the whistle-blowers silenced. On January 1, 2020, when Wuhan police authorities announced that eight individuals had been "dealt with" for spreading rumors about an unidentified pneumonia, no one seemed to question the announcement publicly. Neither individual citizens nor professional journalists tried to find out who the eight individuals were and exactly what they said and where. Fighting online rumors had become a new normal in a time of positive energy. Rumors and other forms of deception did fill cyberspace to the extent that netizens wanted rumor-mongers to be punished. Used to news about crackdowns on internet rumors, readers presumably took this story as just another piece of such news. Little did they know that the "rumors" spread by the eight individuals were actualities that would affect everyone's life profoundly. By the time they woke up to the truth, however, the virus had shut down the city of Wuhan.

3

PEOPLE'S WAR

HARDCORE

The lockdown of Wuhan marked the official launch of China's war on COVID-19. The efficacy of this national mobilization has been touted by Chinese media and acknowledged by the World Health Organization. What is less known is how the mobilization unfolded on the ground, how policies were enforced, and how citizens responded. Let's start with policy enforcement.

Called a "people's war of disease prevention and control,"[1] the national mobilization was led by a centralized command system.[2] At the top of this command chain were Xi Jinping and the CCP Politburo. Then there was the Leading Group for Novel Coronavirus Prevention and Control led by Premier Li Keqiang. A Central Guiding Group led by Politburo member and Vice Premier Sun Chunlan was dispatched to Wuhan to guide work there.

Emergency national mobilization measures were implemented. Makeshift hospitals were built in record time, adding 100,000 hospital beds and making it possible to hospitalize all COVID patients. More than 42,000 medical professionals from around the country, including military medics, descended on Wuhan to help staff the local hospitals. They were given a heroic name—"reverse travelers" (*nixing zhe* 逆行者), meaning people who run toward not away from danger.

The lockdown suspended traffic in and out of Wuhan. Residents were required to wear face masks in public spaces and to refrain from leaving home.[3] Although no stay-at-home order was issued until February 10, few left home. And when the stay-at-home order did come, it was the strictest ever. A system called "closed management" (*fengbi guanli* 封闭管理) was enforced in Wuhan on February 10 and closed down all residential communities, with only essential workers allowed in or out.[4] Organizers and volunteers of residential communities (*shequ* 社区) played a key role in enforcing the closed management while delivering essential services such as groceries.[5]

Warlike scenes, some more violent than others, appeared across the country. Outside Hubei province, people from Hubei were stigmatized. Gas stations and highway rest areas turned away vehicles with Hubei license plates for fear of contamination. In one story, a fifty-year-old truck driver with a Hubei license plate had left Hubei on January 7 to transport goods in several provinces. When Wuhan was locked down, he was on his way back to Hubei from Sichuan province, but he was not allowed to enter rest areas or get off the highway. On January 29, local police in Shaanxi province found him sleeping in his truck on the highway with his emergency lights on. When questioned by the police, he burst into tears and said that he had wandered on the highway for about twenty days.[6]

Social media were full of stories and photographs of villagers in rural areas setting up road barricades or even destroying roads to prevent vehicles from passing through. In one village, a family with members who had recently returned from Wuhan found its door sealed from the outside with a large red banner pasted on the door: "This family has returnees from Wuhan. Please don't visit." One graphic video shows law enforcement officers beating up citizens who were not wearing face masks and shaming them by parading them in public. Another video shows an incident in the city of Xiaogan in Hubei province in which a group of people stormed into a private home and smashed the mahjong table at which a family of three were playing.[7]

Visiting relatives and friends to bring them New Year's greetings is an enduring New Year custom. Although the practice was prohibited this year, not everyone complied. To stop people from making such visits, slogans with violent language appeared in public spaces in both rural and urban areas, such as "Even if it's your in-laws who have come to visit, do not let them in"; "If you run around visiting people today, pneumonia will visit you tomorrow"; and "Face masks or ventilators—choose one or the other." The latter slogan is like a curse: those who don't wear face masks will get so sick that they will need ventilators to save their lives.

Images of these slogans spread quickly when posted online. The Communist Youth League of the city of Fuzhou posted a collection of such viral slogans on its Weibo account with the comment, "Although they may look 'cruel' and 'hardcore,' these slogans achieved the purpose of propaganda."[8] Legal scholars questioned the legality of many of these acts. Netizens were amused by the slogans' bluntness but thought they were necessary for the extraordinary circumstances. Ning, a psychology counsellor, pondered why there was not only tolerance but also public support for such "hardcore" measures: "Why is it that when people unleashed their anger on those who did not wear face masks or who were suspected cases of COVID but did not report themselves, there was no public outcry? It seems that such harsh condemnation comes from love. Perhaps everyone involved, including the onlookers, saw the 'goodness' of human nature in the 'toughness' of these condemnations. People's words may be harsh, but they have a gentle heart."[9]

For others, images of people with red armbands storming into private homes were alarming reminders of Red Guard behavior in the Cultural Revolution. One commentator considered such behavior an abuse of power: "While the virus of a disease poisons the health of the human body, power, once it has mutated, is like a virus that poisons the human heart."[10] In his diary entry on February 17, commenting on the video about the storming of the private home, Xiao Yin 小引 warned that the coronavirus had created secondary disasters, such as this kind of violence. He was worried that such violence might enjoy broad public support.[11]

LOUDSPEAKERS

One facet of the campaign against COVID-19 is particularly revealing of its warlike character—its loudness. The hardcore slogans were loud if they were read or broadcast, as sometimes happened. But the loudest noise came from loudspeakers. In the Mao era, wired radios and loudspeakers were a ubiquitous part of Chinese life. They were used for political propaganda, campaign mobilization, and labor discipline.[12] In villages, for example, loudspeakers would blast out reminders in the morning to villagers that it was time to head to the field and start work. By the late 1970s, these wired networks had covered 90 percent of China's numerous villages. The advent of television culture in the 1980s led to the decline of the use of loudspeakers. In recent years, however, loudspeakers are being reinvented and revived as part of the national program of "building a new countryside." In the digital age, the old-style wired networks have been transformed into digital and internet networks of loudspeakers. In the early 2010s, there were already grassroots initiatives to revive and update the traditional loudspeaker system in rural areas in Fujian by connecting it to internet networks. Similar initiatives were launched in 2016 in Hunan and in 2017 in Hebei.[13] On November 7, 2017, CCTV reported a story about a "new countryside loudspeaker project" in the city of Shijiazhuang in Hebei province. Within a year of the airing of this story, the new loudspeaker project had been expanded to two hundred cities and counties around the country.[14] In the city of Cangzhou, for example, from 2017 to 2020 loudspeaker broadcasting was introduced to 5,659 villages.[15] These developments were boosted by policies issued in 2017 by the then State Administration of Press, Publication, Radio, Film, and Television to build a national emergency broadcasting system. "Let every village be wired with loudspeakers" (*cuncun xiang* 村村响) became a new campaign-style slogan.

This new digitalized loudspeaker infrastructure was activated after Wuhan was locked down. On January 28, 2020, the Cangzhou municipal party department in charge of personnel appointment issued a notice requiring "the full use of loudspeaker platforms throughout the city to transmit all the information, commands, and requirements about the fight against the coronavirus to every single household at the fastest speed."[16] In a compilation of thirteen cases of loudspeaker broadcasting during the Wuhan lockdown, Chinese researchers found that five of the thirteen cases adopted the broadcasting style of parents lecturing their children (*jiazhang xunhua shi* 家长训话式), while five other cases used folk cultural forms such as slippery jingles (*shunkouliu* 顺口溜) and Henan-style opera (*yuju* 豫剧). Only in one case in Fujian province did the speaker use a "gentle encouraging" style.[17]

It is not surprising, therefore, that such village-style broadcasting was recorded in lockdown diaries. Mr. Sheng went back to his village hometown in Henan for the Lunar New Year, where he was stuck after the epidemic outbreak. In his diary on January 29, he wrote about the use of the loudspeaker in his village:

Before I got up in the morning, at about 7:00 or 8:00 a.m., the village loudspeaker began shouting. Like yesterday, it was propagating about the novel coronavirus, warning villagers not to visit relatives or friends, but to wear face masks, maintain good ventilation, wash hands frequently, etc. I had thought that some real person was shouting over the loudspeaker and it would be done once everything was said. But then it was played and replayed, and the whole day was spent broadcasting two speeches. When it first started, I had the dreamy feeling of being back in the television and films of the 1960s and '70s.[18]

Loudspeakers carry a sense of raw power. In the early days of the lockdown, many hand-made videos and audios of loudspeaker broadcasting were posted online. Some of these show village leaders blasting out harsh warnings to villagers in colorful local dialects, as in the following example:

Villagers, attention please. Villagers, attention. I have something to say. What about? Based on my observations these days, I found our village has some problems. Many villagers have lots of problems. Let me tell you, tell you. First, I've been shouting over the loudspeakers for a few days. You all know our roads are closed. You are not allowed to visit relatives or other families. You're not allowed to run around. Yesterday, the whole day, many people were running around. Do you not fear death, or are you morons? Just stay home! Don't run around. Don't visit anyone. Some people are playing mahjong, and organizing mahjong parties at home. Do you really not fear death? Or is money more important? Don't think I'm giving you an earful. If something [bad] happens to you, I tell you, you don't know where to go to cry. These days, the higher-ups have very strict rules. All the rules prohibit you to visit relatives or others. So you just play mahjong if you can't visit relatives? I broadcast yesterday and the day before yesterday. But some people just wouldn't listen. They took this matter like wind blowing past the ear. So your families are all made of iron? All molded in steel? Your families have no fear? How can you be like this? You run around in the street and even organize mahjong parties. What are you up to? Don't say I'm giving you an earful. Let me tell you, if something happens to you, it will be too late to cry.[19]

The sense of urgency that the village head conveyed in his loud and strong Henan accent was hard to translate, but the rhetoric he used and the threats he shouted out to his fellow villagers left no doubt about his seriousness. Here we have a grassroots figure of authority yelling at his fellow villagers in unmasked, violent tones to urge them to obey quarantine orders.

In the French philosopher Louis Althusser's famous illustration of an ideological subject, an imagined police officer hails an individual, "Hey, you there!" The moment the hailed person turns around in response, that person becomes a subject of the state. Hailing, or interpellation, is how ideology recruits its subjects.[20] In Althusser's theory of ideology, a police figure personifies the power of the state. Thus, when the police figure hails a random individual in the street, it is literally also the state hailing its citizens.

Was the village head in Henan province hailing his villagers like a police officer hailing citizens in the street? Yes and no. A village head is, after all, the grassroots leader in the Chinese state's administrative structure. By invoking the "strict rules" of the higher-ups, he recognized his role in this hierarchy. But he did not appeal directly to the law or threaten to call the police on fellow villagers. Instead, he appealed to family morality and primordial fears of death. He repeatedly asked: "Do you really not fear death?" "Your families have no fear?" He warned his villagers that if they didn't listen to him, they would regret it "if something happens to you." His was the stern voice of a paternal grassroots leader, who probably knew everyone in his village and sincerely wanted to convince them to stay home through moral persuasion. The bluntness of his language betrayed an earnestness about matters of life and death.

Although Althusser emphasizes the power of ideologies to form willing subjects, his example of a police officer hailing an individual in the street cannot preclude the possibility of the individual either ignoring or hailing back at the police. In reality, people do hail back, not as docile subjects but as active citizens. Hailing by state agents can create its own opponents and interlocuters as well as its subjects.

The Wuhan lockdown provided unique conditions for a politics of hailing, yelling, shouting, banging, and screaming. The ubiquitous wearing of face masks in public spaces meant that mutual recognition between individuals could no longer rely solely on visual cues as in the past. If you could not see the masked face of someone gesturing at you from across the street, a surer approach to mutual recognition was to yell at each other. Voice or sound became more important for public communication than it had been previously.

BLUNT FORCE

In cities, the war on COVID-19 also had a loud and moral character. In his diary entry on March 11, Mr. Fu, a university professor in Wuhan, wrote about the calming effects of the sounds from mobile-broadcasting patrol vehicles near his home:

> Every morning, community patrol vehicles would pass through the streets nearby, blasting out announcements about coronavirus control and prevention through their loudspeakers. In fact, in an age of extremely

developed information and communication channels, this form of propaganda and announcements is no longer necessary. Plus, the content of the broadcast is quite long. Before a sentence is finished, the vehicle has already turned the street corner. Even its remaining echoes are blocked by the high-rise buildings. However, the sound of this broadcast is calm and metallic. To some extent, it seems to have an effect on calming emotions and reducing fears. To put it another way, as a form of expression for public service, this kind of broadcasting represents a certain kind of authority and truthfulness.[21]

On February 28, Ms. Yan, a community volunteer, wrote in her diary that a community staff member used a boombox to blast out the following warning at the entrance to the community where she stood guard as a volunteer:

Residents: The epidemic is very serious. Please do not leave your home. Do not leave home. If you leave home, you're seeking your own death! If one person gets infected, the whole family suffers. If the whole family are infected, the whole apartment building will suffer. If anyone has a fever in your family, please call community phone numbers. . . . You'd rather get drunk yourself than attend a party. You'd rather get drunk yourself than running around outside. You'd rather sit your sofa to tatters than going out to make trouble.[22]

Here again was a loud message of moral persuasion. It did not invoke any of the strict lockdown rules or regulations. Instead, it warned the listeners not to jeopardize the well-being of their families and entire communities. If you want to get drunk, fine, do it in your own home because if you go out to party with others, you may put your family at risk.

February 2020 was the month when the war on COVID-19 was at its most austere stage. The strict regimen of community isolation was full of hailing and yelling. On February 8, Xiao Yin recorded an episode that brought back to him memories of the Cultural Revolution. He wrote that the community where he lived had been sealed off and the entrance was guarded strictly by three people in full protective gear. Just as he was going to walk out of the entrance, one of the three guards hailed him loudly to stop and have his temperature taken. This reminded Xiao Yin of his childhood experiences:

> When I was small, a kind of cooperative defense and management system was common. We all lived in apartments assigned by work units. There was not enough police force to patrol the community. So a method of people's war was invented: Every household would take turns to take on the responsibility, and everyday there would have to be a guard at each building. At the same time, the neighborhood committee organized a group of retired grannies and grandpas to patrol the alleys and streets wearing red armbands and carrying a radio. As soon as they spotted anyone idling, they would shout a loud shout: Stop! And the person would instantly stop, whether it was a class enemy, an enemy agent, or a petty thief.[23]

In the current situation, the red armband became the white protective gear, and the radio set was replaced by a thermometer gun. For Xiao Yin, when it came to the exercise of state power and violence, not much had changed since the Cultural Revolution.

Why did the war on COVID-19 take so many violent forms? Xiao Yin's story suggests that the shape of the war is not entirely new, but there is a historical connection. The people's war on COVID-19 may differ in form from the various iterations of people's war in the Cultural Revolution, but the logic of state violence persists. Of course, Xiao Yin was not the only one to discern such a connection. Years ago, the novelist Yu Hua wrote vividly about the logic of revolutionary violence underlying both the Cultural Revolution and the developmental state in the reform period. When giant bulldozers knocked down old houses and forced their residents to relocate in the name of urban development and economic growth, the same kind of state violence was at work.[24] As Elizabeth Perry argues, the warlike enforcement of policies during the Wuhan lockdown was an enactment of a familiar political logic with roots in the Chinese Communist revolution.[25] This political logic was at work in the fight against SARS in 2003[26] and in other areas of contemporary life, such as China's recent war on pollution. The political scientist Denise van der Kamp documents a story about the crackdown on pollution violations in the city of Linyi in Shandong province. In February 2015, the mayor of the city was summoned to Beijing to discuss how to address his city's pollution crisis because environmental inspectors from Beijing had uncovered serious violations. Upon returning to Linyi, he ordered fifty-seven of Linyi's largest factories to stop production: "At the stroke of midnight, authorities cut off electricity to an entire industrial park, although some factories were still in the midst of production. In the ensuing weeks, local authorities ordered a further 412 factories to reduce production and forcibly dismantled several smaller, older factories, costing the city 60,000 jobs."[27]

Calling this behavior "blunt force regulation," van der Kamp argues that such behavior occurs not because state institutions are strong but because they are weak—too weak to exercise adequate oversight of bureaucrats and party officials. Blunt force regulation can "scare bureaucrats into taking action" and reduce bureaucratic discretion, and "by reducing enforcement to a one-off, short-term intervention, blunt force regulation makes the threat of punishment more credible."[28]

Blunt force may take multiple forms. It can be as violent as storming into people's private homes, but it is applied mostly with determined patience by community staff or volunteers and sometimes even by one's neighbors. For it to work, blunt force often puts on a human face. Beginning on February 10, 2020, residential communities in Wuhan were put under closed management with strict control of entry and exit.[29] About a week later, from February 17 to February 19, 2020, the entire Hubei province conducted a concentrated, trawl-like inspection to identify individuals who met the criteria for any one of the "four categories" of infection so that they could be monitored or treated for coronavirus: confirmed cases of COVID-19, suspected cases, suspected cases with fever, and those who had close contact with confirmed cases of patients.

These were blunt-force policies, but they were enforced on a human scale, thanks to the gigantic community organizations already in place in China. In his diary on February 17, Ye Qing 叶青 discussed how a city of 11 million carried out a thorough inspection in just three days. One method was to count the lights in the apartment windows. On the night of February 16, all community grid members (I discuss the community grid later) joined the efforts to count which apartments had their lights on. Another method was to go from door to door to inquire about residents' health conditions. Inspectors could also check electricity meters to see whether the apartments were occupied or not, or they set up automated phone calls. The responses to automated calls would be automatically converted into text messages for community staff to access.[30]

Ye Qing is a deputy director of the Bureau of Statistics in Hubei province and a professor of public finance at Zhongnan University of Economics and Law. He works with numbers, and his lockdown diary is full of them. He started every diary entry with a detailed tally of the number of new confirmed cases, total confirmed cases, total deaths, and new deaths for Wuhan, Hubei province, and China as a whole. He often accompanied these tallies with figures and graphs. His diary documents numerous examples of the warlike mobilization and policy enforcement. On February 24, he reported that there were 2,043 deaths and 64,786 confirmed cases in Wuhan. He then reported in some detail that throughout the nation the reopening of the economy was accelerating and that seven provinces had downgraded their state of emergency to level 3.[31]

But his focus for February 24 was the province-wide inspection. He wrote that police stations throughout the province formed 2,258 investigation teams, which organized 19,168 work teams, each comprising two police officers, one health commissioner, and one local cadre. With the support of more than 150,000 village and community cadres and volunteers, the teams conducted door-to-door inspections of 4.27 million people in Hubei province within three days and uncovered 9,479 four-category people, who were then hospitalized or put under quarantine. Of these 9,479 cases, 6,609 were in Wuhan.[32] While commending the effectiveness of the inspection, Ye Qing was appalled that so many cases still had not been taken care of.

Inspection teams, however, sometimes encountered resistance. In one incident, inspectors in Wuhan knocked on the door of a Ms. Jiao, who was a "suspected case." No one answered the door. The inspectors waited outside and tried to persuade the resident to open the door. Ms. Jiao eventually responded, but she and her family refused to be quarantined in a hospital. The inspection team visited Ms. Jiao several times before she finally agreed to move to a hospital. Incidents like this were common. Thirty were reported in the city of Yichang.[33]

COMMUNITY GOVERNANCE

The entire structure of urban community governance was mobilized in the fight against COVID-19, including residential communities, homeowner associations (*yezhu weiyuanhui* 业主委员会), and property-management companies (*wuye gongsi* 物业公司). These entities are involved in different aspects of the management of residential communities, but the relations among them are not always straightforward. Before China's housing reform reintroduced private home ownership in the 1990s, neighborhood committees were the grassroots organizations in urban areas.[34] With the growth of private home ownership, urban homeowners began to organize their own associations to represent homeowners' interests vis-à-vis property-management firms.[35] For the party–state, however, when homeowner associations are too assertive or confrontational, they become a source of social instability and consequently a cause for worry.[36]

Under Xi Jinping's predecessor Hu Jintao, an initiative called "social management innovation" (*shehui guanli chuangxin* 社会管理创新) was introduced to improve grassroots urban governance and tackle social conflict.[37] "Grid governance" (*wangge hua guanzhi* 网格化治理) was part of the initiative. In grid governance, communities and neighborhoods in cities are divided into grids, with each grid consisting of dozens or hundreds of households. Staff members from residential committees cover designated grids. As a grassroots CCP institution, a residential committee works with homeowner associations and property-management firms on a range of issues from service provision to surveillance, community watch, and daily policing. In form and rhetoric, the goal of this governance structure is to enhance residents' self-governance. In reality, it is a mechanism for the deeper penetration of the party–state into citizens' lives.[38]

The following story illustrates a day in the life of a grid staff member during the Wuhan lockdown and how yelling became part of her job. On the morning of February 21, 2020, grid staff Li Yin left home to start a day of door-to-door inspection in her community. She was dressed in personal protective equipment (PPE) and brought with her a pen, a notebook, a thermometer, and a register of the residents in her community. Li Yin works in Min'an Residential Community of Huangpo District in Wuhan. The community has 2,308 households. Her own grid, the fourth grid of the community, has 292 households with a head count of 881. During the inspection from February 16 to February 18, she and seven other grid staff members covered all 2,308 households in three days. Some buildings were locked up to prevent visitors from entering. Inspectors could not enter, either, so she had to yell to the residents inside the apartments to check on them. She told reporters that her throat turned hoarse because of the shouting. She would yell questions such as "How many people are in your home now?," "Does anyone have a fever?," and "Do you have any difficulties that need help from the community?" She kept a list of the community residents who had fever symptoms and would check on them by phone or instant messaging. She got in touch with one individual who had to be moved to a designated quarantine site because the individual had had close contact with a confirmed COVID patient. The person was reluctant to go but eventually agreed when Li Yin said transportation service would be provided for free.[39]

After health codes (*jiankang ma* 健康码) were developed, they quickly became a tool of community governance. Health codes are mobile applications for users to check and report health conditions—fever or other symptoms. If "everything is normal," the health code would show green. Otherwise, it showed red. If people's health codes showed red, they would be barred from entering grocery stores and other public facilities.

Health-code apps developed by Tencent and Alibaba's Alipay were and continue to be in wide use. For example, Tencent's health code, installed on its popular platform WeChat, was developed in early February 2020. By the time the lockdown was lifted in Wuhan, the app had been adopted by more 900 million users nationally.[40] With 903 million internet users in China as of March 2020, this means almost all internet users were using Tencent's health-code app. In community governance, residents are requested to use health codes to report their health conditions daily to community staff, a requirement that presents challenges to the elderly and to people without smartphones. Community volunteer Ms. Yan raised this question when community staff showed up on March 10, 2020, to persuade residents to install and use health codes. The answer she got was that if the elderly did not know how to use the health code or didn't have a smartphone, they could get their children to help them. Their children could input their health information for them and print a hard copy for them to carry if they wanted to leave home. Ms. Yan was not convinced. "What about the elderly who live alone?," she wondered.[41]

HOMEOWNERS OSTRACIZE ONE OF THEIR OWN

Besides the blunt exercise of state power, community pressure was conducive to broad-based citizen support and effective enforcement of policy.

Mr. Fu documented one such case in his diary. On February 7, he wrote that a woman in her seventies in his community was diagnosed with COVID, but she continued to live in the community and did not report her condition to the community office. After staff in the community office found out about her health status, they did not inform other residents but instead tried to find a hospital bed for the patient—not an easy thing to do when all the hospitals were at full capacity. When they did secure a bed in the community hospital, the patient refused to go. At this point, other residents and the homeowners' association learned about her. They requested that the community office enforce quarantine regulations and reported the case to the Mayor's Hotline and the headquarters for COVID prevention and control. They designated the two elevators in the building where this COVID patient lived "Normal" and "Abnormal" and asked the patient and her family members to use the one designated "Abnormal."[42] At around 3:00 p.m. on February 9, pressured by the homeowners' association, the community office once again tried to persuade the patient to be hospitalized. The patient agreed, but when she found that the vehicle transporting patients was going to a temporary shelter hospital, she got off halfway there. When community staff and police contacted the woman again, she insisted that she would only go to a regular hospital, not a temporary shelter hospital, and the automobile driving her to the hospital must not be too crappy. The negotiation lasted until 11:00 p.m. but was unsuccessful. That night, the patient's daughter was spotted using the "Normal" elevator when she went downstairs to dump trash. The patient and her daughter were defiant.[43]

Mr. Fu provided updates about the case in his diary entry on February 10. He wrote that late at night on February 9, after repeatedly calling 110 (China's 911), residents received a promise: the patient would be sent to a hospital before 8:30 in the morning. The following morning, they were relieved to see in their WeChat group that the patient had been admitted into the community hospital. Around noontime, however, the woman was spotted outside the gate of the residential community, trying to reenter. The homeowners' WeChat group exploded with anger. About ten people rushed to the main entrance to block the woman from entering. The guard told them the patient had just left and might have gone to another entrance. The ten people then dashed to the other gate. Meanwhile, a community staff member arrived on the scene and asked the agitated crowd to calm down. The staff called the patient and found that she was on her way back to the community hospital.[44]

At 4:00 p.m. on February 10, the patient's daughter tried to drive out of the community. When stopped by the guard at the entrance, she said she was going to deliver some personal items to her mother. Other residents explained that the personal items could be delivered by the community office and that her vehicle should not leave the community. But she drove out anyway and on her way threw a sanitary hand wipe onto the roadside. At about 6:00 p.m., she came back and was stopped at the entrance by other residents. The two sides debated for hours until the woman called the police. At the request of the police, the woman was let back in on the condition that she would leave the community with her child before midnight. They left at 11:35 p.m. and checked into a quarantine hotel.[45]

In her book *Risk and Blame* (1992), the anthropologist Mary Douglas writes that when a disease is perceived as a source of pollution, it becomes a threat to the community. The person who has the disease becomes blameworthy. The threat of community-wide pollution can be used as "a weapon for mutual coercion": "There is nothing like it for bringing their duties home to members of the community. . . . Who can resist using it who cares for the survival of the community?"[46] The story Mr. Fu tells shows how united the community residents could be and what lengths they would go to try to kick one of their own out of their community. The perceived immorality of the patient and her daughter, who refused to use the elevator marked out for them and defiantly threw garbage on the road, made the community residents only more determined to move her to a quarantine venue.

A GONG-BEATING WOMAN

To some extent, the people's war on COVID-19 was a war of the state and state agents hailing and yelling at ordinary citizens. Order and discipline were enforced vociferously, sometimes by residents on their own peers, as shown in Mr. Fu's story. Although most people followed COVID-related regulations to the letter, not everyone was compliant. Small acts of evasion and resistance were common. Some refused to give up old routines, such as the grandma who wanted to go out to buy steamed buns (see chapter 6). They tested the limits of the rules by making up stories and innocent lies. There were also louder forms of public resistance, where instead of state agents hailing citizens, citizens yelled at the state.

On February 9, Arlie wrote about an incident on the previous day.[47] A video showed a young woman crying out desperately for help on the balcony of her apartment building. The woman was beating loudly on a metal wash basin as if it were a gong. She has since become known as "the gong-beating woman" (*qiaoluo nü* 敲锣女). While knocking on the basin, she cried out in a strong Wuhan dialect: "Help! Help us! I don't want to trouble you like this, but I am really helpless. Please help save our lives." The woman's mother was sick, but the daughter could not get her admitted into a hospital because all of the hospitals were over capacity.

The video went viral, and the woman's cries for help filled Chinese cyberspace with pity. The video moved Arlie to tears. The following day, with the public attention generated by the video, the woman and her mother were successfully admitted into a hospital. They both tested positive for COVID-19, received treatment, got well, and were happily discharged from the hospital on April 10.[48]

This story has a surprise ending that I will recount later, but the point here is that the gong-beating woman's howling succeeded in getting her and her mother hospitalized when hospital beds were an extremely scarce resource. She was literally crying out into the air, not to any particular person or hospital. Yet given that citizens expected the state to be responsible for their well-being, no one would miss her point: her cries for help were directed at public authorities in Wuhan.

What is especially interesting is that although the woman was knocking on a wash basin instead of a gong, she was instantly named the "gong-beating woman" on social media. Beating a gong to cry out for help and air grievances was not a new invention but an age-old practice in the repertoire of protest dating back to imperial times.[49] The practice in the past was to hang a gong in front of the office of the county magistrate so that those who had serious grievances to bring to the magistrate could beat the gong to make a petition. It is unclear when this practice started and how common it was. It is detailed in a handbook about government and administration written by Liu Heng 刘衡 (1775–1841), a benevolent county official in the Qing dynasty. Entitled *An Ordinary Official's Ordinary Words* (庸吏庸言), it has a chapter on sounding the gong (*mingluo* 鸣锣). Sound the gong, it states, "to report an official who detains people without a warranty"; "to report an official who blackmails and takes bribes"; "to report a murder"; "to report theft, burglary, and cases of bride kidnapping (*qiangqin* 抢亲)"; and so forth.[50]

This ancient practice of sounding the gong to air grievances never quite died out. A quick online search for the phrase "beating a gong to air grievances" (*qiaoluo mingyuan* 敲锣鸣冤) brings up contemporary cases. As recently as October 2020, *China Economic Weekly* (中国经济周刊) reported a story of construction workers in Beijing beating a gong in front of a business firm to demand payment of their wages.[51] On June 30, 2018, an auntie in Jincheng of Shanxi province was often seen crying loudly while beating a gong in front of the city's intermediate court, attracting crowds of spectators.[52]

Making loud noise to catch public attention, such as by beating a gong, is a time-tested tactic of popular protest everywhere. The protest that brought down President Fernando de la Rúa's government in Argentina in December 2001 has been called the revolt of pans and pots because a key part of the protest—*cacerolazo*—involved women taking to the streets and banging their pots and pans.[53] More recently, after the Myanmar military seized power in a coup in February 2021, citizens protested by banging pots.[54] Making noise, or *nao* 闹 in Chinese, has always been an important means of protest.[55]

A CONTRIBUTION TO CRITICAL AUNTY STUDIES

Making loud noise to catch public attention, such as by beating a gong, was not the only way of airing grievances during the Wuhan lockdown. Angry and frustrated residents often directly shouted back at state agents and party officials. On February 22, 2020, a WeChat audio file nicknamed "Wuhan Swearing Aunty" (汉骂大嫂) or simply "The Wuhan Swearing" (汉骂) went viral on social media. It was the recording of an anonymous Wuhan woman venting her anger, spiced up with swear words, at a party secretary of the residents' community and the manager of a neighborhood supermarket. Speaking as a homeowner, she was angry that the residents' community staff tried to shirk their responsibilities and that the supermarket took advantage of residents by selling bundled groceries to them. Carrots would be sold together with onions, ginger, or even toilet paper, so even if customers wanted to buy only carrots, they would still have to buy them with whatever the carrots were bundled with.

Whereas state agents hailed citizens to get them to abide by the rules of community isolation and quarantine, the Wuhan aunty's swearing speech was a case of counterhailing in response to the problematic implementation of some policies:

> You are bamboozling us. We just want to buy a bag of rice, but it has to be bundled with toilet paper, soy sauce, and stuff. Brute! Motherfuckers!. . .

If we complain, you will say, "OK, *you* come and work as community volunteers."

That's all you can say. What else can you do?

What good have you done? Write it down and let us take a look. Bullshit!

Secretary Zhu [of the residents' community], I'm glad you happen to be in this [WeChat] group! Let me tell you why I am so angry today. From the time when this group was set up to now, I can tell you our homeowners association tried to contact your office numerous times. Not a single response [from you]!... Yes, you work on the front line. It's true you're busy. But that's your job! And we're doing our job.[56]

The Wuhan aunty swore loudly and unabashedly in a strong Wuhanese dialect. She was clearly aware of her citizenship rights when she shouted that it was the party secretary's job to work on the front line. Her speech won applause on social media. Ping, a retired teacher in Wuhan, wrote in her diary that the speech had cathartic effects on a city in distress:

The Wuhanese swearing of the Wuhan aunty stirred up your feelings like waterfalls pouring down high mountains. It showered thorough joy and gratification on so many Wuhan people. . . . To be fair, she scapegoated community workers for the ineptitude of the government. All the resentment people had accumulated in their hearts poured out with the rhythmic rise and fall of the top-grade Wuhanese swearing. Wuhan people have obeyed government orders. You said there was no human-to-human transmission. I trusted you. You said there was limited human-to-human transmission. I trusted you too. You told us not to go to the hospital on our own but wait for the community to help us. I waited. You decided to lock down the residential neighborhood. I stopped leaving home. But how to solve my food problem? You just paint some cakes for me to look at. When people begin to go hungry, aren't they going to be angry?[57]

Ping's diary also makes clear that the targets of the swearing, even though unspecified, could not be anyone but government authorities: "One order after another came from the Wuhan government. Community cadres were the ones to execute the orders. If people could not be admitted into hospitals and have family members dying at home, aren't they going to blame you? If they cannot buy vegetables, or their babies run out of powdered milk, or women run out of sanitary napkins, aren't they going to blame you?"[58]

For Ping, there were moral obligations between state authorities and citizens. Citizens trusted government information about COVID-19 and followed rules and regulations. They did not question the stringent policies of lockdown and community isolation. But if the government prohibited citizens from leaving home, she reasoned, then it should at least solve residents' food problem. Otherwise, the implicit trust and mutual obligations would be broken, and citizens would be entitled to protest.

The "Wuhan swearing aunty" was one of the most memorable episodes of the lockdown. But like the gong-beating scene, the story of this cursing woman is a familiar tale about tough and fearless aunties. Stories about Chinese square-dancing aunties, for example, abound in both Chinese and English media. Square dancing is popular as both a physical and a social activity, especially among retired and elderly women. Due to space constraints, contingents of these aunties may take their dancing anywhere they can, including martyrs' cemeteries, which often have large, open spaces. This became such a social issue that in 2017 China's Central Administration of Sports issued regulations for square dancers, stipulating specifically that dancers cannot congregate in solemn places such as martyrs' cemeteries.[59] In another story, when the global gold price plunged in April 2013, Chinese aunties, in this case dubbed "Chinese DAMA" by *Bloomberg*, rushed to purchase gold, thus leading to the biggest one-day increase in the global gold price in 2013.[60]

Tales of tough and fearless aunties, however, are not unique to Wuhan or China but are found across cultures and historical eras, so much so that online manifestos on aunties and books about aunties have been published.[61] Even academic conferences on critical aunty studies have been organized.[62] In early 2021, a call for papers for a special issue on critical aunty studies for the academic journal *Text and Performance Quarterly* announced:

This special issue . . . invites submissions that consider the globally ubiquitous and notoriously unruly aunty figures that appear in sitcoms,
memes, theatre, literature, drag, politics, and our everyday lives. "Aunty"
is often employed to describe women of one's parents' generation—you
may know her as ajumma, ayi, tannie, tantie, tía, tita, cioty, khala, or
mausi. She occupies the threshold of the nuclear family, whether or not
she is related; she is a liminal figure who might surveil the family's boundaries or perhaps facilitate transgressions. Aunty is a label that brings
both gravity and familiarity to performers in the public sphere: Aunty
Maxine, Kamala "chitthi," Anita Yavich as "Resistance Aunty," Smriti
Irani as "Aunty-national," drag legend Tita Aida, podcasts such as Bad
Brown Aunties and Ya Gay Aunties. These aunties acquire their moniker
not just through age or kinship, but through performance: melodramatic
speech, maximalist fashion, searing glances, muscular femininity, and
distinct hairstyles. . . . In her incarnation as the opinionated and judg-
mental grand dame, she takes no bullshit, defiantly lays bare her thoughts,
and perhaps even basks in the precision of her cuts.[63]

The Wuhan swearing aunty can undoubtedly count as a proud new addition to this hall of fame of multicultural aunties, a Chinese contribution to
global aunty cultures.

FAKE! FAKE!

Throughout the lockdown, citizens continued to hail back at party leaders, sometimes on social media, sometimes offline but catching national
attention through social media. Another famous counterhailing incident
happened on the morning of March 5, 2020, when Vice Premier Sun Chunlan, head of the Central Guiding Group, was inspecting a residential community in Wuhan. In preparation for the visit, the property-management
office had apparently arranged for volunteers to deliver groceries to the
residents—what was really a show staged to impress party leaders. While

Vice Premier Sun was touring the compound with her entourage, angry voices came banging out of the windows of the high-rise apartments: "Fake! Fake! Formalism!" (*Jiade! Jiade! Xingshi zhuyi!* 假的! 假的! 形式主义!). Residents yelled to the vice premier that the grocery delivery she saw was fake and that the property-management office had not been doing a good job in assisting them during the lockdown.

In her diary on March 6, Guo Jing shared her responses to this incident. She wrote that in the morning the head of the property-management office in her own community sent a WeChat notice to residents to tell them they could fetch free and discount vegetables handed out by the government. She wrote that ever since her community had been locked down in mid-February, residents had been promised discount vegetables, but this was the first time it was actually happening. "Many measures taken to assist people's livelihood sound very good, but when it comes to implementation, it is a different matter." She then commented on the "Fake! Fake!" incident the day before: "This is not the first time that Wuhan people have voiced their grievances during the epidemic. I hope these cries of discontent do not just lead to some pro forma discussion."[64]

In the "Fake! Fake!" case, such cries produced instant results. After her inspection, Vice Premier Sun called a meeting with provincial and municipal leaders to address citizen complaints. Mr. Amber was moved by Vice Premier Sun: "She is at such an advanced age but has stood by us Wuhan people all the time. She never abandons us or gives up on us. I am moved. I solute her Excellency!"[65] At the age of seventy, Sun Chunlan is the oldest of the ten-member executive meeting of the State Council and the only female member. Mr. Amber saluted her not only as a high-ranking government leader but also as a senior citizen looking after the affairs of her fellow citizens, the figure of a caring mother or aunt. For Mr. Amber, Vice Premier Sun's dedication at her age gave her an aura of moral authority.

Ye Qing found the citizens' outcries to the vice premier "quite effective": "These shouts will probably lead to the penalty of a few officials, but they were beneficial to the residents. The municipal government immediately sent staff to visit all the 3,000 households in the community and to find out about the concrete issues to be resolved. You wouldn't know the truth without yelling. Yell, and you know the truth. More importantly, this case should serve as a general lesson for solving common problems." Ye Qing continued: "The vice premier immediately requested provincial and municipal leaders to carefully study the situation. She said that it was quite normal for the masses to have grievances. It reminded us that we were not doing a good enough job in providing the basic life necessities to community residents. Do not hide conflicts. Respect facts. Solve problems in a timely fashion. Resolve conflicts. Reject any formalism or bureaucratism."[66]

About two weeks later, in his March 23 posting, Ye Qing wrote about the case again: "Residents' shouts of 'Fake, Fake' from Wuhan high-rise buildings to Vice Premier Sun Chunlan exposed formalism."[67]

Ye Qing is not the usual government official. An internet celebrity known as "China's most unconventional official" (*zui linglei guanyuan* 最另类官员), he is a delegate of the provincial Chinese People's Political Consultative Conference. In his lockdown diary, he often discussed problems or loopholes in government policies and offered policy recommendations. His diary projected a refreshing image of a government official—smart, thoughtful, well informed, and outspoken. His was a voice of reason.

Ye Qing loathed formalism and bureaucratism. He repeatedly called on the government to tackle these problems. In one of his earliest diary entries, dated February 1, he told a story about the party boss of Jiangsu province making an undercover visit to a village to inspect how the social isolation policy was being enforced at the grassroots level. When his vehicle arrived at the village, he was blocked from entering. The party secretary then revealed his identity and commended the guards for enforcing the policy strictly. Ye Qing wrote: "If the guards had been notified in advance, the provincial party secretary would surely get a greenlight all the way and wouldn't be able to see any problems. Formalism and bureaucratism can harm people to death. I hope party secretaries at all levels will adopt this style of 'undercover visits.'"[68]

Ye Qing's diary entry for March 13 probed further the need to fight formalism and bureaucratism in the war on COVID-19. In his own words, "The fifty days have shown that the correct choice is to fight coronavirus and bureaucratism and formalism together." He pointed out that prior to the lockdown there were efforts to cover up problems, and journalists had to act like detectives to get the true stories. Later, the change of leadership in Hubei province and Wuhan city led to a change in leadership style. The new leaders tried to solve problems quickly, as happened in the "Fake! Fake!" incident. Ye Qing mentioned another example in his diary. Two days earlier, on March 11, a trash-collection truck was spotted delivering groceries in residential areas, causing an instant outcry on social media. Party authorities responded by removing the responsible official. As Ye Qing noted, this speedy response to public opinion was a lesson learned from the lockdown: "In fifty days, Wuhan residents have seen the true face of the coronavirus; they have also seen the true face of bureaucratism and formalism. They hate bureaucratism and formalism to the bone and oppose bureaucratism with shouts and curses. No one will dare to find excuses for bureaucratism and formalism again." He also cautioned against internet censorship: "Be very very careful about deleting postings. Don't delete postings without even thinking about it. The postings may have correct content."[69]

On WeChat, readers praised Ye's daring criticisms. One reader wrote: "Brother, you spoke boldly. Let's wait and see [how things will change]." Another wrote: "Thank you from a fellow native of northern Fujian! You are an official who speaks truth and puts your words to practice. Ordinary people are scared of formalism and bureaucratism. Formalism and bureaucratism exist everywhere in the grassroots. You are the pride of northern Fujian people." Another reader offered advice about how to overcome bureaucratism and formalism: "The most effective approach to resisting bureaucratism and formalism is openness. People must have the right to speak. The majority must be allowed to speak instead of just watching a small minority of 'actors' performing."[70]

GRATITUDE POLITICS

The day after the "Fake! Fake!" incident, the drama of mutual hailing between citizens and party officials took a surprising and almost comical turn. As if responding to the previous day's incident, Wuhan party secretary Wang Zhonglin said at a meeting of the Wuhan anti-COVID headquarters that Wuhan needed "gratitude education" to teach its people "to be grateful to the general secretary [Xi Jinping], grateful to the Communist Party, to obey the party, follow the party, and create strong positive energy." Wang added: "Wuhan people are a heroic people, but also a people who know how to be grateful." Wang's speech was quoted in a news story in the March 7 issue of *Changjiang Daily*, the official outlet of the Wuhan Municipal Party Committee, which highlighted Wang's message by also posting it on the paper's Weibo account.[71]

Following the reconstruction of the Sichuan earthquakes in 2008, people in Sichuan were called upon to show "mandatory gratitude" to the Communist Party. Schoolchildren were subjected to "gratitude education" to inculcate this culture of gratitude.[72] In the middle of the COVID-19 pandemic, seeing that gratitude was being demanded of the people by both Donald Trump in the United States and by CCP leaders in China, the political scientist Christian Sorace wrote that behind the "warm edges" of gratitude "lies the moralising and silencing accusation of being ungrateful. What does it mean when gratitude is no longer a spontaneous emotional response but *something that is asked from us*?"[73]

In the case of Wuhan, netizens promptly rejected Wang Zhonglin's call for gratitude and mocked its stupidity and heartlessness. Xiao Yin captured the initial social media reaction when he wrote that his entire computer screen was covered with this news: "Today is March 7, 2020. When I turned on my computer, I saw the whole screen covered with the word 'gratitude.' Some people were rather sly and pungent. They said China now has another Thanksgiving Day. I was shocked. I hurried to scroll back to read what came before. It turned out what was taking up all of the computer screen was a piece of news about Wuhan: [the call] to conduct a deep gratitude education among all the residents of the city."[74] The whole "gratitude" brouhaha quickly turned into another online protest. The pushback against Wang Zhonglin's gratitude speech was so strong that the *Changjiang Daily* deleted its Weibo posting on it soon afterward. In a clear snub to Wang in a speech made on March 10 on an inspection tour of Wuhan, Xi Jinping said, "The party and the people thank the people of Wuhan."[75]

Wang Zhonglin's call for gratitude presupposed a subject–ruler relationship between citizens and the CCP. For Xiao Yin, this was the relationship between emperors and their subjects in imperial China, but as the Wuhan aunty made clear in her swearing speech, modern citizens did not accept this relationship. They believed that it was the job of the party and government officials to work for citizens' well-being.

Furthermore, Wuhan residents felt it was an insult to be told how to be grateful. They knew who to be grateful to, and they had already expressed their gratitude in numerous ways. They were most grateful to the medical workers on the front line, to the cleaning and delivery workers who provided the essential services for their daily life, and to the volunteers. That is why there were strong emotional outpourings whenever there were reports of the death of medical workers. As one WeChat reader commented, "Ordinary people are not stupid. They do not need be told whether they should be grateful or grateful to whom."[76]

For many netizens, party leaders should be held accountable for their initial mishandling of the epidemic. Why demand that gratitude be given to officials whose inaction and irresponsibility had caused the epidemic crisis in the first place? That is why diarists such as Fang Fang insisted on holding party officials accountable.

Other people felt that Wang Zhonglin's call for gratitude violated a fundamental value of humanity. As the sociologist Georg Simmel puts it, gratitude is "the moral memory of mankind."[77] For the good turns they receive, people are naturally bound in a relationship of gratitude to the giver. It is in their memory. A reminder to feel grateful implies an accusation that they are ungrateful. As one reader of Xiao Yin's diary noted, gratitude (gan'en 感恩) is a beautiful word in the Chinese language, but now it has been abused and ruined.[78]

Again, leaders' demand for gratitude from their peoples in both the United States and China during the COVID-19 pandemic was nothing new; a history of gratitude education in both countries dated back much earlier. In the Mao era, PRC citizens were taught to be thankful to Mao and the CCP for saving them from the misery of an "old" society. But as the gratitude education in postearthquake Sichuan shows, it has gained new currency in the past decade. In the United States, as the communication scholar Jeremy Engels writes in his book *The Art of Gratitude* (2018), Americans are "confronted with a booming gratitude industry." This gratitude industry is part of the self-help and positive-psychology movements. Its purpose "is to make Americans more comfortable living lives in debt. Intentionally or not, the work of contemporary gratitude authors serves to mollify the American citizenry, so that as we count our blessings and take stock of our many interpersonal, social, and political debts we are less likely to speak out about social and economic injustice."[79]

Two different political systems and two different political cultures converge on the same politics, or rather nonpolitics, of gratitude. The goal is the same: to put people in a position where "they are less likely to speak out about social and economic injustice." In both countries, this gratitude education or industry may backfire, as we see from the waves of American resistance in recent years and from netizens' protest against Wang Zhonglin's call for gratitude education.[80]

4

LOCKDOWN DIARIES

A DELIVERY DRIVER'S DIARY

Old Ji is a forty-something delivery driver employed by Meituan, one of China's biggest online platforms for shopping and retail services. After Wuhan was locked down, Old Ji posted his first Weibo message on January 24, 2020: "#Wuhan novel coronavirus# It's coming to me closer and closer." The message was posted with two photos. One photo shows three people in full PPE entering a building in a residential community. The other is of an "urgent notice" issued by the property-management office of his community, notifying residents that a couple had contracted the virus and were under quarantine at home.[1] The notice urged residents not to leave home but if they had to, to wear face masks. From then to the end of the lockdown, Old Ji put up about four hundred posts on Weibo, averaging five a day. Most of them were as short as the one quoted, but there were also longer ones depicting in detail what he was doing on his job and what he saw and felt as he drove around Wuhan making his deliveries. He used various hashtags, such as "chitchat" (*xuxu daodao* 絮絮叨叨), "guarding Wuhan" (*shouhu Wuhan* 守护武汉), "seeking help" (*qiuzhu* 求助), and "#Wuhan diary#" (*Wuhan riji* 武汉日记). For him, these Weibo posts were his Wuhan diary.

In another post on January 24, Old Ji forwarded a short video showing health-care workers in Wuhan Tongji Hospital having their Lunar New Year's Eve dinner. For most Chinese families, this is the most important dinner of the year, but the video showed the frontline medical workers eating instant noodles. Old Ji commented: "As a delivery guy (*waimai xiaoge* 外卖小哥) in Wuhan, I feel guilty. I'm so sorry!" And then immediately in his next post, he wrote: "I feel ashamed to see frontline medical workers eating instant noodles on New Year's Eve! I'm going back to work tomorrow. As much as possible, I'll take delivery orders to hospitals."[2]

His first post the next day showed a map of his delivery route: "My first delivery order of the New Year was sent to the Zhongnan Hospital of Wuhan University."[3] Thus began Old Ji's busy life as a delivery man while Wuhan was under lockdown. His Weibo postings documented this life in detail, showing aspects of lockdown life that would otherwise have remained little known. One post on January 26 was a direct quote from a customer: "Mom cooked a meal. Please deliver it to my father. My father is a frontline physician. Thank you, delivery brother!" And then another post:

> (Be warned about clicking image 6.) When I was about to get off work, I received an order to help a girl who was not in Wuhan to look after her cats at home. She has been away from Wuhan for four days. And . . . when I entered the room, my glasses were foggy and I didn't see clearly. I thought there were dead mice on the floor. And . . . and . . . they turned out to be dead kittens. [Crying emoji here.] One of her cats gave birth while she was away. The owner of the cats was on WeChat with me. She was choked with sobs. What the fuck can I do? Sigh.[4]

In later posts, Old Ji would share other stories about cats, including taking an order to find a missing cat and ending up chasing the cat on the rooftop of a high-rise building.

Old Ji drove around town on a battery-operated moped. More than once, while he was making deliveries, his moped battery died, and he got stuck. This happened on January 27:

I didn't calculate the battery power properly. My moped broke down! Before the breakdown, I took a supermarket purchase order and delivered a big bag and a small bag of snacks. But the small bag was stolen! We're still observing the New Year and this happened? I hope the small bag of snacks was taken by someone who really needed it. If you ate it out of hunger, I would be happy. But please be merciful toward us delivery drivers! This is a time of hardship. We are in the same boat! (Although this makes me feel much better, I still have three kilometers to walk my moped. Who knows how I feel?)[5]

On February 7, the day Li Wenliang died, Old Ji received a mysterious order: "Please deliver a bouquet of flowers to the venue for mourning Dr. Li Wenliang." And so he did. After putting his flowers amid a mountain of flowers already there, he bowed in front of Li's picture and then left.

Although Old Ji did complain about the hardships of his job from time to time, he generally came across as a strong and optimistic person in his diary posts. When he decided to get back to work on Lunar New Year's Day, it was because he was moved by the dedication and sacrifice of health-care workers and he wanted to help out by delivering goods and services to people in need. His Weibo postings of his delivery experiences documented his daily struggles as well as those of other Wuhan residents.

As in other countries, however, delivery workers in China have a precarious existence. Because they work for corporations that use apps to run their businesses, they are at the mercy of algorithms. In September 2020, the popular magazine *People* published a long-form investigative report about delivery workers that drew national attention to their dire conditions. The story found, for example, that delivery workers are involved in a disproportionately high number of traffic accidents, hitting others or being hit, because they are forced to drive at high speeds to meet their delivery deadlines. The algorithms of the delivery apps calculate the fastest route for each delivery and give them the shortest possible time to make it. Delivery workers are, as the title of the story goes, "stuck in algorithms."[6]

And yet, stuck as they were in the algorithms, delivery workers rose to the occasion of the lockdown to offer their services to a city in need. As

Old Ji's story shows, he was moved to action by the personal sacrifices made by the health workers. And he endured hardships as he made his delivery rounds. How was this possible? What should we make of Old Ji's story? Answers to these questions may be gleaned from the wealth of online diaries produced during the lockdown.

AN ART OF ENDURANCE

After the city of Wuhan was shut down, many residents started writing "lockdown diaries," which they shared on social media. These early diaries presumably inspired others to write, and within weeks there was an explosion of online lockdown diaries. Most of them ended when the lockdown was lifted on April 8, but some continued. Their authors represent a broad spectrum of the Chinese urban population. There are more women than men among the diarists: twenty-eight (61 percent) of the forty-six diarists cited in this book are women. They have diverse professions, however, and include high school teachers, graduate students, university professors, poets, novelists, retired teachers, lawyers, frontline health-care workers, government officials, feminist activists, social workers, professionals in media industries, a Christian, and a delivery driver. Two diaries were produced by COVID patients.

Given the diverse authorship, the contents of the diaries are also wide ranging. Some are rich with descriptions of daily life and personal feelings. Others are sparse in personal details, focusing instead on news of the day. On the ideological spectrum, there are diaries by liberal authors such as Fang Fang, the poet Xiao Yin, and the feminist activist Guo Jing, but a few diaries have strong nationalistic tones. Most fall somewhere in between, with relatively few ideological intonations. Fang Fang's diary is the best known, but there are many other valuable and informative diaries. About a dozen diaries have been published since the end of the Wuhan lockdown. If I did not make special efforts to collect or use these published diaries, it is because they lack the original context of online reader interaction and in that sense are incomplete.

Most lockdown diaries were written in the traditional diary form. Their authors called them "diaries" (*riji* 日记), and entries typically started with information about dates, weather, and in some cases the latest tally of COVID-19 cases. Most were one to two pages long, and longer entries often came with photographs. The most popular online platforms for posting lockdown diaries were WeChat and Sina Weibo. Video diarists (or vloggers) shot short videos on cell phones and then uploaded them to video platforms such as YY, Red, and Douyin (the Chinese version of TikTok). All of these lockdown-diary forms documented both personal and collective struggles. The abrupt shutdown of a city of 11 million people stunned China and the world, and the diaries brought home the visceral realities of the closed city.

Diary writing requires self-discipline and perseverance. Even in ordinary times, it takes effort to keep a diary. A pandemic-induced lockdown exacerbated the hardship. Wuhan diarists had to overcome the obstacles of time management, boredom, mental and physical exhaustion, and censorship. Writing and posting diaries during the lockdown was both an ordeal and an accomplishment. In enduring the lockdown like others around them, diarists were also enduring the consequences of their commitment to iterative online publishing: keeping up with repeated posting on social media and managing responses. Each iteration carried forward and partially reenacted the entries that came before it, so the whole series of diary entries became an ongoing dialogue with both the self and the diarist's networked audiences. Writing a lockdown diary became a practice of endurance art.

In *Performing Endurance: Art and Politics Since 1960* (2018), Lara Shalson examines the intentional performance of endurance in both art and life. Conventional wisdom associates endurance with pain, ordeal, and hardship, but Shalson also directs attention to endurance as a *form*. Using Chris Burden's performance *Shoot* in 1971 as an example, she suggests that all performance art of endurance has a simple structure: "It involves a plan and a following through of that plan," except that the plan "can never guarantee its outcome in advance."[7]

In the same way, commitment to writing a diary does not mean the diarist will follow through. Diarists face both personal challenges and external forces beyond their personal control. As a repetitive activity, diary writing can come to feel monotonous—a challenge to diarists' willingness to persevere. The effort to follow through turns diary writing into an act of endurance.

As the COVID-19 pandemic spread globally, lockdown diaries appeared in other countries, but their volume is far smaller than the diaries that came out of Wuhan. Why did they thrive in China? Because no other city in the world experienced a lockdown quite like the one in Wuhan. Cities in other countries hit by the pandemic may have suffered far more casualties, but Wuhan experienced the first shock. Wuhan residents knew nothing about the pandemic when it first broke out. They were taken by surprise. And when it did dawn upon them that a SARS-like disease had broken out, they immediately recalled the horrible scenes of the SARS crisis in 2003. The abrupt lockdown of a city as gigantic as Wuhan drove home the gravity of the situation. Even before any stay-at-home orders were issued, residents voluntarily confined themselves to home. And the city's lockdown was the most drastic of its kind. No other city in China or the world was sealed off as abruptly, decisively, and tightly as Wuhan, and no other city was locked down for as long. The lockdown suspended all outbound and inbound traffic—air, railway, highway, waterway. Traffic within the city was highly controlled. Starting on February 10, a system called "closed management" was strictly enforced in Wuhan.[8] It closed down all residential communities, and only essential workers were allowed in or out.[9] It was under these conditions that so many lockdown diaries appeared online and attracted so many readers. The boom of lockdown diaries in Wuhan reflects an acute public awareness of the seriousness of the health crisis and a desire to document an unprecedented historical event.

ZHANG KANGKANG'S MISSING DIARY

Diaries have a complicated history in the PRC. Some diaries were prepared for propaganda. One of the best-known propaganda diaries is *Lei Feng's Diary*, which was first published in 1963 in the national campaign to promote Lei Feng as a revolutionary hero. Lei Feng was a soldier who died in an accident in 1962 at the age of twenty-two. His published diary contains sixty-one entries filled with accounts of the good deeds he performed in his daily life. His diary was thus a proof of his devotion to the party and Chairman Mao, the key criterion of a revolutionary hero promoted in the years leading up to the Cultural Revolution.[10]

But diaries could also be viewed as sources of ideological impurity and pollution. They could be seized by authorities and used against their authors.[11] Under these conditions, writing about private thoughts and feelings in diaries took special caution and courage. It is for this reason that in the early days of the Wuhan lockdown the Wuhan native and dissident intellectual Ai Xiaoming 艾晓明 warned about the impossibility of diary writing in China.[12]

Still, even in the intensely ideological environment of the Chinese Cultural Revolution, there were those who used diaries to document their private lives and personal feelings.[13] The well-known novelist Zhang Kangkang 张抗抗 once recounted a personal story about the diary she had kept as a teenage girl.[14] In 1969, two of her diary notebooks were seized by Red Guards in search of evidence against her boyfriend, the leader of a rival faction of Red Guards in another high school. In her notebooks, she had written about her most intimate feelings for the young man. She felt brutally violated and dreaded what might befall. Surprisingly, nothing happened. No one ever mentioned her diaries to her, and she was too scared to ask. The following spring she left her hometown Hangzhou as a sentdown youth and gradually forgot about her lost diaries.

Eleven years later, in 1980, by which time Zhang Kangkang had become a well-known writer in Beijing, she received a letter from a man called Guo Dajiang 过大江, who asked her whether she had lost two diaries in 1969. It turned out that Guo Dajiang had kept her two diary notebooks for eleven years. To make a long story short, Guo was a teenager in 1969 and one day found himself alone in the office of the Propaganda Department of his school. Quite by accident, he found two notebooks in the drawer of a desk. He opened the notebooks to discover they were the diary of a young girl. He took the notebooks home with him, read them that night, and was mesmerized. He had read nothing like that before. The personal feelings described in this diary were entirely different from the diaries published for propaganda. They opened a new world to him. Later on, Guo Dajiang was sent down for seven years, but he always kept and treasured the two diary books. He was in college in 1980 when he saw Zhang Kangkang's name in the media and decided to contact her.

Zhang Kangkang's story shows both the potential risks of diary writing and its profound meaningfulness to its author as well as, in Zhang's case, to an unexpected reader. Times may have changed with the profusion of blogs, microblogs, and vlogs in fashion in today's digital age. But, curiously, all of the authors of the Wuhan lockdown diaries chose to call their writings "diaries," not "blogs." Perhaps the word *diary* (*riji* 日记) carries a deeper historical sense and resonance. We think of the diaries left behind from great wars and other extraordinary events of the past. The Wuhan lockdown diaries certainly have an extraordinary significance both to their authors and to their millions of readers. They are the "epics of everyday lives" in a city under lockdown.[15]

ONLINE SEX DIARIES AND DEATH DIARIES

The immediate predecessors of lockdown diaries, however, are not diaries of the Cultural Revolution generation but rather blogs and personal home pages. In the United States, according to one account, online diaries first appeared in 1994.[16] In China, they came a few years later. Many of the personal writings that appeared on personal home pages in the late 1990s were diary-like, although blogging came closest to the traditional genre of diary writing. In fact, the concept of the blog and the practice of blogging in China owe their popularity to the online diary of one particular blogger—Muzimei 木子美. A young woman based in Guangzhou, Muzimei began to serialize her diary about her sexual exploits on her blog hosted by blogchina.com on June 19, 2003. These blog entries were explicit in sexual content, a daring challenge to mainstream sexual mores. The sociologist James Farrer's study quotes the following from Muzimei's diaries: "When I write my sex columns, I think that the liberation of human nature is more important than just writing about the body. The truth that people express in sexual intercourse is difficult to find in other everyday experiences. Nakedness and sexual intercourse are the most effective ways to express human nature."[17] By October 2003, Muzimei's blog had become famous (or infamous to her critics), attracting tens of thousands of hits daily. It was instrumental in popularizing blogs in China.[18]

Another genre of online diary focuses on dying and death. Endurance is a key part of the meaning of this genre as authors record their own experiences of dying of a terminal illness. In China, death is as much of a taboo topic for public talk as sex, if not more so. But the internet helped to break the taboo. The first online diary about death appeared before blogs came on the scene. In 2000, the popular online literature website Under the Banyan Tree serialized the online diary of Lu Youqing 陆幼青, who had terminal cancer.[19] Another influential online diary about dying was written by Yu Juan 于娟 and posted on Sina's blog site. A lecturer at Fudan University, Yu was diagnosed with breast cancer in December 2009 at the age of thirty-one. In May 2010, she started blogging about her experiences as a hospitalized cancer patient. By the time she died on April 19, 2011, she had posted about seventy entries. Some call her diary a "cancer diary"; others call it a "life diary." It is both—her fight against cancer was a fight for life. It was her will to live, her ability to endure, that touched so many readers. On April 6, 2011, less than two weeks before her death, she wrote about her birthday celebration. The most important thing in the celebration was signing the contract to publish her diaries. She was happy about publishing them because "as more people read the stuff I wrote with my life, they could [attend to their health] by avoiding small errors. They would not be squandering their health like I did, they would not be squandering their happiness like I did, until the day when they could only type on the keyboard and stare at the screen realizing with remorse that it is too late." She celebrated her birthday at home in the morning. In the afternoon, her condition deteriorated, and she had difficulty breathing. "I can't breathe. I can't breathe," she wrote.[20] The next morning she was rushed back to the hospital, less than two days after she had checked out of it.

Chinese internet culture was at its most diverse and dynamic in the 2000s, despite all the censorship. Online writing of all varieties flourished, challenging cultural norms and orthodoxies. Muzimei's sex diaries and Yu Juan's cancer diaries are only two examples of a vast galaxy of online personal writing that predated online lockdown diaries.

COMBATING COVID BY STAYING HOME

While delivery workers such as Old Ji shuffled around town, the vast majority of residents stayed home. But staying home was not about idling away time but rather a key tactic in the war on COVID. Doing nothing but staying at home was viewed as an act of citizenship and quickly became a national norm.

Home confinement had its emotional and physical tolls, and diarists wrote frequently about their mood swings. Diaries written in the first week of the lockdown depict residents' initial responses—scenes of apocalypse in Wuhan, panic shopping, feelings of personal helplessness as well as hope and the determination to fight the virus. By late February, Wuhan's lockdown had been in effect for a month, and diarists reflected on their month-long experience of lockdown. In some diaries, there was a shift in personal emotions from sadness and anxiety to inner peace, although a sense of uncertainty remained strong. As Tao Tao 桃桃 wrote on February 21: "Life in these thirty days changed from shock to sadness, to anger, to frustration, to busyness, to joy. I believe all of us experienced the same sequel of changes. I have gradually found peace."[21]

Some diarists reported that they had become used to staying at home after a month, while others continued to agonize over the uncertainties of the lockdown. Here is an excerpt from an entry on February 18:

> I finally realized that people have a very strong ability to adapt. Since the pandemic started, my life of living at home has become fixed. I'm used to being at home. Except for the three meals of the day, our family are all busy with their own lives. My husband often reads his favorite novels in front of his computer. My son has time for playing online games besides making some phone calls about work. Besides preparing meals and

cleaning the house, I can do my own things. To describe this period of my life, I even think of using the phrase "a quiet and good life" (*suiyue jinghao* 岁月静好). The pandemic is gradually being contained. It won't be long before it is over. In the future, I will surely look back at this unusual period of "good life" with fondness and nostalgia.[22]

The mingling of feelings of hope and pain continued through early March. As the previous chapter shows, some of the major online protests happened in early March. But there were also online celebrations of hope and solidarity, even on the same days as protests. March 6 was a day of protest, but a small incident on the same day triggered emotions of hope. On the afternoon of March 5 in Wuhan People's Hospital, Dr. Liu Kai 刘凯 and a college student volunteer named Gan Junchao 甘俊超 were taking an eighty-seven-year-old COVID patient for a CT scan. The patient was lying in a transport trolley. They had to pass through a large open space on their way to the CT room in another building. It was four o'clock in the afternoon, and the sky was hazy, but the setting sun was shining through the haze and lighting up the distant sky with a warm golden color. Dr. Liu paused the trolley for the elderly patient to take a look at the setting sun while Gan Junchao snatched a photo of the two sun watchers on his phone. In the photo shown on this book's cover, with his back facing the viewer, Dr. Liu in his heavy protective gear stands next to the trolley looking to the distance as the prone patient slightly raises his head and points his feeble fingers at the sun. The photo gives off an aura of warmth, tranquility, and hope. Posted on social media and reprinted by major news media, it was an instant hit. At a time of suffering in a virtual war on the pandemic, it conveyed hope. Lan Xi 阑夕 wrote that the photo gave him a magical feeling: "The dead are resting in peace, the living are strong. Each and every one of these difficult days must be cherished. Each and every one of these photo shots must be remembered."[23] The feminist activist Xiao Meili painted a water color of the photo and accompanied it with the following reflections: "Under conditions of pressure and anxiety, many people had a sense of serious deprivation. And the two of them cared enough to stop and watch the sunset. This is like you still maintain your habit of growing flowers even though you were living in plight. This act represents life beyond bare existence. It transcends the 'if others can manage, why can't you?' kind of admonition. I suppose this is why the image moves me."[24]

By mid-March, COVID-19 had been contained in China but was rampant in other countries. In the United States, where the novel coronavirus was declared a national emergency on March 13, incidents of racism against ethnic Chinese and Asian Americans increased significantly.[25] Far-right conservatives' protests to defend the choice not to wear face masks were widely reported.[26] These stories were translated into Chinese and circulated on Chinese social media, causing much alarm and fear. Many diarists took note. Mr. Yun, for example, who started posting diary entries on January 27, had by March 18 posted forty-nine entries and wrote that he would now turn his attention to overseas. His son was studying in the United Kingdom, and incidents of racism against Chinese students there worried him. For several days, he posted diaries in the form of letters to his son, offering advice about how to manage his stay-at-home life in a foreign country.[27]

In recording their daily emotional and physical struggles, diarists also shared new understandings of self and social relationships with families, friends, and neighbors. In her diary on May 5, Jiang wrote that she spent her morning in her parents' home. She first went grocery shopping and then did laundry and cleaning for her parents: "When I was shopping in the supermarket, I felt the presence of people around me. I thought to myself that all these people were there to provide support for their own families. . . . I realized that the pandemic made me experience many feelings that I had never experienced before."[28]

ENDURING LIFE

How did diarists of the Wuhan lockdown practice their "art of endurance"? Initially, diarists had no idea how long the lockdown would last, and few expected it to last as long as it did. The unknowable nature of the end point caused anxiety. Diarists were conscious of the number of days the city had been under lockdown. They counted the entries they had written. "Lockdown Diary 12, 12th day of lockdown, February 3, 2020," Tao Tao wrote at the top of her entry for that day. "Lockdown Diary (60), March 22, 2020, Sunday," wrote Chu Ma 楚马 and Xuan Yue 炫悦.[29]

February 21, the thirtieth day of the lockdown, was taken as a milestone. Fang Fang started her diary entry for that day by saying: "The thirtieth day of the lockdown. My Heavens. It's been so long."[30] Tao Tao wrote, "It's been 30 long days. If I hadn't been writing, I would surely not remember the number of days. Thinking back to a month ago, I felt that it was another world."[31] To live with this intense awareness of the passage of time, reflected in the counting of every passing day even while one was completely incapable of knowing when such days would come to an end, was to endure. In this sense, endurance was to remind oneself constantly that one was living with an unknown future.

Diarists endured self-doubt. Some felt that life was so upside down that keeping a daily account of personal life might be too trivial. Others refused to entertain any self-pity despite feeling powerless. Guo Jing initially hesitated about starting a diary. She did not wish to be seen as a miserable victim and did not feel she was among the most unfortunate. She did not want to admit that she was a victim because "it took courage to recognize one's powerlessness." She then pondered the meaning of keeping a diary from an activist's perspective: "As a gender-equality advocate, I know better than others that to solve a social problem, it is first necessary to tell it. I decided to try to keep a diary because I do need support now."[32] Writing and sharing her diary with others became a way of managing self-doubt and powerlessness.

Lockdown diarists had to endure mental and physical exhaustion. Typing Chinese characters is slower than typing the English alphabet. Thus, even writing a one-page entry can be time-consuming, and posting it on social media requires additional labor. After finishing her entry on January 27, 2020, Guo Jing was so exhausted that she had to lie in bed for a couple of hours: "It never occurs to me that writing a diary is so mentally and physically exhausting. The lockdown freezes time and space but at the same time magnifies our emotions and feelings. I've never paid so much attention to myself."[33]

For Mr. Yun, a college professor of Chinese literature in Wuhan, writing had been a habit of life, "as important as breathing and sleep."[34] But during the pandemic, he could not post every day for lack of time and energy. Before posting anything, he had to revise, proofread, and insert photo images. There were many details to take care of. After losing sleep one night, he realized that it was because he had spent so much time on his diary the previous day that it took up his daily workout time.[35]

This practical endurance was common among diarists who were front-line health-care workers, COVID-19 patients, and volunteers who had time to write only after a long day's work. Dr. Zha, a physician sent from Shanghai to Wuhan, wrote sixty-seven diary entries during her sixty-eight days in Wuhan. Her entry on February 18 consisted of just the following: "It is so hard to balance between all kinds of good wishes and reality. Today was the most exhausting day for me since I came to Wuhan. I don't want to do a thing. Don't even have the strength to talk."[36]

Diarists who joined Peace of Mind, a collective diary-writing project in a WeChat community, had to keep up with others in the project. In her entry on April 5, Ying, who lived in a city in the Northeast, wrote: "Today I still have my diary to write. It was already past midnight when I checked the watch. Life is so busy every day. Only after I have finished all the stuff did it occur to me I still have a diary to complete. . . . But going to bed peacefully after finishing writing it is also a nice feeling. I enjoy the sense of fullness in keeping a diary, although at the same time I am a bit resistant about recording the trivialities of daily life."[37]

Ms. Gu shared a similar experience. She had gone out for dinner at a friend's place. Back home, she realized that she had to prepare to teach the next day, and she was already feeling sleepy. Suddenly remembering that she hadn't written in her diary, she hurried to do that: "Persisting in an activity not for any particular goal, but just for the sake of doing it. Not doing it makes you feel uneasy: a small thing like keeping a diary is like this. It is probably the same in the case of so many people who have done so many good deeds."[38]

Diarists must also endure the risks and realities of internet censorship, a topic I examine in chapter 7. Suffice it to say here that a few of the diarists I followed closely on WeChat had to navigate censorship carefully. They complained about the difficulty of putting up daily postings because of it.

Finally, diarists had to endure both attention and its absence. To post entries on social media is an invitation for reader engagement. Neglect or fame is a constant source of anxiety. While diarists wanted their works to be read, they could not control their readers' responses. Tao Tao, a mother of a twelve-year-old boy, wrote: "There are many things I want to write about—dreams, love, and even my trivial everyday life. Some things I wrote first, and then cut later. I want to be known but fear to be known. I want to be understood but do not want to be controlled. There are secrets in my memos and self-murmuring in my draft folder. I'm open-hearted and frank, but I still fear being misunderstood."[39]

A Wuhan native and a well-known novelist, Fang Fang wrote the best known of all the lockdown diaries. From late January to late March, she posted sixty diary entries on social media. She wrote mostly of her observations and reflections about the pandemic and the havoc it was wreaking on her native city. She called on the public to hold government officials accountable for their actions or inaction and mourned the dead in moving words. For her sharpness, empathy, and insights, she endeared herself to the hearts of millions of readers. Each diary entry was a social media sensation. Her readers would wait long hours at night to read new entries because she posted at night—usually before midnight but sometimes at 2:00 or 3:00 a.m. On April 10, 2020, about two weeks after Fang Fang had stopped writing her diary, the *Guardian* reported that "on Weibo, 'Fang Fang Diary' has had 380m views, 94,000 discussions, and 8,210 original posts, peaking last week."[40]

The success of Fang Fang's diary brought on scrutiny and personal attacks. Her detractors initially blasted her for being too critical and "negative," complaining that her entries lacked "positive energy." Then in late March when news came that an English version of Fang Fang's diary would be published in the United States, she was called a traitor. By making it available to U.S. readers, the accusation went, she had "handed over ammunition" to U.S. politicians, who were already blaming their own pandemic failures on China. Fang Fang had criticized Chinese government leaders for mishandling the pandemic, and her critics could now point out that China had done much better in dealing with it than the United States. Her diary drew the ire of nationalists. Fang Fang fought back on Weibo and continues to this day to endure the consequences of posting her diary.

SELF-MOBILIZATION

Writing and sharing diaries online were also a means of coping with the ordeals of an unprecedented lockdown. Just as the fight against COVID-19 everywhere is often depicted as a war, so lockdown diaries share some of the features of war diaries. In his study of diaries written by Nationalist soldiers and commanders in the War of Resistance against Japan in 1937–1938, the historian Aaron William Moore finds that these military diaries were used "to mobilize oneself for war."[41] In fact, Nationalist military commanders often required soldiers to write diaries as a means of cultivating self-discipline and recording military experiences. As an example of such "self-mobilization," Moore quotes an entry from the diary of Platoon Commander Cai Yizhong 蔡以中, which he wrote while war was building in Shanghai in 1937: "These past five years, our people have suffered indignities and deception that have added to our fury; at the same time, however, they have also become a source of boundless inspiration."[42] Other military diaries of self-mobilization described in fiery rhetoric hatred of the enemy and the bravery of fellow countrymen. Those that described heavy losses, casualties, and the fierceness of enemies also expressed a firm belief that the enemy would be defeated.

Lockdown diarists were engaged in self-mobilization in ways similar to the war diarists of the 1930s. Keenly aware of the unprecedented nature of the Wuhan lockdown, diarists saw themselves as witnesses to history and were determined to leave personal records through diary writing. They reflected on the meaning of keeping a diary. Mr. Amber, a Wuhan native who worked in the telecommunications industry, was staying with his parents in Wuhan and kept a diary throughout. The last entry of his diary, written on the last day of the lockdown, sums up his total output: seventy-six diary entries for seventy-six days, totaling 143,000 words, plus forty poems and some occasional essays. A self-conscious diarist, he explained to himself repeatedly why he was keeping a diary and reminded himself again and again to persevere to the end of the lockdown. On January 28, the sixth day of the lockdown, he wrote that his original intention in keeping a diary was to document his and his family's life so that more people could understand Wuhan and the lives of its people:

> My diaries are a running account, but the records are true. Therefore, in my heart I feel that my "Lockdown Diary" is meaningful. Maybe meaningful only to myself. One day when I look back from my old age, she will be the "Grand Historical Record" ("Shiji" 史记) of part of my life.[43] It is said that there are two most valuable words in the world. One is *self-discipline*. The other is *persevere*. Self-disciplined people keep changing themselves. People who persevere change fate. I must persevere. I will persevere [in my diary writing] till the end of the anticoronavirus and stay-home life![44]

Writing and sharing diaries helped their authors overcome the hardships of life under lockdown. Both fighting COVID and keeping a diary depended on perseverance. Keeping up with diary writing created a sense of accomplishment. Ms. Long told herself:

> To do one thing well requires a strong will. It requires a clear goal as guidance. Giving up is easy. When there are hardships, obstacles, and one difficulty after another, one must overcome laziness and cheer oneself on, in order to persevere. Only in this way can one act more effectively. Neither the continuation of the pandemic nor the busy work schedule after the resumption of class has caused me to skip even a single day of diary. I have written close to 100,000 words. The daily habit of writing makes me overcome all difficulties. Nothing can stop me from writing, rain or wind.[45]

Fighting a pandemic called for a collective will and a belief in science. In his first diary entry, dated January 23, 2020, Lan Xi wrote about the importance of unity:

> Yesterday, I said in my WeChat Moments that I always disliked the phrase "united like a city wall" (*zhongzhi chengcheng* 众志成城). Now that I'm

taking a fresh look at it, it appears much more pleasing. "United like a city wall" means when united, the will of the people can turn into a strong city wall. A city wall may not block the virus, but as long as it stands there, it can maintain a sense of safety inside the wall. Do not destroy or damage this wall. This is a wall made of the will of 10 million people.[46]

The "10 million people" were the population of Wuhan. Lan Xi was mobilizing himself and his friends to stand united against the virus when faced with the challenges of an abrupt lockdown, such as rising grocery prices and the circulation of misinformation. Ten days later, on February 1, Lan Xi wrote about what individuals should do in the face of misinformation as he reflected on a wave of panic purchasing of the traditional Chinese medicine *shuang huang lian* 双黄连 rumored to be a cure for COVID-19:

> *Shuang huang lian* became a hot commodity overnight. This shows without a doubt that tricks aimed to fool people can always find a way of catching their attention unscrupulously. The lack of common sense is not frightening. What is frightening is to . . . put sorcery on the alter at a time when science is needed most. . . . Public life is made up of you and me. All we can do is to maintain self-discipline. Take care of ourselves. Take care of people we love. Make sure to act on correct ideas, respect professionalism, respect logic. Don't yield to stupidity.[47]

Here Lan Xi was using his diary to mobilize himself and the public to trust science, not "sorcery," in an environment where people were easily swayed by misinformation.

Diary writing was also a means of managing the personal anxieties of stay-at-home lives. Some diarists carried on extended self-dialogues with themselves. Tao Tao posted seventy-six lockdown-diary entries. On February 26, she wrote about her effort to practice self-discipline by paying her respects to the Japanese novelist Haruki Murakami:

> For twenty years, Haruki Murakami persevered: getting up at 5 in the morning to start writing. For him, daily writing was like going to work. He would write for four to five hours. Nothing could stop him. Even if he

wasn't able to write anything, he would still sit there. When time was up, he would get up like it was time to get off work and then go running. He would run at least 10 kilometers every day. Every year, he would run at least one marathon. A person who can spend decades in exactly the same way like one day and do things every day in a carefully regimented way deserves a lot of respect. . . . I have a special liking toward such people. . . . A week after the lockdown, I began to pay respect to this kind of disciplined life. I no longer spent all my time eating, sleeping, and watching TV dramas. I began to follow a daily schedule. I find that these days, among my friends, some have started working out, others are honing their cooking skills, and still others have taken up calligraphy. Everyone is making self-improvement quietly. . . . I want to learn from them. . . . I would like to make progress together with my self-disciplined friends. This ordeal is Heaven's plan, and we will complete it together.[48]

In this entry, Tao Tao encouraged herself to practice a more disciplined daily routine by following her friends and a famous Japanese writer as her models.

The diverse experiences learned through the sharing of pandemic diaries as well as the sense of community developed in this process were sources of self-mobilization. In her one hundredth and last entry, written on May 23, 2020, Jiang reflected:

When I wrote down the number 100, it means this "Peace of Mind" diary project has come to an end. Although we will no longer keep diaries, we will continue to live lives with or without peace. I don't know what I should write by way of conclusion. Individuals' attention span, thinking, and experience are all limited. By sharing our writings online, we experience so many different lives all at once. It enriches my perspectives. . . . By documenting our ordinary lives, a group of ordinary people create a strong sense of vitality together. There is happiness in this process.[49]

The day before, in her ninety-ninth entry, Jiang had reminisced, "I remember in my first 'Peace of Mind' pandemic diary, I wrote the following sentence: 'I wonder what things will be like when my diary reaches its hundredth day.' How time flies. Tomorrow will be the hundredth day. And these diaries have kept a record of my life in this period."[50]

Pandemic diary writing formed diary communities.[51] Being part of an online community motivated participation. For pandemic diarists, the feeling of being acknowledged by readers, even through small acts such as liking and retweeting their diary entries, turned into self-motivation. Some would tell themselves to write better and write more. Mr. Yun, for example, often reported how happy he was to see that a particular day's posting had reached hundreds of views or how flattered he was to receive compliments from friends or former teachers. When he finished his entry for March 6, he felt both tired and happy—happy because of the positive responses he received from friends, colleagues, and students. Readers' encouragement made him want to publish his diary, but then he thought to himself that perhaps his diary was not good enough:

> This morning, I read "News from Plagued Wuhan" (来自疫区武汉的消息) posted by the WeChat public account "Xiao Yin's Poetry." This was its forty-fourth diary posting. Xiao Yin is wiser and more far-sighted than I am and has a stronger will. His diary has more depth and breadth. Only when I compare [my writing] with superior writers do I see my distance from others and realize there is a great deal of room for self-improvement and self-enhancement. If I just congratulate myself behind my own closed doors and indulge in good feelings about myself, I would be stuck in the same place forever.[52]

Mr. Yun enjoyed the attention of his readers, but he also read other people's lockdown diaries. By reflecting on his experiences as both writer and reader in the larger community of diary writing, he expressed a sense of accomplishment but motivated himself to improve.

A PARABLE OF WUHAN

As an endurance art, lockdown diaries both are of their moment and seek to transcend it. Even after diarists stopped writing, what they had endured while they were writing lived on in other forms and in forms beyond their control.

That so many people wrote and posted diaries during the Wuhan lockdown is both surprising and not surprising: surprising because the authors voluntarily committed themselves to enduring the hardships and uncertainties of their acts of writing and sharing in pandemic times; not surprising because, despite the hardships, the acts and processes of writing and sharing diaries were simultaneously self-motivating and self-mobilizing. They were a means of mobilizing personal feelings, energies, and will power to persist and persevere—to persist and persevere not only in writing and posting diaries but in fighting the pandemic. Writing a lockdown diary was a symbolic act whose true significance goes far beyond the personal, just as the outcomes of an act of endurance art go far beyond the performance itself.

Diary writing epitomized the larger war on the pandemic in Wuhan. Millions of people there committed themselves to the practices of endurance in similar ways, albeit not necessarily through writing. Health-care workers, volunteers, patients, delivery workers, students, teachers, parents, grandparents, young and old—all were enduring hardships and making sacrifices during the lockdown. They all were engaged in self-mobilization in one form or another. The authors of lockdown diaries emerged from these millions of people. Their stories of endurance are a parable of the endurance of the entire city of Wuhan.

5

FIRE AND THUNDER

PAIN STYLE

At age forty, Dr. Cai Yi 蔡毅 was the head of the Pain Department of Wuhan Central Hospital. During the lockdown, his first post on Sina Weibo was about the death of his colleague Li Wenliang. Each sentence of the page-long message was put in a separate line, so the entire post looked like a poem, an elegy. Addressing Li as "brother," the message read like a long howl of anger, sadness, and pain.

By the time the lockdown was lifted on April 8, Cai Yi had posted about thirty Weibo messages and had become an internet celebrity. His diary-like postings offered a rare and detailed insider perspective on the life and work of medical professionals in Wuhan. Almost all of his postings were like character portraits, telling the stories of his brave colleagues and friends and condoling every death in his hospital.

The posting that made Cai Yi famous was put up on February 11. A story about "little people" who died of COVID-19, it opened with four plain words: "Mr. Lin passed away." Then he continued: "Who was Mr. Lin? I don't even know whether his name was Lin Jun 林军 or Lin Jun 林君 or Lin Jun 林均![1] But almost every old-timer in Wuhan Central Hospital knows him. He was not the head of the hospital or the party secretary. He was only the owner of the small mart at the entrance of our campus on Nanjing Road."[2]

Dr. Cai recalled what a wonderful person Mr. Lin had always been. With just a phone call to him, he would quickly deliver bottled water to a doctor's office. He would receive express deliveries for staff in the hospital. Hospital staff could take something from his store and pay later (and it would be OK if someone forgot to pay). And Mr. Lin was always smiling and never complained. Dr. Cai lamented that there were many kind people like Mr. Lin around, and yet they were invisible. "It is only when they are suddenly gone that we discover how important they were in our lives."

In the days ahead, Dr. Cai would write stories about everyone in his hospital who died of coronavirus—six in all as of June 2020. Five of them were physicians, and one an administrative staff member. He wrote of their colorful personalities, their hard work, their sacrifices, and their humility and kindness as human beings. The pathos of sorrow in these writings was as deep as an earnestness to learn from their examples. They were stories of remembrance and condolence. Readers found them both heart-rending and inspiring. Because Cai was a physician in the hospital's Pain Department, his fans jokingly called his postings "pain style" (*tengtong ti* 疼痛体). Even the funniest of his postings brought tears to his readers.

Cai Yi not only mourned the dead but also wrote about the living, especially about colleagues who, like him, worked on the front line. These postings were humorous even when he was recounting the hardships of work and life. On March 12, Cai told a moving story about a female colleague. Wuhan Central Hospital has two campuses. Next to its Houhu campus is the Home Inn, which had been converted into temporary dormitories for the hospital's employees. By March 12, Cai Yi had lived in the hotel for forty-five days. Initially, he and all of his colleagues at work lived there. For a long time, they never visited their own homes for fear of bringing the virus to their families. Later, when the pandemic situation improved, some female colleagues would take their laundry back home. He once gave a ride to a nurse in his department who had just gotten off her night shift and wanted to pay a quick visit to her family. When they reached the entrance to the nurse's residential compound, she did not enter. Instead, she handed some bottled milk to her husband, who was waiting inside the gate with their child. She did not hug her husband or child. They exchanged a few words before she left hurriedly. The moment when she turned her head away from her husband and child, Cai Yi saw tears in her eyes and was deeply touched. Everyone was fighting the battle in their own way, Cai wrote: "They do not have any grandiose words. It is just one small family after another persevering with great tenacity and optimism and bearing the hardships of separation between husband and wife, mother and child!"[3]

Cai Yi wrote his social media diaries after work. At work, he embodied the same kind of bravery and self-sacrifice he saw in his colleagues. The policy for frontline medical professionals was a two-week work shift. After two weeks, they would be replaced for a new shift. By February 11, Cai and his team had worked for fourteen days straight, and it was time for them to turn over their work to a new team. But when he learned that the new team did not have enough personnel to staff it, he and his team members decided to stay on. Eventually, he was "forced" to leave work on February 17 for the sake of his personal health and safety. He wrote on February 9: "I have never had as strong a sense of professional identity as I do now."[4]

As if in immediate response to Cai's March 12 posting about the sacrifices of medical workers, Ye Qing wrote on March 13 that fifty days of lockdown experience proved unequivocally that "in the fight against the coronavirus, medical workers are the frontline soldiers, while academicians are the generals."[5] By "academicians," he meant distinguished scientists such as Dr. Zhong Nanshan. Zhong played a key role in the decision-making process in the war on the virus and would later be awarded the Order of the Republic. Academicians are few and far between, but there are many frontline soldiers like Dr. Cai, and they literally put their lives on the line. The nature of their work exposed them to health risks, but they showed no fear. As Cai said in a later public interview about their experiences at the beginning of the lockdown: "We were fighting with our own lives. We had no way of protecting ourselves. We didn't have enough supplies. Not enough ventilators or face masks. The temporary department for [COVID] patients was hastily created. It was so urgent. Then patients just poured in. They kept pouring in. You couldn't stop them. They were so sick. They stood at the entrance. Were you going to turn them away?"[6]

There could be many reasons for such bravery and sacrifice—duty, responsibility, professionalism, compassion for patients, and more. But the image of medical workers as frontline soldiers suggested that bravery may also derive from the power of comradeship in times of war. As J. Glenn Gray wrote in his classic work *The Warriors: Reflections on Men in Battle* (1959), military comradeship is a communal experience, the feeling of belonging together in battle. While comradeship may be called into being by external conditions such as the defense of one's country, ultimately in the heat of battle "the fighter is sustained solely by the determination not to let down his comrades."[7]

Cai and his team did not hesitate to continue to work even after they had completed their shift because they were moved by the sacrifices made by their colleagues, some of whom had lost their lives. The sense of comradeship that came from working closely together in a time of danger gave him strength. It was when he got off work and returned to his hotel room that he was sometimes overwhelmed with loneliness. His posting on March 12 continued:

It's actually better to be at work because after work, when people return to the hotel, they could not visit one another. They all have to lock themselves up in their own rooms. The cell phone becomes the best way of killing time. . . . But when you browse your WeChat moments, you could easily see news of colleagues getting infected and even dying. Obituaries and mourning messages about colleagues around you keep popping up in the WeChat Moments. They hurt. Since you're all by yourself, and there is no need to hide your feelings, you just cry. Crying becomes normal![8]

FIRE GOD MOUNTAIN AND THUNDER GOD MOUNTAIN

In 2018, Wuhan had 398 hospitals and thousands of grassroots health facilities (*jichu yiliao weisheng jigou* 基础医疗卫生机构) such as community health centers (*shequ weisheng fuwu zhongxin* 社区卫生服务中心) and clinics.[9] After Wuhan was locked down, 55 hospitals, including Wuhan

Central, were designated as special hospitals for treating COVID-19 patients. But they were far from adequate. They did not have enough beds to hospitalize the growing number of patients. To solve the bed-shortage problem, a special hospital with 1,000 beds, called Fire God Mountain Hospital 火神山, was built in ten days and opened on February 2, 2020. Another special hospital with 1,600 beds, called Thunder God Mountain Hospital 雷神山, was built in twelve days and opened on February 6. The names of the two special hospitals allude to ancient Chinese beliefs about the correspondence between vital human organs and the Five Elements of nature. The Five Elements—metal, wood, water, fire, and earth—are in a relationship of mutual nourishment and antagonism. In the *Yellow Emperor's Classic of Internal Medicine* (皇帝内经), an ancient work on Chinese medicine, the lungs correspond to the element of metal, but fire vanquishes metal. Thunder is associated with lightning and therefore fire, and in the hexagrams of the *Yi Jing* (易经, *Book of Changes*), mountain means "stop." Thus, the names "Fire God Mountain" and "Thunder God Mountain" symbolized the vanquishing of the lung disease by fire and thunder.[10] Supernatural powers and ancient wisdom were invoked in the naming of the hospitals to aid contemporaries in their war on the disease.

The construction of the two special hospitals was turned into a national media spectacle through livestreaming. CCTV livestreamed the construction to viewers all over the country (and the world) through multiple cameras installed at different spots of the construction sites. The livestreaming continued nonstop twenty-four hours a day every day, and viewers could log in to watch at any time. Tens of millions did. Many logged in regularly; some jokingly called themselves "cloud supervisors" (*yun jiangong* 云监工). They did not just sit and watch but actively participated in the process remotely by leaving comments on the livestreaming website. By the time the two hospitals were completed, viewers had left more than 780,000 comments. They praised the construction workers and cheered the people of Wuhan. Colorful nicknames were given to the workers and vehicles operating at the construction sites, turning them into dramatic characters. For example, the welding teams were given the nickname "Emperor Wudi of Welding" (焊k武帝) after Emperor Wudi of Han (汉武帝) because the Chinese characters for the term *welding* and the name for the Han dynasty are homophones. Similarly, concrete mixer trucks were called "Emperor Concrete Carriers" (送灰宗) after Emperor Huizong of Song (宋徽宗), the pronunciation of which sounds like the term for a person who transports concrete.[11]

In the end, the livestreaming of the construction of the Fire God Mountain and Thunder God Mountain Hospitals turned the otherwise monotonous construction projects into a true drama of fire and thunder in the war on COVID. A sense of community grew among the regular viewers.[12]

Meanwhile, beginning on February 3, 2020, a total of sixteen *fangcang* 方舱医院, shelter hospitals or literally "ark hospitals" (alluding to Noah's Ark), were built by converting existing public venues such as stadiums and exhibition centers. The first three were constructed overnight.[13] As in the building of the Fire God and Thunder God Hospitals, the construction of these shelter hospitals continued day and night.[14] The sixteen facilities had a total capacity of 14,000 beds. Whereas the Fire God and Thunder God Hospitals admitted patients with severe symptoms, the makeshift hospitals were for patients with light and moderate symptoms. Chinese policy makers decided against home isolation of patients with mild to moderate symptoms because that could put family members at risk, could be psychologically taxing, and presented difficulties for providing medical care, monitoring, and referral.[15] One of the many functions of a shelter hospital was that it not only made it easier to provide medical care by putting patients under the same roof but also provided space for organizing social activities to build a sense of community.[16] This was the kind of human connection that even healthy people, not to mention patients, needed during the lockdown. The numerous shelter hospital diaries and vlogs written during the lockdown convey a clear sense of community in them.

AH-NIAN'S STORY

"Ah-Nian 阿念" is the web name of Wu Shangzhe 吴尚哲. A twenty-six-year-old Wuhan native employed in Beijing, she traveled back home to Wuhan on January 19, 2020, for the Lunar New Year holiday. She has two pandemic diaries. One diary, which I call "Ah-Nian's Weibo Diary," consists of her Weibo postings. The postings were relatively short, but she often put up more than one a day. These social media posts are a new type of diary suited to the social media age. Her first Weibo Diary entry was dated February 14, one day after she was diagnosed with COVID-19. The other diary, published in print as *Wuhan Girl Ah-Nian's Diary* (武汉女孩阿念日记) in August 2020, ran from January 19 to April 16, 2020. She wrote this diary retrospectively from mid-March to mid-May based on her Weibo postings, videos that she shot on her phone, audio diaries she did with media channels, as well as her postings on WeChat Moments. The published version is longer and more detailed.[17]

Ah-Nian developed a fever on January 28. For fear of exposure, she did not want to see a doctor, and pharmacies were either closed or had run out of medical supplies. After she complained of her fever in WeChat Moments, her friends began to look all over Wuhan to find pharmacies and purchase medicine for her. One friend delivered traditional Chinese medicine to her home. On February 9, her eighty-nine-year-old maternal grandma got sick, and Ah-Nian's father requested the whole family follow a self-quarantine arrangement. As the only child of the family, Ah-Nian was made to stay in the family's master bedroom, and her father would deliver meals to her. She wrote on February 10: "This virus was so cruel. It turned family members into strangers. Although we lived in the same home, our life was like that of roommates in big cities who don't interact with one another."[18]

On February 11, seeing that Grandma was not getting better, Ah-Nian's parents took her to a hospital. Left alone at home, Ah-Nian could not sleep. At around 2:00 or 3:00 a.m., her father called from the hospital and told her that her grandma had probably gotten infected, so he was coming back home to pick up Ah-Nian for a test. Standing in the middle of the living room, Ah-Nian thought to herself: "If our whole family are infected with this disease and die one after another, then this home will become completely empty. Can I come back after today's testing? What will happen to our pets if bad things happen to us? Will they also get sick?"[19]

Ah-Nian and her father took COVID tests that morning. Two days later, they checked the results online via their phones. Her father's result was negative. She made a screenshot of her own result and shared it in her family's WeChat group. "See, I'm negative, too," she wrote. After looking at her screenshot closely, though, her father said: "How come? You're positive?!" She saw her result was indeed positive. Her father looked at his phone and then at her; "his eyes were full of such fear and pain as I had never seen before. Then he began to murmur to himself: 'How can you be positive? How can you be positive?!' "[20] Shortly afterward, she received a phone call from a community staff member. The community office had received notification of her diagnosis and asked her to get ready to move to a shelter hospital. Ah-Nian saw her father's reaction: "Dad stood with his back facing me, his two hands pressing down on the table. This abrupt news of pain and sadness seemed to have sucked all the energy out of him. He would probably have collapsed if he were not holding onto the table."[21] Ah-Nian had never seen her father so broken.

Community workers soon arrived and drove her to a shelter hospital called "Wuhan Lounge." The next day Ah-Nian started posting diaries on Sina Weibo and vlogs on Douyin. Her Weibo postings were mostly short, some as brief as one phrase or one sentence, but their brevity conveyed a special urgency and force. Her first posting on Weibo starts with: "Shelter Hospital Diary Day 1: #Valentine'sDay#. My residential community sent a police car to take me to the shelter hospital. . . . I will try to be the most optimistic girl in the hospital." Her second posting on Weibo, put up on the same day, goes: "Shelter Hospital Diary: The patient in #72 bed suddenly burst into loud howling with her hands reaching forward. She was not speaking clearly and was trembling. My heart sank. I hurried to the help desk to get a nurse. I thought she must be suffering badly from the disease, but it turned out it was because of her personal relationships."[22]

Ah-Nian posted every day on Weibo. Day 4: "Yesterday I was crying; today I'm smiling. Life is just as capricious as this." Another posting on Day 4: "Everyone *says* one should be strong. Why doesn't anyone teach you *how* to be strong?" She also wrote:

> Today I offered my virgin square dance!!
> But . . . I couldn't follow [the steps].
> Every day, friends urged me to do the square dance. While videochatting, my mom also told me to join. . . . Ah, you have no idea how good the Square Dance Sister No. 1 is!! I thought all I needed to do was to sway left and right. In reality, the disco was followed by Mongolian dance and then by Xinjiang dance. . . . Who would have thought that these vigorous

people were mostly shouldering the burden of broken families and the pains of sick bodies? It moved me to tears to watch.[23]

While Ah-Nian was in the shelter hospital, her eighty-nine-year-old grandmother, who had contracted the coronavirus earlier, was put in ICU in the Thunder God Mountain Hospital, so Ah-Nian requested to be transferred to Thunder God Mountain to look after her grandma. Her request was granted, and she moved there on February 19. Before the transfer, she wrote on Weibo: "I'm determined and will never turn back" (*yiwu fangu* 义无反顾). In a separate posting on the same day, she noted that her transfer was neither an impulsive act nor about personal sacrifice: "My goal is to try to get out of the hospital together with Grandma."[24]

Ah-Nian was a COVID patient with light symptoms. Her decision to transfer to a hospital for patients with severe symptoms to look after her grandmother was viewed as a heroic act. It made national news. People's Net posted one of Ah-Nian's vlogs on the video platform Miaopai on February 25. From then to March 14, when she was checked out of the shelter hospital, Ah-Nian regularly posted diaries about her daily life and her grandma, showing the care and kindness of medical workers and fellow patients. One day, for example, she felt that her hospital pajamas were too big for her because she was very short, so she cut off a strip from each leg. Seeing this, the aunty in the bed next to her offered to sew up the loose threads for her.

The saddest moment for Ah-Nian was March 6, the day that her grandma passed away. She had promised her mother that she would go home with her grandma. Now she said: "I did not finish my job." On March 13, she wrote that although she often felt sad and in pain, she tried hard not to be emotional when writing about her life. "I'm optimistic by nature. I'm lucky to be telling my stories in this [optimistic] way. . . . But I do hope to hear the different voices that other people want to express—crying, laughter, doubts, anger."[25]

Ah-Nian checked out of the shelter hospital on March 14 and was moved to a quarantine venue for fourteen days of observation. Life during quarantine had surprises of its own. She found that friendship during the pandemic crossed age groups. She had never thought she would be making handicrafts with two middle-aged men or taking walks and chatting with three guys her father's age. She appreciated her experiences in this period.[26] It was also during quarantine that she started writing the diary that would be published as *Wuhan Girl Ah-Nian's Diary.* Compared with her Weibo Diary, the published diary contains more painful details. Ah-Nian told me that in the midst of the crisis she tried to suppress her negative feelings when posting on Weibo, but when she wrote about her experiences in retrospect, she recalled and wrote about more painful feelings: "I received some private messages [on Weibo]. One person told me that when alone at home and feeling afraid, seeing me and my videos eased her fear. That made me realize that if I could give people a little bit of hope, that would be a very good thing. But when the crisis passed and things . . . calmed down, many of my negative feelings began to show up when I was writing my book."[27]

AH-BU'S STORY

Ah-Bu 阿布, mother of a three-year-old daughter, was also hospitalized in the Wuhan Lounge. She posted her first COVID vlog on January 27, 2020, on the social media platform Red. Known in Chinese as Xiaohongshu 小红书 (Little Red Book), Red is similar to Instagram. Ah-Bu's first vlog was a recording she made from her home. As the camera moved left and right taking in the high-rise buildings outside, loud voices shouting "Wuhan, jia you!" came from the background. *Jia you* 加油, literally "add oil," is a common way of saying "cheers" and offering encouragement (see chapter 8 for more about *jia you*). Some of the screams coming from the background of the video were hoarse and sharp, striking a note of sadness and distress. Several vlogs later, on February 7, Ah-Bu filmed herself. Speaking to her phone camera, she reported that she had been diagnosed with COVID and was at a designated spot waiting to be picked up and taken to a shelter hospital. Wearing a down coat, she cut a solitary figure in the wintry cold. The following day she reported that by the time she was admitted into the hospital, it was 2:00 a.m. She was starving and ate a very late dinner. February 8 was the Lantern Festival, and she was happy that patients were given as part of their meals the traditional festival food—boiled sticky rice balls (*tangyuan* 汤圆). However, she wrote in the space beneath the video that the hospital facilities were poor. The mobile bathrooms were big enough for several hundred people but dirty: "Maybe it is because there are not enough supporting staff, but we have to deal with it. The war has begun. The only way is to go forward and protect the most important people dearest to your heart."[28] Her vlog entry on February 9 shows footage of the interior space of the hospital, which she reported was divided into four zones. There were police officers, cleaners, as well as medical workers. She noted that the patients were in different moods: some optimistic, others irritable, and still others full of complaints.[29]

Ah-Bu's vlog on February 10 made her famous. It was a video of a group dance inside the hospital. A song was playing in the background. Leading the dance was a female medical professional in full PPE with a face mask and protective eye glasses. Although the PPE made her look bulgy, her dance moves were spirited and graceful, prompting a viewer to comment jokingly that she must be an "undercover professional dancer among the medical professionals." As Ah-Bu's camera moved left and right, it showed some patients dancing along, while others held up their phones to record or photograph the dancers. In the comment section of the video posting, a viewer asked for the name of the song. Ah-Bu responded that it was a Mongolian song called "Fire-red Sa Rilang" (火红的萨日朗). The video had more than 200,000 views and close to 2,000 comments when I checked on June 19, 2020. Many viewers commented that they were moved to tears to see such cheerful dancing in the hospital. Some observed that it was a really tough job for the medical workers, who not only provided medical service but also helped create an uplifting atmosphere. One person wrote that a granny who was dancing with her hands up in the air reminded her of her own grandmother. Another called on viewers to help medical workers fight the virus by staying home: "I've tried hard to control my emotions since the virus started. This afternoon, when I saw this video, I couldn't hold my tears any longer. We're all ordinary people; life is not easy for any of us. Let's do our own share, try not to leave home, and protect ourselves."[30]

The group-dance video went viral and was shown on national television programs. There were discussions of it in my own WeChat Moments. Some viewers were critical, noting that the joyful atmosphere was incompatible with the cruel realities of the pandemic. Others felt that official media were using the video for propaganda. Both were true, but they were not the whole story. Perhaps more importantly, Ah-Bu's group-dance vlog went viral because it delivered a message of hope and joy in an oppressive atmosphere of distress and fear. February 10, 2020, was the peak in the number of daily confirmed new cases and new deaths in China. It was on February 10 that the Wuhan Municipal Headquarters for Preventing and Controlling COVID-19 announced that all residential communities in Wuhan would be put under strictly closed management.[31] Just the day before, on the night of the Lantern Festival, more than 6,000 medical professionals had arrived in Wuhan to provide support, showing the urgency of the situation. Guo Jing wrote on February 10 that "Wuhan was a mess."[32] Dr. Cai Yi wrote movingly about Mr. Lin's death on February 11. Arlie wrote on February 11 that "nowadays Wuhan people are like chickens in a chicken coop. They shiver and tremble, fearing that they will be the next to be infected."[33] In the middle of these stories of urgency, death, and fear, Ah-Bu's video struck a much-needed note of optimism and unity, hence its popularity.

Ah-Bu joked that she was a reporter and photographer in a war zone. Many of her vlogs were about the people she called "warriors" or "fighters dressed in white" (*baiyi zhanshi* 白衣战士): the doctors and nurses working in the shelter hospital. To reduce chances of infection, medical workers were not allowed to bring personal belongings into the shelter hospital, not even their cell phones. Ah-Bu offered to document their lives for them and their families with her own phone. She would ask them to say their names in front of her camera and make recordings of them at work. One vlog shows a doctor explaining her health condition to her. In another video, she holds up a note card. When she first received the note, she thought it was from a doctor, but it turned out to be thanks to Ah-Bu from a nurse in the Anhui medical team for sharing her vlogs and for her optimism and strength. Next to her vlog on February 13, Ah-Bu wrote a long passage introducing the various medical teams working in the shelter hospital. About one hundred "fighters" were from fifty-three different hospitals in Gansu province. There were also medical teams from Guangdong, Anhui, and Fujian provinces. One of the male nurses told her that his newborn son was just two months old when he left the family and came to Wuhan.

The medical teams staffing the hospital were divided into seven groups, each consisting of thirteen or fourteen members. Each team worked for a six-hour shift. To save PPE and time, most of them did not eat or drink anything on their shift. They wore diapers to avoid using the bathroom.[34] Ah-Bu's vlogs about medical workers showed their personal sacrifices and dedication. One viewer commented: "Hopefully after this fight against the epidemic, there will be no more incidents of attacking medical workers."[35]

PREPANDEMIC RELATIONS BETWEEN PATIENTS AND MEDICAL WORKERS

This viewer's random comment about "incidents of attacking medical workers" brings up an entirely different kind of relationship between medical professionals and patients in China, one of conflict and violence. In the war on COVID-19, medical workers won universal praise for their hard work and sacrifice. The whole society, not just patients and their families, held them in awe. The most frequently used phrase to refer to medical professionals was "angels dressed in white" (baiyi tianshi 白衣天使). Such a harmonious relationship was the result of a united war against a common virus. In ordinary times, however, the relationship between patients and health-care workers has been less than harmonious. Since the 1990s, it has become increasingly strained, to say the least. Incidents of patients and their families physically attacking, hurting, and even killing doctors have been on the rise.[36] As early as 2010, the influential medical journal the Lancet reported that the personal safety of Chinese physicians was under threat as doctors became victims of violence.[37] According to "White Paper on the Professional Conditions of Medical Practitioners" issued by the China Medical Doctors Association in 2015, 59.79 percent of the 2,638 respondents in the national survey reported being the targets of verbal violence, while 13.07 percent reported being the victims of physical violence. Only 27.14 percent did not report any violence. In comparison with surveys conducted in 2009, 2011, and 2013, the white paper of 2015, which was based on a survey taken in 2014, showed an increase in the number of physicians being harmed in incidents of violence.[38]

In its survey report for 2017, the China Medical Doctors Association found a slight decrease in physical violence against medical professionals. In 2017, 34 percent did not report being the targets of violence, as opposed to 27 percent in 2014. But, overall, the social environment of medical practice had not improved significantly. Half of the respondents in 2017 believed they did not receive recognition for their work and close to half of them did not want their children to go into the medical profession.[39]

In an online survey of 643 orthopedist trainees and 690 neurosurgeon trainees conducted between 2017 and 2018, researchers found that about 40 percent of respondents had experienced workplace violence in the previous five years. Less than 10 percent of respondents were satisfied with their pay, and more than 70 percent would not encourage their offspring to become a doctor.[40]

A study of 150 medical conflicts from 2002 to 2016 found that only 6 of the 150 cases did not escalate. In the other 144 cases, the conflict escalated, mostly into physical violence. In 30 of these 144 cases, patients and their families occupied hospital facilities; 29 cases involved patients or their families physically attacking and injuring medical workers; 26 cases involved damage of hospital property; in 20 cases, patients and families verbally threatened medical workers or attempted to restrain their personal freedom.[41] As recently as 2019, two female physicians at work were stabbed to death, one in Gansu province by a patient, the other in Beijing by a patient's family member. The murder in Beijing was particularly gruesome and provoked public uproar. The incident happened in the early morning of December 24. Ms. Yang Wen, age fifty-one, was a doctor in the emergency department of her hospital. Her patient was a ninety-five-year-old lady who had had cerebral infarction. When Dr. Yang first saw her on December 4, the patient was vomiting and delirious. The patient's family refused to let the doctor perform any examinations and requested only an IV drip. When the patient's condition did not improve, though, the family blamed the doctor. In the days before the incident, the family, especially Sun Wenbin, the son of the elderly patient, quarreled with and threatened the medical staff. Although these behaviors were reported to the hospital administration, no special measures were taken to protect the medical staff. In the early morning of December 24, when Dr. Yang was sitting at her desk, Sun Wenbin walked up behind her and slashed her throat in an extremely cruel way. Dr. Yang died the next day. In the public uproar that followed, netizens questioned the way the hospital had managed the situation. Despite clear signs of potential violence, the hospital management did not take precautions to protect their staff. Dr. Yang was seen as the victim of her own good-heartedness because she was kind enough to take in a patient who would likely have been turned away by other hospitals.[42] The growing frequency of violence against health-care workers has forced many hospital personnel to be cautious in admitting patients.

This violence exposes some of the deep-rooted problems in China's medical system. When China started to reform the system in 1992, the country was still in the early stage of its market reform. At that time, the medical reform aimed to reduce government financing and introduce market mechanisms to support hospitals, but it led to surging medical costs and was declared a failure in 2005.[43] When a new round of medical reform started in 2009, the emphasis shifted to rebuilding hospitals as government-supported public institutions. The guiding principle of the new medical reform was that hospitals ought to be "state led," but the market would still be given a role. In practice, public hospitals continued to become more commercialized. They competed for profits. The mechanism driving this profit orientation was the practice of tying employees' salaries to hospital revenues. Under this system, it became common knowledge that doctors would overprescribe medicine and tests: the more tests and prescriptions, the more revenue for the hospitals. Patients were often at the mercy of hospitals and their staff. Over time, this practice eroded trust between patients and health-care professionals. When patients felt that they were treated unjustly but had limited resources to initiate legal proceedings, they resorted to violence.[44] In response to these problems, as recently as 2019 the government launched another round of reform of the medical system. The goal is to shift from treatment-based curative care to population-based health prevention and management.[45] It is too early to know the effects of this deepening of the reform. One may hope that the new forms of relationships between patients and health-care workers forged in the war on COVID-19 will be an opportunity to achieve longer-term positive change.

FEMALE MEDICAL WORKERS
SHAVE THEIR HEADS

Given this history of strained relationships between medical professionals and patients, the new sense of mutual understanding and support during the lockdown was remarkable. Much of it is attributable to the exceptional circumstances of the pandemic. But national crises and disasters do not touch all people in the same way. As the dire polarization in the United States shows, a national unity of purpose cannot be taken for granted. National mobilization depends on leadership and acts of citizenship.

More than 42,000 medical professionals were dispatched to Hubei province from around the country to make up for the shortage of physicians and nurses there. In ordinary times, medical expenses are a main source of conflict between patients and doctors. During the lockdown, the government covered hospitalization costs for all COVID-19 patients. Patients received free medical treatment, free medicine, free meals, and free services.[46] The government's financial subsidy of patients preempted potential conflicts arising out of medical costs.

Incidents of violence did occur, but law enforcement and public-security authorities cracked down quickly. On the night of January 29, 2020, for example, in Wuhan No. 4 Hospital, which had just been designated a special hospital for treating COVID patients, a Dr. Gao was beaten up and injured by a patient's relative. The doctor was exposed to the virus when his PPE and face mask were torn by the assailant. On the same day, the Department of Public Security in Hubei province issued a public notice to crack down on such criminal behavior in medical facilities.[47] About a week later, on February 7, the National Health Commission, the Supreme People's Court, the Supreme People's Procuratorate, and the Ministry of Public Security issued a joint notice on protecting the safety of medical professionals in the war on COVID. The notice acknowledged the occurrence of incidents of violence against medical workers and specified seven types of criminal behavior to be prosecuted, the first type being "beating, deliberately harming, or killing medical workers."[48] In short, policy and law makers took strong measures to guard the personal safety of medical professionals after the war on COVID started.

But the social environment of support for medical workers created through national mobilization policies and crackdowns could also have oppressive effects, especially on women. On February 17, the official Weibo account of Everyday Gansu Web put up a posting with the headline "They Shaved Their Pretty Hair and Geared Up to Go on a Mission." The story was about fifteen female health-care workers from the Gansu Provincial Maternity and Child-Care Hospital who reportedly voluntarily cut their hair and shaved their heads to show their determination to fight the coronavirus. They would leave their hometown Lanzhou that afternoon and travel about 1,000 miles to Wuhan to join the war on the pandemic.[49] Accompanying the Weibo posting was a close-up video showing several men cutting the women's hair and shaving their heads, with onlookers standing around. On the floor in the background stood travel-size luggage, suggesting that the head shaving was done right before nurses' departure. The background also suggested that the women were not even in a hair salon but in the lobby of a building of their own hospital. Several women were visibly in tears. After cutting off a lock of hair from one woman, a male barber held the hair in front of her eyes, while she turned her head away in visible pain, unable to look at her own hair.

The Everyday Gansu Web's posting was celebratory, praising the young women's head shaving as a symbolic act of bravery and self-sacrifice. But the video prompted a public outcry. Netizens found it hard to believe that these women voluntarily had their heads shaved. They protested that it must be another of those public performances staged for show and publicity—just another example of formalism, this time at the expense of female health-care workers. For some viewers, this video showed that an outdated logic of propaganda is still at work in China today. One commentator wrote that it was a form of propaganda that bluntly glorified personal sacrifice for the sake of a higher good. There is nothing wrong about sacrificing for a higher good, the commentator added, but the orchestrated publicity of it betrays the indifference of the larger entity (the nation) toward the individual.[50]

In her diary on February 18, the feminist activist Guo Jing pointed to the gendered character of this incident: "Was it necessary to shave their heads? Did they agree to do it?" Then she commented, "Women's bodies have never belonged to themselves. There are always people who have more power than women to direct their bodies."[51] Arlie wrote about the video at length. She was so angry she trembled after watching it: "There is no way you can see from the video that they shaved their heads willingly. It was brutal from beginning to end. . . . They all had tears in their eyes and looked like they were reluctant and wronged." Arlie abhorred how the camera dramatized the scene and turned the miserable women into a spectacle for public consumption: "Some people may feel sympathetic, angry, and [that the scene is] unbearable to watch; others may find it thrilling, pleasurable, and exciting."[52] Of all Arlie's diary entries, this was the angriest one. It illustrates the general sentiments of outrage at the release of the video by the main official media channel of Gansu province.

DESPAIR AND HOPE AT WUHAN CENTRAL HOSPITAL

Amid the newfound harmony between medical workers and patients as well as the concerted government efforts to crack down on violence against medical workers, Wuhan Central Hospital remains a puzzle.

Wuhan Central Hospital is a large comprehensive hospital covering a broad range of medicine. It has two campuses—one on Houhu, the other on Nanjing Road. The Houhu campus is only a few minutes' walk from the South China Seafood Market, where the earliest cases of coronavirus were reported. Perhaps due to this proximity, the hospital treated some of the earliest coronavirus patients in December 2019.

Wuhan Central Hospital is infamous not only for the heavy casualties among its staff during the lockdown but also for its administration's utter silence about the ill treatment of its staff. Li Wenliang was the first death in the hospital. His humiliation by the hospital's administrators and the police and then his death from COVID-19 put him in a national spotlight. By early June 2020, five more of his colleagues had died of COVID-19, and more than 230 of the 4,000 employees in the hospital had contracted the disease.[53] Each death made national headlines. With each death, Wuhan Central Hospital came under greater scrutiny. The public outrage did not come just from ordinary netizens on social media. Even official media channels published long stories questioning what was going on in the hospital. The nationalistic newspaper *Global Times* (环球时报), not particularly known for its critical voice, carried a long story on March 16 with a headline that the pandemic was like a magic mirror that exposed the monstrous face of Wuhan Central Hospital.[54] Through interviews with eight medical workers in the hospital, the reporter uncovered horrendous stories about how the hospital management had treated its employees. For example, although by late December the hospital had already treated patients with SARS-like symptoms, the hospital management prohibited its staff from openly talking about the disease and even from wearing face masks. Even after the lockdown had started and the Red Cross Society of Hubei Province began to offer support funds to medical workers who had contracted coronavirus, the hospital did not allow its staff to apply for the funds for fear of attracting unwanted attention to the many cases of COVID there. The hospital administration was preoccupied with guarding its public image, even at the cost of exposing the lives of its frontline workers to known risks.[55]

In his diary on April 2, a retiree named Mr. Lao wrote about Wuhan Central Hospital, where his daughter was a physician. He reported that his daughter knew before New Year's Day that her hospital had admitted several patients with SARS-like symptoms. Although she did not know whether there was human-to-human transmission, as a precaution she asked her parents to move their travel plans ahead of their original schedule. She told him not to tell anyone else because her hospital had prohibited the employees from saying anything. At that point, Wuhan Central Hospital was badly in need of protective supplies, yet the hospital management refused to accept donations from private citizens. In desperation, his daughter and her colleagues decided to solicit donations of supplies through personal networks.[56] The shortage of PPE meant that some of the frontline healthcare professionals worked without proper protection. Lao's story about his daughter confirmed news stories about how the hospital's inscrutable policies exposed its employees to the risks of the disease.

The most curious part of the story is the hospital administrators' silence in the face of wave after wave of public outrage. Before his death, Li

Wenliang had already disclosed in media interviews that he had been censured by hospital administrators and the police. With his death and then the death of several other physicians in the following weeks, major media channels published detailed investigative reports, further revealing the hospital administration's missteps. Public denunciations of the administrators also came from their own staff members, such as Dr. Ai Fen (see chapter 7). There were public calls for the hospital's party secretary Cai Li and director Peng Yixiang to resign, yet neither of them made any public response. The party secretaries of Wuhan city and Hubei province had been removed from office for their inept responses to the pandemic, yet public calls for the resignation of the Wuhan Central Hospital administrators were futile.

On August 27, 2020, long after the lockdown was lifted, Cai Li was removed from her position and replaced, but nothing was said about the reasons for her replacement. It was not clear whether she was fired or simply resigned. Netizens again pressed in vain for an explanation.[57]

Months after the lockdown ended, Dr. Cai Yi, the celebrity physician known for his pain-style Weibo postings, continued to post regularly on Sina Weibo. On September 2, 2020, he wrote that a few days earlier he had posted some reminiscences about the pandemic in the lockdown period. But then he apologized to his fans for bringing back sad memories and announced that he would wait for a few years before posting his memoir: "My colleagues and fellow Wuhanese have just crawled out of the trauma with great difficulty. Now I am taking them back to that period again with my stories. That's not good. I'll wait for a few years and post them when things have faded in memory."[58]

Cai reported, however, that as time passed, the adverse effects of the pandemic were receding, and his colleagues were back to work as normal. Despite all the problems Wuhan Central Hospital went through during the lockdown, he was still proud of it: "Wuhan Central Hospital has a history of 140 years. Although it suffered heavy losses, we still have 4,000 brave members. It's only a matter of time before we are reborn from the ashes."[59]

6

CIVIC ORGANIZING

ANIMAL RESCUE

Gu Meng is an animal lover in the city of Huangshi near Wuhan. Her dream is to live with animals. After Wuhan was shut down, pet owners who happened to be away from home could no longer return, thus leaving their dogs and cats alone. On January 25, after seeing a pet owner's plea for help in a WeChat group, Gu Meng started recruiting volunteers to help feed the pets. Her request was met with enthusiastic responses. Within just one day, she had set up five WeChat groups for volunteers in five different districts of Wuhan, about 1,000 people in all.

One challenge Gu Meng faced was how to arrange for volunteers to enter locked homes without causing safety concerns for homeowners. Their solution was to request volunteers and pet owners to exchange copies of their ID cards. With the pet owners' permission, volunteers would hire a locksmith. The locksmith would open the locked doors for the volunteers, who would then feed the pets. The process would be livestreamed for the owners to watch from afar or recorded for viewing later.[1]

In the recording where Gu Meng shared her story about animals in Wuhan, she audibly sobbed several times when she mentioned the pitiable situation of the abandoned pets. And she was moved by the work of so many volunteers who braved the risks of exposure to drive around town and feed the pets. One volunteer adopted seventeen cats and five dogs.

Gu Meng was among the first to organize animal-rescue efforts after the city was shut down, but she was by no means the only one. There were other groups like hers. The Wuhan Small Animal Protection Association, a grassroots volunteer organization, went into action on January 26, 2020, when it issued its own rescue plan. The plan contained the QR codes of three WeChat groups in three different districts of the city. The association invited pet owners who needed assistance to scan the code and join one of three WeChat groups. It also announced that when its staff entered households, the process would be recorded for or livestreamed to the pet owners.[2] In its WeChat notice the following day, the association announced that it had received 550 requests for assistance within just one day.[3] One of the challenges for the volunteers was that many residential communities were closed, so it would take a lot of patience just to persuade the guards to let them in. Even so, within a little more than a week, they had helped four hundred families to feed their pets.[4]

PSYCHOLOGICAL COUNSELLING

Life during the lockdown exacerbated the mental problems already haunting Chinese society.[5] Together with the Beijing Federation of Social Psychological Work and the Beijing Pro Bono Foundation, the Beijing Huizeren Volunteer Development Center launched Beijing–Hubei iWill Volunteer United Action to provide online psychological counseling to residents in Wuhan. A summary report about the project published in June 2020 characterized iWill Volunteer United Action as a model of government–society collaboration (zhengshe xiezuo 政社协作), meaning that the project was organized by social organizations in collaboration with government agencies. Both the Bureau of Civil Affairs in Beijing and related government agencies in Hubei and Wuhan committed their support to the project.[6]

The iWill initiative recruited about 2,000 volunteers from around the country. Because of the nature of the work, most of the volunteers were female professionals in social work and psychological counseling.[7] Yuan, a psychological counsellor in a counseling firm in Beijing, signed up as a volunteer on January 28, 2020. Her story gives a glimpse of how volunteer counseling worked in one case:

> My shift as a psychological counseling volunteer was at night. I would join a WeChat group of Wuhan residents to offer psychological channeling and support. Initially, I had thought that residents would be full of anxiety and fear. But when I entered the group for my first shift, I saw that everyone was posting their dinner photos. This episode left the deepest impression on me. At that point, I saw the happiness of living human beings who have an instinct to live joyfully even if they are in pain. To use somewhat grandiose language, isn't this about the resilience of life?
>
> In the residents' chat group, some residents would often ask me directly about their symptoms. Inevitably, they would show signs of panic, fear, and even anger. We would rely on social workers to find resources, find physicians to explain symptoms, and bring other counsellors to allay their emotions. . . . From January 28 to February 24, I volunteered 133 hours. . . . On the last day of my volunteering, when it was time to say good-bye to the WeChat group and the residents, I realized that my nightly shift had become a habit and a daily routine.[8]

While most volunteers, like Yuan, provided online counseling, the project also needed other types of services to be done. Han and Yin were two college students in the northeastern city of Harbin. As volunteers, their responsibilities were to process data related to the project, such as statistical tables and reports. This work required patience, care, and technical skills. Both were pleased, however, that they could contribute to the fight against COVID-19 in this way and without having to travel to Wuhan.[9]

AN ANTI-DOMESTIC-VIOLENCE CAMPAIGN

Guo Jing was part of an online network that organized an anti-domestic-violence campaign called Anti-Domestic-Violence Little Vaccine.[10] A social worker and feminist activist, Guo had already been concerned about issues of domestic violence prior to the pandemic. After the lockdown started, she and her friends became aware of the growing incidence of domestic violence and the difficulty for victims to seek help. They offered an online workshop to call attention to domestic violence and then in collaboration with a private foundation for rural women's development launched their anti-domestic-violence campaign.

Guo's diary postings on Weibo became her organizing tool. In her post on March 4, 2020, she reported that their anti-domestic-violence campaign had received enthusiastic responses. To encourage victims to speak up against domestic violence, she shared her personal story of the violence in her own parents' home. The following day, emphasizing the importance of bystander intervention, she shared a story about a friend who effectively intervened and stopped domestic violence in a neighbor's family.

As a key part of the campaign, the organizers published an open letter and called on volunteers to join the campaign by printing out and posting the letter in their own residential buildings and neighborhoods. The letter stated that stay-at-home living during the lockdown may have caused an increase in family conflicts and tensions. It called on family members to respect one another and avoid violence of any form. In cases of violence, whether in one's own family or in a neighbor's family, it advised reporting to the police or community offices. The letter included several articles from China's Anti-Domestic-Violence Law in an appendix.

Posting the letter in public spaces was not as easy as it may sound. In her diary post on March 6, Guo Jing wrote that many individuals felt nervous about it, as if they were thieves. Because public spaces are usually occupied by commercial ads or political slogans, citizens rarely feel entitled to post their own information. Therefore, putting up the open letter on anti–domestic violence was both a means of supporting victims and an assertion of citizens' right to use public space for sharing information.[11]

Several days later, Guo Jing shared the story of a campaign participant in Guangzhou. This volunteer was excited about joining the campaign after she learned about it from friends, but when it was time to do the actual work, she dithered and procrastinated. She thought to herself that maybe she should go out at night to post the letter but then changed her mind because at night she could not take a nice photo for posting on social media. Then she thought maybe she could start with the elevator right next to her apartment, which would be safer. And still she hesitated. Finally, though, the "whistle-giver" protest incident (see chapter 7) gave her the nudge to go out and post the letter in public. But even then she was so nervous and afraid that she was very vigilant of her surroundings. She eventually posted three copies of the letter in three different locations in her neighborhood. On Weibo, where Guo Jing posted this story, the first reader comment was: "So true! When I was doing it, I also had fear. I clearly knew I was doing the right thing but was still afraid."[12]

ONLINE FAN CLUBS

Another form of civic mobilizing during the Wuhan lockdown was done by online fan clubs, alumni associations, and self-organized WeChat groups. Fan clubs (*fensi houyuan hui* 粉丝后援会) are online organizations built to support their celebrity idols—pop singers, film stars, and so on. Young women are such an important part of these fan clubs that on the Weibo account of one club, some messages address the fan followers directly as "dear girls."[13] An important way of supporting their idols is to do fundraisers and other promotional activities, which require speedy mobilization and meticulous organization. Fan clubs have accounts on major social media platforms, where members interact with their idols and each other. Through these routine interactions, fans build group solidarity and connectivity while honing their organizing skills. The social influence of online fan clubs goes beyond idolatry: the clubs have also flexed their muscles in organizing cybernationalist protests, giving rise to the phenomenon of "fandom nationalism."[14]

Fan club participation was remarkable in the early stage of the war on COVID-19. On the first day of the lockdown, a Weibo account called "82 King Street the Dreamer" went into action. This Weibo account is one of the many fan groups of the popular singer Cai Xukun. Fans' conversations in the comment section suggest that Cai's fans are mostly young professional women. On January 24, the account posted a message informing its followers that the group had raised and paid a total of 57,500 RMB (approximately U.S.$8,986) to purchase 30,000 surgical masks and 250 disposable PPE to be shipped to hospitals in Hubei. In an update two days later, it informed its followers that the purchased supplies had been shipped using SF Express courier.[15]

Zhang Yunlei is a performer of *xiangsheng* 相声, a traditional art form similar to standup comedy. His fan club on Weibo started raising funds to purchase medical supplies for hospitals in Wuhan on January 24, 2020. By January 28, a total of 328,350.37 RMB (approximately U.S.$51,315) had been raised. Insisting on the importance of being transparent about the donations, the fan club posted thirty-two pages of the Weibo IDs of all club members who had made donations as well as the amount of each individual's donation. The thirty-two pages listed 3,200 individual donors who had contributed anywhere from one to hundreds of yuan to the funds. These postings attracted thousands of user comments. Many happily announced they had found their names on the list; others praised the donors for their loving hearts.[16]

According to one media report, as of February 5, 2020, nineteen fundraising projects were launched under the Weibo hashtag #To Fight Coronavirus, We Take Action# (*kangji feiyan, wo'men zai xingdong* #抗击肺炎, 我们在行动#) (on Weibo, hashtags include a second hashmark). These projects raised 36.89 million RMB (approximately U.S.$5.8 million) and involved the participation of 1.19 million people. Sixty-six percent of all participants were members of various online fan clubs, who contributed 88 percent of all donated funds.[17]

In the highly commercialized entertainment industry, online fan clubs are an innovative form of promoting celebrities.[18] On Weibo, although celebrities may serve as nodes of these online fandom networks,[19] at the core of the clubs is a meticulous organizational structure with clearly defined roles for individual fans. A typical fan club, for example, has organizational departments for publicity, data processing, and video and text editing as well as teams for fighting negative publicity of the celebrity the club promotes.[20] There are often negative news or portrayals of idols on social media, and such views are considered particularly damaging to the idols if they become trending topics on Weibo. Fans monitor the web closely for such negative information. As soon as they detect trending topics that are unfavorable to their idols, they mobilize rapidly and bombard Weibo with positive comments.[21]

Critics have argued that social media platforms and the entertainment industry exploit the young fans' emotional labor by turning their postings into data and profit.[22] But fans do derive personal joy and pleasure from being part of a community. On January 24, just the second day of the lockdown, Zhang Yunlei's fan club announced on Weibo that the club had donated 1,000 medical protective glasses to a hospital in Wuhan on behalf of all his fans. In the comment section, fans left more than 1,000 enthusiastic responses of support and solidarity. Some said, "I'm so proud to be a fan of Zhang Yunlei." Others said, "Let's unite and work together to overcome the ordeal." Still others expressed their willingness to make more donations whenever it was necessary.[23] On March 12, when the same fan club posted a report of all its donations during the lockdown, it again drew more than 1,000 responses. Fans expressed their appreciation for the club's transparency in handling the donations. Numerous people expressed hope that the COVID crisis would end soon: "Let's wait for spring and blooms together," and "Our idol gives us strength. We fans will follow closely and perform good deeds with confidence in the future."[24]

#StandByHer#

#StandByHer# (#予她同行#) was a hashtag campaign launched by the Shanghai native Liang Yu 梁钰.[25] She began to call attention to Wuhan frontline female medical workers' hygiene needs in early February 2020. She had been engaged in online public debates about feminist issues for years and had amassed more than 200,000 followers on Sina Weibo.[26] Her online celebrity status helped her cause. On February 6, she posted that if all medical workers needed PPE, then female medical workers must also be in need of feminine hygiene products as well. She asked her followers: "Are there reliable channels and ways of donating lady pants to frontline female medical workers?"[27] The responses to her question were enthusiastic. Others wanted to make donations, too, but did not know how. That night Liang Yu asked online fan club girls (*fanquan nühai* 饭圈 女孩) for information about channels of fund-raising. Again, she received quick responses and found out that she would have to work with a charity organization authorized to do fund-raising projects. Through a volunteer's alumni network, Liang found a willing sponsor—Lingshan Charity Foundation based in the city of Wuxi. She and four volunteers spent the night of February 10 writing a project proposal, which they submitted to Lingshan Charity Foundation the next day, and it was immediately approved. They officially launched their fund-raising campaign website on February 11. By the following morning, the campaign had raised more than its target goal of 2 million RMB (approximately U.S. $313,000).[28]

From then to March 24, 2020, when the campaign ended, volunteers working on the ground in Wuhan had delivered feminine hygiene products to 84,500 women in 205 hospitals or medical teams in Wuhan.[29] During this period, Liang Yu made daily posts on her Sina Weibo account, usually multiple ones. These posts include detailed public announcements and updates about the campaign, such as information about daily spending, donations, and hospitals that received donations as well as occasional features on volunteers. Liang's daily Weibo posts resemble a diary in their meticulous chronicling of daily activities. Besides maintaining public transparency about donations, the daily chronicling served the triple goal of the campaign—to support female medical workers, promote female pride, and enhance the visibility of women's labor.

In assessing the meaning of the campaign, Liang attached importance to its professionalism. For her, female pride was above all the pride in women's labor and their professional achievements. Their skills, efficiency, high standards, stamina, and generosity are as good as anyone's. The campaign volunteers' work in raising funds and delivering donations was proof of the value of women's labor:

> Why do so many people want to see some values in us and try to attribute bravery and meaning to our action?. . . We really don't have so

much meaning to speak of. But please see the rigor and high standard of our fund-raising proposal, the professional ethical criteria and competence in the reports we published daily for the sake of transparency, the speed and efficiency in delivering donations, and our team's ability to cooperate and coordinate work. Please see our labor and our professional competence. Really, I feel that from the perspective of professional public-charity projects, our #StandByHer# action is truly a very valuable case for study, isn't it? It would be a shame to look at it purely from a gender perspective.[30]

#MakeWomenLaborersVisible#

After she started the #StandByHer# campaign, Liang Yu received questions and criticisms that what frontline medical workers needed most were medical supplies such as PPE, not "that female thing." When she and her team contacted hospitals to inquire about the need for feminine hygiene products, if the person who answered their phone was male, the answer was likely to be no. And yet on social media, they received direct messages from female medical workers explicitly requesting these products. Thus, from the very beginning, #StandByHer# was a campaign for multiple causes—a charity project to donate feminine hygiene products to frontline female workers as well as a campaign to promote the visibility of female labor and to raise awareness of feminine hygiene needs. This struggle for visibility was promoted with the hashtag #MakeWomenLaborersVisible# (#看见女性劳动者#), used alongside #StandByHer#.

The invisibility of female labor in Chinese media has long been a feminist concern. On September 22, 2019, CCTV posted a message on its Weibo account to salute the laborers working in extreme summer heat. Accompanying the message were nine photographs of police officers, firefighters, street cleaners, and delivery workers—all of them men. The following day, the online feminist collective on Weibo, @CatchUp, protested the erasure of women's labor in the CCTV posting and called on netizens to take photographs of laboring women and post them with the hashtag #MakeWomenLaborersVisibile#. However, this hashtag did not gain traction until it was used with the #StandByHer# hashtag in February 2020.[31] As in the #MeToo and #BlackLivesMatter movements in the United States, the power of a hashtag is coeval with the critical event of which it is a part.[32] A critical event such as the war on the epidemic exposed the invisibility of female labor and made it more urgent than ever to value women's labor. As a timely reminder of the meaning of women's work, the hashtag #MakeWomenLaborersVisibile# went viral during the lockdown.

After volunteers started working on the project, they found that the voices of female medical workers had been drowned out. Xiao Xiong was one of the first volunteers to join the campaign. She realized that the issue was not that these medical workers did not need feminine hygiene items but that some of them were just too shy to talk about it because they viewed female physiology as very personal and private. Others did articulate their needs, but their voices were neglected. Their message was either not relayed to the hospitals' logistics and supplies departments or, if it was relayed, not taken seriously. Medical supplies were the top priority. Xiao Xiong and Liang Yu felt, however, that women's needs should not be sidelined. Their first challenge was to find the voices that had been ignored. They made hundreds of calls to hospitals and found that in the hospitals they were able to reach, about 60 to 70 percent of all the medical workers were female. For example, there were more than 5,000 female medical workers in Wuhan Tongji Hospital, 5,700 in Wuhan Union Hospital, 1,300 at Wuhan Jinyintan Hospital, 600 in Wuhan Hankou Hospital, and 1,000 in the Xincheng Branch of Wuhan Tongji Hospital. As of February 7, 2020, none of these hospitals had received donations of feminine hygiene products.[33]

Among Chinese feminist circles, Liang Yu and her #StandByHer# campaign are controversial. More radically oriented activists argue that Liang is no feminist, that she manipulated the feminist label to attract online traffic (*zhuan liuliang* 赚流量) and build personal fame, and that she is too close to the political establishment to have any critical stance toward the party–state.[34] Although these criticisms may be valid, there is no denying that as a self-organized charity and female-visibility campaign,

#StandByHer# succeeded in mobilizing large numbers of resources and volunteers. The stories of its volunteers contain especially meaningful experiences of men and women in the fight against COVID.

VOLUNTEERS FOR #StandByHer#

Volunteers from diverse backgrounds left the safety of their homes to join #StandByHer# and other civic efforts to fight COVID-19. In a posting on February 15, Liang Yu talked about her transportation team. She started with Di Zi, who she said was driving around Wuhan "fearlessly." Once she asked Di Zi whether her parents worried about her doing this volunteer work, and Di Zi told her she actually didn't have a driver's license, so her mother was driving her around. Liang was shocked, but Di Zi brushed it aside, saying that their team had all kinds of people—a video arcade owner, a clothing shop owner, a cosplayer, a TMall shop owner, a photographer, a motorcycle lover, and a graffiti painter.[35]

One Weibo user commented: "coser, graffiti youth, motorcycle lover—at first glance they look like the 'not-so-serious type,' and yet they are doing these dangerous and great things." Another one commented: "It feels like it's precisely because they have the courage to engage in these 'not-so-serious' preoccupations that they can rise to the occasion in these special times. I truly respect their courage. If I were in these circumstances, I wouldn't dare to venture out of home."[36]

Theirs are stories of bravery, hard work, humor, and toughness under duress. Di Zi was a fan of Italian soccer. When I checked on April 15, 2020, the background image of her Weibo timeline was a soccer game. A Wuhan native and a PhD student studying botany in the United Kingdom, Di Zi once worked as an in-country soccer journalist for Tencent. Before the epidemic outbreak, she was doing research in Beijing and had returned to Wuhan to spend the Lunar New Year with her family, as she did every year. She joined the #StandByHer# action as one of the earliest members of its transportation team, accompanied by her mother every day to pick up donations from a warehouse and then deliver them to hospitals in Wuhan.

The lockdown turned out to be a special time for mother and daughter. In her mother's words,

> Because of the lockdown, she had to stay at home for this long. This is a joyful thing to me. Maybe she will never have another chance of staying at home for such a long time. We can do things together. We have so much time to spend together and talk. That's why if she needs to go out to do volunteer work, I'm happy to accompany her. Mothers are all like this. If I follow her and watch over her, I can always remind her. This way I feel less anxiety too. It's better than letting her run around outside on her own.[37]

Mr. Wen was a volunteer driver on the delivery team. Every morning he would drive to a warehouse in the suburbs of Wuhan to pick up the donated supplies. Because the city was closed to traffic, he would have to show multiple permits to get to the warehouse and back. He would spend half an hour to one hour loading the supplies onto his truck and then drive for another hour or two to another warehouse in the city. Once Mr. Wen transported the supplies to the second warehouse, other team members would decide what supplies to send to which hospital and then load their own cars for delivery to the hospitals. By that time, it was usually late afternoon. Only then could Mr. Wen catch a quick lunch.[38]

The forty-eight-year-old Ms. Xie was a manager in a provincial airline logistics department. She was staying home during the lockdown. When she saw the #StandByHer# campaign on Weibo on February 10, she joined as a volunteer and became the leader of the logistics and transportation team. Logistics and transportation were the most difficult part of the campaign. The vehicles used would need special permits to go around town. Some of the donations and purchases came from other provinces, which required long-distance transportation. Ms. Xie overcame these difficulties by mobilizing the social networks she had built on her job as a manager in a major logistics firm.[39]

Blue Bird was a data analyst. As a volunteer, she was responsible for designing and creating the digital image files of the campaign's daily announcements. To ensure that the announcements could be posted in a timely way the next day, she and her team would often work late into the night. For example, the announcement for March 14 was a summary of the campaign activities up to that point—ten images showing lists of detailed expenses, procured and delivered goods, receiving hospitals, and so on. They worked until 5:00 a.m. to finish this job.[40]

Sister Dong was in her forties and the owner of a small business on Alibaba's TMall e-commerce platform. When she was fifteen, her mother died, and she moved to Wuhan to make a living as a migrant laborer. She joined the volunteer team after seeing news about it on WeChat. She knew the streets of Wuhan well and thought she could help. She donated the warehouse of her own firm as a temporary storage space for the donations they received. An optimistic person, she said, "In fact Wuhan people are not as depressed and afraid as they are made to look. Wuhan people are actually very optimistic and very strong."[41]

Wei Qiangqiang was a Wuhan native. At thirty-one years of age, he was a motorcycle fan. He said if the epidemic had not happened, he would have just been playing with his motorcycle. When he saw recruitment information for volunteer drivers, he decided to join. He said he didn't have money to contribute but could at least do some small things such as delivering donations with his car. He had a one-year-old son, so both his wife and he were worried about exposure to COVID-19, but he still volunteered. Every day after returning home, he took extra care to disinfect himself. And he would still help with some housework and bathe his baby. Because he needed to spend time on child care in the morning, he usually went on delivery rounds in the afternoons and evenings.[42]

A VOLUNTEER IN A
RESIDENTIAL COMMUNITY

Volunteering was organized in multiple ways and by multiple social organizations. The volunteer activities recounted so far in this chapter were organized by individual animal lovers, feminist activists, charity foundations, nonprofit organizations, and online fan clubs—all nonstate actors and organizations. But state organizations, including universities, schools, government bureaucracies, and residential communities were also directly involved in organizing volunteer work in the war on COVID.

Ms. Yan was a graduate student in a college in Beijing. Trapped home while visiting her family in her hometown near Wuhan, she signed up to be a community volunteer. Her residential community, like other such communities in China's urban governance system, was a party-led grassroots organization. Signing up to be a volunteer did not mean she would be working in her own community, though. She could be deployed to other places, even to villages near her city. But luckily for her, she wrote in one of her thirteen diary postings, she was assigned to a relatively easy job as a guard in an old residential community.[43] The community had about a hundred households, and most residents were retired senior citizens. Her job was to guard the entrance and check people in and out. Her diary entry about her first day at work provides a detailed record of the daily activities of a residential community, especially how strictly the quarantine policies were enforced. As a volunteer, she tried to be as strict as possible in enforcing the rules.

On February 20, as noted in her diary, Ms. Yan left home at 11:40 a.m. After passing several COVID checkpoints set up in the streets, she arrived at the gate of the community where she would work at 12:10 p.m. A community staff member, Sister Tang, was there. Sister Tang was explaining to her about her job when a person dressed in PPE showed up and asked whether there was a woman in her fifties living in this community. The PPE guy was looking for a suspected case of the coronavirus disease. After confirming that no such person lived there, he hurriedly left. At 12:30 p.m., two lunchboxes were delivered to the volunteers at the gate. At this point, Sister Tang's shift was over. Before leaving, she told Yan to watch out for an eighty-year-old grandma who lived by herself in this community and who always wanted to go out to buy steamed buns (*mantou* 馒头). At 1:08 p.m., a man in his thirties walked by and asked for a pair of gloves. Ms. Yan gave him the gloves and asked what they were for. The man told her he was going to visit his wife in the hospital, where he had to wear gloves to be allowed entrance. At 2:35 p.m., an elderly woman in her eighties appeared, and Yan guessed who she was.

"Where are you going?" Yan asked.

"I'm going to buy something to eat. I haven't had lunch yet."

"How come? Didn't one of our volunteers send a lunchbox to you at noon?"

"No, I haven't had lunch," the old lady insisted.

At this point, a patrol guard who was passing by intervened. When he heard the old lady hadn't had lunch, he offered to fetch her a free chicken lunch, but the old lady said she did not eat meat. "I only want to eat steamed buns," she said. Ms. Yan could now tell for sure she was the lady Sister Tang had told her about. The grandma eventually took some instant noodles from the volunteers and agreed to return to her apartment.

At 3:10 p.m., a man on a bike requested entry to the community. He was let in after he showed his ID card to prove that he was a delivery person for a nearby supermarket. At 3:30 p.m., a young man asked to exit the community because he needed to do some banking. Yan told him that all the banks were closed and turned him back. At 3:50 p.m., a middle-aged, no-nonsense-looking woman asked Yan to help her open the gate. Yan asked her what for. She said she had to go out and pick up something. Ms. Yan lied to her and said she didn't have the key to the gate. Annoyed, the middle-aged woman turned back. At 4:20 p.m., another middle-aged woman on a share-bike came up to the gate from the outside and requested entrance. She said her parents were not in good health, and she wanted to take a look at them. Yan was sympathetic but told the woman she couldn't enter now but could come back the next morning because no visitors were allowed in the afternoon. The middle-aged woman said she could leave her own community only every three days, so she would have to wait for another three days before she could come back. Yan softened and told her she would let her in secretly but asked her not to stay long. At 4:45 p.m., shortly before Ms. Yan's shift ended for the day, another woman came and asked to enter. Yan said no. The woman explained that she would not enter the building but would only talk to her father from outside his window on the first floor. Yan let her in and heard her ask her father whether he still had food. The woman left after a short exchange with her father.[44]

Ms. Yan's personal experience as a volunteer guard at a residential community illustrates how seriously the personnel put in charge of enforcing the regimen took their job. It also shows how state-organized volunteerism works on the ground. Some scholars have argued that "Chinese volunteering has been incorporated into the state's ruling scheme by developing a state-controlled volunteer service system."[45] Ms. Yan's story shows that the system of volunteering was mobilized effectively during the lockdown to support the party's community work. Although Ms. Yan was a volunteer for a party-led residential committee, her job to assist community management was not so different from the work of other non-party-led volunteers such as those described earlier in this chapter. The boundary between state and nonstate organizing was not always so clear during the lockdown. In times of crises such as the COVID-19 pandemic, both types of volunteering become useful means of mobilizing grassroots support.

WHERE ARE THE NGOs?

The stories of civic organizing and volunteering recounted so far in this chapter are reminiscent of similar stories in the wake of the Sichuan earthquake in 2008, with one major difference: in 2008, more than three hundred NGOs descended on the earthquake areas to provide or coordinate disaster-relief efforts,[46] whereas in 2020 there was little mention of even the terms *nongovernmental organization* or *civil society*.

NGOs were not completely absent in 2020. The Wuhan Small Animal Protection Association and the Beijing Huizeren Volunteer Development Center are NGOs. There were others too, but, overall, much fewer than in 2008.[47] The bigger difference was in language. NGOs were such an important part of the earthquake disaster relief that Chinese media and scholars alike proclaimed 2008 the "Year of Civil Society" or "Year One of Chinese Civil Society."[48] The anthropologist Gao Bingzhong 高丙中 and the communication scholar Yuan Ruijun 袁瑞军 from Peking University opened the introduction to their *Blue Book on Civil Society Development in China* (中国公民社会发展蓝皮书), published at the end of 2008, by declaring that "China has entered the doorsteps of civil society."[49]

By 2020, however, as discussed in chapter 2, Western-style NGOs and civil society had become politically suspect. CCP documents warned about the dangers of Western notions of civil society.[50] New legislation was introduced for managing domestic and international NGOs.[51] NGOs may still be operating, but they avoid calling themselves NGOs or civil society organizations.

Civil society has always been a contested concept in China. For its critics, the concept originates in modern Western political discourse and is loaded with values and assumptions that render its applicability in China (or in East Asia more broadly) problematic.[52] Thus, even as the concept entered public discourse, a number of alternative concepts were still being used and even preferred, such as *minjian* 民间 (unofficial or "among the people"), *caogen* 草根 (grassroots), and simply *shehui zuzhi* 社会组织 (social organizations). These three concepts denote a status outside of the CCP and the government establishment—China's official realm. "Social organization" is the official name given to nonprofit social groups, private foundations, and social service organizations such as organizations set up for charity, education, and poverty alleviation. The management of such organizations comes under the Regulations for the Registration and Management of Social Organizations, publicized in 2018.[53] *Caogen*, "grassroots," is part of a new vocabulary borrowed from the language associated with global citizen action.[54] In the Mao period, *jiceng* 基层 was the equivalent for the English word *grassroots*. Literally meaning "foundation" or "infrastructure," *jiceng* is a term with a revolutionary history. The hallmark of Mao's organizational approach, the mass line, was based on the assumption that the CCP's voice should penetrate into the very fabric of Chinese life—the *jiceng* or foundation.[55] With the development of NGOs since the 1990s, however, the more literal Chinese translation of *grassroots*, *caogen*, has become a favored term for grassroots social organizations.

Minjian is sometimes translated as "unofficial." Literally meaning "among the people," it is the opposite of the official—that is, the court in imperial times and the government and the Communist Party in China today.[56] A related term used in imperial times but revived in popular culture is *jianghu* 江湖. *Jianghu*, literally meaning "rivers and lakes," is the realm outside of the court. With its Daoist origin, the term suggests an inclination to reject worldly aspirations in favor of a carefree life.[57] *Minjian* is sometimes translated as "popular," minus the class connotation that *popular* in *popular culture* has.[58] When Stuart Hall talks about culture of the popular classes, he is referring to working-class culture.[59] *Minjian* intellectuals in China are not of the working class.

Citizens and civic groups involved in volunteering in the war on COVID-19 refer to their organizations as *minjian*, "grassroots" or "social organizations" rather than as NGOs. Some do not view their groups as organizations (*zuzhi* 组织) at all. Organization is the monopoly of the CCP, which calls itself "the Organization." Thus, any organization outside the purview of the CCP can be suspect, and civic groups avoid using the term *zuzhi* to refer to themselves if they can. Instead, they call themselves by their actual names: online fan clubs, volunteer groups, WeChat shopping groups, WeChat reading groups, Weibo fan groups (*fensi qun* 粉丝群), Douban groups (*douban xiaozu* 豆瓣小组), and so forth. It is revealing that the nonprofit organizations that initiated the Beijing–Hubei iWill Volunteer United Action characterize their project as a government–society collaboration.[60]

WOMEN'S ROLE

As the stories in this chapter show, women played key roles in civic organizing during the Wuhan lockdown. They did so in part because the issues around which they organized, such as feminine hygiene and domestic violence, directly concern women. Women also dominate the professions of social work and counseling. It is notable, however, that most initiatives of civic organizing aimed to provide social service. They were consistent with state policies concerning the war on COVID. The anti-domestic-violence campaign might be an exception. Although China has an anti-domestic-violence law, a grassroots campaign independently launched by activists to mobilize citizen action around the country still had a radical side to it. If feminist activism such as the anti-domestic-violence campaign remained strong in a political environment inhospitable to civil society, that is because it was riding on the momentum of a new, radical feminist movement in recent years.

This new feminist movement was born in a series of public performances between 2012 and 2015, precisely the period when civil society came under attack in official discourse. This new feminist activism involved a younger generation of feminists who adopted new and more radical tactics. Unlike their senior colleagues, who were mostly scholars and professionals seeking social change from within the establishment, the younger generation assumed confrontational postures and staged eye-catching performance art to deliver their messages.[61]

The first and arguably still the most influential instance of a staged message was the "injured bride" performance in Beijing. On Valentine's Day in 2012, three young women appeared in the Qianmen pedestrian quarters, a popular tourist spot right next to Tiananmen Square. Dressed in white bridal gowns splattered with red paint to represent blood and holding signs such as "Love is not an excuse for violence," they called attention to the issue of domestic violence by dramatizing it.[62] Five days later, on February 19, several young feminists staged a public performance in Guangzhou: they occupied a men's toilet to voice their demand for gender equality by highlighting the shortage of public bathrooms for women.[63] Later that year, on December 2, 2012, the "injured bride" performance was reenacted, this time in five cities—Beijing, Shanghai, Hangzhou, Xi'an, and Dongguan.[64] This five-city performance took place *after* Xi Jinping took office and right before the crackdown on internet activism and civil society in the summer of 2013. And despite the crackdown in 2013, radical feminist performance activism continued through 2015. One of the more influential instances involved Xiao Meili. In 2013, Xiao took a 1,200-mile walk from Beijing to Guangzhou to raise public awareness about sex abuse of children in schools.[65] In 2015, after five feminist activists were detained in Beijing, Xiao wrote in support of them and explained why China's young feminists had turned to performance art as a favored form of action: "Many women before us have taken the accommodationist route, but little has changed. Strong public pressure is necessary. We cannot afford to go about our campaign quietly. Since public protests and demonstrations are banned, we rely on a unique platform—performance art—to challenge social conditions. We've taken our message to the streets and subways and fought for a safe public space for women."[66]

The performance art of the young feminists after 2012 attracted mainstream media attention and put their cause in the public limelight. On March 7, 2015, when five of them were planning to launch a new action to raise awareness about sexual harassment, police detained them. Their detention prompted an international uproar and brought them global fame, turning them into global icons of China's young feminists.[67]

The young feminists performed their way onto the world stage at a time when public space for civil society in China was shrinking. Why were they so bold and dramatic in their actions? The sociologist Li Jun 李军, a feminist activist, argues that women's issues have traditionally been less politically sensitive in China, so that even when the control of media and civil society was tightening, media could still cover such events. The drama of the feminists' performances also helped greatly. The performances were designed to attract public attention. When media, especially commercial and metropolitan newspapers, were finding fewer issues of public interest to cover due to growing control of what they published, they turned their attention to these feminist performances.[68]

The detention of the Feminist Five in March 2015, however, marked the narrowing of political space even for the feminist cause. Although some activists persisted in China, others moved to the United States, where they became diaspora activists. They continued their cause while attending graduate school.[69] By the time the #MeToo movement swept the United States in late 2017,[70] these diaspora activists were ready to join their American activist friends in the streets of New York. Meanwhile, the global #MeToo movement inspired an indigenous #MeToo movement in China in early 2018. Victims of sexual harassment in universities, NGOs, and media industries in China broke their silence on social media. Their stories received overwhelming public support, and China's #MeToo movement was born. The momentum of the movement forced some employers to fire some of the accused individuals, resulting in the downfall of prominent professors and media celebrities.[71] At the time of the COVID-19 outbreak, that momentum was still being felt. It is not surprising, then, that feminist activists not only organized to support residents and medical workers in Wuhan but also launched a campaign to raise public awareness of domestic violence.[72]

ONLINE–OFFLINE CONVERGENCE

Since the advent of the internet, people have talked about an offline–online divide, implying not only that they are two different worlds but also that the online world is less real and less meaningful than what happens in the "real" (offline) world.[73] Again and again, the Wuhan lockdown stories show to the contrary that the offline and online worlds are parts of the same world. Cyberspace is not a separate realm. The exigencies of the lockdown simply blended the offline and online worlds more seamlessly. Moving between online and offline activities is a problem to be dealt with but has become as natural as an everyday routine.

With more than 70 percent of the 1.4 billion Chinese online as of December 2020 and almost all of them equipped to go online with mobile phones,[74] the digital and network infrastructures in China are powerful enough that internet access is no longer an issue in urban China. Smartphones and social media apps have become so prevalent that volunteers and activists rarely complain about internet access or other technical difficulties. Indeed, there is little explicit mention of the internet or social media except when censorship kicks in. Setting up WeChat groups, for example, is an easy and taken-for-granted way of coordinating activities. It is no surprise that Gu Meng started her organizing efforts to rescue pets by setting up such groups. Nor did anyone seem to think using smartphones to livestream onsite animal rescue work to pet owners was anything particularly innovative. It happened naturally because livestreaming, both for the streamers and for their audiences, was already a ubiquitous aspect of popular culture and contemporary life.

If there was still something miraculous about online activism ten years ago, the convergence of online and offline civic participation in 2020 shows that it has been routinized. Admittedly, such an online–offline connection has always been a feature of online activism. Both in the Wuhan lockdown period and earlier, offline activist events were often organized through online action. In many cases in the past, the goal was to organize an event offline. Once the event had occurred, mobilization would end. But in the anti-domestic-violence campaign discussed earlier, the offline acts of posting hard copies of the open letter in volunteers' neighborhoods were only one link in a chain of action, albeit a critical one. Just as important was the act of bringing the women's stories back online. Participants were scattered in different parts of the country,[75] but when their stories were posted on social media and marked with the same hashtag, those acts aggregated the women's diverse experiences into a common reservoir of personal testimonial, witnessing, and participation. This common reservoir of personal stories in turn inspired more volunteers to join the campaign. In short, online and offline are two sides of the same action.

This online–offline convergence was true of both the #StandByHer# campaign and the online fan clubs' fund-raising efforts. The main goal of online fan clubs was to raise funds and donations for residents and hospitals in Wuhan. This would entail offline action, especially transportation, but the organizing and accounting took place online. All of the fan clubs took special care to publish online the lists of donations they received in order to maintain the transparency and accountability of the campaign and to recognize the contributions made by individual fans. A key part of the #StandByHer# campaign was the daily chronicling of activities and expenditures on Weibo. Again, it was not just a matter of transparency but also a matter of visibility—of making women's labor visible, which was one of the campaign's main goals.

Creativity has long been viewed as a notable feature of Chinese internet culture and politics. Creative uses of the web help netizens to stay active and engaged in a controlled cyber and political environment. Such creativity will always be important. However, if the convergence between online and offline action has become a routine and taken-for-granted feature of civic organizing, more attention needs to be paid to the mundane and habitual uses of the web and social media.[76] Their "taken for grantedness," to borrow from the communication scholar Rich Ling's study of mobile phones, means that such habitual uses have become an existential condition of life.

If all members of your social groups are users, then the social expectation is that you are a user too.[77] Sharing personal sentiments on social media or coordinating group activities on WeChat are facts of contemporary life, at least until newer technological forms overtake them. Meanwhile, whether for civic organizing or for other purposes, netizens habitually turn to social media, and moments of creativity are likely to flare out of these web habits.

7

GAME OF WORDS

"I'd Fucking Talk About It Everywhere"

In his diary on March 11, 2020, Xiao Yin wondered aloud if Wuhan's lockdown were made into a film, what kind of a film it might be: "How are we going to document these months of tragedy, suffering, sorrow, and heroism? How to write about the life, death, and loss of each and every concrete individual?" He flashed back to December 2019, when Dr. Ai Fen of Wuhan Central Hospital was censured by her supervisors for disclosing information about a novel SARS-like disease to her colleagues. For Xiao Yin, Ai Fen's story should be a key scene in his imaginary film.[1]

Ai Fen was a trending topic on social media on March 11. On the previous day, the magazine *People* had published an interview with her on its WeChat account. Called "The Whistle-Giver" (发哨子的人), the story was quickly censored. To keep it "alive" on the web, netizens joined what they called an online relay (*wangluo jieli* 网络接力). One after another, as if they were passing the baton, they posted and reposted remixed versions of the original censored story on social media. On WeChat, for example, I found myself and many of my contacts drawn into the relay as we forwarded these postings. So many people participated that Xiao Yin called this event "a spectacular battle between censorship and countercensorship."[2]

Many other important media stories were censored during the lockdown period, so why did the censoring of this particular story provoke such protest?

"The Whistle-Giver" told an explosive story, confirming public suspicions of a possible cover-up in the early phase of the epidemic. It also revealed for the first time that besides "whistle-blowers" such as Dr. Li Wenliang, there was also a "whistle-giver," as Ai came to be called. And all this information was conveyed in strong emotional language.

The journalist who interviewed Ai Fen anticipated the explosive effect of her story. About a week before the interview was published, she told readers on Weibo: "I've prepared a bomb for you to read." In it, Ai Fen revealed that on January 2, 2020, she was excoriated by her hospital's supervisory department for "single-handedly ruining the wonderful situation of Wuhan's development" by disclosing information about the coronavirus. This was a serious accusation. An individual charged of "ruining" an entire city's development would surely incur serious disciplinary action. Crushed by this accusation, Ai stopped mentioning the coronavirus disease to anyone again, not even to her husband. Meanwhile, the city was locked down, and Ai's hospital suffered the biggest casualties of all the hospitals in Wuhan. By the time she did the interview on March 2, three of her colleagues had died of COVID-19. She regretted not speaking up sooner. Her tone in the interview conveyed her pent-up anger: "If I had known things would come to this, I wouldn't have cared about any censure. I'd fucking talk about it everywhere, right??" (Zao zhidao you jintian, wo guanta piping bu piping wo, laozi daochu shuo, shi bu shi? 早知道有今天，我管他批评不批评我，老子到处说，是不是?).[3]

Dr. Ai's angry words shocked the public. Who would have expected to hear "I'd fucking talk about it everywhere" from a well-educated physician in a published interview by a well-respected magazine? And who would have expected that a well-respected magazine with an official background would publish such a daring story? "I'd fucking talk about it everywhere" turned into an instant internet meme.

"I'd fucking talk about it everywhere" is not a literal translation. The Chinese original defies a literal translation. The term *laozi* 老子, here referring to

Ai herself, cannot be simply rendered as "I." Better translated as "daddy I," it is a common masculine expletive and curse word. Translating it as "I'd fucking talk about it" conveys that flavor of defiance in the original Chinese.[4]

"The Whistle-Giver" contains another story. The circumstance described in the embedded story had happened a month earlier and was itself one of the most iconic events of the Wuhan lockdown—the story of Dr. Li Wenliang. A thirty-four-year-old ophthalmologist, Li Wenliang was Ai Fen's colleague and one of the first to disclose information about the coronavirus (chapter 9 tells Li Wenliang's story). After Li died of COVID-19 on February 7, netizens staged one of the first major online protests of the lockdown period. By embedding that protest within "The Whistle-Giver," the online relay refreshed the memories, emotions, and symbols of that earlier protest. The embedded earlier protest doubled the power of the new protest. There was also a direct narrative connection. By then, everyone knew Li Wenliang was a whistle-blower, but no one knew there was also a whistle-giver. From whistle-blower to whistle-giver and back—this recursive story chain multiplied the emotional power of the relay protest. Linking the two characters, the whistle-blower and whistle-giver, was the whistle itself. The whistle had become a new symbol of dissent. To keep the whistle blowing became a powerful motivation for carrying on the relay.

"erehwyrevE tI tuobA klaT gnikcuF d'I"

Although creative and playful forms are common in online protest everywhere, the online relay was still a strikingly innovative form. The "original" text was relayed in forms designed to thwart censorship algorithms and to attract readers. The first remixed form I saw on my WeChat timeline showed the original text in reverse order, sentence by sentence. Thus, a sentence such as "I'd fucking talk about it everywhere" became "erehwyreve ti tuoba klat gnikcuf d'I." The reversed text is a playful assertion of the original text's right to existence by whatever means possible.

When reversed, Chinese characters are more readable than the English alphabet. Chinese readers would immediately know that it was a word game for mocking censorship. This creative rearrangement of "The Whistle-Giver" inspired at least fifty-two different versions.[5] There were versions in foreign languages, such as German, English, French, Italian, Vietnamese, Japanese, and Korean. Some versions were in ancient oracle-bone scripts or in local dialects such as Cantonese and Sichuanese. There were renditions in Morse code, Braille, emojis, computer-programming language, and even the Elvish language Quenya. There were also versions in cartoons, audio files, and Mao-style calligraphy. Clearly, the original text could be reproduced in as many forms as were imaginable. Figure 7.1 shows an emoji version. Figure 7.2 shows a "monument version" (*jinianbei ban* 纪念碑版).

FIGURE 7.1 Emoji version of Gong Jingqi 龚菁琦, "The Whistle-Giver" (我是发哨人), *People* (人物), March 10, 2020 (partial view).

纪念碑版：

纪念碑

FIGURE 7.2. Monument version of Gong, "The Whistler-Giver."

Most of these creative formats are not quite readable, and that was the point. Programmed computer codes for censoring the web do not understand the content of a text. They recognize forms. Thus, anticensorship efforts work best by inventing new forms. By substituting different symbols for the censored vocabularies or images, netizens produce new textual forms to elude censors.

In track-and-field races, a relay involves multiple runners, with one passing the baton to the next until the anchor reaches the finish line. The goal of the online relay of "The Whistle-Giver" was to keep the story "alive" on the web through posting and reposting. Such a "game," as it was called by some netizens, invited massive participation. Internet celebrities such as Fang Fang played an important role. Fang Fang's online diary writing was a major media event in its own right, with each posting receiving millions of views. Whatever she wrote about in her diary became instant national news. By focusing on Ai Fen's story, her diary entry on March 11 gave the relay a major boost:

> From yesterday to today, the name of Dr. Ai Fen of the Central Hospital has been circulating on the whole web. Internet blocking and murdering have caused popular anger. People posted it after it was deleted, posted it again after it was deleted again, as if they were playing a game of relay. One relay baton to the next. In all kinds of languages and all kinds of styles, so that the censors cannot delete them all or wipe them out. In the confrontation between deleting and reposting [the deletions], it became a sacred duty in people's heart to keep this article alive. The sense of sacred duty came almost from a subconscious awakening: to protest it is to protect ourselves. Once things have reached this stage, web managers, can you still delete them all?[6]

This diary posting received more than 10,000 user comments. They capture well the dynamics of the protest:

> The miraculous thing about this article is that it popped up again after being deleted, then deleted again and then popped up again repeatedly. It even appeared in the formats of computer codes, reverse writing, and oracle bone language. This miraculous event is no longer due to an article. It is because it has turned into a ritual for defending rights! This situation shows where people's hearts lie. Are there no others who feel goosebumps on their back?[7]

> Today's deleting—reposting—deleting again—reposting again—this is the internet version of a people's war.[8]

> All the deleting and blocking of postings is futile and ineffective. Because there are far more people who support you than people who want to

censor you. Could they delete people's angry hearts? This is an old world. It smells of rottenness everywhere.[9]

These reader comments expressed anger, helplessness, and sympathy. As negative emotions out of tune with the mainstream ideology of positive energy, they amounted to a refutation of the mainstream discourse.

The participation of regular netizens kept the game going by posting, cross-posting, liking, and commenting on the relayed texts. These were creative acts of citizenship under circumstances of tight internet censorship.[10] Certainly, Chinese netizens have always been creative in managing censorship,[11] but their confrontations with it this time were extraordinary.

Cross-posting Ai Fen's interview on social media was not a simple repetitive act but a transformative one as well.[12] Each reposting reenacted the emotions contained in the original texts, especially Ai's anger. It also recreated the emotions conveyed in the reinvented forms of the relayed texts, such as the humor and satire in the emoji and Elvish representations. Each reposting invited new audience participation. Readers joined the relay by sharing their personal emotions and moral outrage:

The coronavirus situation saddens us. Our hearts ache for our doctors. The authorities make us angry.[13]

I'm grateful to the author for this work of conscience. I cried while reading it. I was so sad and angry after finishing it.[14]

We must show support for Dr. Ai Fen through the internet relay until truth is revealed. Afterward we should also regularly check to make sure she will not be subject to unjust treatment!!!![15]

The game of relay exposed censorship to more people than ever before. Ordinary internet users who would not normally experience censorship in their daily lives might see the relayed postings in their WeChat Moments. The relay of Ai Fen's interview also generated intensive public discussion. Users on WeChat or Weibo rallied in support of Ai and condemned censorship by sharing their personal experiences with it. One person commented, "This is the third time I'm reposting it [the interview]. The first time it was censored. The second time I cut and pasted it into the comment section paragraph by paragraph. That helped to preserve the complete text, albeit slowly and with difficulty (. . . it took an entire afternoon, which gave me a sense of accomplishment)."[16] This individual's personal experience of reposting the relayed article shows that the online relay was about persistence. Acts of persistence gave participants a sense of accomplishment.

CHINESE MEDIA IN EXCEPTIONAL TIMES

Many scholars have examined countercensorship practices in China, but the COVID-19 pandemic presented a different context. It was a national crisis. By unsettling routines and disrupting habits, it created not only uncertainty but also new openings. The same thing happened in the wake of the earthquakes in Sichuan in 2008. As the communication scholar Maria Repnikova shows in her book *Media Politics in China* (2017), Chinese media opened up briefly after the earthquakes as critical journalists used their time-tested tactics to negotiate the boundaries of critical reporting.[17]

The lockdown of Wuhan was a different kind of crisis, but one of comparable magnitude nonetheless. Information was critical. The entire nation was anxious to know exactly what was happening in Wuhan, yet local media were not keeping the public informed. The *Changjiang Daily* had compromised its credibility throughout January when it failed to cover the local coronavirus situation. Under these circumstances, commercial media provided the much-needed information through creative and daring investigative reporting. They acted more quickly than state media to cover the lockdown. The popular financial news outlet *Caixin* created a special epidemic section on its website, which became the most comprehensive information hub of daily cases and investigative reports. *Caixin* was also the first to publish an interview with Dr. Li Wenliang on January 31. Li Wenliang's statement that "a healthy society should not have just one voice" became an unofficial banner of citizen struggles for the openness of media and the internet throughout the lockdown period.[18]

Other major commercial media agencies also covered the Wuhan lockdown extensively.[19] To see how bold some of their stories were, consider the censored ones. On March 23, a group of journalism students published an article titled "41 Disappeared News Reports About the Pandemic." An instant hit that was soon censored, it examined media reports about the coronavirus outbreak from January 23 to March 13, 2020, and found that forty-one stories had been censored. Throughout February and the first half of March, a mainstream media story was censored from the web almost every day. The three media outlets censored the most were *Caixin*, *Caijing Magazine* (财经杂志), and *Jiemian News* (界面新闻)—all commercial news media. The censored stories were mostly hard news and in-depth investigations. They were more likely to be stories about medical personnel, patients, problems in government decision making, and the daily hardships in Wuhan. The public sentiments covered in these stories tend to be negative feelings of anger, anxiety, and frustration.[20]

Although most of the forty-one censored stories were published by mainstream media agencies, there were four exceptions. Three of the four exceptions were first published on WeChat's public accounts, and one was published in *Changjiang Daily*, the official paper of the CCP Wuhan Municipal Committee. The latter was about Wuhan party secretary Wang Zhonglin's call for Wuhan people to show gratitude, which I discussed in chapter 3.[21] It was deleted from the web not because it was too critical but because it triggered an online backlash.

The story in *Changjiang Daily* was the only exception in a long list of censored stories that were in-depth investigative reports about the pandemic. That these stories were published at all was remarkable. Media crackdowns after 2013 had "tam[ed]" critical journalism.[22] Many media professionals quit their jobs in legacy media to seek new careers elsewhere. Those who stayed on had to navigate a new political environment. Some of them continued to hold onto the ideals of journalistic professionalism. The editors and journalists at *Sanlian Lifeweek* (三联生活周刊) who covered the COVID-19 situation in Wuhan exemplify the persistence of journalistic professionalism. From January 20 to February 26, 2020, *Lifeweek* published more than one hundred stories about the outbreak. One of its associate editors, Wu Qi, happened to have returned to Wuhan for the Lunar New Year holiday. After the lockdown started, *Lifeweek* sent five more reporters to Wuhan. The team of six produced high-impact stories about the early days of the epidemic. When asked whether *Lifeweek* had switched its focus to covering hard news, Wu Qi said that the professionals at *Lifeweek* had never given up their values and dreams of producing journalism of social significance: "The values of these *Sanlian* people have always been very pure; they want to produce journalism with public and social significance. Their values never changed."[23]

The story about the forty-one censored reports was an example of critical journalism. Given the political context, it was a bold decision to research and write the article. Even more remarkable, it was the initiative of journalism students. For them, the media environment had not just *become* more open or relaxed. The students did not seek prior approval to write the report. They did it because they wanted to. Meanwhile, the censorship machine was still in full production.

In the agitated atmosphere of the early period of the lockdown, the censorship apparatus behaved unpredictably. Stories published by official media outlets could be censored. Even a high-impact official magazine produced by the all-powerful Xinhua News Agency could be subject to censorship. Called *China Comment* (半月谈), the magazine published an article on February 20, 2020, titled "Daring to Speak Up Is a Precious Attribute!"[24] The article started by discussing the abrupt spike in the number of confirmed cases of coronavirus in Hubei province from 1,638 on February 11 to 14,840 on February 12, noting that the spike was due to revised diagnostic criteria. It commented that although this spike in numbers might look frightening, it really was not because what was frightening was untruthful numbers. It concluded by emphasizing the importance of speaking truth: "To sum up in one sentence: Let people speak the truth, the skies will not collapse!" (Zongzhi yijuhua: Rangren jiang zhenhua, tian tan bu xialai 总之一句话: 让人讲真话, 天塌不下来!). In the online version of this article, the sentence "Let people speak the truth, the skies will not collapse!" was used as the headline. In an environment that had silenced truthful voices such as Li Wenliang's, this was a daring statement from the editors of the magazine, which may have caused the article to be cut from the web even though it was published in a Xinhua News Agency magazine.[25] The removal of an op-ed published in a high-level official magazine may suggest that China's censorship machine had its idiosyncrasies, or it may reveal a hidden rationale of censorship—authorities are more worried about the online dissemination of information than about print magazines. After all, the article from *China Comment* as well as the forty-one censored media stories existed in print versions, but they were removed from the web. In the internet age, censorship authorities are more worried about access to information on the web than via print.

"BOLD AND CAREFUL"

Censoring an official magazine such as *China Comment* was an exception, not the norm, though. The routine targets of censorship were and are not party media such as *China Comment* but rather netizens, commercial media, and other nonparty media entities. On February 1, Xiao Yin wrote that during the day he had archived ten postings for future use on his WeChat account, but when he opened them again that evening, five of the ten were already gone—a "death rate of 50 percent," as he put it. On February 28, he noted that he had written thirty-eight diary entries, yet only about a dozen of them survived censorship. The others were removed for unknown reasons. Even in some of the diary postings that were not censored, the comment function had been disabled by the WeChat platform.[26]

What is permitted and what is not, however, are not always predictable; some postings may be deleted for no obvious reason. The lesson for ordinary users is to be cautious about what to say and how to say it. In his diary of February 9, Mr. Mei wrote that when he tried to use his WeChat account that afternoon, he found it had been closed for one day because he had retweeted a rumor. Mr. Mei wondered who could always tell exactly which posting was a rumor and which was not: "Li Wenliang's rumor later became a precautionary warning. It took the authorities over a month to make a judgment. How can I, an ordinary person, tell within two or three minutes whether a posting is a rumor or not?"[27]

Diarists cultivated strategies for coping with censorship. Patience and persistence were essential. For Mr. Yun, one must be "bold and careful" (*danda xinxi* 胆大心细) when operating a WeChat public account: to be bold means to be brave in voicing one's views publicly; to be careful is to express oneself with caution. "Think over in your mind what can be said and what cannot be said," he wrote.[28] How can one be bold and cautious at the same time? Mr. Yun's words captured an absurd and yet common feature of Chinese internet culture.

Xiao Yin was one of the most critical diarists, and he coped with censorship very carefully. On March 2, 2020, he told readers that it took him an hour and a half to publish his entry for that day. It simply would not go through despite his repeated attempts to post it. He checked his use of words meticulously. In the end, it went through after he changed one word in the following passage: "Even when the epidemic situation is so grave, we still see that some people are lax and lazy in doing their job. There are always people who depend on the operations of the monster machine and benefit from the dividend of the rules. The same danger has another manifestation. To make sure that they don't get into trouble, some people would rather move farther to the left [of the ideological spectrum]. You never get into trouble for singing praise."[29]

The next day Xiao Yin revealed the one-word secret. The original text that had prevented his diary from being published was the word *left* in "farther to the left" (*zuo yidian* 左一点). He was able to publish the entry after he changed *left* to *radical* (*jijin* 激进). It is not exactly clear why *left* was a more sensitive word than *radical*. One possibility is that being "leftist" in one's ideological orientation could allude to the leftist politics of the Mao era.

When it became too difficult for someone to personally put up postings, friends came to the rescue. When Guo Jing encountered difficulty in posting her diary entries on Weibo, a friend helped her publish them on a WeChat public account. When Fang Fang's Weibo account was suspended for two weeks in early February, a friend based in the United States, Er Xiang 二湘, published them on her own WeChat public account. Er Xiang had to fight censorship, too, though. She documented her frustrations in an editor's note written after Fang Fang stopped writing her diary.

When Er Xiang started publishing Fang Fang's diaries, she used a WeChat public account she had named "Er Xiang's Seventh-Dimensional Space." But the account was repeatedly closed, and she was forced to open new accounts and move from one to another like a guerilla publisher. After her Seven-Dimensional Space was closed, she opened the WeChat accounts Eighth-Dimensional Space, Ninth-Dimensional Space, Tenth-Dimensional Space, and, finally, Eleventh-Dimensional Space. She wrote:

> The articles were deleted one after another (one day I received three deletion notifications). The Seventh-Dimensional Space was shut down twice. The Ninth-Dimensional Space was taken back [by the platform]. The Tenth-Dimensional Space does not allow user comments. . . . Once an article was deleted just one hour after it was posted. I had a deep sense of powerlessness. The machine confronting me was gigantic, and I was just like a tiny ant. After that article was deleted, Fang Fang said: Do we still want to publish? I said: yes. I am a stubborn person. I remember most deeply that the article entitled "Wrong, Wrong, Wrong" failed to go through after even more than ten attempts to post it. Eventually I had to post a notice to say "I've tried my best." But soon, readers began to post chunks of Fang Fang's diary in the comment section, one after another like a relay, until the entire diary was posted.[30]

This stubborn refusal to give up was sometimes accompanied by strong feelings of anger and frustration. A diarist calling himself "Second Uncle" 二叔 wrote often about his frustrating experiences with censorship. February 28, 2020: "An article I wrote yesterday was deleted by the platform. I said nothing but a few truthful words. I'm really angry and helpless." Then March 31, 2020: "I wrote an article yesterday and posted it at midnight. By 9:00 a.m. this morning, it had been censored. So fast. Although I feel very frustrated and angry, all I can do is feel frustrated and angry."[31]

He never stopped writing, though. By July 19, he could no longer hold back his anger. His entry for that day was simply called "Anger" ("Nu" 怒):

"I didn't spread rumors. I didn't slander anyone. I just commented on a few things. I didn't attack anyone. Less than an hour after I posted it, it was censored. There was no reason at all. All that is left is anger!"[32]

FANG FANG FIGHTS TROLLS

Fang Fang faced even bigger challenges. Not only were her diary postings often deleted or blocked, but she was also the target of vicious attacks from anonymous trolls, or *penzi* 喷子 in Chinese. Fang Fang started complaining about troll attacks in early February. When Weibo suspended her account, it was because of complaints lodged against her by anonymous users.[33] On February 3, she wrote about the importance of remembering those who had wrongfully died in the epidemic. For this, she became the target of an online essay on February 6, the first published attack on her.[34] From then on, the attacks continued nonstop. On February 18, Fang Fang wrote in her diary that the people who had been attacking her were ultra-leftists: "Today, I especially want to say a few words I had been chewing on for a long time: The ultraleftists in China basically exist to ruin the country and the people. They can't wait to return to the Cultural Revolution. They hate the reform and opening. All those who hold different views from them are their enemies."[35]

For Fang Fang, ultraleftists were people who still pined after the politics of Mao's Cultural Revolution. With Mao's death and the end of the Cultural Revolution, they had fallen from grace. Although the Cultural Revolution was officially denounced as "a calamity," it never completely lost its supporters.[36] Their voice becomes louder in times of surging nationalism. Fang Fang complained that even though ultraleftists attacked her with the ugliest and most violent language, their postings were never deleted by the Weibo platform,[37] suggesting that the ultraleftists might have official endorsement.

Detractors made character attacks without engaging the substance of Fang Fang's writing:

Fang Fang, these essays do not look like they were written by you but rather by anti-China forces. Are you petitioning on behalf of the people, or are you just being shameless? Do you think our country does not know how to handle such big matters? You are so rude and peremptory. Do you want to be the municipal party secretary? Not a single Chinese wants to see the situation like today's, except you! All that the country and all the people have sacrificed for the disaster just does not satisfy you. Do you want the country and all the people to suffer more? Who are you? You are a murderer of all the people![38]

Besides anonymous attacks, several well-known leftist nationalists challenged Fang Fang publicly. These individuals are active on nationalistic websites such as guancha.cn and mzfxw.com. One of them is Zhang Hongliang, a Maoist who self-identifies as a member of China's leftists (*zuopai* 左派). Maoists are critical of Deng Xiaoping and other party leaders supportive of the economic reform. Mao's Cultural Revolution was their golden age. Liberal intellectuals are their enemies.[39] Several years ago they launched an online campaign against liberal intellectuals by labeling them as traitors. They also called Fang Fang a traitor of the nation, alleging that the upcoming publication of the English translation of her diary would give ammunition to Western powers who had accused China of spreading the coronavirus.

For years, Zhang has argued that the internet provides the space for a genuine mass movement of the Left against China's elites. In their opposition to public intellectuals, China's Maoist leftists resemble far-right groups in the United States. On March 25, Zhang wrote that their campaign against Fang Fang had achieved a temporary success in denouncing her as a class enemy and a cultural traitor (*wenhua hanjian* 文化汉奸). He warned, however, that the campaign against Fang Fang must not stop at attacking her as an individual:

If we attribute everything to Fang Fang's personal traits, then we are no different from the fifty-cents.[40] . . . The question is: Who has promoted such an anti-CCP and anti-China person to the administrative level of a bureau chief?[41] What factors have caused her anti-CCP works to win literary prizes?... We must not attack Fang Fang independently of the conditions and contexts that had created her or of her position as one who exploits and represses the people, a representative of the elitist one percent.[42]

This passage betrays a bigger goal of the relentless online attacks on Fang Fang. More than just a target, Fang Fang was weaponized. Attacking her was a means of shutting down all criticisms of the party authorities. Who would dare to speak up again if they witnessed the endless and random verbal violence against Fang Fang? Quite a few diarists mentioned that after Fang Fang's diary became a national controversy, they stopped sharing personal views about it on WeChat for fear of alienating friends and family. The attacks on Fang Fang silenced many, but not Fang Fang, who continued to fight back. In her last diary entry, she even thanked those who had attacked her. She said that without their attacks, she would probably not have written so many entries. Fang Fang also believed that their attacks had fully exposed the true nature of the ultraleftists in China: "They exist only to ruin the nation and the people! They are the biggest obstacle to reform and opening! If they are allowed to have their way, they will infect the whole society like a virus. Reform will be bound to fail. China will have no future."[43]

POSITIVE ENERGY IS A "BIG STICK"

What was it exactly that exposed Fang Fang to such vitriol? The accusations made against her could be easily dismissed, as, indeed, she did in her own responses. But one accusation might have been partly true—her diary was critical and "lacking" in positive energy. It was only partly true, though, because Fang Fang had just as many positive things to say about Wuhan. Indeed, as the award-winning journalist Ian Johnson writes in his review, Fang Fang's diary is "the work of someone not trying to challenge the system but simply trying to express in real time what she felt."[44]

As a former president of the Hubei Writers' Association, Fang Fang is part of the official establishment, not a dissident. Yet precisely because she is from within the establishment, her criticisms could be viewed as particularly hurtful and her calls for accountability especially threatening. Her insider knowledge and experience made her criticisms right on target.

The ideology of positive energy has attained a near sacred status in recent years. It appears in official policy documents as much as in popular culture. Party leaders encourage media and citizens to express positive energy, just as self-help and mental health manuals urge their readers to have a positive attitude toward life. An atmosphere of manufactured positivity makes it hard for citizens to express dissent.

The tragedies of the pandemic created the conditions for questioning the ideology of positive energy. Most netizens simply dissented through practice—namely, by voicing and relaying negative emotions on social media. Fang Fang went the furthest by launching a frontal attack on positive energy. She called it by what it really is: "a big stick" with which to threaten and penalize critical voices. In doing so, Fang Fang hit where it hurt most.

This was surely the first time the ideology of positive energy was so directly and publicly challenged since its popularization in 2012. Fang Fang's challenge has a significance that goes beyond the immediate context. But only in that context was her challenge understandable and possible. The hegemonic nature of the positive-energy creed was such that without that context it would have been even more difficult to openly challenge it.

Fang Fang fulminated against positive energy in her entry on March 2. The title of the entry is "Let Posterity Know What Wuhan People Went Through."[45] On March 2, China had 80,151 confirmed cases of COVID-19. There were 125 new confirmed cases and 31 deaths that day. Fang Fang noted with hope that it was the first time the number of new confirmed cases had fallen below 200. Perhaps the lockdown might end sooner than expected, she pondered. In this context, she noted that it was about time to put the issue of accountability on the agenda. She pleaded with journalists to carry on their investigations of what had delayed communication about the disease. She pressed again and again for accountability, arguing that whoever was responsible for the mishandling of the crisis must answer for it.

In that entry, Fang Fang also urged people not to forget the sufferings and sacrifices of Wuhan's residents. Because the pandemic situation seemed to be improving, she was worried that once people got over the most difficult times, they would no longer want to recall past traumas. Those who had died tragically could be forgotten. In all her diary postings up to that point, she had told stories about the sufferings of ordinary people out of the fear that they would be forgotten. To tell their stories is to remember. She also encouraged others to tell their own stories and use personal storytelling as a means of managing trauma.

And yet, Fang Fang continued, in the name of positive energy some people tried to stop others from telling their stories of pain and suffering. For these people, wrote Fang, positive energy was a big stick with which to scare their opponents:

> But a big stick called "positive energy" often hangs over the head of the complainer. This is a big stick with a well-justified name. It is held and raised high by many people. If you cry and vent your feelings, then you are creating panic, you are damaging the antivirus efforts, you are negative energy. To destroy negative energy is the irrefutable moral obligation of positive energy. Ugh. If the affairs of the human world were understood and judged in such simple ways, that would only mean you've wasted your life in this world. If positive energy looks so ignorant and fearless, what is positive about it? Who says that you can't stand up and walk on after finishing your crying and venting?[46]

On Weibo, this posting received more than 8,000 reader comments. Although some attacked her for being unpatriotic, most users hailed her boldness and insight in challenging the discourse of positive energy. User comments broadened and reinforced Fang Fang's critique by adding personal experiences and viewpoints:

> Fang Fang's diaries started large-scale discussions on the internet. It is like another war independent of the antipandemic but no less significant.[47]

> I really don't understand why this diary was quickly banned on its WeChat public account. Doesn't it have enough positive energy? Enough sense of

justice? The reason WeChat provided for deleting it was: Suspected of violating relevant laws and regulations. Obviously, WeChat no longer has any bottom line in order to achieve a pure web.[48]

Truth is labeled negative energy. Rumor and eulogy are called positive energy. . . . Even after the novel coronavirus ends, the brain virus has already grown badly.[49]

With each diary posting, Fang Fang carried on her battle with anonymous trolls. Her entry on March 18 was a critique of her ultraleftist opponents through a personal story of her experiences in the Cultural Revolution. There she made a direct response to an anonymous open letter addressed to her in the name of a sixteen-year-old high schooler, "A Letter to Aunt Fang Fang from a High School Student," which had been posted the previous day. In it, the "high-school student" expressed disappointment that a famous writer such as Fang Fang did not produce works with positive energy. The "student" wrote that as a child he had learned from his mother that people should not show their dirty laundry to outsiders. How could Fang Fang have written all those bad things about Wuhan? The letter writer also said that he had learned from his mother to be grateful to whoever provided food and clothing and asked: "Aunt Fang Fang, whose clothing do you wear? Who gave you your rice bowl?"[50] The rhetorical answer was the Communist Party. The message was that Fang Fang was ungrateful to the Communist Party in her negative descriptions of Wuhan even though she had grown up and prospered under the auspices of the party.

In her response, Fang Fang pointed out that this letter could not have been written by a high-school student. It was clearly not written in the language of a young student. Nevertheless, she would treat it as if it were from one. Fang Fang then recalled in endearing tones what she was like at the age of sixteen. It was 1971, when China was still in the middle of the Cultural Revolution. In 1971, if anyone had told her that the Cultural Revolution was a catastrophe, she would never have believed it and would have argued with the person at all cost because ever since she was eleven, she had been taught that "the Cultural Revolution is good." Fang Fang told the sixteen-year-old letter writer that he was probably at the same stage of growth, but one day he would become a critical and independent thinker, just as she did. Fang Fang thus turned her diary into a lesson about the adverse effects of official ideology on critical thinking.[51]

The barrage against positive energy continued in the online battle over Fang Fang's diary. Dozens of noted scholars and writers rallied in support of her. One of them, a professor of Chinese literature at Hubei University in Wuhan, wrote: "Some people say Fang Fang's diary has no positive functions. I think their biggest positive function is to warn people not to make the same mistakes again. . . . Serious, well-reasoned criticisms based on evidence are not negative energy. They can help overcome difficulties and correct errors. They are full of positive energy."[52] Another expressed similar views:

> I have never liked the phrase "positive energy." Now that I'm writing about it here, I want to say that Fang Fang's diaries are the real positive energy. Only people with a bright heart want to discover and expose darkness; they censure in hopes of improvement; they criticize to make change. . . . What is negative? What does not have positive function? To turn a blind eye to social injustice and the conditions of the subaltern and disempowered groups, to remain apathetic to all the false, ugly, and evil things in society—that is negative; that does not have any positive function. . . . Seventeen years ago and now—haven't we paid high enough costs? If we have more people like Fang Fang, society will develop in a better direction. That's positive energy![53]

CENSORSHIP AND EMOTIONAL PUBLICS

Was the online relay of "The Whistle-Giver" a success? Yes. As a result of the relay, the story not only did not disappear from the web but also became better known. Censorship itself was exposed as never before. More importantly, the chief target of censorship, public emotions, was not wiped out but became stronger as a result. The online relay was made possible by the participation of emotional publics, but it also channeled the outpouring of public emotions. Ai Fen's own emotions were infectious. They helped open the emotional floodgate of a Wuhan under lockdown. The relay was cathartic.

Emotions have long been a driving force of protest in China, online and offline.[54] For party authorities, attacking emotions as uncivil and irrational is a means of suppressing online protest. Accusing Fang Fang's diary of lacking positive energy attacked the allegedly negative emotions in her diary.

In this politics of emotions, however, only so-called negative emotions are targeted because they are the emotions of protest. Positive emotions such as loyalty and gratitude are promoted in official discourse. But as the scene of gratitude politics described in chapter 3 shows, emotions are not easily manipulated or controlled. The Wuhan mayor's call for residents to show loyalty and gratitude to CCP leadership backfired. An effort to inculcate positive emotions of loyalty inadvertently prompted an outpouring of negative emotions of anger. Indeed, as the online relay shows, every attempt to eradicate negative emotions through censorship produced more negative emotions.

Why does censorship persist if it does not work? Perhaps it persists in part because it is built into the CCP propaganda machine. As the machine runs, so do its component parts, and so the game goes on. But censorship, like content moderation on U.S. social media platforms, has also become a business and a profession.[55] Technology companies and government agencies run businesses to monitor online communication for fee-paying clients.[56] Major platforms in China hire growing numbers of content moderators (*neirong shenhe yuan* 内容审核员). At the height of the anticensorship protest in March 2020, *Southern Weekend* (南方周末) reposted a story about content moderation that it had published in 2019. The viral circulation of the story highlighted yet again the prevalence of the content-moderation profession.[57] According to this story, Jinan and Tianjin are the two major bases of the content-moderation industry in northern China, although the industry is also large in other major cities, such as Xi'an, Chongqing, Chengdu, and Wuhan. Personal stories abound on social media about the dreary and depressing nature of the job. New college graduates badly in need of work are the main targets of recruitment, but few want to stay on the job for more than a couple of years.[58]

As a job, censorship is not always done in the same way. Some content moderators may get tired while doing it, others may not be paying close enough attention, and still others may delay performing their job for a few seconds—just in that short time lag, a posting can take on a life of its own. I have come across user comments on Weibo that make precisely these points. One person wrote, for example, "That interview with Dr. Ai Fen is banned from the entire internet, but it appears that there are people [censors] who deliberately missed their fire [chance of deleting it]."[59] A reader of Fang Fang's diary commented: "Those who monitor and surveil the internet are human beings, too, and must have some basic human sympathy. So they keep one eye open and the other closed [thus pretending not to see what needs to be censored]."[60]

When direct censorship fails, however, other institutional forms of discipline may be activated. In the months after Wuhan lifted its lockdown, two individuals who had publicly defended Fang Fang came under troll attack. One was Liang Yanping 梁艳萍, a professor of Chinese literature in Hubei University. The other was the well-known poet Wang Xiaoni 王小妮, a retired professor at Hainan University. Both Liang and Wang were accused of being unpatriotic and "publishing inappropriate speech" (*fabiao budang yanlun* 发表不当言论). In a manner reminiscent of "human-flesh search," trolls dug up Liang's and Wang's social media postings from years back and charged them with insulting China and Chinese culture. According to this charge, Liang was once a visiting scholar at a Japanese university and had often posted favorable views about Japan on Weibo and allegedly once used the derogatory appellation *Chinks* (支那人) to compare Chinese with Japanese. Hubei University started an investigation into Liang at the end of April 2020 and announced in mid-June that she would no longer be allowed to teach. Hainan University also announced an investigation into Wang Xiaoni, but Wang had already retired, and no result of the investigation was announced.[61]

In the midst of these attacks on liberal intellectuals, the gong-beating woman described in chapter 3 made a surprising new appearance. In early February, she had cried out desperately for help to get her COVID-infected mother admitted to a hospital. She won instant public sympathy and support. Fang Fang was one of many who tweeted on Weibo the video of the woman crying out for help. No one doubted that the public attention heaped on the gong-beating woman was instrumental in getting her and her mother hospitalized, where they received medical care.[62] However, a little more than a month later, the woman made a surprise attack on Fang Fang. In a Weibo post on May 14, she claimed that when Fang Fang had retweeted the video about her in February, she had weaponized her, not helped her. Taking a stab at the English translation of Fang Fang's diary, she wrote, "Don't write about me in your book. I don't want to go abroad."[63] The gong-beating woman's Weibo posting was an instant scandal. Many readers compared her to the wolf in the ancient fable of Mr. Dongguo 东郭先生: Mr. Dongguo had saved a wolf from a hunter, but after the hunter left, the wolf wanted to eat Mr. Dongguo.

Second Uncle wrote about this incident in his diary on May 16. He found the gong-beating woman to be a hopeless opportunist. She had turned on Fang Fang because so many others were attacking Fang Fang that it seemed like a safe thing to do. What was especially disconcerting to Second Uncle, however, was not that she was an opportunist—he reasoned there were always opportunists—but that many postings critical of the woman's attack on Fang Fang had been censored. The merit of these postings, he argued, was not to save this woman from moral depravity, which would be a hopeless cause, but simply to express a sense of public outrage and remind others not to degenerate to the same level of lowliness. Second Uncle was also worried that if the gong-beating woman were a product of the environment, then censoring postings critical of her was nothing less than cultivating an environment for more harm.[64] He was worried, in other words, that post-COVID China would return to its pre-COVID condition without learning any lessons. The ideology of positive energy, once challenged by Fang Fang, would return with a vengeance.

8

COVID NATIONALISM

"NEVER UNDERESTIMATE HUMAN STUPIDITY"

In March 2020, as nations around the world closed borders, sentiments of nationalism and xenophobia grew. In the United States, what the sociologist Mark Juergensmeyer calls a COVID "cultural nationalism" appeared. Writing in June 2020, he highlighted media images of angry and largely white males protesting invisible virus cells "thought to be undermining the American way of life."[1] Wearing Donald Trump's MAGA (Make America Great Again) hats and sometimes even holding guns and pistols, these protesters were out in the streets ostensibly to protect their freedom, including their freedom not to wear face coverings. In their conspiracy theories, COVID-19 is either a hoax or a disease created by sinister foreign forces out to destroy the United States. The country's foremost expert on infectious diseases, Dr. Anthony Fauci, became a target of such conspiracy theories and received death threats from Trump supporters for allegedly trying to undermine Trump in an election year.[2] As Trump and officials of his administration called COVID-19 the "China virus" and demanded China pay reparations, they joined a state nationalism with a right-wing populism.

By and large, China's COVID nationalism parallels its U.S. variety, often in direct reaction to anti-China rhetoric in the United States. Initial responses to the coronavirus outbreak in Wuhan were pessimistic and negative. Citizens were critical of how party authorities handled, or mishandled, the crisis. Public attention was focused on domestic situations. Although official media made early efforts to project positive images of China's war on COVID-19, popular nationalism in China did not flare up until mid- and late March, when the pandemic had come under control in China and heavy outbreaks hit Japan, South Korea, Italy, the United States, and many other countries.

Diarists documented this shift of public attention from domestic to international pandemic conditions. Mr. Song started his "Paris Diary" on March 13, when France was just entering a period of lockdown. In his first entry, Song wrote about Sophie Trudeau, the wife of the Canadian prime minister Justin Trudeau, testing positive for COVID-19 and how Sweden had "completely surrendered" to the virus.[3] Sister Meng, a Wuhan native, wrote on March 1, 2020, that fifty-eight countries in the world had reported cases of COVID-19. According to a *Los Angeles Times* report, she wrote, the chancellor of the University of California at Davis, Gary May, had confirmed three cases of possible infection among students, but county health officials refused to disclose their contact history. This refusal prompted Meng to exclaim: "Without publicizing their whereabouts, how could other people know whether they had had any contact with them? How could it be possible to find and control the spread of the disease as early as possible?" In the same diary entry, Meng also wrote that in northern Italy multiple towns were locked down, but in one town residents rallied in a plaza with slogans demanding their freedom. After enumerating a long list of COVID-related stupidities reported in other countries, Meng summed up her thoughts with a quote from Yuval Harari, "Never underestimate human stupidity."[4] At this moment, she was a proud Chinese indignant about the "stupidities" in foreign countries.

"OUR COUNTRY IS THE BEST!"

The effectiveness of China's war on COVID-19 in 2020, frequently compared with the failures in the United States and other foreign countries, strengthened Chinese nationals' patriotic feelings. Sister Meng visited her parents on April 22, 2020. Because they hadn't seen each other for a long time, her parents had a lot to say to her. "What they lamented most is the cruel and miserable conditions of senior citizens in many foreign countries, which have given up treating them and just let them wait to die," she wrote. Her mother told her about a video on WeChat that showed an elderly foreign woman crying out desperately for help. Meng's father told her that there were many deaths in senior homes in the United States and Europe. In contrast, Meng's parents praised China for never giving up on its senior citizens: "Our country even saved a few people above the age of one hundred!" What moved them most was that just a few days earlier they had learned of a 5 percent pension raise for all retirees in China. Her mother said to her: "I never imagined that our country would raise our pension in such difficult times. I called to share the news with your uncle, Aunt Long, grandfather, Aunt Zhang. They all said they didn't expect it. It's so moving!" Her father said, "There are over 100 million retirees in the whole country. Even if each person gets a raise of only 100 yuan, it will be a huge amount! Our country is the best" (Hai shi wo'men guojia hao 还是我们国家好).[5]

Mr. Fei is a Hubei native residing in Guangzhou. When he posted his diary on April 21, the Wuhan lockdown had been lifted for about two weeks, and much of the public's attention had shifted to the resumption of work. But at the same time China's social media world was being torn apart by the polarized positions on the English translation of Fang Fang's diary. Debates about Fang Fang's online diary had been intense from early on, but when news came that English and German translations of it would soon be published in the United States and Germany, the debates turned into an online war. Some people who had initially liked Fang Fang's diary changed positions. Those who previously had not taken a side began to take one. Even close friends and families split into warring factions. WeChat circles became treacherous battlegrounds.

In Mr. Fei's own WeChat circle, several of his well-educated friends who had previously been polite and courteous suddenly turned belligerent. They attacked Fang Fang viciously. What puzzled him most was the change he saw in a woman in her seventies, his mother-in-law's friend, who was a mother figure to him whom he called "Aunt." About ten years earlier, Mr. Fei had suffered from a serious illness, and surgery had left him in great pain for months. It was Aunt who offered to look after him in the hospital. She took such good care of him that he felt he owed his life to her. Aunt often told him that she had a miserable life when she was young. Her family had been poor, but she luckily received help from many kind people, for which she had always been grateful. That is why later in her life, when her own circumstances improved, she wanted to help those in need. She had a Buddha-like heart.[6]

After the lockdown started, Mr. Fei recommended Fang Fang's diaries to Aunt. Initially, Aunt did not express any opinions but did read them. Fei felt that if Aunt did not say anything, that at least meant that she did not dislike the diaries. Several times she had even "liked" the diaries he had posted in his WeChat Moments. However, when she learned that Fang Fang's diary would be published abroad, her attitude changed abruptly. She began to forward postings and videos critical of Fang Fang. In her WeChat comments, she called Fang Fang a traitor. Fei was stunned. He had known Aunt's patriotic feelings but was still greatly puzzled by her drastic change of attitude.

Fang Fang had attracted attacks for her critical depictions of Wuhan, but the voices of support for her had initially far outnumbered her detractors. Yet news of the publication of her diary in English turned the tide. Similarly, in the initial period social media were full of criticisms of the authorities' delayed responses to the epidemic and the chaos and tragedies that had caused. Yet as Western politicians and media intensified their attacks on China, criticisms of government behavior in China decreased, and expressions of patriotism became stronger. When Sister Meng's father said, "Our country is the best!," he sounded utterly genuine, and he was only one of many ordinary Chinese thinking these same thoughts.

The two trends represent China's populist COVID nationalism. But to lump individuals such as Mr. Fei's Aunt and Sister Meng's parents under the umbrella of "COVID nationalists" does little to illuminate the meaning of concrete human experiences. They and numerous others like them may be part of a new wave of COVID nationalism, but it would be too simplistic to dismiss their behavior as mere symptoms of a pathology or as brainwashing by official ideologies. As Mr. Fei notes, Aunt was not anywhere close to being such a person. How, then, should we understand ordinary people like Aunt?

"UNDER THE SAME MOON AND SKIES"

The lockdown of Wuhan was initially met with international support. Donations of medical supplies poured into Wuhan's hospitals from abroad. Foreign governments as well as Chinese diaspora communities sent donations. What were considered the most special of foreign donations came from Japan. A year later, on my WeChat Moments I can still find many postings about the Japanese donations. These postings appeared between January 31, 2020, and the first two weeks of February. They not only praised the friendship of the Japanese but marveled at how much more cultured and "classical" the Japanese were than the Chinese. The cause of the marvel was what had been written on the packaging of Japanese donations. Besides the names of the senders and recipients, the boxes had some additional phrases written on them, such as "How can you say you don't have clothes? I'll share my underskirt with you" (Qiyue wuyi, yuzi tongshang 岂曰无衣, 与子同裳), or "Our mountains and rivers are different, but we live under the same moon and skies" (Shanchuan yiyu, fengyue tongtian 山川异域, 风月同天). The first quotation comes from *The Book of Poetry* (诗经), one of the greatest classics of the august Confucian canon. The second was allegedly written on the gifts that the Japanese prince Nagaya (684–729 CE) sent to Chinese Buddhists in the Tang dynasty (618–907 CE). In return, Jianzhen 鉴真, a Buddhist monk in the city of Yangzhou, traveled across the sea to Japan in 754 CE to teach Buddhism. Thus was born the best-known legend of Sino-Japanese friendship.

The classical Chinese quotations printed on Japanese donations were instantly taken as a sign of Japanese refinement. News reports covering the story elaborated on the historical background and literary allusions of these quotations. Netizens discussed how to translate them into English. Others lamented that the donations sent to Wuhan from inside China lacked "culture"—they only had "Wuhan, jia you" written on them. *Jia you* 加油 literally means "add oil." "Wuhan, jia you!" is equivalent to saying, "Go, Wuhan!" In the excitement about Japanese donations, netizens saw the more colloquial term *jia you* as so much less refined than the classicism of the Japanese.[7]

This national fervor about Japanese donations reflected a fragile national psyche torn between feelings of shame and pride. In social-psychological language, rejection by others results in the lowering of one's feelings of self-worth—hence shame. Conversely, recognition by others creates a sense of self-pride.[8] The enthusiasm about the donations from Japan reflected a sense of pride in being recognized by the Japanese. There was something special about the Japanese using classical Chinese verse to show their support. At the beginning of the epidemic in Wuhan, a sense of shock and helplessness was pervasive. These classical verses of friendship, sympathy, and support from a foreign country were a much-needed boost to the Chinese morale. And that they came from Japan carried special significance. In the past, Japan had usually been the target of nationalistic protest because of the historical memory of the Nanjing massacre committed by Japanese troops in China's War of Resistance against Japan.[9] The publicity about the verses on the aid packages showed how sensitive the Chinese can be to foreigners' perception of them and their country. Recognition by foreign nations would be bountifully acknowledged, while rejection and disrespect would be met with the same. Thus, in her press briefings on February 4, 2020, Chinese Foreign Ministry spokesperson Hua Chunying thanked the Japanese government and the Japanese people for their friendship and support but simultaneously took a stab at a *Wall Street Journal* op-ed published the previous day.[10]

ANTI-CHINESE RACISM

Using the headline "China is the Real Sick Man of Asia" and published on February 3, before the pandemic hit the United States, the *Wall Street Journal* op-ed viewed China's initial response to the COVID-19 outbreak as "less than impressive" and ineffective.[11] The racist headline provoked public outrage. Asian and Chinese Americans in the United States as well as citizens in China demanded an apology from the *Wall Street Journal*. When no apology was forthcoming, the Chinese Foreign Ministry expelled three *Wall Street Journal* reporters. At a press conference on February 24, 2020, the newly appointed Foreign Ministry spokesperson, Zhao Lijian, was asked: "Given that the three reporters expelled had nothing to do with the offensive editorial in question, why were these three particular individuals expelled?" Zhao responded: "I think you should ask [the *Wall Street Journal*] why it published an article that attacks and slanders a nation and its people, why it chose a clearly racist headline, why no one has come forward to assume responsibility so far, and why it refuses to apologize."[12]

Zhao's tough posture at his inaugural appearance as a Foreign Ministry spokesperson won him praise. He was given the nickname "Rejoinder Zhao" 赵怼怼 for his aggressive responses to questions. One diarist wrote about him enthusiastically: "On February 24, the regular press conference of the Foreign Ministry was held in the Blue Hall. The 31st spokesperson of the Foreign Ministry, Zhao Lijian (who is the deputy director of the Department of News in the Foreign Ministry), made his first appearance in the Blue Hall to host his first press conference. He was sharp and domineering. Love him. Have always wanted such a commanding spokesperson."[13] Many netizens welcomed tough responses that challenged foreign misrepresentations of China's efforts to fight COVID-19.

Tensions become particularly unbearable when contemporary insults are added to past traumas. During the COVID-19 pandemic, incidents of racism and discrimination against ethnic Chinese were widely reported around the world. These painful stories invariably spread to Chinese social media users, thus exacerbating a sense of fear of the foreign. Chinese official media covered some of these stories. Chinese students abroad reported personal experiences to friends and families back home. WeChat accounts run by overseas Chinese, of which there are many, translated and distributed such stories to ethnic Chinese communities around the world. Pandemic diaries written by overseas ethnic Chinese and Chinese students in Europe, Australia, New Zealand, Singapore, Manila, Canada, and the United States blossomed on WeChat and Weibo, reaching the same audiences as the diaries produced inside China.

Mr. Yun is a college professor in Wuhan. His diary was often light-hearted and funny, and he came across as a jolly man. His diary on March 18 was addressed as a letter to his son, who was studying in the United Kingdom. Later he would post more diary entries in the form of letters to his son, and other parents who had children in the United Kingdom would seek him out for advice. On March 20, he shared a story from one such parent. The parent told him that four Chinese students, one male and three females, in Southampton were harassed by a group of local teenagers for wearing face masks. The parent asked Mr. Yun's views about the incident. Yun's response was that it was a rare incident that attracted attention only because of the current circumstances. He told the parent that similar incidents had happened in the United States. He added that such place-based discrimination had also happened in both the past and the present in China and abroad. His advice to his own son was: "You should correctly and rationally view the Southampton incident, and there is no need to fear. I've repeatedly told you to be 'brave.' During this period, try to go out as little as possible. Even if you go out, do not try to 'act like you're so special' " (*teli duxing* 特立独行).[14]

Mr. Yun played down what was apparently a serious incident in which one Chinese student was beaten up, two culprits were detained by the police, and the Chinese embassy in the United Kingdom issued a public statement.[15] One of the Chinese students involved in the incident gave a detailed account of her experience on her Weibo account, and her story attracted lots of sympathy for them and anger toward their assailants.

Similar incidents of racism were reported by Chinese diarists in New York, Philadelphia, Sydney, and other global cities. A white man yelled racist and sexual insults at a female Chinese student in New York.[16] Two Asian women were spat at by a white woman in the street of Sydney.[17] The author of Vancouver Pandemic Diary reported a hate-speech incident in Vancouver's Chinatown: on the glass door of the Chinese Cultural Center there, someone wrote, "Let's put a stop to Chinese coming to Canada. Shoot them on the spot."[18] The incident was condemned by Vancouver's mayor, but it shows the dangers that racism posed to overseas Chinese during the pandemic.

The author of the Philadelphia Pandemic Diary wrote about racism on April 20. She started with an incident that happened to her own children in early March. They had just finished school and were heading to the subway station together with several classmates. On their way, someone shouted to them: "Do you have coronavirus?" The author also mentioned other incidents of racism that members of her Chinese church experienced in Philadelphia.[19]

Citing a study issued by the Stop Asian Americans and Pacific Islanders Hate website based in San Francisco, a BBC story on May 27, 2020, reported that more than 1,700 incidents of anti-Asian racism were reported in the sixty days after March 19, 2020. The BBC story recounts the experiences of several interviewees. Thirty-one-year-old Tracy Wen Liu in Austin, Texas, reported that her Korean friend "was pushed and yelled at by several people in a grocery store, and then asked to leave, simply because she was Asian and wearing a mask." After this incident, Liu decided to get her first gun. Kimberly Ha, a thirty-eight-year-old Chinese Canadian, had lived in New York for more than fifteen years. She experienced a traumatizing incident in February. When she was walking her dog, a stranger shouted at her: "I'm not scared of radioactive Chinese people," and "You people shouldn't be here, get out of this country, I'm not scared of this virus that you people brought over."[20]

Not only did ethnic Chinese and Asians become random targets of racism, but Chinese students in the United States were also singled out as targets of surveillance by U.S. government agencies. They became the victims of an increasingly hostile U.S.-China relationship and the Trump administration's anti-immigration policies. Accounts of personal horror stories of being harassed and interrogated by U.S. Customs and Homeland Security officers at airports circulated in the many WeChat public accounts run by overseas Chinese students. Students on their way back to China could be asked to hand over passwords to their mobile phones and social media accounts, their laptops and iPads could be taken from them, and some students were held for so long that they missed their flights.[21]

In response to such incidents of racism abroad, some Chinese students reported feeling a sense of pride as Chinese nationals when they received support from Chinese embassies. At the time, Little Mao was a seventeen-year-old student attending high school in Sheffield in the United Kingdom. He started writing a stay-at-home diary on March 20 when his school was closed down. By April 24, when he flew back to China, he had written thirty-six entries. On March 26, he wrote that the Chinese embassy in the United

Kingdom had started distributing "health kits" to Chinese students there. When he told his landlord and landlady about the health kit he had received, they were even more excited than he. The couple felt that things were quite a mess in the United Kingdom and that there were many things the government could not take care of. China, in contrast, was not only fighting the COVID pandemic vigorously at home but also showing care for Chinese citizens abroad. "I felt like I had just got a shot of cardiac stimulant. My feeling of confidence showed clearly on my face," Little Mao wrote.[22]

Several days later, on March 31, Little Mao attended a virtual meeting hosted by Chinese ambassador Liu Xiaoming. At that meeting, medical experts who had just arrived from China gave lectures on COVID-19 as well as practical advice. Little Mao felt the care and warmth of his compatriots from China: "I felt very fortunate and proud. Although I am facing the pandemic in a foreign country, my strong motherland is standing behind me, supporting me, and protecting me. I believe we will survive this catastrophe safely."[23]

Meanwhile, those who tried to return to China experienced deep frustration because of China's stringent testing requirements for international travelers and the high cost and unpredictability of international flights. Two visiting Chinese students in my own school in Philadelphia spent much of the summer first trying desperately to purchase plane tickets back to China, then worrying about flight cancellations and harassment by security officers at the airport, and finally anxiously and meticulously planning the precise timing of COVID testing so that at the time of boarding they could show proof that their testing results were up to date (within three days before boarding, as of September 2020).[24]

"A NEW EIGHT-NATION ALLIANCE"

The *Wall Street Journal*'s racist headline and the responses it provoked in China were only an early example of the nasty language in what would become a protracted media war between the United States and China. To the Chinese, the most outrageous allegation was that China should be held accountable for the global pandemic and pay reparations. Demands for reparations were reportedly raised in India, Australia, the United Kingdom, and the United States. In the United States, according to a *Bloomberg* story published on May 6, 2020, not only did Donald Trump call on China to pay reparations, but also lawsuits against China had already been filed in Miami, California, Nevada, Pennsylvania, Texas, and Missouri.[25] As the *Bloomberg* report noted, many of these lawsuits were political theater meant to rile up sentiment against China ahead of the U.S. presidential election. A strategy memo for Republican campaigners put it bluntly: "Don't defend Trump, other than the China Travel Ban—attack China."[26] Blaming China was a way of deflecting Trump's failure in tackling the COVID crisis.[27]

The reparation claims made by U.S. politicians and organizations were reminiscent of the humiliating indemnities imposed on China through unequal treaties such as the Boxer Protocol. In August 1900, as the troops of the Eight-Nation Alliance 八国联军 advanced to Beijing on their expedition to quell the Boxer Uprising, they burned villages along the way, summarily executed people suspected of being boxers, and plundered the capital city. In the end, Western powers made the Qing court sign the Boxer Protocol on September 7, 1901. Among other things, the protocol demanded the payment of 450 million taels of fine silver (around 18,000 tonnes, worth U.S.$333 million or £67 million at the exchange rates of the time) as indemnity to the Western nations over a period of thirty-nine years.[28] As the historian Joseph Esherick puts it, this amount was "more than four times the annual revenue of the Beijing government and an even one tael for each Chinese subject."[29]

Against this background, reparation claims made by Western politicians and organizations drew ire from both the Chinese government and Chinese citizens. References to the historical Eight-Nation Alliance appeared often on social media. Some called the foreign countries where COVID reparations claims were made the "New Eight-Nation Alliance." In his diary entry on April 8, 2020, Mr. Wen, a professor in a college in Shandong province, wrote: "It seems as if we were back to 180 years ago, the Opium War of 1840 and the mad colonial era of the West. The historical dregs of a 'U.K.-France Alliance,' a 'New Eight-Nation Alliance,' a 'New Paris Peace Conference' seem to be rising up again."[30]

Chinese official media and the Foreign Ministry responded with official statements. To debunk reparation claims made against China, the *People's Daily* published on its website what it called "ten questions the U.S. needs to offer clear answers to the world," along with interlinear English translations. To publish an article with English in it was unprecedented for the *People's Daily*, suggesting the gravity of the matter.[31] The most eye-catching aspect of the Chinese counteroffensive in the COVID-19 blame game was that prominent Chinese diplomats, including ambassadors, took to Twitter to shout back. Again, the Chinese Foreign Ministry spokesperson Zhao Lijian made the most headlines at home and abroad. In China, he is viewed as a hero and a fighter. In the West, he is dubbed a "wolf-warrior" diplomat, a new species of Chinese diplomat taking China's "media going out" policy to a newly aggressive level. One of Zhao's tweets, posted on March 12, 2020, pointed to the U.S. Army, not to Wuhan, as a potential origin of COVID-19: "CDC [U.S. Centers for Disease Control] was caught on the spot. When did patient zero begin in U.S.? How many people are infected? What are the names of the hospitals? It might be U.S. Army who brought the epidemic to Wuhan. Be transparent! Make public your data! U.S. owe us an explanation!"[32]

Zhao's conspiracy theory stirred up a hornet's nest, turning him into a prime target in Western media. His tweet prompted Twitter management to put a fact-checking note beneath it: "Get the facts about COVID-19." The note is also a link to the following message from WHO: "WHO says evidence suggests COVID-19 originated in animals and was not produced in a lab."[33] But just as reparation claims made by U.S. leaders and organizations were designed to shift blame from the U.S. president, so Zhao Lijian's tweet was less about facts and more a countersalvo to debunk unfounded claims coming from American media. Probably to deflate international criticism, Chinese ambassador to the United States Cui Tiankai later disowned Zhao's conspiracy theory in a public interview.[34]

CHINESE MEDIA'S GLOBAL ASPIRATIONS

Twitter was a different creature ten years ago. According to Twitbase.com, a website that tracked Chinese-language Twitter activity, there were 85,541

Chinese-language twitter accounts as of November 11, 2010. A look at the top-one-hundred Chinese-language Twitterers by number of followers listed on Twitbase.com reveals the categories presented in table 8.1. Although the identity of fifty-one of these accounts was unknown, judged by their content they could not possibly have anything to do with official Chinese media. In other words, ten years ago there were no known Twitter accounts for official Chinese media agencies or individual officials among the top-ranking Chinese users of Twitter. One-third of the top-one-hundred accounts were activists. At that time, Twitter discourse about China was nothing short of subversive. Although Twitter's Chinese users represented a small number, they had large followings and enjoyed high visibility. At the time of Twitbase.com's research (November 11, 2010), the top-ranked person on the list had 62,636 followers; the last person on the list had 7,407

TABLE 8.1 Top-100 Chinese-language users of Twitter, November 11, 2010

Type of user	Number of Twitter accounts
Blogger activists in China	33
Chinese activists in exile	2
Chinese journalists	1
Hong Kong journalists	2
International news agencies (BBC-Chinese)	2
Liberal-oriented Chinese news agencies (*Caixin* and *Southern Weekend*)	3
Information technology entrepreneurs/analysts	2
Chinese celebrities	1
Chinese media scholars	1
Internet magazines	2
Unknown	51
Total	100

Source: Author's classification based on data from Twitbase, November 11, 2010, in Guobin Yang, "Power and Transgression in the Global Media Age: The Strange Case of Twitter in China," in *Communication and Power in the Global Era: Orders and Borders*, ed. Marwan M. Kraidy (London: Routledge, 2013), 170.

followers. All were active users, tirelessly tweeting and retweeting. The top ten on the list had an average of 16,809 tweets and a median of 11,556.[35]

Ten years later, much of Twitter discourse about China in either Chinese or English remains critical. But users who tweet about China are more diverse than before. Ethnic Chinese students, scholars, and journalists working or studying in Western countries bring different voices about China to the Twitter sphere.[36] And as Zhao Lijian's case shows, Twitter accounts representing official Chinese media and state agencies have grown in number and visibility.

In the past decade, Chinese official media have tried to gain a foothold in the global arena by expanding their international presence. Chinese media outlets have joined U.S. social media platforms. Xinhua News Agency, *People's Daily*, CCTV, *China Daily* (中国日报), and China Radio International have become active on Facebook, Twitter, and YouTube. They post information frequently and build their number of followers conscientiously. When I studied these outlets on August 21, 2018, for example, China Radio International's China Plus News Facebook page had more than 20 million followers and 20 million "likes." CCTV's Facebook page had more than 47 million "likes" and 48 million followers. The New China Twitter account run by Xinhua News Agency had 11 million followers, while *China Daily* USA had more than 2 million followers on Twitter.

The global expansion of Chinese media is part of its "going out" policy. The practice of "media going out" is not new. It was integral to China's Third World strategy in the Mao era. Mao's *Little Red Book*, among other things, was translated into dozens of foreign languages and sold or distributed freely around the globe in large quantities, and China Radio International broadcast to the world in multiple languages.[37]

What is new in the recent global expansion of Chinese media is that it is an effort to project positive images about China at a time when global media discourses about China's rise are full of fear and negativity. The global "China rise" talk acknowledges China's economic growth but often frames China as a threat to the U.S.-dominated global order. There is a common perception in China that Western media depictions of China are biased. Chinese nationals are proud of their country's economic rise, but this sense of pride is often spurned by Western media portrayals. An example of these contrary views is the 2008 Olympic Games in Beijing. For the Chinese, hosting such a global event was a hard-won honor. If so many global cities had had the privilege to host the Olympics, why hadn't Beijing had even one single chance? When the International Olympics Committee finally selected Beijing in 2001, the news was greeted with national euphoria. From then to the summer of 2008, the entire nation was mobilized to prepare for the Olympics, but in the months leading up to the opening of the games, there appeared what many Chinese saw as a Western media blitz against China. China was taken to task for its human rights records, and the Beijing Olympics torch relay encountered protests in many cities across Europe and North America.[38]

Partly because of the negative publicity China suffered, the year 2008 became a turning point in its global media strategy. After 2008, the Chinese government increased its investment in the overseas operations of state-run media and reportedly pledged U.S.$6.5 billion to the endeavor in early 2009.[39] In 2010, China launched Xinhua News Agency's twenty-four-hour English-language satellite and cable television network, CNC World, which has correspondents stationed in more than 170 countries. In 2011, China launched a new national strategic plan to develop its cultural industry. Compared with earlier approaches to culture as propaganda independent of commercial interest, this emphasis on the development of a cultural industry marks a policy shift. The language of soft power, a Western social science construct, has influenced the recent emphasis on cultural power. Indeed, a notable feature of China's new approaches to media and culture is the displacement of the Mao-era language of Third World revolution and liberation with a new language of public diplomacy, soft power, branding, and image management. This new language is an amalgam of commercial culture and Western social science. Chinese policy makers have learned this language as they look to communicate more effectively with the world.

Despite the growing global presence of Chinese media, however, their influence is limited. The unabashedly propagandistic nature of China's international media operations does not help to attract audience. Chinese media on Twitter and Facebook are engaged mostly in one-way information transmission. Besides conventional news from official media sources, Chinese media publish on American social media lots of lifestyle information, typically of the kind that has been printed in English-language magazines such as *Peking Review* since the Mao era. Photographs of local food, cute pandas, folk arts, and so forth are among the most common postings. Some scholars have dubbed this form of digital diplomacy "panda engagement" because of the prevalence of panda images. Panda images proliferate because, like cute cats, they attract many "likes" and followers on social media, and the large numbers of followers and "likes" are taken as indicators of the popularity and success of these media channels on Western social media.[40]

Against this background, the rise of a new species of "wolf warriors" is notable for the global media attention they have garnered.

WOLF-WARRIOR STYLE

On July 21, 2020, Manya Koetse, the editor in chief of the website What's on Weibo, published a list of 280 Twitter accounts run by Chinese official media and state organizations. She divided them into five categories. Under diplomatic missions are the Twitter handles of Chinese embassies around the world. The second category consists of individual ambassadors and diplomats, such as ambassador to the United Kingdom Liu Xiaoming (with 67,800 followers). Government and state accounts are the third category. They include the spokespersons of the Chinese Foreign Ministry, such as Zhao Lijian (731,100 followers) and Hua Chunying (579,400 followers). In the fourth category, city and region accounts include various municipal government agencies, such as Visit Fuzhou (@visit_fuzhou), Discover Yunnan (@discoverYunnan), and Zhejiang Tourism (@tourzj1). Many of these city accounts focus on promoting local tourism; some have only a hundred followers. Finally, in the fifth category, official media agencies include all the big ones, such as China Xinhua News (12.6 million followers), the *People's Daily* (7.1 million followers), the *China Daily* (4.3 million followers), and the *Global Times* (1.8 million followers).[41] Koetse notes both the growing influence of some of these accounts and the lack of sophistication of some others.[42] But in general the growing presence of Chinese official accounts on Twitter is a sharp contrast with their near complete absence ten years ago.

Although many of these accounts cultivate their followings using a "panda engagement" approach to tweeting, the recent rise of "wolf-warrior" diplomats shows that a more confrontational and aggressive approach is an effective means of catching attention. In Chinese and Western media, the most visible Chinese officials on Twitter are the two Foreign Ministry spokespersons—Hua Chunying and Zhao Lijian. Geng Shuang is another popular Foreign Ministry spokesperson, but he is not as active on Twitter. Appearing in many viral memes and videos, these Foreign Ministry officials are internet celebrities on Chinese social media, known for being tough and sharp-tongued when answering foreign journalists' questions. What is mentioned most about them is their personal style. Viewers comment on their smiles, laughter, humor, subtle eye expressions, posture, as well as their choice of words.

Hua Chunying, nicknamed "Sister Hua" and "Goddess of Chinese Diplomacy" by her fans, is known for being strong and forceful underneath an appearance of gracefulness and gentleness. She is best known for using an internet catchphrase in her responses to journalists' questions. At a press conference on July 29, 2019, Hua was asked: "On July 26, the U.S. issued a memorandum on developing-country status in the WTO [World Trade Organization], asking the organization to make changes within 90 days of the date of this memorandum, or it may take unilateral actions. As China is mentioned many times in the memorandum, I wonder if you have any comment on it?" After making three points in her response, Hua ended with the following: "When you hear the words and deeds of the U.S. on the status of developing countries in the WTO, I believe you feel just the same as I do. They further reveal how capricious, arrogant, and selfish the country is. Such are not worthy behaviors of the 'world's biggest power.' There is a catchphrase that got popular just recently in China, 'Don't behave like the United States.' I hope some people on the U.S. side can deeply reflect on it."[43]

The original Chinese version of "Don't behave like the United States" is "Zuoren buneng tai Meiguo" (做人不能太美国). A more literal translation might read: "Don't be too U.S. in conducting yourself," where "U.S." is treated as an adjective to mean all the bad things about the United States. No one knows the origin of this internet meme, but after Hua Chunying used it at that press conference, she made both the meme and herself famous.

Fans applauded Hua's public performance during the pandemic. On March 21, a story in the American news publication the *Daily Beast* revealed the White House communication guidelines for U.S. officials to talk about the coronavirus. The key talking point was to blame China for the pandemic. Whereas the Chinese Communist Party "cared more about its reputation than its own people's suffering," the U.S. government cable stated, "the United States and the American people are demonstrating once again that they are the greatest humanitarians the world has ever known."[44] In response to this story, Hua Chunying posted the following tweets on March 22:

> 1/2 Heard about the story of plugging ears while stealing bell? Is this the so-called freedom of information? Don't the American people have the right to know the truth? Will self-deception and smearing China help with epidemic response?
>
> 2/2 Indeed saving lives is more important than saving face! Be honest and responsible![45]

Screenshots and Chinese translations of Hua's tweets were circulated as inserts in online stories.

Geng Shuang is known for being subtle, indirect, but sharp. At a press conference on March 12, 2020, he was asked: "Robert O'Brien, the White House national security adviser, said yesterday that China covered up the virus outbreak in Wuhan, and this likely cost the world two months of time to prepare. What's your comment on this?" After a lengthy response explaining how China had won time for the international community and how some countries were doing much better than the United States, Geng concluded:

> Faced with the pandemic, the guiding consensus for all countries is to join hands and overcome difficulties together. Pointing the finger at others is certainly not constructive, nor will it get any backing. To quote an

ancient Chinese saying, "Turn inward and examine yourself when you encounter difficulties in life." You know what this means? Ha ha. We urge the U.S. official to respect facts and the common understanding of the international community. Every minute wasted on smearing and complaining would be better spent on enhancing domestic response and international cooperation.[46]

"Turn inward and examine yourself when you encounter difficulties in life" (Xingyou bude, fanqiu zhuji 行有不得,反求诸己) is a famous saying from the Confucian classic *Mencius*. Geng asked with a smile whether the journalist knew its meaning. His smile and question "You know what this means? Ha ha" became an internet meme. In WeChat groups about children's education, popular postings appeared with headlines such as "Foreign Ministry's Geng Shuang Shows You the Power of the Chinese Language!"[47] They praised Geng Shuang's fluency with classical Chinese proverbs and quotations. Geng was held up as a model for school kids to learn from because of his mastery of the Chinese language. "Do You Want to Be as Eloquent as Geng Shuang? Then Please Carefully Cultivate Your Cultural Depth," claimed one of these postings.[48] Although these viral stories seem merely to provide inspiring examples for schoolchildren, for the general public their effect was to propagate patriotic pride in using the classical treasures of the Chinese language in retorts to aggressive foreign journalists. Geng became popular for his use of quotations and proverbs and for his "Geng-smiles"—in short, for his style.

Geng Shuang's successor Zhao Lijian is hailed as a heavy-weight boxer who is relentless in throwing verbal punches on Twitter and at press conferences. On March 12, 2020, Zhao posted five messages in both Chinese and English on Twitter with video clips of the U.S. CDC director Robert Redfield testifying to the House Oversight and Reform Committee about how some Americans reported to have died of flu were found to be infected with the coronavirus after their death. "The U.S. owe us an explanation," Zhao tweeted. Ms. Spring wrote about this tweet in her diary on March 12: "Foreign Ministry spokesperson Zhao Lijian posted five consecutive tweets and angrily challenged the U.S. to give us an explanation."[49] "Melon Mass" wrote the following in her diary on March 14:

Zhao Lijian used his personal Twitter handle to question the U.S. even if he did not have firm evidence [about the origin of the virus]. This seems somewhat inappropriate seen from the perspective of China's traditional [diplomatic] style. But it had a critical role in reversing the overwhelming trend of the world blaming the virus on China and was a slap on the faces of the political leaders in the U.S. and some other countries who kept talking about the "China virus" and "Wuhan virus," despite the fact that WHO already named the novel coronavirus "COVID-19" on February 11.[50]

WOLF TOTEM

The wolf has a bad reputation in Chinese culture. A symbol of greed, avarice, aggression, and cruelty, it is a metaphor for bad people. Common Chinese idioms with the word *lang* 狼, "wolf," in them all refer to bad people. "Wolf's heart and dog's lungs" (*langxin goufei* 狼心狗肺) describes people who are ungrateful. "Ambitious as a wolf" (*langzi yexin* 狼子野心) refers to people who have evil ambitions. "Letting a wolf into one's house" (*yinlang rushi* 引狼入室) means letting enemies into one's house or country. The saying "Wolves and *bei* are partners in crime" (Langbei weijian 狼狈为奸) refers to people who do evil together.[51]

In popular culture in the 1980s and 1990s, however, the image of the wolf underwent change. In 1985, the Taiwanese singer Chyi Chin's 齐秦 song "Wolf" (狼) presented the image of a solitary young man who wanders the unlimited expanse of the wilderness, a lone wolf: "I'm a wolf coming from the north, / I walk in the unlimited expanses of the wilderness." Together with Cui Jian's 崔健 song "Nothing to My Name" (一无所有), "Wolf" captures the experiences of alienation and angst of a generation coming of age in the 1980s. Their songs became the sonic icons of the student movement of 1989 when Cui Jian sang "Nothing to My Name" in the Tiananmen Square protest during the hunger strike.[52]

Meanwhile, the new commercial culture also appropriated images of the wolf to represent aggressiveness and competitiveness in an increasingly commercialized Chinese society. The fashion company Septwolves was founded in 1990 and would later become a very successful business. Targeting young male professionals, the company celebrated the competitive "wolf culture" in its branding strategy and featured a running wolf as its logo.

But it is the novel *Wolf Totem* (狼图腾) that marked a national turning point in the saga of wolf culture. Published in 2004, *Wolf Totem* quickly became a best seller and the bible of China's business world, a commercial counterpart to Mao's *Little Red Book*.[53] As of 2008, 4.2 million copies of it had been sold in China, and countless copies had been pirated.[54] The novel is semiautobiographical and was based on its author Jiang Rong's personal experiences. Jiang Rong 姜戎 is the pen name of Lü Jiamin 吕嘉民, who spent thirteen years in the grassland of Inner Mongolia as a sent-down youth from the late 1960s through the 1970s. Upon returning to his home city Beijing in the late 1970s, he became involved in the Democracy Wall movement and later in the Tiananmen movement in 1989.[55] Because of his participation in the Tiananmen movement, he spent a year and a half in jail and upon release kept a low profile and lived a quiet life. He spent many years writing the novel, a secret project that only a few close friends knew he was working on.

The two protagonists in the novel, Chen Zhen 陈阵 and Yang Ke 杨克, are youth sent from Beijing to Inner Mongolia as part of Mao's sent-down campaign.[56] After narrowly escaping a close encounter with a large wolf pack, Chen is both awed by and infatuated with the Mongolian wolf. In the course of the novel, he comes to see the spiritual side of the wolf worship among the Mongolian people. The novel is full of long passages of his reflections on the meaning of wolf culture in comparison with China's ancient Confucian culture. At one point, Chen explains to his friend:

"The wolf totem has a much longer history than Han Confucianism," said Chen, "with greater natural continuity and vitality. In the Confucian thought system, the main ideas, such as the three cardinal guides and the five constant virtues, are outdated and decayed, but the central spirit of the wolf totem remains vibrant and young, since it's been passed down by the most advanced races in the world. It should be considered one of the truly valuable spiritual heritages of all humanity. There'd be hope for China if our national character could be rebuilt by cutting away the decaying parts of Confucianism and grafting a wolf totem sapling onto it. It could be combined with such Confucian traditions as pacifism, an emphasis on education, and devotion to study."[57]

The intense cultural debates following the publication of *Wolf Totem* focused on the question of whether Chinese culture needs more wolf nature. The debates both reflected and fed into the intensifying culture of capitalist market competition happening in China in the mid-2000s. Business firms and government agencies alike put *Wolf Totem* on employees' required reading list to cultivate a wolfish spirit among them. As recently as 2015, a reading festival held by a real estate company in Hangzhou made *Wolf Totem* the required reading for the festival. The slogan of the festival? "Building the best wolf team!"[58]

It was also in 2015 that the Hollywood-style film *Wolf Warrior* (dir. Jing Wu 吴京) was released in China to great box-office success. It is the story of a Chinese military special force fighting a group of foreign mercenaries hired by a drug lord in Southeast Asia. The film's commercial success inspired *Wolf Warrior II*, which was released to even greater success in 2017 as it broke the box-office record in China and became one of the top-one-hundred highest-grossing films of the world.[59] The two *Wolf Warrior* films highlight patriotic themes and the greatness of the Chinese nation. An image that appears toward the end of *Wolf Warrior II* has become iconic. The hero of the movie, played by the director, the same leading actor as in *Wolf Warrior*, comes to an African war zone with his compatriots and African friends. Two African armies are fighting each other. When his fellow travelers are hesitating about how to cross this war zone, the protagonist asks for the Chinese national flag. Using his arm as a flag pole, he holds up the flag high in the air and asks the driver to start driving. As they enter the war zone, the local government and antigovernment forces are engaged in fierce fighting but pause to let the Chinese truck squad pass. The red flag is given the magical power of the totem, and as the symbol of the Chinese nation, it not only radiates the power of the nation but also does so in a war zone on foreign territory. Despite its imperialist overtones, this image is a moment of great national pride for its Chinese audience. Even to this day, video clips of this episode from the film are easily found on Chinese social media.

The label *wolf-warrior diplomacy* is based on the *Wolf Warrior* films, but it is unclear when and how it originated. At a press conference in Beijing in late May 2020, a CNN reporter asked the Minister of Chinese Foreign Affairs Wang Yi: "We've seen an increasingly heated 'war of words' between China and the U.S. Is 'wolf-warrior' diplomacy the new norm of China's diplomacy?" Wang's response was indirect: "We Chinese value peace, harmony, sincerity and integrity. We never pick a fight or bully others, but we have principles and guts. We will push back against any deliberate insult to resolutely defend our national honor and dignity."[60]

Wang's subordinate Liu Xiaoming, Chinese ambassador to the United Kingdom, was more direct. In an interview on CCTV in May 2020, Liu said: "Some people say that China has many 'wolf warriors' now. In my view, if China has 'wolf warriors,' it is because there are 'wolves' in this world. If there are 'wolves,' then there must be 'wolf warriors' to fight them. Therefore, we encourage diplomats at different levels to fight back. Where there are 'wolves,' there will be battles to fight back and defend the dignity and interest of the nation."[61]

LEARNING THE STYLE OF GLOBAL POPULISM

The popular *Wolf Warrior* films are at best just one source of inspiration for China's "wolf-warrior" diplomats. "Wolf-warrior" diplomats are noted for their militant style, but if their style is new for Chinese diplomats, it is not new for Chinese social media. In fact, in the global media arena militant styles are the norm, not the exception. With their breaking news and sensationalizing headlines, many global media agencies, networks, and programs are the unnamed wolf warriors of the world.

In their book *The Outrage Industry* (2013), the political scientist Jeffrey Berry and the sociologist Sarah Sobieraj show that American political-opinion media are an outrage industry. Whether liberal or conservative, American talk radio and cable news hosts are recognizable by a rhetorical style marked by outrage: "Outrage discourse involves efforts to provoke emotional responses (e.g., anger, fear, moral indignation) from the audience through the use of overgeneralizations, sensationalism, misleading or patently inaccurate information, ad hominem attacks, and belittling ridicule of opponents. Outrage sidesteps the messy nuances of complex political issues in favor of melodrama, misrepresentative exaggeration, mockery, and hyperbolic forecasts of impending doom."[62]

These media hosts spew outrageous discourse because outrage sells. To attract large audiences and advertising dollars, media hosts compete to be more outrageous than their rivals. The two authors identify thirteen types of outrageous behavior common in American political discourse, including insulting language, name calling, verbal fighting, character assassination, ideologically extreme language, belittling, and obscene language.[63]

Although the United States may be an extreme case, such over-the-top discourse is common in the age of global populism. Global populism has a common political style among its different national and ideological varieties. According to the political scientist Benjamin Moffitt, this style has three essential elements—an appeal to the people instead of to the elite, the adoption of "low" language and "bad manners" such as the use of swearing and political incorrectness, and the use of "dramatization and performance" to induce or respond to crisis or threat.[64] In all three respects, contemporary populism is aligned with the outrage industry of American political media.

Wolf-warrior diplomacy and COVID nationalism in China share the political style of global populism. China's "wolf-warrior" COVID diplomacy is a direct response to the accusations and threats from incendiary American media and politicians: Chinese diplomats are adopting the rhetorical style of their challengers. If Twitter is their main platform, it is because it is also the platform of U.S. politicians. And just as the American outrage industry uses incendiary rhetoric to attract audiences, Chinese diplomats have turned to incendiary rhetoric in a way they rarely did before. Stories about wolf-warrior diplomats on Chinese social media almost invariably cite a well-known phrase from martial arts novels to characterize their behavior: "Using an opponent's own style [of martial arts] to fight the opponent" (Yi qiren zhidao, huaizhi qiren zhishen 以其人之道, 还治其人之身).[65] The best masters of martial arts not only cultivate their own styles but also learn from their opponents.

THE STYLE OF INDIGENOUS CYBERNATIONALISM

Consciously or unconsciously, China's wolf warriors also tap into China's indigenous history and style of populism as well as into recent waves of cybernationalism. The most familiar historical example used is the populism of the Red Guards. At the height of the Cultural Revolution from 1966 to 1968, the Red Guards and their rivals fought violent verbal battles using low language, and eventually their "bad manners" escalated to physical violence. They did so in the name of the greatest of populist leaders, Mao Zedong. No other leader in the world had mesmerized such large numbers over such a sustained period of time. That is why the younger generation of patriots that has appeared in recent years is compared to the Red Guards.[66]

More precisely, these new patriots are called "Little Pinks" to indicate that they are a fainter version of Red Guards.[67] They made their first historic appearance in cyberspace on January 20, 2016, by launching a cyberattack on the newly elected Taiwanese president Tsai Ing-wen's Facebook page because of her perceived pro-independence position on the question of Taiwan's relationship with mainland China. The main participants in the attack were youth born in and after the 1990s, many of them online gamers and members of online fandom communities. Organizers named their action the "Diba Expedition" (Diba Chuzheng 帝吧出征) because the platform where the action was launched was Baidu's post bar Diba 帝吧, or King Bar, which was Baidu's most popular online message board.

The thing most striking about the Diba Expedition was the form of the attack: the posting of large numbers of emojis, called "emoji packs" (biaoqing bao 表情包), on Tsai's Facebook page. These emoji packs attacked pro-Taiwanese independence positions and expressed pride in mainland

China, even its cuisines. Some of these emoji packs are ridiculously silly; others are plain texts such as "Taiwan belongs to my country"; still others are humorous. But they all are emotional expressions captured in eye-catching images and provocative memes.

The "weapons" of the Diba Expedition had a clear outrage element. All thirteen types of outrage language identified by Berry and Sobieraj can be found in the Little Pinks' repertoire. Insults and swear words were hurled as much as hyperbolic emoji images. But the goal of this outrageous language was not to increase advertising dollars so much as to perform emotions of patriotism and self-heroism. From such performances, participants derive a sense of belonging and personal pride, just as audiences of American outrage talk radio shows "feel included in a like-minded community, have their lifestyles and viewpoints validated, and walk away armed with ammunition for any who might challenge them."[68]

The Diba Expedition gave birth to a new breed of cybernationalists and populists—the Little Pinks. These cybernationalists are the post-1990s cohort, China's digital natives. Cybernationalism or patriotism is not their main preoccupation or even their main form of entertainment. In ordinary times, they are just fans in online fandom communities. Their idols are entertainment celebrities, and what they do is to organize activities in support of their idols. In chapter 6, we saw how some of these fandom communities raised donations for Wuhan using online platforms such as Sina Weibo.

From the beginning of the lockdown, Diba's Official Weibo Account was actively posting messages related to COVID-19, lauding China's efforts to fight the virus, retweeting news from abroad, mocking Western media's negative depictions of China, and praising Chinese wolf-warrior diplomats for taking on Western media. The account remains active, and the style of its postings is direct and adversarial. With more than 1 million followers, its postings receive wide attention. The comments written in response to many of its tweets suggest that Diba followers, like the audiences of American outrage talk radio shows, feel they are part of a "like-minded community." Diba members' support for "wolf-warrior diplomats" betrays an affinity among them.

In short, the rise of China's wolf-warrior diplomacy and COVID nationalism took place in the context of an already emerging culture of cybernationalism and global populism, both of which share the same political style—outrage.

THE EMOTIONS OF NATIONALISM

Benedict Anderson wrote famously about the "profound emotional legitimacy" of nationalism and people's "deep attachments" to their nation.[69] Chinese COVID nationalism was surely characterized by intense emotions. The characters in this emotional theater fall into several groups. There are the diary writers, from all walks of life in urban China. Although they constitute a broad social group, they expressed different feelings about their nation. Some conveyed strong emotions of love, pride, and loyalty. "Our country is the best!," as Sister Meng's father told her.[70] Stories about the worsening conditions of the pandemic in foreign countries intensified these feelings. Meng's father did not necessarily think of himself as a nationalist, but he surely vocalized strong feelings and cared deeply about China's international images.

Fang Fang and her supporters belonged to the same nation as Sister Meng and Mr. Fei's Aunt, but they did not express the same feelings. Although Mr. Fei's Aunt called Fang Fang a traitor, there is no evidence that Fang Fang and her supporters loved their country any less than their critics. Fang Fang's diary may have been critical, but it was also full of sympathy and appreciation of common people's bravery and sacrifices. Fang Fang and her supporters simply expressed their emotional attachments to their nation in different ways.

The most extreme detractors of Fang Fang, the ultraleftists, look back to the Mao era as a golden age. As in the past, ultraleftists are ultranationalists. Unlike in the past, they publish and congregate on their own websites and launch campaigns on social media. They express pride in their nation and hatred of all those who dare to tarnish that nation's image. Their nationalistic emotions do not tolerate difference.

Diplomats are important by virtue of their official positions. Ambassadors and Foreign Ministry spokespeople are the public faces of the nation. In the past, their public visibility was limited, which also limited their public influence. In recent years, though, as they become active on social media, their behavior is watched by audiences at home and abroad. Social media have put them in the global limelight, compelling them to perform to the public. Acting tough with foreigners is a common style of performance on the national and international stage. The pejorative nickname "wolf warriors" that Western media outlets use to characterize these Chinese spokespeople has become a badge of honor at home.

Still another group in the theater of the nation consists of Chinese students and scholars studying abroad. This group not only experienced a worse pandemic situation than their compatriots back home but also became targets of anti-Chinese and anti-Asian racism in foreign countries. As Little Mao's story shows, they entertained strong positive feelings about their nation and were eager to return there. But returning to China turned out to be rough going. China's stringent preboarding criteria of COVID testing for inbound international travelers as well as soaring ticket prices and a drastically reduced number of flights turned efforts to return to China into an ordeal. In this process, feelings of pride and hope became mixed with anger, frustration, and helplessness.

Technically, all of these groups are nationalists, but in reality they differ considerably. It would be misleading to lump Sister Meng's parents and Mr. Fei's Aunt together with Fang Fang's detractors, although they all expressed strong nationalistic feelings. Furthermore, nationalism is associated with a spectrum of emotions. Depending on the context and the social groups involved, the emotions might include fear of the foreign, shame for one's past, pride, and loyalty. These emotions are activated by concrete situations and may change with context. Racism against Chinese in foreign countries may exacerbate fears of the foreign at home, while gestures of international friendship and solidarity create a sense of internationalism. Wolf-warrior diplomats' aggressive rhetoric on Twitter or at press conferences may be as much a performance for their own domestic audience as it is for the international audience. In short, nationalism is a very broad concept that covers a much messier reality. The same rubric of nationalism cannot adequately capture the nuances of heterogeneous social groups in changing social contexts.

9

MOURNING AND REMEMBERING

TIME IS A FLOWING RIVER

Wuhan residents treated April 7, 2020, as if it were a Lunar New Year's Eve. The custom is to stay up through midnight to greet the first day of the new year. On the eve of April 7, many residents did just that because midnight marked the end of the lockdown and the beginning of a new page of history.

Chu Ma was one of those who stayed up late to witness the dawning of a historic new day. He reported that when midnight came, all of the colorful lights in the skyscrapers on the four banks of the two rivers lit up. His diary posting was accompanied by photographs of the lit-up skyline. The lifting of the lockdown would forever be recorded in the chronicles of history. After midnight, as the light display faded away, Chu Ma still did not feel like going to bed. He pondered the meaning of the end of the lockdown: "In seventy-six days, the structures of some families were completely changed. For some people, their outlooks about life have completely changed. Others will have a completely different life in the future. What does not change is the rolling waters of the Yangzi River and the bright moon that has shone over our ancestors and bathed in the spring wind. All the stories are gone with the flowing river. Only history will tell the story of Wuhan many years later."[1]

Chu Ma waxes lyrical in the last entry of his lockdown diary. The flowing river, more often called the "east-flowing river," is an ancient poetic metaphor for the passage of time. Used by poets across the centuries, it is an image of the ephemerality of human affairs. Everything in this world flows by like the water of the great Yangzi River on its eastward course to the ocean. The stories of the Wuhan lockdown and the pandemic will pass in the same way, Chu Ma ruminated.

But the stories of the Wuhan lockdown will not be gone with the flowing river. Nor will they wait to be told in the future. They were being told as it was happening. The lockdown diarists, Chu Ma included, were telling stories of the lockdown every day. The social media chatter, the official propaganda, the mainstream-media reporting—they all were telling stories. But their stories were not the same. Some complemented and illuminated one another. Others competed and clashed. In the end, not all of the stories will survive. The messiness of history will be tamed, whitewashed, and funneled into a clean morality tale in official history textbooks.

That is already happening in China today. Only months after the Wuhan lockdown was over, it has already become a politically sensitive topic for public discussion. Netizens shun the topic on social media, and if they do talk about it, they tend to put it in positive light. Many of the diaries in my collection have disappeared from the web. Meanwhile, official narratives have blossomed with the release of documentary films, a government white paper, and a national award ceremony to mark the victory of the war on COVID.[2] On August 1, 2020, a major art exhibition opened at the National Museum of China in Beijing.[3] There are moving artworks at the exhibition, such as the large portrait of the national hero in the war on COVID— Professor Zhong Nanshan. Another oil painting depicts a medical professional in three different postures of exhaustion, inspired by the many stories of medical workers who fainted or collapsed after long hours of work.[4]

Yet at the same time the exhibition aimed to create a uniform narrative about China's responses to COVID-19. In his speech at the opening ceremony, a vice chairperson of the China Artists Association said that the exhibition would "sing the main melody and propagate positive energy."[5] Although Fang Fang and her fans had made "positive energy" a target of criticism, their critiques had apparently fallen on deaf official ears. What is considered negative energy about China's war on COVID is missing from the exhibition. The plural voices and rich stories of the Wuhan lockdown already run the risk of disappearance. It is thus necessary to devote this final chapter to the politics of mourning and remembering. I focus on the case of Li Wenliang, undoubtedly the single most important story in any account of the collective memories of the Wuhan lockdown.

"DO YOU HEAR THE PEOPLE SING?"

Arlie posted seventy-six lockdown diary entries on her WeChat public account. From them, I learned that she is a young professional, worked in another city but had returned to Wuhan in early 2020 to spend the Lunar New Year with her parents, and then was trapped there by the lockdown. She started her diary on the first day of the lockdown and wrote regularly until Wuhan was opened up on April 8. Like Guo Jing, Arlie wrote in great detail about people's reactions in the first few days of the lockdown. On January 27, 2020, the fifth day of the lockdown, Arlie went out biking with a former classmate, and her entry for that day contains colorful photos of empty street scenes, closed shops, grocery stores, and homeless cats in her neighborhood. Her diary postings were written in quiet but warm tones, even when they were about moments of anger and depression.

Her most memorable entry was written on February 7. There, she mentioned that she had learned that Fang Fang had been banned from Weibo for fourteen days—the same number of days as the quarantine of a suspected COVID-19 patient. Arlie then wrote that the weather in Wuhan had suddenly become cold again after several springlike days: "The feeling of spring that had been built with great efforts dissipated under the counterattack of the bone-chilling cold." She said that she had gotten some good news the day before—her laptop miraculously was working after it had gotten wet and she had buried it in a rice bag. But today it was dead again, and she was in an awful mood. Just as she was mad about her dead laptop, she wrote,

> I still had not recovered from my personal emotional rollercoaster when
> another wave of wailing to mourn the death of Dr. Li Wenliang came as

if drenching down from the skies. Before I went to bed last night, at about 9:30 p.m., I saw news about his death on WeChat. I even forwarded the news and wrote, "I hope this was just a rumor." This morning when I woke up at five, my mobile phone was full of stories mourning his death. Every piece of news shot straight through my heart. I burst into loud crying in bed. I cried for Dr. Li Wenliang's short and tragic life, cried for every ordinary person trapped in this city.

After breakfast, Arlie began to browse Dr. Li's Weibo postings: "When I read the ordinary and small things of daily life [Li had posted], tears came to my eyes again. I kept wiping my tears but could not stop them. I turned off my cell phone to try to escape from the tsunami of emotions that was on the verge of exploding. All I was thinking [about] was his story, the pictures and texts posted by others, and a song that could not be played."[6]

Arlie did not say which song could not be played. She did not have to. Everyone on WeChat or Weibo would know which song she meant. It was "Do You Hear the People Sing?" from the musical *Les Misérables*, a song of people's rebellion. When news of Li's death came, people started posting the song on social media. I saw such posts on my own Weibo and WeChat timelines. But soon the links to the song stopped working. The song had been censored and delisted from online music platforms. Unable to hear it, people such as Arlie made a point of referring to it. All they needed to say was "that song," and others would understand which song they were talking about.

The difficulty of naming the song as well as the persistence in talking about it were symptomatic. Mourning and remembering are not to be taken for granted at any time, but especially not at a time like this. Li Wenliang's death revealed broader patterns of the culture and politics of mourning and remembering during the Wuhan lockdown.

LI WENLIANG'S DEATH

Li Wenliang, shown in figure 9.1, was one of the whistle-blowers of the spread of a dangerous virus in Wuhan whose story I have mentioned in

FIGURE 9.1 Dr. Li Wenliang (1986–2020).

previous chapters. He contracted the illness he had warned people about and died from it.

The exact timing of Li's death was initially a matter of contention. *Life Times* (健康时报), a public-health newspaper run by *Global Times* (which is a subsidiary of *People's Daily*), was the first to report that Dr. Li had died at 9:30 p.m. Beijing Time on February 6, 2020. The World Health Organization tweeted its condolences on Li's death at 11:25 p.m. Yet at 12:58 a.m. Beijing Time on February 7, the *Global Times* posted the following message on Twitter: "Update: Li Wenliang is currently in critical condition. His heart reportedly stopped beating at around 21:30. He was then given treatment with ECMO [extracorporeal membrane oxygenation]."[7] Li Wenliang's employer, Wuhan Central Hospital, announced at 3:48 a.m. on February 7 that Li had passed away at 2:58 a.m.

The gap between the initial announcement of death at 9:30 p.m. and Wuhan Central Hospital's notice of Li's death at a later time triggered immediate speculation. Some suspected that Wuhan Central Hospital may have deliberately delayed the announcement to the wee hours of the morning to avoid public outrage. When word spread online that Li had not died but was still in ECMO treatment, netizens jumped to social media to post prayers. Arlie also prayed. For once, netizens sincerely hoped that the news of Li Wenliang's death was a rumor. The irony of this characterization of the news was deliberate. Dr. Li had been disciplined for "spreading rumors" when in fact he spoke the truth.

Li Wenliang's death prompted national mourning. Arlie was not the only diarist in our story who was overcome by sadness over it. Having followed Fang Fang's diaries closely, I knew Fang Fang would surely write about Li Wenliang as well. And so she did: "There were so many tears they turned into waves on the Internet. Tonight, Li Wenliang passed to the other world riding the waves of people's tears."[8]

Like Arlie, Guo Jing learned about Li Wenliang's death on the night of February 6. After the lockdown started, Guo had developed a daily routine of video chatting with friends after dinner. For these conversations, she and her friends would pose discussion questions. For February 6, not knowing that Dr. Li would die that night, they happened to choose death as their discussion topic. Guo Jing shared her story about her grandparents with her friends. Due to China's single-child family-planning policy, after Guo's mother became pregnant with her brother, Guo was sent to live with her grandparents and did not rejoin her parents until she was seven years old. She was so attached to her grandparents that when they died, she did not know how to face it for a long time. She did not know who to talk to or how to talk about it because people shun talking about death in China. Guo's friends shared their own thoughts and anxieties about death as well. It was in the middle of these conversations that someone screamed, "Li Wenliang died!"

After the video chat, Guo browsed her WeChat Moments, where people were saying that they wished the news of Li's death were a rumor. She wrote:

But we cannot randomly define what is a rumor. We cannot change what we don't want to believe into rumors. I lay in bed, and tears came to my eyes. Soon I started sobbing. My mind was full of "why's." I didn't know how I fell asleep. In the morning, I woke up several times and then turned around and went back to sleep. I didn't really fall asleep. Just didn't want to get up and face the reality. Eventually I got up and turned on my cell phone. It was full of news about Li Wenliang. . . . I began to cry again. What should I do to survive in such an absurd world?[9]

Guo Jing decided she must do something. She did her usual morning exercise and then went out for a walk:

I must tell other people about Li Wenliang. We should remember him. Recently very few people would go to the river walk, but I often do, and I have gotten to know a manager of the park. I went there today and asked the manager: "Do you know Li Wenliang died yesterday?" After I said it, I thought to myself: "How do *I* know exactly when Li Wenliang died? Some people said his heart stopped beating at around 9:30 p.m., but then he was put on ECMO. This morning, the Weibo account of Wuhan Central Hospital announced at 3:48 a.m. that Li Wenliang died at 2:58 a.m." He replied: "I know. I saw the news on my phone. It's hard to talk about this." I said: "Li Wenliang was the first person to send out information about the pneumonia. He was accused of spreading rumors. And now he is dead. It is so sad."[10]

Why were so many people so saddened by Li Wenliang's death? Why did they mourn Dr. Li the way they did?

AN ABSOLUTELY ORDINARY PERSON

Wuhan residents and netizens throughout the nation were saddened because they saw themselves in Li Wenliang. The way they were locked up at home made them feel they were just like Li Wenliang—vulnerable and powerless. As Fang Fang wrote,

Experts had said that things would turn better on the Lantern Festival Day [the fifteenth day of the Lunar New Year]. Now it doesn't look like the turning point is coming. Yesterday came news of Li Wenliang's death. Today's news is that there will be another 14 days of lockdown. Ugh. People who are not in Wuhan cannot understand the trauma we suffer in our hearts. It is far more than a matter of being quarantined at home. Wuhan people badly need consolation and emotional release. Is that why Li Wenliang's death broke everyone's heart and made them all want to scream and wail?[11]

People knew Li Wenliang had contracted the coronavirus. Just a week earlier, Li had announced on Weibo that his test result was positive. But the news of his death still came as a shock. To an already emotionally drained city, it was the last straw.

When Wuhan was sealed off, no one knew how long the lockdown would last. By February 7, two weeks into the lockdown, there were no signs of an end to it. The disease was still spreading, and the tolls were heavy. As figure 9.2 shows, the number of new confirmed cases per day throughout the nation had been increasing steadily, starting with 259 on January 23 and reaching 3,887 on February 4. This number dropped to 3,694 on February 5 and then 3,143 on February 6. Just when it seemed as if the tide were finally turning, though, the number rebounded to 3,399 on February 7. Daily death tolls had also been growing. There were 8 deaths on January 23 and 16 on January 24. The following two weeks saw a steady increase to the twenties, thirties, and forties per day until the number of daily new deaths hit 65 on February 4, 73 on February 5 and 6, and 86 on February 7 (figure 9.3).

When the lockdown started, the Hubei provincial and Wuhan municipal governments were ill prepared to manage the crisis. The incompetence of party leaders was on full display when they did not have answers to basic questions at press conferences. There were public calls for the removal of inept officials, but the only action taken before February 7 was the removal of a vice president of the Hubei provincial Red Cross Society. Not until February 13 did the Central Party authorities in Beijing remove the top party leaders in Hubei province and Wuhan city and appoint their replacements.

In short, at the time of Dr. Li's death the pandemic situation looked grave, the tolls were high, and the prospects of containing the spread

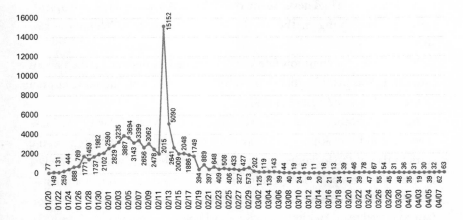

FIGURE 9.2 Daily new confirmed cases of COVID-19 in China, January 20–April 8, 2020.

Source: Data provided by Dydata (www.dydata.io).

Note: The spike in numbers on February 12, 2020, was caused by a modification of diagnostic criteria.

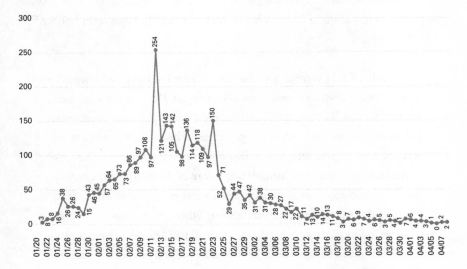

FIGURE 9.3. Daily new deaths caused by COVID-19 in China, January 20–April 8, 2020.

Source: Data provided by Dydata (www.dydata.io).

were gloomy. Life had never seemed so fragile. An acute sense of helplessness and pain hung in the air. In Dr. Li's tragic fate, Wuhanese saw themselves.

This sense of a common fate was heightened as netizens talked about how Dr. Li was just like them—an ordinary person with the same human desires and weaknesses, likes and dislikes.

Like many others, Lan Xi started a diary on the first day of the lockdown. He did not skip a single day until he announced on March 22, the sixtieth day of the lockdown, that his entry for that day would be the last because Wuhan was no longer different from other cities and no longer special. An information technology entrepreneur and internet commentator, Lan Xi is well read. He cited John Rawls when discussing issues of equity in the lockdown crisis and quoted Stefan Zweig on violence and resistance. Rather reticent about his daily life, he devoted most of his entries to commentaries on social issues. On February 7, he reflected on the meaning of Li Wenliang as a hero. He first compared Li with Dr. Jiang Yanyong, the key whistle-blower of SARS in 2003. A letter Dr. Jiang had sent to domestic and international media in April 2003 exposing the severe situation of SARS had led to the resignation of China's health minister and the mayor in Beijing.[12] Lan Xi wrote,

It's true that Dr. Li Wenliang was different from Dr. Jiang Yanyong, who defied all odds seventeen years ago. When we call Dr. Li Wenliang a hero, it is not because he accomplished some great deeds. After he heard about the novel coronavirus, out of his goodness of heart, he warned his colleagues to take precautions. . . . Did he reverse the course of history? Maybe not. . . . Even if he himself was aware of the need to take precautions, he underestimated the contagiousness of the virus and lost his health and then life even as he was treating others. That's why Dr. Li Wenliang was more like our own friend. You and I all know a few people like him. They have a basic sense of justice and a passion and a kind heart for the world. They have fears, could swallow personal grievances, are willing to follow their superiors' instructions, and do their job conscientiously. Is he still a hero? Of course.[13]

Lan Xi also quoted a passage from Stefan Zweig's study of Leo Tolstoy to explicate the meaning of Li Wenliang's heroism: "But a person must never use a weapon that he disapproves of. True strength, believe me, does not respond to violence with violence. It makes impotent through acquiescence. It is written in the gospel." Following this passage, Lan Xi commented: "This was what Dr. Li Wenliang did. He didn't harm anyone. People studied every detail of his Weibo timeline from beginning to end. Nobody found any dark spot. Patriotic, hard-working, honest, friendly—he was all this. Such a person should not have died."[14]

On social media, netizens expressed similar sentiments, hailing Li as an ordinary guy just like everyone else. Some wrote obituaries based on Li's Weibo postings. One such obituary, titled "Fifty Small Things About Li Wenliang," contained the following list:

> He liked eating.
> His wife is pregnant with their second child.
> His colleagues said he was a shy person.
> His New Year wish for 2020 was to be a simple person.
> He called his five-year-old son "Little Li."
> He liked posting his son's photos on Weibo.[15]

Another, longer obituary was prepared after its author perused Li Wenliang's Weibo postings for three hours. Here, I have abbreviated and adapted sections of it:

> Li Wenliang was born in the '80s. He loved fried chicken, hot pot, and Japanese sushi. He liked posting food photos on Weibo, but some of them were quite "ugly." He used to play badminton but gained weight in recent years. "Even my dad's figure is better than mine," Li wrote on Weibo. Once, he wanted to eat oranges, so he ran in his slippers in the rain to buy them. In 2013, after the Ya'an earthquakes, he made two monetary donations via WeChat. One day, he went shopping after work and saw cherries costing 158 yuan per *jin* [1 *jin* = 1.10231 pound]. He took a photo of it and posted it on Weibo with the comment "Can't afford."

That is the image of a hero who could not be more ordinary or more down to earth—a loveable guy with a sense of humor and a kind heart. People mourned him because he was just like them.

"BLOW THE WHISTLE FOR WUHAN"

The massive public mourning for Li Wenliang was also due to the shared feeling that Dr. Li had been wronged and that the wrongs he had suffered had worsened his health and hastened his death. Mourning was a means of expressing protest and demanding accountability.

On the morning of February 7, some Wuhan residents gathered and placed flowers at the entrance to Wuhan Central Hospital, where Dr. Li had worked. On the flowers were written dedications such as "Long Live Our Hero" and "A true person who spoke the truth." On the popular short-video platform Miaopai, a video of eight automobiles slowly parading the evening streets of Wuhan on February 7 was viewed millions of times. One of the car owners said on camera that they were parading the street to mourn Li Wenliang and celebrate the bravery of the eight whistle-blowing doctors who had been disciplined by the police.[16] Far up in the north, on the outskirts of Beijing, where it had just snowed, people wrote "Farewell to Li Wenliang" in the snow on the banks of the Tonghui River. Bouquets of flowers were placed in the snow. Images of these tributes were circulated online. About these activities in Beijing, one comment on Weibo stated: "People in our area are meek but still have a little bit of courage; they are resigned but still harbor a little bit of resistance. Their courage and resistance are hidden in the snow on the banks of Tonghui River, in the flowers, and in the sounds of whistling."[17] In spirit, these remarks are similar to Stefan Zweig's point about how the powerless can make power impotent through acquiescence.

The most remarkable memorial action was "blow the whistle for Wuhan." Like most online actions, it is not clear who started it, but when I got up on the morning of February 7 Eastern Standard Time, which was the evening of February 7 Beijing Time, my Weibo and WeChat Moments were full of postings about it. Everyone seemed to be retweeting it. The action plan started with the following:

> Tonight, I blow the whistle for Wuhan.
>
> All Wuhan people, Hubei people, and friends all over the world who care about the epidemic:
>
> At 9:00 tonight, let us turn on the lights in our homes and blow the whistle to condole Dr. Li Wenliang—Wuhan's whistle-blower who exposed the epidemic!
>
> Let us use our lights and whistles to memorialize (*jidian* 祭奠) all the family members, friends, neighbors, colleagues, and compatriots who died in the epidemic and to whom we haven't even had a chance to say farewell.
>
> Let us use lights and whistles to build our unity! Let us give encouragement to all those who are in illness and pain and who are desperately seeking medical help! Let us give support to the medical personnel who are fighting at the front line! Let us all persevere to the end! We are determined to see light!

The action plan then provided detailed information about the time and methods of the memorial:

> 8:55–9:05: Lights off. Silent mourning of our hero and all the dead
>
> 9:00–9:05: Hold anything with lights in your hand (cell phone, flashlights, lights) and point them toward outside your window while blowing your whistle (or some other sound-making device)!
>
> 9:05: Memorial ends. (Please keep your windows closed all the time to prevent the spread of the virus.)[18]

The action was a success. Pointing the lights of cellphones or flashlights so that they would shine outside the window was a fitting symbolic act, resembling the lighting of a vigil candle. "Blow the whistle" was an ingenious idea: given the circumstances of the lockdown, there was nothing more suitable for mourning the death of a whistle-blower. But who would have whistles at home? It was a challenge that people overcame by downloading whistling software from the web. As Guo Jing wrote in her diary on February 8,

> Last night when I chatted with my friends, we all saw that people started an online memorialization activity. . . . We all downloaded a whistle software. We tested it and felt that the sound volume was rather low. Someone found a video for making your own whistle and tried to make one, but it was unsuccessful. Where I lived, the buildings outside had sparse lights. At 9:00 p.m., I saw dim lights shining out of some parts of these buildings. At that moment, we were each other's light in the darkness. This was a light that broke the blockade.[19]

The "blow the whistle for Wuhan" action was a self-organized celebration of Dr. Li Wenliang as a heroic whistler-blower of the coronavirus. Even before his death, Li had already been hailed as a whistle-blower, a label he rejected because he never thought of himself as such. He said he just wanted to warn his friends and classmates about a SARS-like disease, and he even resented it when he learned that screenshots of his WeChat messages had been posted in other WeChat groups.[20]

Although Li did not see himself as a whistle-blower, his seemingly minor decision to warn his friends about what seemed to be another SARS outbreak was a moral act. He knew he was not allowed to leak the information, but he did so anyway. He probably did not think about the consequences. He said he simply did it out of concern for his friends. His act is reminiscent of what the anthropologist Charlotte Bruckermann calls "rumor as moral action" in writing about an earthquake scare in Shanxi province in 2010. It was only two years after the Sichuan earthquakes of 2008, and the memory of the casualties from collapsed shoddy constructions was still fresh. To make things worse, residents in Shanxi already had suspicions about the quality of their own housing. Thus, the spread of the earthquake rumor became a means of expressing their misgivings about the role of housing developers and local officials in housing projects. A rumor thus became a form of moral action. Bruckermann found that the spread of the rumors was neither spontaneous individual action nor organized group action. Rather, people transmitted the news to their friends and relatives out of a moral obligation: "The obligation towards mutual responsibility in relation to housing risks revealed that protecting one's own life is inseparable from preserving life as shared with others."[21] When Li Wenliang leaked information about the coronavirus out of concern for his friends, the same sense of moral obligation must have crossed his mind. He acted simply out of a good conscience.

The "blow the whistle for Wuhan" was only part of a national outburst of virtual memorialization of Dr. Li Wenliang. Dubbed an "online national funeral" (*wangluo guozang* 网络国葬), the memorialization raged on social media. Netizens retweeted and commented on news of Li Wenliang's death. A beautiful obituary of Li written in the ancient style of the *Records of the Grand Historian* (史记, first century BCE) was circulated widely. Artists posted portraits and photographs of Li, such as the one shown in figure 9.1, which became popular internet memes.

A POET'S WORRY

Like others diarists, the poet Xiao Yin wrote about Li Wenliang on February 7. Unlike others, however, he did not think virtual memorialization was a powerful enough form of action: "Don't think you can change anything with a flash rally or by turning off the lights for a little while. . . . We need more reflections and more sober-headed reflections, so that more powerful efforts to transgress and broaden boundaries can be launched. Have we woken up in the middle of the whistling? Not necessarily."[22]

A published poet and a Wuhan native, Xiao Yin had started his diary about Wuhan even before the lockdown was imposed. His first entry was posted on January 21, a plea to airlines to allow free cancellations when travelers started changing their plans after Zhong Nanshan warned that the coronavirus could be transmitted among humans. Born in 1969, Xiao Yin's personal heroes are from the past. He continues in his February 7 entry about Li Wenliang:

I have always dreaded mourning and memorializing. But in recent years, my seniors gradually all passed away, so I have been going to funeral homes more often. This is a very sad thing. Sometimes I thought that in their own times, they were all so full of talents, so daring and outspoken, that they were so far ahead of us. We no longer have Lao She or Ba Jin or Shen Congwen. We don't have Fu Lei or Jian Bozan. Where is our moral responsibility, our conscience? We don't even have the courage to say one line of truth. . . . All we dare do now is to turn off our lights and hurl two shouts at the vast and dark skies.[23]

The people he mentioned were among the most famous and courageous intellectuals in modern China. Xiao Yin felt that there are no longer such courageously outspoken intellectuals in China today and that the virtual memorialization of Li Wenliang did not go far enough. Much more needed to be done. He called for the construction of a monument in Wuhan: "The monument shall be called 'The Rumor-Monger.' It will caution us that in this world there will always be brave people who will cross the line and there will always be fighters who will transmit 'rumors' in their pursuit of truth. I hope this monument will be built. It will be an unforgettable 'turning point' of this catastrophe." And he was excited to report that a memorial had been set up on a blockchain in honor of Li: "It turns out that today someone set up a monument on Ethereum in honor of Dr. Li Wenliang at the block height 9432824. Dr. Li Wenliang and his heroic act will forever be remembered on the blockchain, never to be changed, never to be erased."[24] Figure 9.4 shows a screenshot of the blockchain memorial dedicated to Li Wenliang on Ethereum.

A VIRTUAL WAILING WALL

Xiao Yin's idea of a "rumor-monger" monument did not materialize, but a virtual monument did come into being soon after Li Wenliang's death— Li's Weibo account has since been transformed into a virtual wailing wall and a fertile site of memorialization.

Li Wenliang posted his last message on February 1, announcing that he had tested positive for the coronavirus. His death prompted a collective

FIGURE 9.4. Screenshot of Li Wenliang memorial on Etherscan.io.

Source: https://etherscan.io/address/0x6e46d3ab7335fffb0d14927e0b418cc08fe60505#code.

rush to re-read and comment on his Weibo postings. Thousands of images of burning candles and RIP messages were left in the comment section. People expressed disbelief:

> Just now someone on Weibo said you died. Could I trouble you to tell them it's a rumor?

> Dr. Li, some people are spreading the rumor that you died. Please post a Weibo message to prove them wrong.[25]

Li Wenliang's Weibo account was called the "wailing wall of the Chinese internet" (*hulianwang kuqiang* 互联网哭墙)[26] and a "tree hole" (*shudong* 树洞).[27] One person wrote: "Dr. Li, some people suggest that Wuhan should build a memorial to commemorate the fight against the coronavirus, but here it has already become a memorial. On it are carved people's hearts, sympathy, reflections, encouragement, warmth, reminiscences, memory. . . . I hope this memorial will 'stand' forever."[28]

Li's Weibo page has come alive since his death. When I checked on February 19, 2020, I saw 454,797 comments on his last posting; on March 18, 2020, there were 636,637; on May 11, 2020, there were 955,613. Soon afterward, the number of comments exceeded a million, and the Weibo platform shows only "million+," with no exact number. Invoking the concept of affective publics,[29] the Chinese communication scholars Zhou Baohua 周葆华 and Zhong Yuan 钟嫒 argue that user comments on Li Wenliang's Weibo account have transformed it into an "extended affective space."[30] No matter what label scholars adopt, the point here is that users visit Li's Weibo account to share personal feelings and comment on current affairs.

Netizens went there to say hello to Li and tell him recent news in the fight on COVID, as in the following comment posted on February 11, 2020, four days after his death:

> Old Li, are you asleep? Let me tell you, I saw a video today. It was a Reuters interview with Academician Zhong Nanshan. Mr. Zhong was full of tears when he mentioned you. He said he believed you were a hero and he was proud of you. He said that's what Chinese doctors were like. Mr. Zhong

and you were among the most respected doctors today. The senior one is still fighting, but you're gone already. But Mr. Zhong holds you in such high regard; that is at least a kind of condolence. You are both heroes who dare to speak the truth.[31]

They went there to confide in Li about their personal relationships, schools, jobs, and families:

I haven't been with my girlfriend for three months. She is in Shanghai. I'm in Beijing. Air tickets are very cheap, but I don't know when this is going to end and things can return to normal.

Dr. Li, I have good news: Junior and senior high schools in Guangxi will start the semester on April 7.

I miss my dad. He has died for almost twenty years.[32]

March 18, 2020, was a historic day for Wuhan. It was the first day after the lockdown that zero new cases were reported. In the morning of March 19, Beijing Time, Dr. Li's Weibo account exploded with user comments sharing the good news with him.

Others protested to Dr. Li that the high-level team sent on February 8 to investigate his death still had not issued its report: "The investigation team about you still hasn't issued any conclusion. Who knows what they are thinking! We all await the day when the conclusion is released. In fact, we don't need them to make any conclusion about you. They are not worthy of you."[33]

As people were making these complaints, that very evening at 7:00 p.m., CCTV announced that the investigation team's report had just been released. The report concluded that the local police station had overstepped its responsibilities when it issued a letter of warning to Li Wenliang. As soon as the report was released, Wuhan police authorities issued an apology on Weibo to Dr. Li and his relatives. On social media, netizens expressed disappointment at the report, arguing that it put the blame on the lowest-level bureaucracy (the local police station) and exonerated party officials at higher levels. They rushed to Li Wenliang's Weibo account to report the news:

> I saw the investigation result about you. I'm so disappointed with this government.

> Dr. Li, the investigation report is out. The police station is the scapegoat. Are you satisfied? I am not!

> Hero: Did you hear it? They rehabilitated you. The Public Security Department of Wuhan has publicly apologized.[34]

Meanwhile, other users reminded the Sina Weibo management not to delete Li Wenliang's account so that they could continue to have this space for commemoration. Back on February 7, right after Li's death, one person wrote: "Please don't delete this account. Please keep this space for people to mourn and remember and come to visit whenever we miss you." On the morning of March 19, the following comments appeared:

> I'm here to post a comment because I hope this Weibo account will not be canceled by the system and the comment function is not closed, so that we and our posterity will forever remember this hero!

> Will this [wailing] wall be torn down? If it is torn [down], where do we go to cry? Does anyone have a backup account?[35]

These comments are reminders of the fragility of cyberspace as a virtual memorial in China, where unannounced deletions of personal social media accounts happen so often that they have a name of their own—"account bombing" (*zhahao* 炸号). Thus, although Li Wenliang's Weibo account is still functioning and still allows user comments as of this writing, its fate is hard to tell.

Both the power and the limits of this virtual wailing wall lie in its form. Technically, as long as Sina Weibo does not close or delete the comment function of Li's Weibo account, this popularly anointed virtual wailing wall will endure, and netizens may visit it at any time to browse or leave comments. A wall is an open structure. In the past, walls served as public spaces for expression and protest. This was the case for the Democracy Wall movement in Beijing in 1978 and 1979.[36] The virtual wailing wall serves similar functions. But the limits of a wall, digital or stone, are also clear. The Democracy Wall was eventually demolished. The virtual wailing wall may be removed by Sina Weibo's editors at their discretion. In fact, it disappeared briefly on June 19, 2020, when the comment section suddenly became invisible, but it reappeared after netizens responded with angry protest. This shows the fragile nature of the virtual wall but also suggests that users can help to sustain its longevity by actively and continually using it.

SUSTAINING AND CO-OPTING MEMORIES

Anniversaries are a means of sustaining collective memories. By reminding contemporaries of past struggles, sacrifices, and unfulfilled dreams, they rouse people from dulled habits and spur new ideas and action. In the Tiananmen movement in 1989, for example, student protesters tried to reinvigorate their movement by celebrating the seventieth anniversary of the May Fourth movement and issuing a New May Fourth Manifesto.[37] Also, every year since 1989, June Fourth, the day of the military crackdown at Tiananmen, has been marked with remembrances around the world in both open and covert forms.[38]

Barely a month after Li Wenliang's death, March 5, 2020, was the fiftieth anniversary of the death of Yu Luoke 遇罗克 (1942–1970). At the age of twenty-seven, Yu Luoke was executed as a political prisoner on March 5, 1970, during the Chinese Cultural Revolution, because of essays he wrote attacking a hidden hereditary caste system within the CCP. On the basis of his analysis, Yu Luoke called on oppressed youth to rise up in rebellion against the injustices of the new feudal system.[39] A fearless advocate of equality and individual rights for all citizens, he lost his life for his ideals. Though rehabilitated after the Cultural Revolution, Yu Luoke is not widely known in China. His is a story of political subversion, and subversive tales are suppressed in China's tightening political environment in recent years. A book dedicated to his memory was published in Beijing in 1999, but it would not have been possible in 2019. Yet from March 5 to the days after Li Wenliang's death, netizens posted writings by or about Yu Luoke on social media. By remembering Yu, people reminded themselves of the meaning of freedom and equality as well as of the sacrifices of martyrs in the past.

But commemorating Yu Luoke on March 5, 2020, was also a means of remembering Li Wenliang because Li's death was also related to his speech. The famous poet Bei Dao 北岛 once wrote a poem in memory of Yu Luoke that contains the following line: "In an age without heroes, I just want to be a human being." Fang Fang quoted this line in her diary on March 5, where she compared Li to Yu.[40]

Popular memorialization turned Li Wenliang into a national symbol of compassion and a people's hero. It forced party authorities to respond. Instead of bluntly censoring these memories of Li, party authorities appropriated them to their own advantage. Signaling a recognition of Li's prominence in public memory, official media outlets issued brief obituaries after his death and dispatched a high-level team to Wuhan to investigate the case. Even more revealingly, at a press conference after the release of the investigation report, a high-ranking party official claimed that Li Wenliang was a member of the CCP and not a dissident.[41] In early April 2020, right before the Qingming Festival, the traditional memorial day in China, fourteen medical workers who lost their lives in the war on COVID, including Li Wenliang, were officially anointed as national martyrs,[42] and the 2020 Qingming Festival was made National Mourning Day.

Li Wenliang never claimed that he was a whistle-blower. He was made into a people's hero by the people. But party authorities, by claiming him as one of their own, attempted to co-opt the collective memory of him to show that the party, too, was on the side of the people.

The first anniversary of Li's death was on February 7, 2021. Not surprisingly, social media were full of postings commemorating him. His photos and stories from a year ago were reposted. Netizens visited his Weibo account, sent him greetings, and updated him about current affairs. Among the most touching of the anniversary commemorations was a small incident that the poet Xiao Yin recorded in his WeChat message on February 7, 2021.

He wrote that a year had passed since Li's death and that his death had been a wake-up call to the world: "I hope this call will not weaken with the passage of time." He then remembered an incident the day before when he went out to see a friend. He was in a taxi. As the taxi was crossing the tunnel through the Yangzi River, the driver suddenly sighed: "Today is Small Year [Xiao Nian 小年].[43] Tomorrow is Li Wenliang's [anniversary]."[44] A taxi driver who was driving a customer suddenly uttering these words as if out of nowhere—this shows well that Li Wenliang lives on in people's memory.

BLOCKCHAIN MEMORY

Exactly a year before this incident, on February 7, 2020, Xiao Yin had worried about the ephemerality of memory. He had feared that Wuhan's traumatic history would soon be forgotten, and he knew from experience that virtual memorials are vulnerable to censorship. That is why he was excited to hear that a memorial had been created for Li Wenliang on the blockchain, where he believed it would stand forever.[45]

The ephemerality or permanence of the digital sphere has been an enduring question for scholars since the early days of the internet. Websites and the information on them are constantly refreshed. Many disappear as technologies evolve. Others are censored.[46] There is something fundamentally ephemeral about the web. But at the same time the web has its own memories. Disappeared information or websites may leave traces; they may be stored somewhere through the magic of computer programming, which leads the media scholar Wendy Chun to ask: "Why and how is it that the ephemeral endures?"[47]

Are virtual memorials ephemeral or enduring? Perhaps they are both.[48] Monuments built with stones may seem to last, but they, too, can be destroyed. Recall how all the Mao statues dotting China's public spaces disappeared overnight after the Cultural Revolution. For virtual memorials to endure on the web, it takes not only maintenance, storage space, and technological upgrades and migrations[49] but also, in China especially, efforts and strategies to manage censorship.

More than a decade ago, I studied the virtual memorialization of the Chinese Cultural Revolution in the 1990s and early 2000s, when many websites were set up by China's first generation of internet users for critical reflections on the Cultural Revolution.[50] All of those memorial websites are long gone now. Today, few people even know they ever existed.[51] These now-gone virtual memorials of the Cultural Revolution attest to the ephemeral nature of the web.

Yet Wendy Chun's notion of the enduring ephemeral is insightful. The ephemeral sites on the web may well disappear and become invisible, but they leave digital traces. This is not only because the web has memory[52] but also because people have memories and will use the web to share them. Nowadays, hardly anything explicit about the Tiananmen protest in 1989 can be found on the Chinese web, but savvy netizens and readers can communicate about it in coded language. Over the history of the Chinese internet, many popular websites were shut down, censored, but memory narratives about them are scattered on the web, thus retaining their traces.[53] Some disappeared websites become part of a vernacular internet folklore, perhaps even a "netlore of the infinite" in the sense that it is continually perpetrated through digital memory practices of one kind or another.[54]

The vast amounts of digital material created during the Wuhan lockdown, such as the lockdown diaries and the many forms of virtual memorialization recounted here, may disappear one day. Many have already. But those that disappear may leave traces. Some are stored in the personal archives of savvy readers. Others live in the online chats among friends. Some live on in this book. The disappeared may even reappear as they find their way into alternative digital archives. The memories of the Wuhan lockdown will persist for a long time to come, and even the mighty Yangzi cannot easily wash away the great stories of Wuhan in the year 2020.

CONCLUSION

For about a year while I was writing this book, a series of dramatic scenes kept playing and replaying themselves in my mind. Scenes of streets, residential communities, temporary hospitals, even private homes in Wuhan. Of sadness, helplessness, hope. Some scenes contained striking visual imagery of slogans and internet memes; others had noisy loudspeakers or citizens yelling at authorities. There were scenes of volunteers delivering groceries or rescuing animals and scenes of diarists battling censorship. These scenes were alive with drama. They had characters in action or, in the case of quarantine and stay-at-home living, civic inaction. In retrospect, it was this long series of scenes that made up the drama of the Wuhan lockdown.

But how did these scenes—and the drama—happen? Why?

Surely, they reflect the exigencies of the exceptional circumstances of a pandemic crisis. Extraordinary events call forth extraordinary behavior. But even the most unthinkable behavior, such as the tank man on Tiananmen Square in 1989, is understandable in its context.[1] A scene of action, according to Kenneth Burke's theory of human motives, is both the setting and the realization of purposeful human acts.[2] Urban sociologists point to urban scenes as "constellations of establishments and activities, in which cultural practices are articulated."[3] Scholars of popular music consider music scenes as effervescent moments of cultural production or "momentary transformations within dominant cultural meanings."[4] Viewing scenes as processes rather than as stable contexts, sociologists posit that "scenes are works-in-progress. They are never final, but always coming and going."[5] In short, scenes are dynamic moments of action in concrete settings. Not structures or institutions, they enact and encapsulate social structures and institutions in powerful ways.

The "Fake! Fake!" incident recounted in chapter 3 was a scene of conflict between citizens and party authorities, where citizens challenged authorities by voicing their concerns loudly (albeit anonymously from their apartments in their high-rise buildings), and authorities responded by convening a meeting to address citizen concerns. Although the scene happened in a residential compound in Wuhan, it turned into a national event when phone recordings of residents' cries of "Fake! Fake!" were posted on social media. This scene crystallizes social conflict on multiple levels. It shows that citizens were daring enough to speak truth to power, but it also shows the benign face of party leaders who were attentive to citizen discontent. Social media amplified the voices of protesting citizens but at the same time made them vulnerable to censorship. The resulting picture of Chinese politics is not black and white but multicolored, with layers of meaning and complex dynamics and relations. If history is too messy for totalizing explanations or omniscient visions, then a "scenic" approach, so to speak, promises contextualized knowledge. This does not mean that a focus on specific scenes will not produce general insights. As constellations of complex social and political dynamics, scenes encapsulate larger dynamics. Zooming in on scenes in contemporary China is like opening a window onto shifting episodes of social life in a longer historical process. Offering a "scenic" view invites dialogue and refuses any form of reductive and deterministic understanding.

In the final pages of this book, I highlight four broader, theoretical themes underlying the concrete scenes of the Wuhan lockdown: politics of appearance, active citizenship, moral feelings, and digital infrastructures. Each scene in this book enacted some configuration of these four themes.

POLITICS OF APPEARANCE

For at least twenty days before Wuhan was shut down, the city was full of festivities as residents prepared for the biggest holiday season of the year. COVID-19 was already spreading, but the Wuhan Municipal Health Commission was either silent about it or, when it did issue public notices, reassured the public that the novel coronavirus showed no evidence of human-to-human transmission. Meanwhile, medical professionals who tried to warn their friends and families about the coronavirus were silenced by their employers and the police; party leaders of Wuhan and Hubei held their annual "two congresses" and New Year gala performances; and communities such as Baibuting proceeded with their annual communal feast. A once-in-a-year opportunity for publicity and spectacle was not to be missed. This obsession with appearance and putting on a good show blinded party authorities to the urgency of an epidemic outbreak.

Appearance is at the heart of social and political life everywhere. We dress up differently for different occasions. Politicians speak in different tones or styles depending on whether their audiences are public or private. Organizations, businesses, and nations distinguish themselves from others by cultivating their own images and brands—their appearances. Appearance is vital because appearance is what we see, and other people's positive or negative perception of our appearance defines us in beneficial or harmful ways.

However, when the concern for appearance is taken to its extreme, especially in politics, it can be disastrous.

An obsession with appearance is endemic to CCP politics and bureaucracy. Party leaders strive to show to their superiors and constituencies how wonderful things are and, conversely, to hide whatever might hurt their public image. That is why after Dr. Ai Fen in Wuhan Central Hospital shared information about the coronavirus with her colleagues, she was chastised for "single-handedly ruining the wonderful situation of Wuhan's development."[6] How could a single person ruin an entire city's development? From her supervisors' perspective, a single piece of negative news could tarnish the shining image of Wuhan, which the city's leaders were trying to maintain.

The harms of this practice, dubbed "formalism" in official discourse, are well known to citizens and party leaders alike.[7] Even Mao characterized formalism as a "contagious disease infecting the Communist Party" and a "poison" whose "spread would wreck the country and ruin the people."[8] Yet Mao was nevertheless the grandmaster of formalism, manicuring a holy appearance of himself directly conducive to his personality cult.[9] If formalism proves hard to eradicate, it is because those who want to remedy it are condemned to practice it at the same time. At a fundamental level, what matters *is* appearance. Reality *is* appearance. That is why even official campaigns to eradicate formalism take on features of formalism.[10]

If maintaining a positive public image is critical to the personal career advancement of individual bureaucrats, for national party leaders and the CCP as a whole it is a matter of regime legitimacy. Because appearance may be tied to regime legitimacy, censorship becomes a means of sustaining appearance by eradicating undesirable content. Image building hinges on representations, which must be controlled. But censorship is more than an instrument of disappearance. Censorship can happen through excess, such as by flooding the web with distracting information.[11]

The flooding of the web is not always done by censors, however, if by "censors" we mean the specific institutions and personnel directly involved in controlling speech. Many other institutions, state and nonstate, are engaged in the job of flooding the web. Propaganda departments, internet platforms, and, increasingly, algorithm-operated bots (robots) are all part of a state ideological apparatus that functions to produce legitimacy and consent in a society. The production of ideological discourses and scripts is a key aspect of this apparatus. The concepts of civility and positive energy are the recent favorites in the arsenal of ideological discourses. Fang Fang was attacked by online trolls precisely because she exposed the true face of the positive-energy ideology by pointing out that it is often used as "a big stick" with which to threaten and penalize outspoken citizens.

The language of positive energy has its popular appeal—hence its effectiveness as a big stick because it is more than a script of propaganda. It is deeply tied to social practices. As the anthropologist Li Zhang shows in her book on the rise of psychotherapy in China, Chinese society is an anxious society troubled by depression and other mental-health issues. A psychotherapy industry, which fetishizes positivity, has arisen to meet popular needs for counseling and treatment.[12] The language of positive energy is smuggled from this booming health industry and turned into a magical weapon of propaganda and censorship. It provides a convenient and sometimes even convincing excuse for filtering speech for the sake of maintaining the appearance of harmony, prosperity, and positivity. It was under this facade of positivity that the early COVID-19 whistle-blowers were hushed.

In crucial ways, the lockdown of Wuhan was a drastic step to make up for regulatory failures in the weeks prior to it. Resulting from an obsession with appearance, those failures ended up damaging it. All the "decisiveness" of subsequent policy making among the top party leadership was meant to repair that damaged image. Without drastic action, the virus could get so out of control that the legitimacy of the CCP would be in jeopardy. That explains what WHO called China's "all-of-government, all-of-society" approach to COVID-19.[13]

But once the machine was turned on, it worked marvelously, and an appearance of war replaced the facade of harmony. The emergency lockdown and subsequent quarantine and stay-at-home orders were implemented effectively, sometimes with blunt force but more often through community organizing and grassroots persuasion. Civil servants and party members in government bureaucracies were "sunk" down to communities to assist in grassroots organizing. Volunteers were recruited from all walks of life to perform essential duties, such as guarding and patrolling residential compounds. Policies and daily COVID case numbers were issued through apps on mobile phones; automatic notifications were sent to residents multiple times a day.

An appearance of war was achieved through the governing of space and time. The lockdown exerted strict control over public and private space. Residential compounds guarded their entrances vigilantly, prohibiting residents from leaving home and nonresidents from entering. Public venues such as shopping centers and restaurants were shut down. Entering establishments that provided essential services, such as grocery stores, pharmacies, and hospitals, required the scanning of health codes installed on mobile phones. Citizens' movement in public spaces was subject to surveillance and discipline. In residential compounds, community staff, volunteers, and fellow homeowners watched residents' movement closely. Violators of quarantine and stay-at-home orders were reported, cajoled, and persuaded into compliance.

A battle for time defined all stages of the people's war on COVID-19. The construction of special and temporary hospitals in the early period of the lockdown was about speed. No material or human resources were spared to expedite the constructions. The national mobilization of support for Wuhan—for instance, by transporting health-care workers and supplies from all over the country—was about speed. For Wuhan and China as a whole, the fight in which they were engaged was for time lost and time delayed.

But if it was a battle for time, it was also one that had to be seen, that had to be made into a spectacle. That was why the nation's major television network CCTV livestreamed the construction of the Fire God Mountain and Thunder God Mountain Hospitals, which produced the spectacular effects of attracting live mass participation. That was also why female health workers shaving their heads (or, rather, having their heads shaved) before setting off for Wuhan could be turned into a media spectacle to show their determination to fight in the war on COVID. In short, although the politics of appearance assumed different forms before and after the Wuhan lockdown, what remained the same was the preoccupation with appearance.

ACTIVE CITIZENSHIP

Keeping up with appearances requires citizen cooperation. Yet citizen cooperation is never automatic, nor can it always be coerced or coerced for long—hence, the role of propaganda, ideology, education, and discipline. A whole apparatus of governance is at work to cultivate loyalty and induce cooperation. Nevertheless, it may not work, and yet Chinese authoritarianism has endured. Why?

This puzzle has long preoccupied scholars. One of the first concepts proposed to explain it is "authoritarian resilience." Articulated in 2003 by the political scientist Andrew Nathan, authoritarian resilience remains a key concept in the study of Chinese politics.[14] Nathan's original article on the concept used it to address a burning question of the time: How did the Chinese regime survive the crisis of the Tiananmen protest in 1989? He argues that China's political system underwent a process of institutionalization that allowed it to adapt and survive. Institutionalization is evident in (1) the increasingly norm-bound nature of China's succession politics, (2) the increase in meritocratic criteria for promoting political elites, (3) the differentiation and functional specialization of institutions, and (4) the establishment of institutions for political participation and appeal that strengthen the CCP's legitimacy among the public at large.[15] With a focus on elite politics, the concept of authoritarian resilience emphasizes the dynamism and adaptability of political institutions. The concept has since inspired a whole family of adjectives to modify *authoritarianism*, such as *responsive*, *consultative*, *deliberative*, *participatory*, *negotiated*, and *bargained*.[16] The term *responsive authoritarianism*, for example, is used to characterize a government that responds to citizen demands by making policy changes.[17]

Although there are many studies of citizen activism and protest in China, they tend to wonder how these forms of citizen participation are possible at all in the face of the state's formidable power.[18] The question of how responsive authoritarianism may depend on an active citizenry—a matter of symbiosis—has not attracted enough attention. For state institutions to be responsive, they must have citizen demands to respond to in the first place. And citizens must be willing to make claims, voice concerns, and act in some manner; they must not be resigned to their fate or give in to cynicism or sullenness. If a mayor's online forum for gathering citizen input is to work, citizens must submit requests and questions. If government bureaucrats are to be held accountable through public supervision, and if party media are not doing the job of supervision, social media exposure and criticism become essential. But, again, citizens would have to care enough to act. In a society of citizen withdrawal, apathy, and disengagement, there would be no institutional responsiveness of any kind to speak of. Responsive authoritarianism is symbiotic with an active citizenry.

What is an active citizenry? It has been proposed that "an active citizen evinces a sense of efficacy and is willing to openly confront and assert her interests against the powerful."[19] A sense of efficacy is central, but an active citizen does not always have to "openly confront and assert her interests against the powerful." Citizens use diverse forms and tactics in expressing and asserting their interests. The key is to engage rather than to disengage.

The political scientist Engin Isin distinguishes between "activist" and "active" citizens, proposing that activist citizens are creative, but active citizens are not: "While activist citizens engage in writing scripts and creating the scene, active citizens follow scripts and participate in scenes that are already created."[20] It is not always possible, however, to tell when citizens are writing their own scripts or following existing scripts. The boundary between writing and following scripts is fluid and ambiguous. Acting out existing scripts may sometimes entail creative improvisation and may germinate new scripts. Many of the contentious incidents studied in this book, such as the "gong-beating woman," achieve creativity by following existing scripts rather than writing new ones.

In my view, being activist or active may be a matter of whether citizens are committed to specific social change causes or not. By virtue of a relationship to an -ism, an activist is committed to one or more causes, such as environmental protection or anti–domestic violence. Thus, those committed to social change causes may be viewed as activists. They often join formal or informal organizations to pursue their causes. Active citizens are not necessarily committed to social change causes but are nevertheless concerned with social issues and may take action out of such concerns. Active citizens may turn into activist citizens, and vice versa. In any society at any historical moment, there are more active citizens than activist citizens. In societies like China, where the state is suspicious of organized citizen action, citizens may be active but not activist because becoming an activist may invite unwanted attention from the authorities.

The stories in this book showcase both activist and active citizens. These citizens organized fund-raising campaigns, donated money, and worked as volunteers. They carried on political talk on social media with friends, families, colleagues, and strangers. Voices demanding government account-ability were loud and persistent on social media. As party authorities hailed citizens, citizens hailed back. And in several high-profile cases such as the one involving residents yelling at the inspecting Vice Premier Sun Chunlan, party leaders listened. They were responsive.

The extraordinary circumstances of the pandemic expanded the mean-ings of citizen acts. Active citizenship was not confined to daring acts such as loudly hailing back at party officials. Writing and sharing diaries online were acts of citizenship. Documenting the social impact of the pandemic by recording personal experiences has clear historical significance, but diarists also inspired readers and viewers with their acts of endurance and self-mobilization and contributed to the building of online diary communities.

Strictly following the regimen of quarantine and stay-at-home orders required self-discipline and sacrifice; it benefited family and collective well-being. As such, it was also a moral act of citizenship, a form of active inac-tion.[21] The uncertainty about how long the lockdown would last created tre-mendous anxiety. As the lockdown diaries show, managing daily life with such uncertainty was a daily ordeal. And yet the diarists and citizens at large endured.

MORAL FEELINGS

Why do citizens act? Some may be acting in the age-old tradition of rules consciousness or out of a growing rights consciousness.[22] The term *rules consciousness* refers to action based on and justified by existing rules of the state. Instead of challenging the authorities, such actions affirm the legiti-macy of existing political arrangements. The term *rights consciousness* refers to awareness of one's citizenship rights. As such, it may "evolve into a more far-reaching counterhegemonic project."[23] The stories of the active citizenry in this book evince both rules consciousness and rights consciousness. In either case, however, the individuals involved spoke or acted with strong feelings and emotions—anger, indignation, love, pride, sadness, and more.

Active citizens have strong moral feelings, conveyed through strong emotions, as well as an awareness of rights and rules. Emotional publics are moral publics.

In Harold Garfinkel's sociological experiments, when people's common-sense assumptions about appropriate behavior were violated, they responded with "astonishment, bewilderment, shock, anxiety, embarrassment, and anger."[24] A moral grammar guides social behavior; violating it draws emotional responses.

For a long time, studies of state–society relations have focused on the self and on individuals acting in relation with the state,[25] where individuals are presumed to be autonomous persons unbound by social relations. Such an image of the self is not true in China, if it is ever true anywhere at all. Citizens taking public action in China are entangled in a web of social relationship: self, party–state, family, friends, and more. This relationship is regulated not just by laws and regulations but also by moral obligations that are rooted in the party's own political rhetoric (such as "to serve the people heart and soul"), by the duties and obligations of modern citizenship, as well as by enduring ethical principles of family and friends, such as filial piety, loyalty, sincerity, and reciprocity.[26]

Pandemic governance did not always rely on top-down legalistic and administrative approaches. Moral persuasion and personalistic relations mattered no less.[27] A pandemic moral economy was at work. Village leaders implored fellow villagers to follow quarantine rules by warning them of the risks they could pose to their families if they did not. Community volunteers helped home-bound residents with groceries and food delivery instead of just telling them to follow the rules. Citizens cooperated with government authorities out of a sense of civic responsibility. They complained and protested only when party authorities failed to fulfill their official duties. The Wuhan aunty's swearing speech went viral on social media because her remarks contained the force of moral persuasion. Her strong emotional expressions showed that what she said was sincere and heartfelt.

Citizens' adherence to quarantine and stay-at-home policies demonstrated a deep concern for the well-being of family, friends, and community. Medical professionals lived in chartered hotels instead of returning home after work because they did not want to risk taking the virus to their loved ones. They carried on at work for long hours and days out of their duty to care for the health of the people but also, as in the case of Dr. Cai Yi in chapter 5, out of a sense of comradeship forged in the middle of a "battle." Diarists wrote about fighting the virus through "inaction." Out of love for her family, Ah-Nian moved from a facility for light-symptom patients to one for patients with serious symptoms just so she could look after her grandmother.

The pandemic revived a basic wisdom of life that gets forgotten in the hustle and bustle of ordinary times: what matters most are family and community. When life becomes exceptionally fragile and vulnerable, it feels more precious than ever before. Never before did Ah-Nian think about what might happen if her entire family got infected and were to "die one after another."[28] Now she worried. These worries about loved ones transmogrified into a determination to take all necessary precautions to stay healthy by staying at home.

A moral community functions by informal rules and personalistic relations as much as by formal laws and regulations. Urban residential communities are such moral communities. In the past in China, they were work-unit communities—people who worked together also lived in the same gated communities. Although contemporary residential communities are no longer work-unit based, they are still tightly knit. Residents have access to shared public spaces; they participate in similar activities in these spaces, such as square dancing. Community residents are not strangers. They are a society of acquaintances bound by mutual obligations. The community's physical togetherness is further enhanced by its online connectivity. Homeowners in the same residential community are linked through WeChat groups. In ordinary times, these WeChat groups are spaces for socializing and information sharing. During the lockdown, they became hubs for coordinating daily activities such as grocery shopping and delivery and for COVID monitoring and surveillance.

DIGITAL INFRASTRUCTURES

When I began studying the Chinese internet more than twenty years ago, it was a brave new world with promises of an ever-brighter future. People talked about the internet as magic,[29] a new homeland for collective belonging, a public square for free expression, and a world of martial arts, or *jianghu* (江湖)—that is, a world outside of the purview of the state power where heroic individuals stand up for justice.[30] From the late 1990s through the first decade of the new millennium, the number of internet users and the size of internet businesses in China grew in proportion with the frequency and scale of citizens' voices online.

Over time, those earlier visions of the internet have faded. The number of internet users in China reached 989 million as of December 2020, and the character of Chinese internet culture and politics has also been changing. In recent years, a process of party-sponsored platformization has changed the ecosystem of the Chinese internet. The Chinese propaganda apparatus, which initially lagged behind the development of the internet, has caught up. Social media accounts run by party, government, and state media agencies have penetrated Chinese cyberspace. Party media agencies maneuver for power and influence online by mimicking the strategies of commercial platforms (such as by using clickbait headlines). Meanwhile, in the fierce competition for attention and revenues, private social media platforms are increasingly commercialized.

For ordinary people, the internet has become more of a daily utility. If in its early days it was embraced with a near religious fervor, today it has become a practical tool integrated into everyday life and work. Going online via smartphones and computers is now a taken-for-granted daily routine. However, because of that routinization, the internet's continuing significance in China may not be fully appreciated.

The stories in this book attest to the routine nature of the internet as well as its continuing significance. The experiences of people during lockdown were inextricably tied to the infrastructural support of the internet. The whole galaxy of digital networks—social media, smartphones, apps—was essential to government agencies in fulfilling basic functions, to essential workers in performing their work, to citizens in meeting daily livelihood needs, to educators and students in conducting virtual classes, and to volunteers and activists in organizing public support.[31] And the only reason readers and viewers like me who lived elsewhere could follow what was happening on the ground in Wuhan is that it was also happening on social media.

Digital infrastructures and social media platforms are more than a matter of technology. Long before online communities were mobilized for the pandemic, they had made their presence known: online fan clubs, WeChat shopping groups, WeChat reading groups, Weibo fan groups, Douban groups, and so forth. I am a member of dozens of WeChat groups—informal groups with affective ties that make them affective communities. The remarkable thing about civic organizing during the Wuhan lockdown is that informal social media groups turned into organizing hubs, showing that at a time when organized civil society is on the retreat, an informal online society remains strong.[32] This online society is not oppositional to the state. It is not even political because it consists primarily of leisure, hobby, and professional groups. They are precisely the kind of grassroots civic groups whose collapse in American society Robert Putnam lamented twenty years ago.[33] If they are alive and well in an authoritarian polity but not in a democracy, democracy is not cast in a good light.

In China's online society of fans and friends, feminist groups are particularly strong and resilient. They adopted more radical tactics when NGOs and other civil society organizations were under attack. In a sense, though, it is not surprising that feminist activists took their action to a more radical level. When reflecting on the feminist movement in contemporary China, the veteran feminist activist Lü Ping said, "In its early period, China's feminist movement was at the vanguard of Chinese civil society."[34] In the new political environment, Chinese feminists continue to be at the forefront of social activism, and their activism hinges on their use of the internet. The Feminist Five came on the scene by staging radical forms of performance art, but they won international fame only when the photographs of their radical performances were posted on Twitter. China's #MeToo movement rode the wave of the global movement, but, again, it was on social media that Chinese activists exposed sexual harassment. During the Wuhan lockdown, feminist groups organized anti-domestic-violence campaigns via social media. As civil society continues to retreat, an online society of fans and friends built on digital infrastructures of commerce and service will continue to be socially engaged.

Certainly, we must not underestimate how official institutions, such as the Weibo accounts of *People's Daily* and the China Youth League, sway online sentiments and opinion[35] or how profit-driven businesses turn these platforms into de-politicized spaces of consumerism, entertainment, and voyeurism. Nor is it helpful to underplay the ways in which the party–state wields its coercive and ideological power to shut down open communication. The questions are: Under these conditions, how will the evolving digital infrastructures intermesh with state politics? Will citizens remain as active as they were during the Wuhan lockdown? The myriad scenes depicted in this book provide no simple answer but point instead to the coexistence of multiple vulnerabilities and possibilities.

NOTES

PREFACE

1. The World Health Organization officially named the novel coronavirus disease "COVID-19" on February 11, 2020. See World Health Organization, "Novel Coronavirus (2019-NCoV) Situation Report—22," February 11, 2020, https://www.who.int/docs/default-source/coronaviruse/situation-reports/20200211-sitrep-22-ncov.pdf. WHO declared COVID-19 a pandemic on March 11, 2020. See World Health Organization, "Novel Coronavirus (2019-NCoV) Situation Report—51," March 11, 2020, https://www.who.int/docs/default-source/coronaviruse/situation-reports/20200311-sitrep-51-covid-19.pdf.

2. In her study of what she calls China's "third revolution" under Xi Jinping, Elisabeth Economy notes that "the ultimate objective of Xi's revolution is his China dream—the rejuvenation of the great Chinese nation" (*The Third Revolution: Xi Jinping and the New Chinese State* [Oxford: Oxford University Press, 2018], 10).

3. Joseph W. Esherick, *Reform and Revolution in China: The 1911 Revolution in Hunan and Hubei* (Berkeley: University of California Press, 1976).

4. Stephen R. MacKinnon, *Wuhan, 1938: War, Refugees, and the Making of Modern China* (Berkeley: University of California Press, 2008).

5. Roderick MacFarquhar and Michael Schoenhals, *Mao's Last Revolution* (Cambridge, MA: Belknap Press of Harvard University Press, 2006), 211. For a detailed analysis of the Wuhan Incident and the Cultural Revolution in Wuhan, see Shaoguang Wang, *Failure of Charisma: The Cultural Revolution in Wuhan* (Hong Kong: Oxford University Press, 1995).

6. *New York* magazine recently reported, "As early as the spring [of 2020], the former Portuguese diplomat Bruno Maçães was suggesting that indifference in Europe and the U.S. reflected a kind of pandemic Orientalism. When China put Wuhan into lockdown, he told me, the intervention was doubly and catastrophically discounted by the NATO

states. The disease was dismissed as a culturally backward outgrowth of wet markets and exotic-animal cuisine, and the shutdown was seen not as a demonstration of extreme seriousness but as a sign of the reflexive authoritarianism of the Chinese regime (and the imagined servility of its population)" (David Wallace-Wells, "How the West Lost COVID," *New York*, March 15, 2021, https://nymag.com/intelligencer/2021/03/how -the-west-lost-covid-19.html). Notable exceptions to this "pandemic Orientalism" are the early stories by Peter Hessler and the Wuhan dispatches by Chris Buckley in the *New York Times*. See Peter Hessler, "Letter from Chengdu: Life on Coronavirus Lockdown in China," *New Yorker*, March 23, 2020, https://www.newyorker.com/magazine/2020/03 /30/life-on-lockdown-in-china; Peter Hessler, "Nine Days in Wuhan, the Ground Zero of the Coronavirus Pandemic," *New Yorker*, October 5, 2020, https://www.newyorker .com/magazine/2020/10/12/nine-days-in-wuhan-the-ground-zero-of-the-coronavirus -pandemic; and Chris Buckley, "Wuhan Dispatch: Losing Track of Time in the Epicenter of China's Coronavirus Outbreak," *New York Times*, February 5, 2020.

7. Mr. Amber's Diary, February 7, 2020. English translations of direct quotations of web postings and diaries are my own. Original data are kept in a personal archive. Throughout this book, citation information is omitted to protect bloggers' anonymity.

8. I thank Elizabeth Perry for helping me to articulate these tough questions.

9. See Ken Plummer, *Documents of Life 2: An Invitation to a Critical Humanism* (London: Sage, 2001). The essence of a personal document is that it is "an account of one person's life in his or her own words" (Plummer, *Documents of Life 2*, 18). Diaries and letters are the classical documents of life. Other varieties include autobiographies, memoirs, and oral histories as well as materials such as photographs, videos, and audio recordings. One of the pioneering and most important sociological studies of immigrant experiences, the five-volume work *The Polish Peasant in Europe and America* by the Chicago sociologists W. I. Thomas and Florian Znaniecki, was based on 754 private letters and an autobiography. See William Isaac Thomas and Florian Znaniecki, *The Polish Peasant in Europe and America*, vol. 1 (Boston: Gorham Press, 1918). Gail Hershatter, *The Gender of Memory: Rural Women and China's Collective Past* (Berkeley: University of California Press, 2011), a study of the experiences of rural women in the Chinese Revolution in the 1950s and 1960s, is based on oral histories with the villagers Hershatter studied. Similarly, Guo Yuhua 郭于华, *The Stories of the Sufferers* (受苦人的讲述) (Hong Kong: Chinese University of Hong Kong Press, 2013), a sociological study of the suffering of villagers, is based on many years of interviews and oral histories.

10. My collection of overseas pandemic diaries did not aim to be exhaustive. They are of interest to me to the extent that they illuminate pandemic experiences inside China.

1. FESTIVITIES, INTERRUPTED

1. I first introduced Guo Jing's lockdown diaries to English-speaking readers on February 3, 2020. See Guobin Yang, "The Digital Radicals of Wuhan," Center on Digital Culture and Society, February 3, 2020, https://cdcs.asc.upenn.edu/guobin-yang-2/. Guo

Jing's diary was published in Taiwan on March 27, 2020. See "*Wuhan Lockdown Diary Published. You May Not Know Who the Author Is*" (《武汉封城日记》出版了, 你可能不知道作者是谁), March 27, 2020, https://xw.qq.com/amphtml/20200327A04SQ800. Without the original context of online interaction and reader comments, however, the published diary becomes a static product. For this reason, I use only the original postings of Guo's diary.

2. Guo Jing's Diary, January 23, 2020.

3. Guo Jing's Diary, January 24, 2020.

4. Guo Jing's Diary, January 27, 2020.

5. Xiao Meili, Weibo posting, February 12, 2020, quoting Xu Meiwu.

6. Xiao Meili, Weibo posting, February 12, 2020.

7. The word *netizen* is often credited to Michael Hauben, who first used it in an article in 1992, but it never quite caught on in the English language. See John Horvath, "Death of a Netizen," *Telepolis*, July 27, 2001, https://www.heise.de/tp/features/Death-of-a-Netizen-3451797.html. The Chinese term *wangmin* 网民 is standard usage for referring to any internet user. There is no better translation of it than "netizen." For a discussion of its meaning, see Guobin Yang, *The Power of the Internet in China: Citizen Activism Online* (New York: Columbia University Press, 2009), 217–18.

8. Zhu Juanjuan 朱娟娟 and Lei Yu 雷宇, "Eight People Investigated and Dealt with for Spreading Untruthful Information About Wuhan Pneumonia" (8人散布武汉肺炎不实信息被查处), *China Youth Daily* 中国青年报, January 2, 2020, https://www.sohu.com/a/364171325_119038. All translations of Chinese texts are mine unless otherwise noted.

9. "Eight People Dealt with According to Law for Spreading Untruthful Information About Wuhan Viral Pneumonia" (8人因网上散布"武汉病毒性肺炎"不实信息被依法处理), Xinhuanet, January 1, 2020, http://www.xinhuanet.com/2020-01/01/c_1125412773.htm.

10. Mr. Mei's Diary, January 17, 2020.

11. Mr. Mei's Diary, January 20, 2020.

12. Ms. Spring's Diary, January 14 and 20, 2020.

13. "At Wuhan Baibuting Community, a Social Worker's Unsuccessful Request to Neighborhood Committee Leaders to Cancel the Ten-Thousand-Family Meal" (武汉百步亭社工: 曾和居委会领导反映取消万家宴, 但没成功), *The Paper* (澎湃), February 12, 2020, https://news.sina.com.cn/o/2020-02-12/doc-iimxxstfo816064.shtml.

14. "Wuhan Baibuting Community: Residents Cook Ten-Thousand Family Meal to Cheer a Beautiful Life" (武汉百步亭社区: 居民烹制万家宴为美好生活加油), *Guangming Daily* (光明日报), January 19, 2020, http://difang.gmw.cn/hb/2020-01/19/content_33495078.htm. See also Qian Gang, "As an Epidemic Raged, What Kept Party Media Busy?," *China Media Project* (blog), January 30, 2020, https://chinamediaproject.org/2020/01/30/too-busy-for-an-epidemic/.

15. Qian, "As an Epidemic Raged, What Kept Party Media Busy?"

16. Baibuting Community 百步亭社区, "Working Nonstop! What Do the 57 Community Workers from Beijing Learn During Their Five-Day Visit to Baibuting?" (步履不停! 北京57名社区工作者来百步亭5天学到了啥?), WeChat, November 17, 2019, https://mp.weixin.qq.com/s/1ZxuxrhREfq83XcTzIewrA.

17. Baibuting Community 百步亭社区, "Vice Minister of Central United Front and Party Secretary of All-China Federation of Industry and Commerce Xu Lejiang Visit Baibuting Community" (中央统战部副部长、全国工商联党组书记徐乐江考察百步亭社区), WeChat, November 25, 2019, https://mp.weixin.qq.com/s/oG_hVIehyUtn6giQrT cc5w.

18. Baibuting Community 百步亭社区, "Solving the Secret to Baibuting Police Station's Receipt of National Honor" (喜获全国性荣誉 解开百步亭派出所的 "枫桥密码"), WeChat, December 2, 2019, https://mp.weixin.qq.com/s/v_i3ZqP2WoQ8hY9JWay4Ag.

19. Fang Fang's Diary, January 20, 2020. Posted in the March 6, 2020, entry.

20. "Chronicle of Wuhan COVID-19 (December 2019–January 20, 2020)" (武汉新型冠状病毒肺炎大事记2019年12月–2020年1月20日), *Caixin* (财新), January 20, 2020, http://www.caixin.com/2020-01-20/101506242.html.

21. Wuhan Municipal Health Commission 武汉卫健委, "Notice Concerning the Current Pneumonia Condition in Our City" (武汉市卫健委关于当前我市肺炎疫情的情况通报), December 31, 2019, http://wjw.wuhan.gov.cn/front/web/showDetail/201912 3108989.

22. Tan Jianxing 覃建行, "'Whistleblower' of Novel Coronavirus Li Wenliang Says Truth Is More Important Than His Rehabilitation" (新冠肺炎 "吹哨人" 李文亮: 真相比平反更重要), *Caixin* (财新), January 31, 2020; the original web link has been removed, but the article is archived at https://project-gutenberg.github.io/nCovMemory-Web/post /59185d41627a723c19bae95bab17dafe/.

23. Xie Linka, quoted in Tan Jianxing 覃建行 and Wang Yanyu 王颜玉, "Another COVID-19 'Whistleblower' Goes Public" (新冠肺炎又一"吹哨人"现身), *Caixin* (财新), February 1, 2020, http://china.caixin.com/2020-02-01/101510173.html.

24. Gong Jingqi 龚菁琦, "The Whistle-Giver" (发哨子的人), *People* (人物), March 10, 2020, currently available at https://medium.com/coronavirus19/%E4%BA%BA%E7%89%A9 -%E5%8F%91%E5%93%A8%E5%AD%90%E7%9A%84%E4%BA%BA-26e2c5b64394.

25. Ai Fen, quoted in Gong, "The Whistle-Giver."

26. Police letter of warning to Li Wenliang, quoted in Tan, "'Whistleblower' of Novel Coronavirus."

27. Xie Linka, quoted in Tan and Wang, "Another 'Whistleblower' of COVID-19 Goes Public."

28. Wuhan Public Security Department Weibo announcement, quoted in Zhu and Lei, "Eight People Investigated and Dealt with."

29. Wuhan Municipal Health Commission 武汉卫健委, "Notice Concerning the Condition of an Unidentified Pneumonia" (关于不明原因的病毒性肺炎情况通报), January 3, 2020, http://wjw.wuhan.gov.cn/front/web/showDetail/2020010309017.

30. Wuhan Municipal Health Commission 武汉卫健委, "Notice Concerning the Condition of an Unidentified Pneumonia" (关于不明原因的病毒性肺炎情况通报), January 5, 2020, http://wjw.wuhan.gov.cn/front/web/showDetail/2020010509020.

31. Wuhan Municipal Health Commission 武汉卫健委, "Notice Concerning the Condition of an Unidentified Pneumonia" (关于不明原因的病毒性肺炎情况通报), January 11, 2020, http://wjw.wuhan.gov.cn/front/web/showDetail/2020011109035.

32. "Saddening! 29-Year-Old Physician Xia Sisi from Wuhan and Dr. Huang Wenjun from Xiaogan Both Die of COVID-19" (悲痛! 武汉29岁女医生夏思思、孝感黄文军医生, 均因感染新冠肺炎去世), *Xinmin Evening News* (新民晚报), February 23, 2020, https://k.sina.cn/article_1737737970_6793c6f201900urdw.html.

33. Wuhan Municipal Health Commission 武汉卫健委, "Notice Concerning the Situation of the Novel Coronavirus Pneumonia" 关于新型冠状病毒感染的肺炎情况通报, January 18, 2020, http://wjw.wuhan.gov.cn/front/web/showDetail/20200119 09074.

34. Wang Hongchun 王洪春, Wang Feixiang 王飞翔, and Sun Zhao 孙朝, "Zhong Nanshan Says Novel Coronavirus Transmits from Human to Human" (钟南山: 新型冠状病毒存在人传人现象), *Beijing News* (新京报), January 21, 2020, http://www.bjnews.com.cn/news/2020/01/21/677199.html.

35. "Wuhan Time: The Puzzle of the Twenty Days from the Arrival of Experts Team to the Lockdown" (武汉时间: 从专家组抵达到封城的谜之20天), *Economic Observer* (经济观察报), February 7, 2020, http://www.eeo.com.cn/2020/0207/375826.shtml.

36. Zhou Xianwang, quoted in Rebecca Ratcliffe and Michael Standaert, "China Coronavirus: Mayor of Wuhan Admits Mistakes," *Guardian*, January 27, 2020, https://www.theguardian.com/science/2020/jan/27/china-coronavirus-who-to-hold-special-meeting-in-beijing-as-death-toll-jumps.

37. Qian, "As an Epidemic Raged, What Kept Party Media Busy?"

38. Fang Fang's Diary, March 18, 2020.

39. Fang Fang's Diary, March 18, 2020.

40. Edward Wong, Julian E. Barnes, and Zolan Kanno-Youngs, "Local Officials in China Hid Coronavirus Dangers from Beijing, U.S. Agencies Find," *New York Times*, August 19, 2020, https://www.nytimes.com/2020/08/19/world/asia/china-coronavirus-beijing-trump.html.

41. Yongshun Cai, "Irresponsible State: Local Cadres and Image-Building in China," *Journal of Communist Studies and Transition Politics* 20, no. 4 (2004): 22, 23.

42. Sun's Diary, February 22, 2020.

43. "19th CPC Central Committee Concludes Fourth Plenary Session, Releases Communiqué," Xinhuanet, October 31, 2019, http://www.xinhuanet.com/english/2019-10/31/c_138518832.htm.

44. Honglong Zhang et al., "Surveillance and Early Warning Systems of Infectious Disease in China: From 2012 to 2014," *International Journal of Health Planning and Management* 32, no. 3 (July 2017): 331–32; Yang Hai 杨海, "Why Is Reporting of the Epidemic Situation in the Early Period in Wuhan Suspended at One Point?" (武汉早期疫情上报为何一度中断), *China Youth Daily* (中国青年报), March 5, 2020, https://new.qq.com/omn/20200305/20200305A0O3MV00.html.

45. Zhang et al., "Surveillance and Early Warning Systems."

46. Yang, "Why Is Reporting of the Epidemic Situation in the Early Period in Wuhan Suspended?"

47. Paul Thiers, "Risk Society Comes to China: SARS, Transparency, and Public Accountability," *Asian Perspective* 27, no. 2 (2003): 241–51. See also Deborah Davis and Helen F.

Siu, eds., *SARS: Reception and Interpretation in Three Chinese Cities* (London: Routledge, 2006).

48. World Health Organization, "Timeline of WHO's Response to COVID-19," June 29, 2020, https://www.who.int/news-room/detail/29-06-2020-covidtimeline.

2. ROAD TO APOCALYPSE

1. Ian Johnson, "Calls for a 'Jasmine Revolution' in China Persist," *New York Times*, February 23, 2011, https://www.nytimes.com/2011/02/24/world/asia/24china.html.
2. Guobin Yang, "Contesting Food Safety in the Chinese Media: Between Hegemony and Counter-Hegemony," *China Quarterly* 214 (2013): 337–55.
3. Yang, "Contesting Food Safety in the Chinese Media."
4. "Premier Wen Jiabao Talks with Netizens Online" (温家宝总理与网友在线交流), Xinhua Web and Chinese Government Web, February 27, 2011, http://ask1.news.cn/, in author's archive.
5. Andrew Jacobs, "Village Revolts Over Inequities of Chinese Life," *New York Times*, December 14, 2011, https://www.nytimes.com/2011/12/15/world/asia/chinese-village-locked-in-rebellion-against-authorities.html.
6. Barbara Demick, "Chinese Toddler's Death Evokes Outpouring of Grief and Guilt," *Los Angeles Times*, October 21, 2011, https://www.latimes.com/archives/la-xpm-2011-oct-21-la-mobile-china-toddler-death-story.html.
7. Maihaozi 卖耗子, "New Discovery on Weibo! A 20-Year-Old General Manager of 'Red Cross Commercial Society,' All Sorts of Wealth Show-Off! Hurry Up and Go See!" (微博又有新发现, 20岁 "红十字会商业总经理", 各种炫富! 火速围观!), Tianya, June 21, 2011, http://www.tianya.cn/publicforum/content/funinfo/1/2691682.shtml.
8. Guobin Yang, *The Power of the Internet in China: Citizen Activism Online* (New York: Columbia University Press, 2009); Bingchun Meng, "From Steamed Bun to Grass Mud Horse: E Gao as Alternative Political Discourse on the Chinese Internet," *Global Media and Communication* 7, no. 1 (April 1, 2011): 33–51; David K. Herold and Peter Marolt, eds., *Online Society in China: Creating, Celebrating, and Instrumentalising the Online Carnival* (London: Routledge, 2011).
9. For a detailed account, see Yang, *The Power of the Internet in China*, chap. 5.
10. Jian Xu, *Media Events in Web 2.0 China: Interventions of Online Activism* (Brighton, U.K.: Sussex Academic Press, 2016), chap. 4.
11. Xu, *Media Events in Web 2.0 China*; W. Lance Bennett and Alexandra Segerberg, *The Logic of Connective Action* (Cambridge: Cambridge University Press, 2013); Guobin Yang, "The Dramatic Form of Online Collective Action in China," in *Methodological and Conceptual Issues in Cyber Activism Research*, ed. Asia Research Institute (Singapore: National University of Singapore, 2012), 137–57.
12. Eduardo Navas, *Remix Theory: The Aesthetics of Sampling* (New York: Springer-Verlag/Wien, 2012), 65.

13. For more work on remix culture, see Lawrence Lessig, *Remix: Making Art and Commerce Thrive in the Hybrid Economy* (New York: Penguin, 2008); Vito Campanelli, "Toward a Remix Culture: An Existential Perspective," in *The Routledge Companion to Remix Studies*, ed. Eduardo Navas, Owen Gallagher, and xtine burrough (London: Routledge, 2014), 68–82.

14. Nectar Gan, "Why China Is Reviving Mao's Grandiose Title for Xi Jinping," *South China Morning Post*, October 28, 2017, https://www.scmp.com/print/news/china /policies-politics/article/2117421/xi-jinpings-latest-grandiose-title-aims-take.

15. Susan Shirk, "China in Xi's 'New Era': The Return to Personalistic Rule," *Journal of Democracy* 29, no. 2 (Apr. 2018): 24, 23.

16. Andrew J. Nathan, "China's Changing of the Guard: Authoritarian Resilience," *Journal of Democracy* 14, no. 1 (February 5, 2003): 6–17.

17. Ezra F. Vogel, *Deng Xiaoping and the Transformation of China* (Cambridge, MA: Belknap Press of Harvard University Press, 2013).

18. Ting Gong, *The Politics of Corruption in Contemporary China: An Analysis of Policy Outcomes* (Westport, CT: Praeger, 1994); Melanie Manion, *Corruption by Design: Building Clean Government in Mainland China and Hong Kong* (Cambridge, MA: Harvard University Press, 2004); Andrew H. Wedeman, "The Intensification of Corruption in China," *China Quarterly*, no. 180 (2004): 895–921.

19. Ling Li, "Politics of Anticorruption in China: Paradigm Change of the Party's Disciplinary Regime 2012–2017," *Journal of Contemporary China* 28, no. 115 (2019): 47–63.

20. Li, "Politics of Anticorruption in China," 55.

21. Jiangnan Zhu, Huang Huang, and Dong Zhang, "'Big Tigers, Big Data': Learning Social Reactions to China's Anticorruption Campaign Through Online Feedback," *Public Administration Review* 79, no. 4 (2019): 501.

22. The term *color revolutions* is often used to refer to a series of popular protests in former Soviet countries, specifically the Rose Revolution in Georgia, the Orange Revolution in Ukraine, and the Tulip Revolution in Kyrgyzstan from 2003 to 2005. Lincoln A. Mitchell considers the role played by the international democracy assistance community as a key element of these "revolutions." See *The Color Revolutions* (Philadelphia: University of Pennsylvania Press, 2012), 11.

23. J. M., "*Tilting Backwards*: Whoever Wrote It, a New Policy Paper Is Making Xi Jinping's Government Look Chillingly Retrograde," *Economist*, June 24, 2013, https://www .economist.com/analects/2013/06/24/tilting-backwards.

24. "Document 9: A ChinaFile Translation: How Much Is a Hardline Party Directive Shaping China's Current Political Climate?," ChinaFile, November 8, 2013, https://www .chinafile.com/document-9-chinafile-translation.

25. See, for example, Hu Angang 胡鞍钢, "Why Is People's Society Superior to Civil Society" (人民社会为何优于公民社会), July 19, 2013, http://theory.people.com.cn/n/2013/0719 /c40531-22248498.html.

26. Edward Wong, "Clampdown in China Restricts 7,000 Foreign Organizations," *New York Times*, April 28, 2016, http://www.nytimes.com/2016/04/29/world/asia/china

-foreign-ngo-law.html; Yu Zhang, "Chinese NGOs Receive Less from Overseas Backers as New Law Stresses National Security," *Global Times*, May 26, 2016, http://www.globaltimes.cn/content/985341.shtml.

27. Xijin Jia, "China's Implementation of the Overseas NGO Management Law," trans. Cameron Carlson and Gabriel Corsetti, *China Development Brief*, March 6, 2017, http://www.chinadevelopmentbrief.cn/articles/chinas-implementation-of-the-overseas-ngo-management-law/.

28. Amnesty International, "Laws Designed to Silence: The Global Crackdown on Civil Society Organizations," February 21, 2019, https://www.amnesty.org/en/documents/act30/9647/2019/en/.

29. Mao Zedong, quoted in Mark Selden, *The Yenan Way in Revolutionary China* (Cambridge, MA: Harvard University Press, 1971), 274.

30. Li Hongpeng 李洪鹏 and Fu Chenlin 傅辰林, "Unveiling the Secret of the Omnipotent 'Chaoyang Masses': 130,000 Registrants, up to 500 Yuan Monthly Stipend to Activists" (揭秘万能的 "朝阳群众": 13万人注册, 积极分子每月补贴最高 500 元), *Evening News of the Rule of Law* (法制晚报), September 22, 2017, http://news.sina.com.cn/o/2017-09-22/doc-ifymeswc9046559.shtml.

31. Chen Yuxi 陈宇曦, "Chaoyang Masses APP Goes Alive! Its Main Function Is: Reporting" ("朝阳群众"APP 上线! 它的主要功能就是: 举报), *News from the Paper* (澎湃新闻), WeChat Account, February 13, 2017, https://m.sohu.com/n/480621134/?wscrid=95360_1.

32. Li and Fu, "Unveiling the Secret of the Omnipotent 'Chaoyang Masses.'"

33. Javier C. Hernández, "Professors, Beware: In China, Student Spies Might Be Watching," *New York Times*, November 1, 2019, https://www.nytimes.com/2019/11/01/world/asia/china-student-informers.html.

34. "Notice Concerning Selecting Outstanding Student Information Officers and Updating Information About Student Information Officers" (关于评选优秀学生教学信息员及更新学生教学信息员的信息的通知), September 26, 2017, in the author's archive.

35. "Notice Concerning Awarding Bonus Points to Student Information Officers in the 2015–2016 Academic Year" (关于2015–2016学年学生教学信息员能力分加分的通知), September 21, 2016, in the author's archive.

36. "College Holds Meeting to Commend Outstanding Student Information Officers for the 2018–2019 Academic Year and Provide Training to Student Information Officers" (学校召开2018–2019学年度优秀学生教学信息员表彰暨学生教学信息员培训会), November 7, 2019, in the author's archive.

37. "[Name Omitted] University Regulations for Student Information Officers" ([Name Omitted] 大学学生教学信息员工作制度), February 22, 2017, in the author's archive.

38. "Solution: Let 'Student Information Officers' Do Surveillance Work" (举措: 发挥 "学生教学信息员"的监控作用), April 30, 2019, in the author's archive.

39. Hernández, "Professors, Beware."

40. Javier C. Hernández, "What Happened to the Chinese Professor Who Was Reported by a Student?" (被学生举报的中国大学教授后来怎么?), *New York Times* (Chinese), November 13, 2019, https://cn.nytimes.com/china/20191113/china-informer-professor/.

41. See Prasenjit Duara, "The Discourse of Civilization and Pan-Asianism," *Journal of World History* 12, no. 1 (2001): 99–130; Nicholas Dynon, "'Four Civilizations' and the Evolution of Post-Mao Chinese Socialist Ideology," *China Journal* 60 (2008): 83–109; Ralph A. Litzinger, *Other Chinas: The Yao and the Politics of National Belonging* (Durham, NC: Duke University Press, 2000); Guobin Yang, "Demobilizing the Emotions of Online Activism in China: A Civilizing Process," *International Journal of Communication* 11 (2017): 1945–965.

42. The notion *wenming* resembles the idea of civilization in Western modernity as analyzed by Norbert Elias: "The concept of 'civilization' refers to a wide variety of facts: to the level of technology, to the type of manners, to the development of scientific knowledge, to religious ideas and customs. It can refer to the type of dwelling or the manner in which men and women live together, to the form of judicial punishment, or to the way in which food is prepared. Strictly speaking, there is almost nothing which cannot be done in a 'civilized' or an 'uncivilized' way" (*The Civilizing Process: Sociogenetic and Psychogenetic Investigations*, rev. ed. [Oxford: Blackwell, 2000], 5).

43. Elizabeth J. Perry and Li Xun, "Revolutionary Rudeness: The Language of Red Guard and Rebel Worker in China's Cultural Revolution," in *Twentieth-Century China: New Approaches*, ed. Jeffrey N. Wasserstrom (New York: Routledge, 2002), 221–36.

44. Deng Xiaoping 邓小平, "Implement the Policy of Adjustment, Maintain Stability and Unity" (贯彻调整方针, 保证安定团结), in *Selected Works of Deng Xiaoping*, vol. 2 (邓小平文选第二卷) (Beijing: Renmin chubanshe, 1994), 367.

45. Dynon, "'Four Civilizations' and the Evolution of Post-Mao Chinese Socialist Ideology," 93.

46. As Christopher A. Ford puts it, "The growing emphasis upon Chineseness in the regime's self justificatory political narrative was an important part of what Hu termed 'channeling public opinion' (i.e. censorship and propaganda work), and Party–State officials in the 2000s increasingly came to speak of the country's system of media controls and political content management as 'civilized Web management' . . . characterized by 'online cultural products with a harmonious spirit'" ("The Party and the Sage: Communist China's Use of Quasi-Confucian Rationalizations for One-Party Dictatorship and Imperial Ambition," *Journal of Contemporary China* 24, no. 96 [2015]: 1036).

47. Peidong Yang and Tang Lijun, "'Positive Energy': Hegemonic Intervention and Online Media Discourse in China's Xi Jinping Era," *China: An International Journal* 16, no. 1 (March 15, 2018): 1–22.

48. Sun Liping 孙丽萍, "Top Ten Catchphrases Released: 'Positive Energy' Tops the List" (2012十大流行语发布: "正能量" 位居榜首), Xinhuanet, December 30, 2012, http://news.cntv.cn/2012/12/30/ARTI1356856488818287.shtml.

49. Xi Jinping, quoted in Sun, "Top Ten Catchphrases Released."

50. Yang and Tang, "'Positive Energy.'"

51. Rogier Creemers, "Cyber China: Upgrading Propaganda, Public Opinion Work, and Social Management for the Twenty-First Century," *Journal of Contemporary China* 26, no. 103 (January 2, 2017): 98.

52. Yang and Tang, " 'Positive Energy' "; Zifeng Chen and Clyde Yicheng Wang, "The Discipline of Happiness: The Foucauldian Use of the 'Positive Energy' Discourse in China's Ideological Works," *Journal of Current Chinese Affairs*, February 23, 2020, https://doi.org/10.1177/1868102619899409.

53. Derek Hird, "Smile Yourself Happy: Zheng Nengliang and the Discursive Construction of Happy Subjects," in *Chinese Discourses on Happiness*, ed. Gerda Wielander and Derek Hird (Hong Kong: University of Hong Kong Press, 2018), 106–28.

54. Ian Chambers, quoted in Chris Weedon, Andrew Tolson, and Frank Mort, "Introduction to Language Studies at the Centre," in *Culture, Media, Language*, ed. Stuart Hall et al. (London: Routledge, 1980), 182, emphasis in original.

55. "Public Opinion Office of People's Net Issues June Report on the Degree of Consensus in Online Opinion" (人民网舆情监测室发布6月网络舆论共识度报告), *People's Daily Online* (人民网), July 10, 2015, http://yuqing.people.com.cn/n/2015/0710/c210107-27283825.html.

56. Edward Wong and Austin Ramzy, "China Keeps Lid on Information, as Hopes Dim in Yangtze Ship Disaster," *New York Times*, June 3, 2015, https://www.nytimes.com/2015/06/04/world/asia/hopes-dim-for-survivors-of-yangtze-cruise-ship-media-control.html.

57. Wong and Ramzy, "China Keeps Lid on Information."

58. David B. Nieborg and Thomas Poell, "The Platformization of Cultural Production: Theorizing the Contingent Cultural Commodity," *New Media and Society* 20, no. 11 (2018): 4276. Also see Jeroen de Kloet et al., "The Platformization of Chinese Society: Infrastructure, Governance, and Practice," *Chinese Journal of Communication* 12, no. 3 (July 3, 2019): 249–56.

59. De Kloet et al., "The Platformization of Chinese Society," 252.

60. Guobin Yang, "Introduction: Social Media and State-Sponsored Platformization in China," in *Engaging Social Media in China: Platforms, Publics, and Production*, ed. Guobin Yang and Wei Wang (East Lansing: Michigan State University Press, 2021), xi–xxxi.

61. Communication scholars once characterized China's media industries as "party-market corporatism." See Chin-Chuan Lee, Zhou He, and Yu Huang, "Party–Market Corporatism, Clientelism, and Media in Shanghai," *International Journal of Press/Politics* 12, no. 3 (2007): 21–42.

62. Xi Jinping 习近平, "Speech at the 12th Study Session of the CCP Politburo" (在中国中央政治局第12 次学习会议上的讲话), January 25, 2019, http://www.wenming.cn/specials/zxdj/xzsjhwm_43255/201905/t20190524_5126562.shtml.

63. Xi Jinping, "Speech at the Meeting About Balancing COVID-19 Prevention and Control with Economic and Social Development" (在统筹推进新冠肺炎疫情防控和经济社会发展工作部署会议上的讲话), February 23, 2020, http://www.wenming.cn/specials/zxdj/xzsjhwm_43255/202003/t20200304_5454781.shtml.

64. Yong Zhong, "The Chinese Internet: A Separate Closed Monopoly Board," *Journal of International Communication* 18, no. 1(2012): 19–31.

65. Susan Leong, "Sinophone, Chinese, and PRC Internet: Chinese Overseas in Australia and the PRC Internet," *Digital Asia* 3 (2016): 117–37. See also Guobin Yang, "A Chinese Internet? History, Practice, and Globalization," *Chinese Journal of Communication* 5 (2012): 49–54.

66. For more discussion of the communication patterns on WeChat, see Eric Harwit, "WeChat: Social and Political Development of China's Dominant Messaging App," *Chinese Journal of Communication* 10, no. 3 (July 3, 2017): 312–27; and Yujie Chen, Zhifei Mao, and Jack Linchuan Qiu, *Super-Sticky WeChat and Chinese Society* (Bingley, U.K.: Emerald, 2018).

67. Jose van Dijck, *The Culture of Connectivity: A Critical History of Social Media* (New York: Oxford University Press, 2013); Alice Marwick, *Status Update: Celebrity, Publicity, and Branding in the Social Media Age* (New Haven, CT: Yale University Press, 2013).

68. Tarleton Gillespie, for example, draws attention to how platforms shape information policy to seek limited liability for what users say on them ("The Politics of 'Platforms,'" *New Media and Society* 12, no. 3 [2010]: 347–64). Ori Schwarz's study of Facebook goes further to argue that digital platforms "engage in intensive legislation, administration of justice and punishment, and develop eclectic governing and legitimation apparatuses consisting of algorithms, proletarian judicial labor and quasiconstitutional governing documents" ("Facebook Rules: Structures of Governance in Digital Capitalism and the Control of Generalized Social Capital," *Theory, Culture, and Society* 36, no. 4 [2019]: 117). For a comprehensive study of the social impact of platforms, see José van Dijck, Thomas Poell, and Martijn De Waal, *The Platform Society: Public Values in a Connective World* (New York: Oxford University Press, 2018).

69. Min Jiang, "Internet Companies in China: Dancing Between the Party Line and the Bottom Line," *Asie Visions* 47 (2012), https://ssrn.com/abstract=1998976; Yuezhi Zhao, *Media, Market, and Democracy in China: Between the Party Line and the Bottom Line* (Urbana: University of Illinois Press, 1998). For a classic text on Chinese politics, see William A. Joseph, ed., *Politics in China: An Introduction*, 3rd ed. (Oxford: Oxford University Press, 2019).

70. Maria Repnikova, *Media Politics in China: Improvising Power Under Authoritarianism* (Cambridge: Cambridge University Press, 2017).

71. Rebecca MacKinnon, "Liberation Technology: China's 'Networked Authoritarianism,'" *Journal of Democracy* 22, no. 2 (2011): 32–46; Min Jiang, "Authoritarian Informationalism: China's Approach to Internet Sovereignty," *SAIS Review of International Affairs* 30, no. 2 (2010): 71–89.

72. Rongbin Han, *Contesting Cyberspace in China: Online Expression and Authoritarian Resilience* (New York: Columbia University Press, 2018); Guobin Yang, ed., *China's Contested Internet* (Copenhagen, Denmark: NIAS Press, 2015).

73. Margaret E. Roberts, *Censored: Distraction and Diversion Inside China's Great Firewall* (Princeton, NJ: Princeton University Press, 2018); Yizhou (Joe) Xu, "Programmatic Dreams: Technographic Inquiry Into Censorship of Chinese Chatbots," *Social Media + Society* 4, no. 4 (November 11, 2018), https://doi.org/10.1177/2056305118808780.

74. Patrick Shaou-Whea Dodge, "Imagining Dissent: Contesting the Facade of Harmony Through Art and the Internet in China," in *Imagining China: Rhetorics of Nationalism in an Age of Globalization*, ed. Stephen John Hartnett, Lisa B. Keränen, and Donovan Conley (East Lansing: Michigan State University Press, 2017), 311–38; Ya-Wen Lei, *The Contentious Public Sphere: Law, Media, and Authoritarian Rule in China* (Princeton, NJ: Princeton University Press, 2017); Jing Wang, *The Other Digital China: Nonconfrontational Activism on the Social Web* (Cambridge, MA: Harvard University Press, 2019); Yang, *The Power of the Internet in China*.

75. Stephen J. Hartnett, "Google and the 'Twisted Cyber Spy' Affair: U.S.-China Communication in an Age of Globalization," *Quarterly Journal of Speech* 97 (2011): 411–34; Yu Hong and G. Thomas Goodnight, "How to Think About Cyber Sovereignty: The Case of China," *Chinese Journal of Communication* OnlineFirst (2019), https://doi.org/10.1080/17544750.2019.1687536; Jiang, "Authoritarian Informationalism"; Jinghan Zeng, Tim Stevens, and Yaru Chen, "China's Solution to Global Cyber Governance: Unpacking the Domestic Discourse of 'Internet Sovereignty,'" *Politics and Policy* 45, no. 3 (2017): 432–64.

76. Maria Repnikova and Kecheng Fang call this participatory tendency "authoritarian participatory persuasion 2.0" ("Authoritarian Participatory Persuasion 2.0: Netizens as Thought Work Collaborators in China," *Journal of Contemporary China* 27, no. 113 [2018]: 763–79).

77. Shaohua Guo, " 'Occupying' the Internet: State Media and the Reinvention of Official Culture Online," *Communication and the Public* 3, no. 1 (2018): 19.

78. Headlines quoted in Peng Lan 彭兰, "Short Videos: The 'Genetic Modification' and Recultivation of Video Productivity" (短视频: 视频生产力的 "转基因"与再培育), *Journalism and Mass Communication Monthly* (新闻界), no. 1 (2019): 34–43.

79. See Yang, "Demobilizing the Emotions of Online Activism in China."

3. PEOPLE'S WAR

1. The idea of a "people's war" originated in Mao's guerrilla warfare in the War of Resistance against Japan in the 1930s and 1940s. It was made famous in Lin Biao's grandiose treatise *Long Live the Victory of People's War! In Commemoration of the 20th Anniversary of Victory in the Chinese People's War of Resistance Against Japan* (Beijing: Foreign Language Press, 1965), https://www.marxists.org/reference/archive/lin-biao/1965/09/peoples_war/index.htm. Fighting a people's war became a slogan of factional battles in the Cultural Revolution, when Red Guards imagined they were fighting a people's war against internal and external enemies. To those with memories of the Cultural Revolution, the rhetoric and many of the practices of a people's war against COVID-19 were not new.

2. China Watch Institute et al., *China's Fight Against COVID-19*, April 21, 2020, https://enapp.chinadaily.com.cn/a/202004/21/AP5e9e2c60a3100bb08af0898c.html?from=timeline&isappinstalled=0.

3. Hubei Provincial Headquarters for Preventing and Controlling COVID-19湖北省新型冠状病毒感染肺炎疫情防控指挥部, "Notice of Wuhan Municipal Headquarters for Preventing and Controlling COVID-19" (湖北省新型冠状病毒感染肺炎疫情防控指挥部通告), January 29, 2020, http://www.hubei.gov.cn/zhuanti/2020/gzxxgzbd/zxtb/202001/t20200129_2016284.shtml.

4. Wuhan Municipal Headquarters for Preventing and Controlling COVID-19 武汉市新冠肺炎疫情防控指挥部通告, "Notice No. 12" (第 12 号), February 10, 2020, http://www.wuhan.gov.cn/zwgk/tzgg/202003/t20200316_972539.shtml; Wuhan Announcements (武汉发布), "Wuhan Municipal Headquarters for Preventing and Controlling COVID-19 Issues Notice to Specify Key Measures for Closed Management of Residential Communities" (武汉市新冠肺炎疫情防控指挥部发布通知, 明确住宅小区封闭管理主要措施), February 15, 2020, https://mp.weixin.qq.com/s/Y4qgZ8VZOHVfCUghprwr_g.

5. Ciqi Mei, "Policy Style, Consistency, and the Effectiveness of the Policy Mix in China's Fight Against COVID-19," *Policy and Society* 39, no. 3 (July 2, 2020): 309–25.

6. "Hubei Truck Driver Trapped on Highway for 20 Days" (湖北货车司机被困高速近20天), *Global Times* (环球时报), February 8, 2020, http://news.sina.com.cn/o/2020-02-08/doc-iimxyqvz1241865.shtml.

7. "Parading in the Street, Slapping the Face, Smashing Mahjong Table—Prevention and Control of COVID Should Follow the Law" (游街、抽耳光、砸麻将桌 . . . 疫情防控也要依法), *China Economic Weekly* (中国经济周刊), February 17, 2020, https://mp.weixin.qq.com/s/lrs2TkTtFBTvJ68PUvh5Zw.

8. Fuzhou Communist Youth League, Weibo account, February 18, 2020, in the author's archive.

9. Ning's Diary, March 3, 2020.

10. "COVID-19 Does Not Give You the Authority of Red Guards, Only Chairman Mao Has That Power" (疫情并没有赋予你红卫兵的权利, 只有伟大的领袖毛主席才有), February 17, 2020, https://mp.weixin.qq.com/s/DDFu92mpFqHIDZv6XDqFqA.

11. Xiao Yin's Diary, February 17, 2020.

12. Jie Li, "Revolutionary Echoes: Radios and Loudspeakers in the Mao Era," *Twentieth-Century China* 45, no. 1 (January 11, 2020): 25–45.

13. Zhang Xuelin 张雪霖, "A Study of the Reconstruction Mechanisms of Loudspeaker Systems in Rural Areas Against the Background of Media Convergence" (媒介融合背景下乡村'大喇叭'的重建及其机制研究), *Journalism and Communication Review* (新闻与传播评论) 74, no. 2 (2021): 87–97.

14. "Strong Revival: Long-Gone Loudspeakers Will Return to More Than 200 Cities and Counties Around the Country" (强势回归: 全国200多市县即将响起久违的 "大喇叭"), *Guangming Online*, January 16, 2019, http://economy.gmw.cn/2019-01/16/content_32362372.htm.

15. Li Chunchang 李春昌 and Zhang Chong 张崇, "No Matter Whether Foreign or Chinese, They Are Good Methods as Long as They Are Useful: Reflections on the Practices of Loudspeakers in the Rural Areas of Cangzhou City" (洋办法、土办法, 管用就是好办法-沧州市农村大喇叭广播的实践与思考), *Hebei Communist* (河北共产党员), no. 4 (2020): 8–10.

16. Li and Zhang, "No Matter Whether Foreign or Chinese."

17. Guo Miao 郭淼 and Hao Jing 郝静, "Virtual Aggregation and Precision Decoding: The Political Functions of Rural Radio Speakers in the Communication of Information About an Epidemic Outbreak" (虚拟聚合与精准解码: 农村广播大喇叭在突发疫情传播中的政治功能), *Journalism and Communication Review* (新闻与传播评论) 74, no. 2 (2021): 101.

18. Mr. Sheng's Diary, January 29, 2020.

19. Loudspeaker announcement quoted in "Village Heads Talk COVID Over Loudspeakers: One More Hardcore Than Another, Funny to Listen" (村长对防疫大喇叭喊话, 一个比一个硬核, 听着听着却乐了), bilibili.com, January 30, 2020, https://www.bilibili.com/video/av85806106/.

20. Louis Althusser, "Ideology and Ideological State Apparatuses (Notes Towards an Investigation)" (1971), in Louis Althusser, *Lenin and Philosophy and Other Essays*, trans. Ben Brewster (New York: Monthly Review, 2001), 170–77.

21. Mr. Fu's Diary, March 11, 2020.

22. Ms. Yan's Diary, February 28, 2020.

23. Xiao Yin's Diary, February 8, 2020.

24. Yu Hua, *China in Ten Words*, trans. Allan H. Barr (New York: Anchor Books, 2011).

25. Elizabeth J. Perry, "Epilogue: China's (R)evolutionary Governance and the COVID-19 Crisis," in *Evolutionary Governance in China: State–Society Relations Under Authoritarianism*, ed. Szu-chien Hsu, Kellee S. Tsai, and Chun-chih Chang (Cambridge, MA: Harvard University Asia Center, 2021), 392.

26. Patricia M. Thornton, "Crisis and Governance: SARS and the Resilience of the Chinese Body Politic," *China Journal* 61 (2009): 24–48.

27. Denise S. van der Kamp, "Blunt Force Regulation and Bureaucratic Control: Understanding China's War on Pollution," *Governance*, March 4, 2020, https://doi.org/10.1111/gove.12485.

28. Van der Kamp, "Blunt Force Regulation and Bureaucratic Control."

29. "All Residential Communities to Be Under Closed Management" (住宅小区一律实行封闭管理), *Changjiang Daily* (长江日报), May 15, 2020. As stated in the research report *China's Fight Against COVID-19*, "Strict management of residential communities was universally adopted. Wuhan adopted a rigid regimen of community isolation. Entry and exit were forbidden except for medical treatment and epidemic prevention-related activities, while community workers took the responsibility to provide essential goods. Checkpoints were established to screen and register access and temperatures were taken on both entry and exit" (China Watch Institute et al., *China's Fight Against COVID-19*, 8).

30. Ye Qing's Diary, February 17, 2020.

31. Ye Qing's Diary, February 24, 2020.

32. The numbers were reported in the news media. See Lü Haiwen 吕海文, "Hubei Public Security Agencies Go All Out to Implement Inspection and Treatment of 'Four Categories of People,' Covering a Total of 4.27 Million People" (湖北公安机关全力做好 "四类人员" 排查送治 共排查核查427万余人), February 24, 2020, http://news.hbtv.com.cn/appgd/p/1792262.html.

33. Lü, "Hubei Public Security Agencies Go All Out."

34. Benjamin L. Read, *Roots of the State: Neighborhood Organization and Social Networks in Beijing and Taipei* (Stanford, CA: Stanford University Press, 2012); Luigi Tomba, *The Government Next Door: Neighborhood Politics in Urban China* (Ithaca, NY: Cornell University Press, 2014).

35. Deborah S. Davis, "Urban Chinese Homeowners as Citizen-Consumers," in *The Ambivalent Consumer: Questioning Consumption in East Asia and the West*, ed. Sheldon Garon and Patricia L. Maclachlan (Ithaca, NY: Cornell University Press, 2006), 281–99.

36. Ngai-ming Yip and Yihong Jiang, "Homeowners United: The Attempt to Create Lateral Networks of Homeowners' Associations in Urban China," *Journal of Contemporary China* 20, no. 72 (November 1, 2011): 735–50.

37. Frank N. Pieke, "The Communist Party and Social Management in China," *China Information* 26, no. 2 (2012): 149–65.

38. Beibei Tang, "Grid Governance in China's Urban Middle-Class Neighbourhoods," *China Quarterly* 241 (March 2020): 43–61.

39. Li Wenfeng 李文峰, "A Day in the Life of a Community Grid Worker in Wuhan" (武汉社区网格员的一天), February 26, 2020, https://www.sohu.com/a/376015496_120209979.

40. "Tencent's Main Achievements in the Fight Against COVID-19" (腾讯抗击疫情的主要工作), April 5, 2020, unpublished document in the author's archive.

41. Ms. Yan's Diary, March 10, 2020. As health codes became widely adopted, they raised privacy concerns among foreign reporters but did not appear to be a main concern among Chinese users. See Paul Mozur, Raymond Zhong, and Aaron Krolik, "In Coronavirus Fight, China Gives Citizens a Color Code, with Red Flags," *New York Times*, March 2, 2020, https://www.nytimes.com/2020/03/01/business/china-coronavirus-surveillance.html.

42. Mr. Fu's Diary, February 7, 2020.

43. Mr. Fu's Diary, February 9, 2020.

44. Mr. Fu's Diary, February 10, 2020.

45. Mr. Fu's Diary, February 10, 2020.

46. Mary Douglas, *Risk and Blame: Essays in Cultural Theory* (London: Routledge, 1992), 6.

47. Arlie's Diary, February 9, 2020.

48. "Heart-Rending! Woman in Wuhan Beat Gong on Balcony to Plead for a Hospital Bed for Her Mother" (心酸! 武汉女子阳台上敲锣为母亲求床位), February 9, 2020, https://v.ifeng.com/c/7tvjdGqD33Y?_CPB_404_R3=; "Woman Who Beats Gong to Cry Out for Help for Her Mom Recovers and Returns Home" (敲锣救母女子痊愈归家), *Beijing News* (新京报), April 12, 2020, https://news.163.com/20/0412/05/FA062JP400019B3E.html.

49. I am grateful to Elizabeth Perry for directing me to the longer history of gong beating.

50. Liu Heng 刘衡, *An Ordinary Official's Ordinary Words* (庸吏庸言), in *An Anthology of Readings for Officials* (官箴书集成), 10 vols., ed. Liu Junwen 刘俊文 (Hefei: Huangshan shushe, 1997), 6:173–226.

51. Yang Lin 杨琳, "Gong-Beating Workers Demand Pay at the Door" (工人上门敲锣讨薪), *China Economic Weekly* (中国经济周刊), October 30, 2020.

52. "Breaking News in Taihang: At Entrance of Court, Aunty from Jincheng Cries Loudly and Beats Gong While Shouting Grievances. What Is Happening?" (太行热点, 晋城大妈在法院门口嚎啕大哭, 敲锣鸣冤, 究竟是怎么了?), Yi Du (read01, 壹读), June 30, 2018, https://read01.com/xDe4G28.html#.YMJDOzZKgUE.

53. Nahed Eltantawy, "Pots, Pans, & Protests: Women's Strategies for Resisting Globalization in Argentina," *Communication and Critical/Cultural Studies* 5, no. 1 (2008): 46–63.

54. Ruby Mellen, "How Pots and Pans Became Tools of Protests, from Chile to Myanmar," *Washington Post*, February 4, 2021, http://www.washingtonpost.com/world/2021/02/04/pots-pans-protests-myanmar-coup/.

55. For recent studies of the sonic character of protest, see Benjamin Tausig, *Bangkok Is Ringing: Sound, Protest, and Constraint* (New York: Oxford University Press, 2019); Joseph Lovell, "The Party and the People: Shifting Sonic Politics in Post-1949 Tiananmen Square," in *Sound Communities in the Asia Pacific: Music, Media, and Technology*, ed. Lonán Ó Briain and Min Yen Ong (New York: Bloomsbury, 2021): 151–70.

56. Quoted in "Who Is the Target of the Top-Grade Wuhan Swearing by the Nationally Famous Wuhan Aunty?" (火遍全国的武汉嫂子, 十级汉骂怒怼的是什么人?), February 25, 2020, http://www.wyzxwk.com/Article/shehui/2020/02/414277.html.

57. Ping's Diary, March 8, 2020.

58. Ping's Diary, March 8, 2020.

59. "China Orders Square Dancing 'Aunties' to Avoid Dancing in Cemeteries, Spreading Superstitious Beliefs," Agence France-Presse, November 15, 2017,https://hongkongfp.com/2017/11/15/china-orders-square-dancing-aunties-avoid-dancing-cemeteries-spreading-superstitious-beliefs/.

60. Chuin-Wei Yap, "China's Consumers Show Growing Influence in Gold Market," *Wall Street Journal*, August 12, 2013, https://www.wsj.com/articles/SB10001424127887323446404579008372464837550; "Chinese DAMA, the World's Top Investment Group Will Be Certified with a Gold Seal from Alibaba," *Bloomberg*, August 23, 2019, https://www.bloomberg.com/press-releases/2019-08-23/chinese-dama-the-world-s-top-investment-group-will-be-certified-with-a-gold-seal-from-alibaba.

61. For two books on aunties, see Laura L. Ellingson and Patricia J. Sotirin, *Aunting: Cultural Practices That Sustain Family and Community Life* (Waco, TX: Baylor University Press, 2010); and Laura L. Ellingson and Patricia J. Sotirin, *Where the Aunts Are: Family, Feminism, and Kinship in Popular Culture* (Waco, TX: Baylor University Press, 2013).

62. I thank Pris Stephanie Nasrat for introducing me to the Critical Aunty Studies conference and the rich resources on the conference website at https://www.criticalauntystudies.com/.

63. "Call for Papers for Special Issue on Critical Aunty Studies," *Text and Performance Quarterly*, 2021, https://think.taylorandfrancis.com/special_issues/text-and-performance-quarterly-critical-aunty-studies/?utm_source=TFO&utm_medium=cms&utm_campaign=JPG15743.

64. Guo Jing's Diary, March 6, 2020.

65. Mr. Amber's Diary, March 7, 2020.

66. Ye Qing's Diary, March 6, 2020.

67. Ye Qing's Diary, March 23, 2020.

68. Ye Qing's Diary, February 1, 2020.

69. Ye Qing's Diary, March 13, 2020.

70. Readers' WeChat comments on Ye Qing's Diary, March 13, 2020.

71. Wang Zhonglin, quoted in Wang Xue 王雪 and Gao Meng 高萌, "Start a Gratitude Education in the Whole City, Form Strong Positive Energy" (在全市开展感恩教育 形成强大正能量), *Changjiang Daily* (长江日报), March 7, 2020, http://cjrb.cnhan.com/cjrb/20200307/8127.htm.

72. Christian P. Sorace, *Shaken Authority: China's Communist Party and the 2008 Sichuan Earthquake* (Ithaca, NY: Cornell University Press, 2017).

73. Christian P. Sorace, "Gratitude: The Ideology of Sovereignty in Crisis," *Made in China Journal*, May 18, 2020, emphasis in original, https://madeinchinajournal.com/2020/05/18/gratitude-the-ideology-of-sovereignty-in-crisis/.

74. Xiao Yin's Diary, March 7, 2020.

75. Xi Jinping, "The Party and the People Thank the People of Wuhan!" (党和人民感谢武汉人民), Xinhuanet.com, March 10, 2020, http://www.xinhuanet.com/politics/leaders/2020-03/10/c_1125692140.htm.

76. "Wuhan, Who Needs 'Gratitude Education' Most?" (武汉, 谁最应接受 "感恩教育"?), WeChat, March 8, 2020, in the author's archive.

77. Georg Simmel, "Faithfulness and Gratitude," in *The Sociology of Georg Simmel*, trans., ed., and with an introduction by Kurt H. Wolff (New York: Free Press, 1950), 388.

78. WeChat reader's comment on Xiao Yin's Diary, March 8, 2020.

79. Jeremy David Engels, *The Art of Gratitude* (Albany: State University of New York Press, 2018), 146, 4.

80. Dana R. Fisher, *American Resistance: From the Women's March to the Blue Wave* (New York: Columbia University Press, 2019).

4. LOCKDOWN DIARIES

1. Old Ji, Weibo posting, January 24, 2020.

2. Old Ji, Weibo posting, January 24, 2020.

3. Old Ji, Weibo posting, January 25, 2020.

4. Old Ji, Weibo posting, January 26, 2020.

5. Old Ji, Weibo posting, January 27, 2020.

6. Lai Youxuan 赖祐萱, "Delivery Drivers Stuck in Algorithms" (外卖骑手, 困在系统里), *People* (人物), September 9, 2020, https://mp.weixin.qq.com/s/Mes1RqIOdp48CMw4pXTwXw.

7. Lara Shalson, *Performing Endurance: Art and Politics Since 1960* (Cambridge: Cambridge University Press, 2018), 9.

8. Wuhan Municipal Headquarters for Preventing and Controlling COVID-19 武汉市新冠肺炎疫情防控指挥部通告, "Notice No. 12" (第 12 号), February 10, 2020, http://www.wuhan.gov.cn/zwgk/tzgg/202003/t20200316_972539.shtml; Wuhan Announcements (武汉发布), "Wuhan Municipal Headquarters for Preventing and Controlling COVID-19 Issues Notice to Specify Key Measures for Closed Management of Residential Communities" (武汉市新冠肺炎疫情防控指挥部发布通知, 明确住宅小区封闭管理主要措施), February 15, 2020, https://mp.weixin.qq.com/s/Y4qgZ8VZOHVfCUghprwr_g.

9. Organizers and volunteers of residential communities played a key role in enforcing the closed management and delivering essential services such as groceries. See Ciqi Mei, "Policy Style, Consistency, and the Effectiveness of the Policy Mix in China's Fight Against COVID-19," *Policy and Society* 39, no. 3 (July 2, 2020): 309–25.

10. Lei Feng 雷锋, *Lei Feng's Diary: 1959–1962* (雷锋日记: 1959–1962) (Beijing: Jiefangjun Wenyi chubanshe, 1963); Mary Sheridan, "The Emulation of Heroes," *China Quarterly* 33 (1968): 47–72.

11. Sang Ye, "Memories for the Future," in *Yang Zhichao: Chinese Bible*, ed. Claire Roberts (Sydney, Australia: Sherman Contemporary Art Foundation, 2015), 27–31.

12. Thomas Chen, "Ai Xiaoming and the Quarantine Counter-Diary," *Los Angeles Review of Books*, March 12, 2021, https://lareviewofbooks.org/article/ai-xiaoming-and-the-quarantine-counter-diary/.

13. The well-known literary scholar Wu Mi 吴宓 wrote multiple volumes of diaries with deeply personal details during the Cultural Revolution. When published, they became valuable sources for studying everyday life in that period. See, for example, Wu Mi 吴宓, *Supplements to Wu Mi's diaries: 1967–1968* (吴宓日记续编: 1967–1968), vol. 8 (Beijing: Sanlian shudian, 2006).

14. Zhang Kangkang 张抗抗, "Lost Diaries" (遗失的日记), in *When We Were in That Age* (那个年代中的我们), ed. Zhe Yongping 者永平 (Beijing: Yuanfang chubanshe, 1998), 628–34.

15. For the phrase "epic of everyday lives," see Batsheva Ben-Amos and Dan Ben-Amos, eds., *The Diary: The Epic of Everyday Life*, 2nd rev. ed. (Bloomington: Indiana University Press, 2020).

16. Jill Walker Rettberg, "Online Diaries and Blogs," in *The Diary*, ed. Ben-Amos and Ben-Amos, 410–23; Lena Buford, "A Journey Through Two Decades of Online Diary Community," in *The Diary*, ed. Ben-Amos and Ben-Amos, 425–40.

17. Muzimei, quoted in James Farrer, "China's Women Sex Bloggers and Dialogic Sexual Politics on the Chinese Internet," *Journal of Current Chinese Affairs—China Aktuell* 36, no. 4 (2007): 24.

18. Introduced in 2002, the Chinese word for "blog," *boke* 博客, is credited to one of the Chinese internet pioneers, Fang Xingdong 方兴东.

19. Michel Hockx, *Internet Literature in China* (New York: Columbia University Press, 2015), 38–54.

20. Yu Juan 于娟, "Diary for a Birthday of Life and Death" (出生入死的生日记事), April 6, 2011, http://blog.sina.com.cn/s/blog_7180e9800100q1ua.html.

21. Tao Tao's Diary, February 21, 2020.

22. Pang Yun's Diary, February 18, 2020.

23. Lan Xi's Diary, March 7, 2020.

24. Xiao Meili 肖美丽, "Sketches of a Pandemic" (疫期小画), April 4, 2020, https://mp.weixin .qq.com/s/FVwLpMZrRu7XhouIg67gMA.

25. Helier Cheung, Zhaoyin Feng, and Boer Deng, "Coronavirus: What Attacks on Asians Reveal About American Identity," *BBC News*, May 27, 2020, https://www.bbc.com/news /world-us-canada-52714804.

26. Jason Wilson, "The Rightwing Groups Behind Wave of Protests Against Covid-19 Restrictions," *Guardian*, April 17, 2020, https://www.theguardian.com/world/2020/apr /17/far-right-coronavirus-protests-restrictions.

27. Mr. Yun's Diary, March 18, 2020.

28. Jiang's Diary, May 5, 2020.

29. Tao Tao's Diary, February 3, 2020; Chu Ma 楚马 and Xuan Yue 炫悦, "Diary of Two Walking Trees" (两颗行走的树), March 22, 2020.

30. Fang Fang's Diary, February 21, 2020.

31. Tao Tao's Diary, February 21, 2020.

32. Guo Jing's Diary, January 25, 2020.

33. Guo Jing's Diary, January 27, 2020.

34. Mr. Yun's Diary, February 14, 2020.

35. Mr. Yun's Diary, February 1, 2020.

36. Dr. Zha's Diary, February 18, 2020.

37. Ying's Diary, April 5, 2020.

38. Ms. Gu's Diary, April 5, 2020.

39. Tao Tao's Diary, April 1, 2020.

40. Helen Davidson, "Chinese Writer Faces Online Backlash Over Wuhan Lockdown Diary," *Guardian*, April 10, 2020, https://www.theguardian.com/world/2020/apr/10 /chinese-writer-fang-fang-faces-online-backlash-wuhan-lockdown-diary.

41. Aaron William Moore, "Talk About Heroes: Expressions of Self-Mobilization and Despair in Chinese War Diaries, 1911–1938," *Twentieth-Century China* 34, no. 2 (2009): 43. I thank Professor Elisabeth Perry for introducing me to Moore's scholarship on war diaries.

42. Cai Yizhong, quoted in Moore, "Talk About Heroes," 43.

43. *Records of the Grand Historian* (史记), written by Sima Qian 司马迁 (c. 145–86 BCE), is often considered the greatest historical work in China.

44. Mr. Amber's Diary, January 28, 2020.

45. Ms. Long's Diary, May 22, 2020.

46. Lan Xi's Diary, January 23, 2020.

47. Lan Xi's Diary, February 1, 2020.

48. Tao Tao's Diary, February 26, 2020.

49. Jiang's Diary, May 23, 2020.

50. Jiang's Diary, May 22, 2020.

51. One of the distinct features of online diaries is the formation of online-diary communities. See Buford, "A Journey Through Two Decades of Online Diary Communvity."

52. Mr. Yun's Diary, March 7, 2020.

5. FIRE AND THUNDER

1. The three names have different characters but the same pronunciation.

2. Cai Yi, Weibo posting, February 11, 2020.

3. Cai Yi, Weibo posting, March 12, 2020.

4. Cai Yi, Weibo posting, February 9, 2020.

5. Ye Qing's Diary, March 13, 2020.

6. Cai Yi, interviewed for China Central Television Station 中央电视台, *Fighting Covid in Unity* (同心战疫), documentary, episode 1, Beijing, September 2, 2020.

7. J. Glenn Gray, *The Warriors: Reflections on Men in Battle* (Lincoln: University of Nebraska Press, 1959), 40.

8. Cai Yi, Weibo posting, March 12, 2020.

9. Wuhan Municipal Health Commission 武汉卫健委, "Brief Report on the Public Health Affairs of Wuhan City in 2018" (2018年武汉市卫生健康事业发展简报), n.d., wjw.wuhan.gov.cn/zwgk_28/tjsj/202005/t20200528_1350027.shtml.

10. Zhang Shancun 张善存, "An Analysis of the Naming of 'Fire God Mountain' and 'Thunder God Mountain'" ("火神山" "雷神山" 命名探析). *Speech and Writing* (语言文字报), March 11, 2020, 3.

11. See "50 Million Netizens Supervise the Fire God Mountain and Thunder God Mountain Hospitals!" (5,000 [Ten Thousands] 万网友监工火神山雷神山!), Wuhan Newscast (武汉新闻广播), February 2, 2020, https://k.sina.cn/article_2286386250_88477c4a0190 0nx99.htm.

12. "Livestreaming of the 'Cloud Work Supervision' of the Fire and Thunder God Mountain Hospitals in Wuhan" (武汉火雷神山医院 "云监工" 直播)Yangshipin.cn, February 5, 2020, https://www.sohu.com/a/370708947_115479.

13. "Wuhan Builds 3 Temporary Hospitals Overnight to Provide 3,400 Beds" (武汉连夜建 三所 "方舱医院" 将提供3,400张床位), *The Paper* (澎湃), February 4, 2020, https://www .thepaper.cn/newsDetail_forward_5776218.

14. "*Hubei Daily* Reporter Visits 13 'Temporary Hospitals' in the Three Towns of Wuhan" (湖北日报全媒记者多路探访武汉三镇13处\ "方舱医院"), *Hubei Daily* (湖北日报), February 6, 2020, https://www.hubei.gov.cn/zhuanti/2020/gzxxgzbd/qfqk/202002/t20200206 _2019958.shtml.

15. Simiao Chen et al., "Fangcang Shelter Hospitals: A Novel Concept for Responding to Public Health Emergencies," *The Lancet* 395, no. 10232 (April 18, 2020): 1305–14.

16. Chen et al., "Fangcang Shelter Hospitals."

17. See Wu Shangzhe 吴尚哲 [Ah-Nian 阿念], *Wuhan Girl Ah-Nian's Diary* (武汉女孩阿念 日记) (Beijing: Beijing Lianhe, 2020).

18. Wu, *Wuhan Girl An-Nian's Diary*, entry for February 10, 2020.

19. Wu, *Wuhan Girl A-Nian's Diary*, entry for February 11, 2020.

20. Wu, *Wuhan Girl A- Nian's Diary*, entry for February 13, 2020.

21. Wu, *Wuhan Girl Ah-Nian's Diary*, entry for February 13, 2020.

22. Ah-Nian's Weibo Diary, February 14, 2020.

23. Ah-Nian's Weibo Diary, February 18, 2020, emphasis in original.

24. Ah-Nian's Weibo Diary, February 19, 2020.

25. Ah-Nian's Weibo Diary, March 13, 2020.

26. Ah-Nian's Weibo Diary, March 26, 2020.

27. Ah-Nian, interviewed on WeChat by the author, November 10, 2020.

28. Ah-Bu's Vlog, February 8, 2020.

29. Ah-Bu's Vlog, February 9, 2020.

30. Ah-Bu's Vlog, February 10, 2020; viewers' comments on Ah-Bu's Vlog, February 10, 2020.

31. Wuhan Municipal Headquarters for Preventing and Controlling COVID-19 武汉市新冠肺炎疫情防控指挥部通告, "Notice No. 12" (第 12 号), February 10, 2020, www.wuhan.gov.cn/zwgk/tzgg/202003/t20200316_972539.shtml.

32. Guo Jing's Diary, February 10, 2020.

33. Arlie's Diary, February 11, 2020.

34. Ah-Bu's Vlog, February 13, 2020.

35. Viewer comment on Ah-Bu's Vlog, February 13, 2020.

36. For a recent study of state responses to doctor–patient conflicts in China, see Xian Huang, "Peace in the Shadow of Unrest: Yinao and the State Response in China," *China Quarterly*, first view (2020), https://doi:10.1017/S0305741020001010.

37. "Chinese Doctors Are Under Threat," *The Lancet* 376, no. 9742 (August 28, 2010): 657.

38. China Medical Doctors Association 中国医师协会, "White Paper on the Professional Conditions of Medical Practitioners" (中国医师执业状况白皮书), 2015, http://www.cmda.net/zlwqgzdt/596.jhtml.

39. China Medical Doctors Association 中国医师协会, "White Paper on the Professional Conditions of Medical Practitioners in China" (中国医师执业状况白皮书), December 2017, http://www.c mda.net/u/cms/www/201807/06181247ffex.pdf. The percentage of respondents who did not want their children to enter the medical profession in 2014 was even higher—close to 60 percent.

40. Jinli Yu, Fei Zou, and Yirui Sun, "Job Satisfaction, Engagement, and Burnout in the Population of Orthopedic Surgeon and Neurosurgeon Trainees in Mainland China," *Neurosurgical Focus* 48, no. 3 (March 1, 2020): 3.

41. Chang Jian 常健 and Xu Qian 徐倩, "A Study of the Role of Various Stakeholders in Doctor–Patient Conflicts—Based on an Analysis of 150 Cases" (医患冲突升级中各类主体作用研究—基于对150个案例的分析), *Journal of the Shanghai Administration Institute* (上海行政学院学报) 18, no. 4 (July 2017): 4–12.

42. Chen Chaoyang 陈朝阳 and Tian Dongliang 田栋梁, "Details of Dr. Yang Wen's Murder Revealed" (杨文医生被害细节曝光), *Medical Field* (医学界), December 28, 2019, https://new.qq.com/omn/20191227/20191227A0OZ6O0o.html.

43. Ziyi Zhang and Jia Zhang, "The Logic and Regulations of China's Medical Malpractice," *Chinese Public Administration* 1, no. 355 (2015): 137–41.

44. "Institutional Reform of the Salary and Compensation System in Public Hospitals Is the Main Trend" (公立医院医生薪酬制度改革是大势所趋), *China Youth Daily* (中国青年报), May 25, 2017, http://www.xinhuanet.com//politics/2017-05/25/c_1121031738.htm; Zhang and Zhang, "The Logic and Regulations of China's Medical Malpractice"; Winnie Yip et al., "10 Years of Health-Care Reform in China: Progress and Gaps in Universal Health Coverage," *The Lancet* 394, no. 10204 (September 21, 2019): 979–1112.

45. "State Council General Office Notice Concerning Key Tasks in 2019 in Deepening the Medical System Reform" (国务院办公厅关于印发深化医药卫生体制改革2019年重点工作任务的通知), May 23, 2019, http://www.gov.cn/zhengce/content/2019-06/04/content_5397350.htm.

46. "All Covid-19 patients, confirmed or suspected, received subsidies from state finance for any medical bills not covered by basic medical insurance, serious disease insurance, or the medical assistance fund. In the case of patients receiving treatment in places where they were not registered for basic medical insurance, their medical bills related to Covid-19 were paid by the local insurance fund first and settled later. As of May 31, the medical bills of 58,000 inpatients with confirmed infections had been settled by basic medical insurance, with a total expenditure of RMB 1.35 billion [approximately U.S.$200 million], or RMB 23,000 per person [approximately U.S.$3,594]. The average cost for treating COVID-19 patients in severe condition surpassed RMB150,000 [approximately U.S.$23,471], and in some critical cases the individual cost exceeded RMB 1 million [approximately U.S.$156,479], all covered by the state" (State Council Information Office of the People's Republic of China, "Fighting COVID-19 China in Action" [in English], Xinhuanet, June 7, 2020, http://www.xinhuanet.com/english/2020-06/07/c_139120424.htm).

47. Hubei Provincial Department of Public Security 湖北省公安厅, "Hubei Provincial Department of Public Security Issues Public Notice: Vigorously Crack Down on Six Types of Crimes Related to Health Care Workers" (湖北省公安厅发布通告: 严厉打击六类涉医违法犯罪), January 29, 2020, https://www.hubei.gov.cn/hbfb/bmdt/202001/t20200129_2016275.shtml.

48. "Notice Concerning Guaranteeing the Personal Safety of Health Care Workers and Maintaining Fine Medical Order During the Novel Coronavirus Prevention and Control" (关于做好新型冠状病毒肺炎疫情防控期间保障医务人员安全维护良好医疗秩序的通知), February 7, 2020, http://www.gov.cn/zhengce/zhengceku/2020-02/08/content_5476128.htm.

49. "Shaving Female Nurses' Heads Before They Go on Their Mission? Beware of Another Kind of Logic" (出征前线女护士集体剃光头? 另一种逻辑同样要警惕), February 18, 2020, https://news.ifeng.com/c/7uAIDphseRN; Yuan Ruting 袁汝婷, "Shaving the Heads of Female Health Workers?" (给女性医护人员 "集体剃光头"?), *China Comment* (半月谈), February 18, 2020, https://www.sohu.com/a/373898748_118900.

50. Comment on "Shaving Female Nurses' Heads."

51. Guo Jing's Diary, February 18, 2020.

52. Arlie's Diary, February 19, 2020.

53. "Why Does the Hospital Where Li Wenliang Worked Have Such Heavy Casualties?" (李文亮所在医院为何医护人员伤亡惨重?), *Caixin* (财新), March 10, 2020, http://china.caixin.com/2020-03-10/101526309.html.

54. Fan Wei 樊巍, "Wuhan Central Hospital Medical Staff Reveal the Truth: Epidemic Is a Magic Mirror for Exposing Demons" (武汉市中心医院医护人员吐真情: 疫情是面照妖镜), *Global Times* (环球时报), March 16, 2020, https://k.sina.cn/article_1974576991_75b1a75f01900q3xg.html.

55. Fan, "Wuhan Central Hospital Medical Staff Reveal the Truth."
56. Mr. Lao's Diary, April 2, 2020.
57. "Cai Li Is No Longer Party Secretary of the Wuhan Central Hospital. Wang Weihua Is the Replacement" (蔡莉不再担任武汉市中心医院党委书记，王卫华接任), *The Paper* (澎湃), August 27, 2020, https://mbd.baidu.com/newspage/data/landingshare?pageTy pe=1&isBdboxFrom=1&uk=9awys12a0MvI-yQe2PRaIw&context=%7B%22nid%22:% 22news_10151716813998933254%22%7D.
58. Cai Yi, Weibo posting, September 2, 2020.
59. Cai Yi, Weibo posting, September 2, 2020.

6. CIVIC ORGANIZING

1. "Saving Pets in Wuhan" (在武汉拯救宠物), audio interview, *Sanlian Zhongdu* (三联中读), n.d., http://ny.zdline.cn/h5/article/fpart.do?artId=85549&mode=&activit yId=0&type=0#.
2. Wuhan Small Animal Protection Association 武汉小动物保护协会, "Owners of Cats and Dogs Left Behind, Please Contact Us" (猫狗留在武汉的主人们，可以联系我们), WeChat, January 26, 2020, https://mp.weixin.qq.com/s/uTY4ha4t504aec5uFlBitA.
3. Wuhan Small Animal Protection Association 武汉小动物保护协会, "The First Day of Our Work: Racing with the Times" (上门第1天，我们在跟时间赛跑), WeChat, January 27, 2020, https://mp.weixin.qq.com/s/1AsdPP_XkquYBsb8x1SoIg.
4. "During the Pandemic, They Rescue Small Animals Stuck at Home in Wuhan" (疫情之下，他们救助那些滞留在家的武汉小动物们), *The Paper* (澎湃), February 4, 2020, https://m.sohu.com/a/370483916_260616/?pvid=000115_3w_a.
5. Li Zhang, *Anxious China: Inner Revolution and Politics of Psychotherapy* (Oakland: University of California Press, 2020).
6. Beijing–Hubei iWill Volunteer United Action Project Team 京颚 iWill 志愿者联合行动项目组, "Report on the Building of Beijing–Hubei iWill Volunteer United Action Information Platform" (京颚 iWill 志愿者联合行动信息平台建设报告), June 2020, http://www.jidian.org.cn/uploads/tx_filemanage/0b75d922501c3dbb6fef8004fb813448.pdf.
7. Beijing Huizeren Volunteer Development Center 北京惠泽人公益发展中心, *Newsletter No. 24*, March 31, 2020, https://mp.weixin.qq.com/s/mRJIEvVxs6lNfo5Ruq9VjA.
8. Beijing Huizeren Volunteer Development Center 北京惠泽人公益发展中心, "500 Autobiographies of the Beijing–Hubei iWill Action" (京鄂 iWill 500 人物志), WeChat, March 25, 2020, https://mp.weixin.qq.com/s/bdP_ZtzTqj_1muvjBdMGUg.
9. Beijing Huizeren Volunteer Development Center 北京惠泽人公益发展中心, "iWill Volunteers in Fight Against COVID (No. 18) (iWill 抗疫行动志愿者 [18]), WeChat, June 5, 2020, https://mp.weixin.qq.com/s/JQINHU4VxiJmn-09gZjq5A.
10. Guo Jing's Diary, March 2, 2020. For a detailed discussion of Guo's feminist activism, see Hongwei Bao, "Diary Writing as Feminist Activism: Guo Jing's Wuhan Lockdown Diary," Modern Chinese Literature and Culture Resource Center, April 27, 2020, https://u.osu.edu/mclc/2020/04/27/guo-jings-wuhan-lockdown-diary/. Also see Hongwei

Bao, "Three Women and Their Wuhan Diaries: Women's Writing in a Quarantined Chinese City," *Cha*, October 17, 2020, chajournal.blog/2020/10/17/wuhan-diaries/.

11. Guo Jing's Diary, March 6, 2020.

12. Guo Jing's Diary, March 10, 2020, and reader's comment.

13. "Little Braid Zhang Yunlei's Fan Club" (小辫儿张云雷粉丝后援会), Weibo post, January 24, 2020.

14. Hailong Liu, ed., *From Cyber-nationalism to Fandom Nationalism: The Case of Diba Expedition* (London: Routledge, 2019).

15. 82 King Street the Dreamer 国王街82号丨梦旅人, Weibo postings, January 24 and 26, 2020.

16. "Little Braid Zhang Yunlei's Fan Club," Weibo posting, January 28, 2020.

17. "When Fan Club Girls Join the Anti-coronavirus War" (当饭圈女孩冲上抗疫战场),*The Paper* (澎湃), March 23, 2020, https://m.thepaper.cn/wap/v3/jsp/newsDetail_forward _6646110.

18. The commercial character of online fan clubs is reminiscent of earlier forms of *minjian* society studied by William Rowe. See William Rowe, *Hankow: Conflict and Community in a Chinese City, 1796–1895* (Stanford, CA: Stanford University Press, 1989), and "The Problem of 'Civil Society' in Late Imperial China," *Modern China* 19, no. 2 (April 1, 1993): 139–57.

19. Weiyu Zhang, *The Internet and New Social Formation in China: Fandom Publics in the Making* (London: Routledge, 2016).

20. Tong Qi 童祁, "Fandom Girls' Battleground for Traffic: Data Labor, Affective Consumption, and Neoliberalism" (饭圈女孩的流量战争: 数据劳动、情感消费与新自由主义), *Journal of Guangzhou University* (广州大学学报) (Social Sciences Edition), no. 5 (2020): 72–79.

21. Tong, "Fandom Girls' Battle for Online Traffic."

22. Tong, "Fandom Girls' Battle for Online Traffic."

23. "Little Braid Zhang Yunlei's Fan Club," Weibo post, January 24, 2020.

24. "Little Braid Zhang Yunlei's Fan Club," Weibo post, March 12, 2020.

25. Conducted with the Chinese hashtag #姐妹战役安心行动#, literally meaning "#SistersFightVirusAtEaseAction#," the campaign's English name is "#StandByHer#."

26. An interview with Liang Yu published on February 14, 2020, mentioned she had 270,000 followers at that point. See Xia Shuang 夏双, "The Frontline Is Not Just Short of Face Masks: We Donated 200,000 Comfort Pants to 35 Hospitals" (前线缺的不止口罩: 我们向35所医院捐赠了20万条卫生裤), February 14, 2020, https://finance.ifeng.com/c /7u3wQvtxuTY.

27. Liang Yu, Weibo posting, February 6, 2020.

28. Pan Di 潘迪, "Sisters: Do You Have Enough Sanitary Towels and Comfort Pants on the Frontline?" (姐妹, 前线的卫生巾和安心裤还够吗?), *NoonStory* (正午), February 17, 2020, https://www.weibo.com/ttarticle/p/show?id=2309404472937712320743; Lai Youxuan 赖祐萱, "A 'War' on Behalf of Women" (一场为女性发起的 '战疫'), *People* (人物), February 22, 2020, https://www.weibo.com/ttarticle/p/show?id=2309404474700771229735#_0.

29. Liang Yu, Weibo posting, March 24, 2020.

30. Liang Yu, Weibo posting, March 3, 2020.

31. Feng Jianxia 冯剑侠, "#MakeFemaleWorkersVisible#: Women's Social Media and Dis-cursive Action During COVID-19" (#看见女性劳动者#: 新冠疫情中的女性自媒体与话语行动主义), *Shanghai Journalism Review* (新闻记者), no. 10 (2020): 32–44.

32. On hashtag activism, see Rosemary Clark, "'Hope in a Hashtag': The Discursive Activ-ism of #WhyIStayed," *Feminist Media Studies* 16, no. 5 (September 2, 2016): 788–804; Sarah J. Jackson, Moya Bailey, and Brooke Foucault Welles, *#HashtagActivism: Net-works of Race and Gender Justice* (Cambridge, MA: MIT Press, 2020). On issues of vis-ibility in online feminism, see Rosemary Clark-Parsons, "'I SEE YOU, I BELIEVE YOU, I STAND WITH YOU': #MeToo and the Performance of Networked Feminist Visibility," *Feminist Media Studies*, first view, June 24, 2019, https://doi.org/10.1080/14680777.2019.1628797; Sarah Banet-Weiser, *Empowered: Popular Feminism and Pop-ular Misogyny* (Durham, NC: Duke University Press, 2018).

33. Lai, "A 'War' on Behalf of Women."

34. For a critical perspective on Liang Yu's feminism, see Lü Ping 吕频, "How Can the Fem-inist Movement Be Sustainable?" (女权运动如何才能存续?), *Matters,* March 21, 2021, https://matters.news/@Nikko. I thank Li Jun and Mengyang Zhao for sharing their views about China's feminist movement.

35. Liang Yu, Weibo posting, February 15, 2020.

36. User comments on Liang Yu, Weibo posting, February 15, 2020.

37. "She Is a Mother, but Also a Volunteer" (是母亲, 也是一位志愿者), #StandByHer# (#予她同行#), WeChat, March 3, 2020, https://mp.weixin.qq.com/s/6qTRvGP3TojEb AohypB8jA.

38. Liang Yu, Weibo posting, February 16, 2020.

39. Pan, "Sisters."

40. Blue Bird 青鸟, "The Needs and Pains of Anti-Coronavirus Frontline Sisters Are Like My Own" (前线抗疫姐妹的需要和痛苦, 与我休戚相关), #StandByHer# (#予她同行#), WeChat, March 27, 2020, https://mp.weixin.qq.com/s/X2WmYV2mDhD-UDXBHx GNew.

41. "Your Smiles Are Like a Flower: Volunteer on the Transportation Team Sister Dong" (你的笑容开出一朵花——车队志愿者之冬姐), #StandByHer# (#予她同行#), WeChat, March 16, 2020, https://mp.weixin.qq.com/s/FKo0jrVGsloha7QBU4uV-g.

42. "With Limited Ability We Do Small Things: Wei Qiangqiang—a Cool and Gentle Father" (咱能力小就办点儿小事儿——魏枪枪: 酷而温柔的奶爸), #StandByHer# (#予她同行#), WeChat, March 2, 2020, https://mp.weixin.qq.com/s/AMmTrps3Dwf8IoVJKO rO4w.

43. Ms. Yan's Diary, February 20, 2020.

44. Ms. Yan's Diary, February 20, 2020.

45. Ming Hu, "Making the State's Volunteers in Contemporary China," *VOLUNTAS*, Jan-uary 2, 2020, https://doi.org/10.1007/s11266-019-00190-9.

46. Bin Xu, *The Politics of Compassion: The Sichuan Earthquake and Civic Engagement in China* (Stanford, CA: Stanford University Press, 2017); Shawn Shieh and Guosheng Deng, "An Emerging Civil Society: The Impact of the 2008 Sichuan Earthquake on Grassroots

Associations in China," *China Journal* 65 (2011): 181–94; Wang Ming 王名, ed., *Report on Civil Society Action in the Wenchuan Earthquake* (汶川地震公民行动报告) (Beijing: Social Science Academic Press, 2008); Zhu Jiangang 朱建刚 and Kin-man Chan 陈健民, "Post-earthquake Disaster Relief: An Opportunity for the Rise of Chinese Civil Society" (抗震救灾: 中国公民社会崛起的契机), *Twenty-First Century* (二十一世纪) 114 (2009): 4–13.

47. For a list of NGOs involved in the anti-COVID fight, see Beijing–Hubei iWill Volunteer United Action Project Team, "Report on the Building of Beijing–Hubei iWill Volunteer United Action Information Platform."

48. Shieh and Deng, "An Emerging Civil Society"; Xu Yongguang 徐永光, "2008: Year One of Chinese Civil Society" (中国公民社会元年), *NPO Surveys* (NPO 纵横), no. 4 (2008): 105.

49. Gao Bingzhong 高丙中 and Yuan Ruijun 袁瑞军, "Introduction: Stepping Into Civil Society" (导论: 迈进公民社会), in *Blue Book on Civil Society Development in China* (中国公民社会发展蓝皮书), ed. Gao Bingzhong and Yuan Ruijun (Beijing: Peking University Press, 2008), 1.

50. J. M., "Tilting Backwards: Whoever Wrote It, a New Policy Paper Is Making Xi Jinping's Government Look Chillingly Retrograde," *Economist*, June 24, 2013, https://www.economist.com/analects/2013/06/24/tilting-backwards.

51. Edward Wong, "Clampdown in China Restricts 7,000 Foreign Organizations," *New York Times*, April 28, 2016, http://www.nytimes.com/2016/04/29/world/asia/china-foreign-ngo-law.html; Yu Zhang, "Chinese NGOs Receive Less from Overseas Backers as New Law Stresses National Security," *Global Times*, May 26, 2016, http://www.globaltimes.cn/content/985341.shtml.

52. For an influential early debate about the applicability of civil society and the public sphere in Chinese contexts, see articles in *Modern China* 19, no. 2 (1993): Mary Backus Rankin, "Some Observations on a Chinese Public Sphere," *Modern China* 19, no. 2 (1993): 158–82; Rowe, "The Problem of 'Civil Society' in Late Imperial China"; Frederick Wakeman Jr., "The Civil Society and Public Sphere Debate: Western Reflections on Chinese Political Culture," *Modern China* 19, no. 2 (1993): 108–38; Philip C. C. Huang, "'Public Sphere' /'Civil Society' in China? The Third Realm Between State and Society," *Modern China* 19, no. 2 (1993): 217–40; Heath B. Chamberlain, "On the Search for Civil Society in China," *Modern China* 19, no. 2 (1993): 199–215; Richard Madsen, "The Public Sphere, Civil Society, and Moral Community: A Research Agenda for Contemporary China Studies," *Modern China* 19, no. 2 (1993): 189–90. For a summary of this debate, see Guobin Yang, "Civil Society in China: A Dynamic Field of Study," *China Review International* 9, no. 1 (2002): 1–16.

53. "The New Draft on the Registration of Social Organisations: 15 Points of Note," *China Development Brief*, August 15, 2018, https://chinadevelopmentbrief.cn/reports/the-new-draft-on-the-registration-of-social-organisations-15-points-of-note/.

54. Michael Edwards and John Gaventa, eds., *Global Citizen Action* (Boulder, CO: Lynne Rienner, 2001).

55. Marc Blecher, "The Mass Line and Leader–Mass Relations and Communication in Basic-Level Rural Communities," in *China's New Social Fabric*, ed. Godwin C. Chu and Francis L. K. Hsu (London: Kegan Paul International, 1983), 63–86.

56. As the China scholar Sebastian Veg puts it, "Because the term *minjian* takes its meaning from the historical dichotomy of *min* (people) and *guan* (officials), in the PRC context it is associated with anything that is 'outside the system' (*tizhi wai*)—that is, any person, group, or activity that is not connected to a work unit (*danwei*) in the official urban administrative system" (*Minjian: The Rise of China's Grassroots Intellectuals* [New York: Columbia University Press, 2019], 7).

57. The term *jianghu* was first used by Zhuangzi 庄子, who lived in the fourth century BCE. See Zhuangzi, *The Complete Works of Zhuangzi*, trans. Burton Watson (New York: Columbia University Press, 2013), 44.

58. Veg, *Minjian*.

59. Stuart Hall, "Notes on Deconstructing the 'Popular,'" in *People's History and Socialist Theory*, ed. Raphael Samuel (London: Routledge and Kegan Paul, 1981), 227–40.

60. Although government–society collaboration in civic organizing is billed as a new model in the anti-COVID war, it is not new. Many scholars have argued that Chinese NGOs seek to work *with* rather than *against* the government as a means of building organizational legitimacy and resources. See Timothy Hildebrandt, *Social Organizations and the Authoritarian State in China*. (Cambridge: Cambridge University Press, 2013); Peter Ho and Richard Edmonds, eds., *China's Embedded Activism: Opportunities and Constraints of a Social Movement* (London: Routledge, 2012). For more recent developments in volunteering and the role of private foundations, see Anthony J. Spires, "Chinese Youth and Alternative Narratives of Volunteering," *China Information* 32, no. 2 (July 2018): 203–23; Weijun Lai et al., "Bounded by the State: Government Priorities and the Development of Private Philanthropic Foundations in China," *China Quarterly* 224 (2015): 1083–92.

61. Note, though, that there is also continuity between the earlier generation and the younger generation of feminists. Among the earlier generation, Ai Xiaoming adopted radical and confrontational tactics in several high-profile events. See Jinyan Zeng, "The Politics of Emotion in Grassroots Feminist Protests: A Case Study of Xiaoming Ai's Nude Breasts Photography Protest Online," *Georgetown Journal of International Affairs* 15, no. 1 (2004): 41–52.

62. Stephanie Bräuer, "Becoming Public: Anti-Domestic Violence (ADV) Activism as a Public Event," *China Development Brief*, August 29, 2014, https://chinadevelopment brief.cn/reports/becoming-public-anti-domestic-violence-adv-activism-public -event/.

63. Ji Xiaocheng 纪小城, "Today in the History of Feminist Activism: February 19: 'Occupying Men's Toilet' Action" (女权史上的今天 2月19日: "占领男厕所" 行动), *Matters*, February 19, 2019, https://matters.news/@jidongjie1984/.

64. Didi Kirsten Tatlow, "A Merry Band of Rights Pranksters," *New York Times*, December 4, 2012, https://www.nytimes.com/2012/12/05/world/asia/05iht-letter05.html; Leta Hong Fincher, *Betraying Big Brother: The Feminist Awakening in China* (New York: Verso, 2018).

65. Meili Xiao, "China's Feminist Awakening," *New York Times*, May 13, 2015, https://www .nytimes.com/2015/05/14/opinion/xiao-meili-chinas-feminist-awakening.html.

66. Xiao, "China's Feminist Awakening."

67. On the application of the label *generation* to the young feminists, see Qi Wang, "Young Feminist Activists in Present-Day China: A New Feminist Generation?," *China Perspectives*, no. 3 (March 2018): 59–68.

68. Jun Li, "Social Movement, Media, and the State: The New Feminist Movement with Communication as Core in Contemporary China (2003–2016)," PhD diss., University of Macau, 2017.

69. Shen Lu and Mengwen Cao, "Thwarted at Home, Can China's Feminists Rebuild a Movement Abroad?," ChinaFile, August 28, 2019, https://www.chinafile.com/reporting -opinion/postcard/thwarted-home-can-chinas-feminists-rebuild-movement-abroad. For a study of Chinese diaspora activists, see Mengyang Zhao, "Solidarity Stalled: When Chinese Activists Meet Social Movements in Democracies," *Critical Sociology* 47, no. 2 (March 2021): 281–97.

70. On #MeToo in the United States, see Clark-Parsons, "'I SEE YOU, I BELIEVE YOU, I STAND WITH YOU.'"

71. For a study of #MeToo in China, see Feng Jianxia 冯剑侠, "'Voice' as Contention: Emotional Labor in #MeToo Movement" (发声"作为一种 抗争: #MeToo 运动中的情感劳动), *Press Circles* (新闻界), no. 10 (2019): 61–71. Also see Jing Zeng, "#MeToo as Connective Action: A Study of the Anti–Sexual Violence and Anti–Sexual Harassment Campaign on Chinese Social Media in 2018," *Journalism Practice* 14, no. 2 (February 7, 2020): 171–90; Qi Ling and Sara Liao, "Intellectuals Debate #MeToo in China: Legitimizing Feminist Activism, Challenging Gendered Myths, and Reclaiming Feminism," *Journal of Communication* 70, no. 6 (2020): 895–916. For a comprehensive collection of online materials related to the #MeToo movement in China, see Zhou Yi 周仪, ed., *#MeToo in China Archives, 2018.1–2019.7* (中国米兔志, 2018.1–2019.7), https://www.equalityrights .hku.hk/post/%E4%B8%AD%E5%9C%8B%E7%B1%B3%E5%85%94%E5%BF%97%EF% BC%882018-1-2019-7%EF%BC%89, in the author's archive.

72. Hongwei Bao, "'Anti–Domestic Violence Little Vaccine': A Wuhan-Based Feminist Activist Campaign During COVID-19," *Interface* 12, no. 1 (July 2020): 53–63.

73. See, for example, Rodney H. Jones, "The Problem of Context in Computer-Mediated Communication," in *Discourse and Technology: Multinodal Discourse Analysis*, ed. Philip Levine and Ron Scollon (Washington, DC: Georgetown University Press, 2004), 20–33.

74. China Internet Network Information Center, "The 45th China Statistical Report on Internet Development," April 2020, http://www.cnnic.net/.

75. By just a week after the anti-domestic-violence campaign was launched, volunteers in twenty-three cities had participated in the action. See Xiao Meili 肖美丽, "Mutual Help During the Pandemic: Volunteers in 23 Cities Join Anti-Domestic-Violence Action and Call on You to Join" (疫期守望互助: 23城反家暴志愿者在行动, 呼唤你的加入, WeChat, March 7, 2020, https://mp.weixin.qq.com/s/D6Ash5XyPKR-5ZvHXkBcZg.

76. For a study of the mundane use of digital media for everyday resistance, see Jun Liu, "From 'Moments of Madness' to 'the Politics of Mundanity'—Researching Digital Media and Contentious Collective Actions in China," *Social Movement Studies* 16, no. 4 (2017): 418–32.

77. Rich Ling, *Taken for Grantedness: The Embedding of Mobile Communication Into Society* (Cambridge, MA: MIT Press, 2012), 35–36.

7. GAME OF WORDS

1. Xiao Yin's Diary, March 11, 2020.

2. Xiao Yin's Diary, March 11, 2020.

3. Gong Jingqi 龚菁琦, "The Whistle-Giver" (发哨子的人), *People* (人物), March 10, 2020. The original essay was posted on *People*'s WeChat public account and then censored. A current version is available at https://medium.com/coronavirus19/%E4%BA%BA%E7%89%A9-%E5%8F%91%E5%93%A8%E5%AD%90%E7%9A%84%E4%BA%BA-26e2c5b64394.

4. For the Cultural Revolution generation, the most famous usage of *laozi* 老子 as a curse word was probably a quote from Mao's lieutenant Marshal Lin Biao 林彪, who allegedly said to his soldiers: "When called upon to die, be brave enough to die. To hell with death! On the battlefield, once fighting starts, I just fucking get ready to die!" Lin Biao's words became a favorite quote for Red Guards involved in factional violence. See Guobin Yang, *The Red Guard Generation and Political Activism in China* (New York: Columbia University Press, 2016), 44.

5. This number is based on several viral postings on WeChat that indicate fifty-two versions. I have personally seen more, so the number should be much bigger. See "52 Versions: They Challenge the Bottom Line, We Challenge the Top Line!" (52个版本，他们挑战底线，我们挑战上线!), March 12, 2020, https://mp.weixin.qq.com/s/4TvKCATQXCzBp4Pk5JDYtw; "52 Versions Document the History of Communication in the Internet Age" (52个版本，记录下网络时代的传播史), March 11, 2020, https://mp.weixin.qq.com/s/EUBzHTyZrHhFaNW2fAa3cw.

6. Fang Fang's Diary, March 11, 2020.

7. Reader's comment on Fang Fang's Diary entry for March 11, 2020, Sina Weibo, March 12, 2020.

8. Reader's comment on Fang Fang's Diary entry for March 11, 2020, Sina Weibo, March 12, 2020.

9. Reader's comment on Fang Fang's Diary entry for March 11, 2020, Sina Weibo, March 14, 2020.

10. The sociologist Melanie White argues that creative acts of citizenship happen when citizens "overcome the force of habit by provoking a genuine encounter that poses the problem of how to act" ("Can an Act of Citizenship Be Creative?," in *Acts of Citizenship*, ed. Engin F. Isin and Greg M. Nielsen [London: Zed, 2008], 46). Drawing on the philosopher Henri Bergson's concept of creativity, White argues that strong expressions of emotion, a wellspring of emotional upheaval, can disrupt the shackles of habit and lead to creative acts of citizenship (50).

11. Rongbin Han, *Contesting Cyberspace in China: Online Expression and Authoritarian Resilience* (New York: Columbia University Press, 2018); Siu-yau Lee, "Surviving Online

Censorship in China: Three Satirical Tactics and Their Impact," *China Quarterly* 228 (2016): 1061–80.

12. The communication scholar Elisabetta Adami argues that crossposting is the "transformative recontextualization of sign complexes" ("Retwitting, Reposting, Repinning; Reshaping Identities Online: Towards a Social Semiotic Multimodal Analysis of Digital Remediation," *LEA—Lingue e letterature d'Oriente e d'Occidente* 3 [2014]: 224).

13. WeChat comment on Yan Shu Lou 燕梳楼, "Who Forced Her to Tell the Truth?" (是谁逼她说出了真相?), WeChat, March 15, 2020, in the author's archive.

14. WeChat comment on Yan, "Who Forced Her to Tell the Truth?," March 15, 2020.

15. WeChat comment on Yan, "Who Forced Her to Tell the Truth?," March 15, 2020.

16. WeChat comment on Yan, "Who Forced Her to Tell the Truth?," March 15, 2020.

17. Maria Repnikova, *Media Politics in China: Improvising Power Under Authoritarianism* (Cambridge: Cambridge University Press, 2017), chap. 5.

18. Tan Jianxing 覃建行, "'Whistleblower' of Novel Coronavirus Li Wenliang Says Truth Is More Important Than His Rehabilitation" (新冠肺炎"吹哨人"李文亮:真相比平反更重要), *Caixin* (财新), January 31, 2020. The original web link of this article has been removed, but the article is archived at https://project-gutenberg.github.io/nCovMemory-Web/post/59185d41627a723c19bae95bab17dafe/.

19. These commercial media agencies include, among others, *Bingdian Weekly* (冰点周刊) of *China Youth Daily* (中国青年报), *China Newsweek* (中国新闻周刊), *Sanlian Lifeweek* (三联生活周刊), *Caixin Weekly* (财新杂志), *Yi Magazine* (第一财经), *China Business Journal* (中国经营报), the *Economic Observer* (经济观察报), *New Beijing* (新京报), *The Paper* (澎湃), *Southern Weekly* (南方周末), Shanghai Media Group (界面新闻), and *Xinmin Weekly* (新民周刊).

20. YouYoungWeekly 有 YOUNG 周刊, "41 Disappeared News Reports About the Pandemic" (消失的41篇疫情报道), WeChat, March 23, 2020. The original article was deleted from WeChat but is available at https://medium.com/coronavirus19/.

21. Wang Xue 王雪 and Gao Meng 高萌, "Start a Gratitude Education in the Whole City, Form Strong Positive Energy" (在全市开展感恩教育 形成强大正能量), *Changjiang Daily* (长江日报), March 7, 2020, http://cjrb.cnhan.com/cjrb/20200307/8127.htm.

22. Jingrong Tong, "The Taming of Critical Journalism in China," *Journalism Studies* 20, no. 1 (January 2, 2019): 79–96.

23. Wu Qi, quoted in "*Sanlian* Weekly Wins Respect: All That Is Behind Its One Hundred Stories About the Pandemic" (赢得尊敬的《三联》, 和百篇疫情报道背后的一切), February 25, 2020, https://new.qq.com/omn/20200225/20200225A0QSGG00.html.

24. Yang Jinzhi 杨金志, "Daring to Speak Up Is a Precious Attribute!" (敢言, 是一种宝贵的品格!), *China Comment* (半月谈), February 20, 2020, http://www.xinhuanet.com/politics/2020-02/20/c_1125603673.htm.

25. "When Truth Is Told, the Skies of Xinhua News Agency Collapse!" (说了真话 新华社的天塌了!), February 23, 2020, https://www.dw.com/zh/%E8%AF%B4%E4%BA%86%E7%9C%9F%E8%AF%9D-%E6%96%B0%E5%8D%8E%E7%A4%BE%E7%9A%84%E5%A4%A9%E5%A1%8C%E4%BA%86/a-52488683.

26. Xiao Yin's Diary, February 1 and 28, 2020.

27. Mr. Mei's Diary, February 9, 2020.

28. Mr. Yun's Diary, February 2, 2020.

29. Xiao Yin's Diary, March 2, 2020.

30. Er Xiang 二湘, "Editorial Notes on Fang Fang Diary: A Beautiful Battle Has Been Fought, a Crown of Justice Is Reserved for Her" (方方日记编辑手记—美好的仗已经打完, 有公义的冠冕为她留存), Er Xiang's Eleventh Dimensional Space (二湘的十一维空间), WeChat, March 25, 2020, https://mp.weixin.qq.com/s/uEf2_9szRBYKohzBoYow9w.

31. Second Uncle's Diary, February 28 and March 31, 2020.

32. Second Uncle's Diary, July 19, 2020.

33. Fang Fang's Diary, February 22, 2020.

34. Fang Fang discusses her February 3 diary entry and the February 6 published attack on her in Fang Fang, "About—About Ultraleftism" (关于 – 关于极左), May 2, 2020, https://mp.weixin.qq.com/s/ZJr-aTCz6cBmW7q-trZF7Q.

35. Fang Fang's Diary, February 18, 2020.

36. A leading voice among China's New Left intellectuals, Professor Xiao Gongqin 萧功秦, discusses ultraleftism in "From Authoritarian Government to Constitutional Democracy," in *Voices from the Chinese Century*, ed. Timothy Cheek, David Ownby, and Joshua A. Fogel (New York: Columbia University Press, 2019), 198–208. For a useful mapping of the intellectual public sphere in contemporary China, see Timothy Cheek, David Ownby, and Joshua A. Fogel, "Introduction: Thinking China in the Age of Xi Jinping," in *Voices from the Chinese Century*, ed. Cheek, Ownby, and Fogel, 1–26.

37. Fang Fang's Diary, February 22, 2020.

38. Weibo comment on Fang Fang's Diary, March 12, 2020, in the author's archive.

39. For a study of cyberattacks on public intellectuals, see Rongbin Han, "Withering Gongzhi: Cyber Criticism of Chinese Public Intellectuals," *International Journal of Communication* 12 (2018): 1966–987.

40. The "fifty-cents" are anonymous online commentators recruited by party authorities to guide public opinion. For a detailed analysis, see Han, *Contesting Cyberspace in China*, chap. 7.

41. Fang Fang is a former president of the Writers' Association of Hubei Province, which her detractors claimed was equivalent to the rank of bureau chief in China's bureaucratic hierarchy.

42. Zhang Hongliang 张宏良, "Focus the Analysis on the Class Basis of the Fang Fang Phenomenon: A Commentary on the Fang Fang Incident" (应主要分析方方现象产生的阶级土壤——评方方事件), March 25, 2020, http://www.mzfxw.com/e/action/ShowInfo.php?classid=12&id=133712.

43. Fang Fang's Diary, March 24, 2020.

44. Ian Johnson, "How Did China Beat Its Covid Crisis?," *New York Review of Books*, November 5, 2020, http://www.nybooks.com/articles/2020/11/05/how-did-china-beat-its-covid-crisis/.

45. Fang Fang's Diary, March 2, 2020.

46. Fang Fang's Diary, March 2, 2020.

47. Reader's comment on Fang Fang's March 2 Weibo posting, March 21, 2020.

48. Reader's comment on Fang Fang's March 2 Weibo posting, March 4, 2020.

49. Reader's comment on Fang Fang's March 2 Weibo posting, March 3, 2020.

50. "A Letter to Aunt Fang Fang from a High School Student" (一位高中生给"方方阿姨"的信), March 17, 2020, https://mp.weixin.qq.com/s?__biz=MzU5NTYyNjQyOQ==&mid=2 247485319&idx=1&sn=dd7e1a0ab17c4d977113f15e3da54012&chksm=fe6e5755c919de43 0123dba0f3cffd9c47f72264d786091917894cc159b14c0853b0688ad497#rd.

51. Fang Fang's Diary, March 18, 2020.

52. Liu Chuan'e 刘川鄂, "Fang Fang Is Full of Positive Energy, Criticism Has More Positive Energy" (方方有满满的能量, 批评是更大的正能量), March 22, 2020, https://mp.weixin.qq .com/s/OZ1wdYXQJyEPD89sKy4jsQ.

53. Wen Xiaodao 文小刀, "Evil People Are Banding Together to Attack Fang Fang" (恶人们 在拉帮结派围剿方方), March 22, 2020, https://mp.weixin.qq.com/s/2GPIfSAkLy0082 e1tuaCUg.

54. Elizabeth J. Perry, "Moving the Masses: Emotion Work in the Chinese Revolution," *Mobilization* 7, no. 2 (2002): 111–28; Yu Liu, "Maoist Discourse and the Mobiliza-tion of Emotions in Revolutionary China," *Modern China* 36, no. 3 (2010): 329–62; Guobin Yang, "Achieving Emotions in Collective Action: Emotional Processes and Movement Mobilization in the 1989 Chinese Student Movement," *Sociological Quarterly* 41, no. 4 (2000): 593–614; Guobin Yang, "Of Sympathy and Play: Emo-tional Mobilization in Online Collective Action," *Chinese Journal of Communica-tion and Society* (Hong Kong) 9 (2009): 39–66; Guobin Yang, "Demobilizing the Emotions of Online Activism in China: A Civilizing Process," *International Jour-nal of Communication* 11 (2017): 1945–965; Jinyan Zeng, "The Politics of Emotion in Grassroots Feminist Protests: A Case Study of Xiaoming Ai's Nude Breasts Pho-tography Protest Online," *Georgetown Journal of International Affairs* 15, no. 1 (2004): 41–52.

55. Casey Newton, "Half of All Facebook Moderators May Develop Mental Health Issues," *Verge*, May 13, 2020, https://www.theverge.com/interface/2020/5/13/21255994/facebook -content-moderator-lawsuit-settlement-mental-health-issues.

56. Rui Hou, "The Commercialisation of Internet-Opinion Management: How the Mar-ket Is Engaged in State Control in China," *New Media and Society*, November 27, 2019, https://doi.org/10.1177/1461444819889959.

57. Wang Weikai 王伟凯, "Jinan: A New Capital for Content Moderation in New Media" (济南: 崛起的新媒体内容审核之都), *Southern Weekend* (南方周末), Douban, March 12, 2020, https://www.douban.com/group/topic/167442068/.

58. "Deep Reflections: Confessions of a Content Moderator" (深思: 一个内容审核员的自白), December 20, 2018, https://new.qq.com/omn/20181220/20181220G1GSGO.html; "Per-sonal Story of a Former Content Moderator: 'Let Me Show You the Content'" (离职内 容审核员的口述: "我把内容扒给你看"), September 7, 2018, http://sa.sogou.com/sgsearch /sgs_tc_news.php?req=xtQwEecADjQWW8S5Ss9P83kHOiGZ-KxvZlJx8T_zWIbRA QTh8SwwvoqUr1dbzQe1&user_type=1.

59. WeChat comment on Yan, "Who Forced Her to Tell the Truth?," March 15, 2020.

60. Reader's comment on Fang Fang's Weibo posting, March 10, 2020.

61. "Hubei University Professor Liang Yanping Publishes Inappropriate Speech" (湖北大学教授梁艳萍发表不当言论), April 28, 2020, https://new.qq.com/omn/20200428/20200428A0GGX200.html;"Hubei University's Newest Notice Concerning Teacher Liang Yanping" (教师梁艳萍事件, 湖北大学最新通报), June 20, 2020, https://www.sohu.com/a/403119569_161795; "Does Hainan University Retired Teacher Wang Xiaoni Publish Inappropriate Speech? A Response from the University" (海南大学退休教师王小妮发表不当言论? 校方回应), April 30, 2020, https://news.sina.com.cn/2020-04-30/doc-iirczymi9215915.shtml.

62. "Heart-Rending! Woman in Wuhan Beat Gong on Balcony to Plead for a Hospital Bed for Her Mother" (心酸! 武汉女子阳台上敲锣为母亲求床位), February 9, 2020, https://v.ifeng.com/c/7tvjdGqD33Y?_CPB_404_R3=; "Woman Who Beats Gong to Cry Out for Help for Her Mom Recovers and Returns Home" (敲锣救母女子痊愈归家), *Beijing News* (新京报), April 12, 2020, https://news.163.com/20/0412/05/FA062JP400019B3E.html.

63. Quoted in "Woman Who Beats Gong to Save Mother, Here She Comes Again!" (敲锣救母的她, 再次敲起了锣!), May 14, 2020, https://mp.weixin.qq.com/s/pd_1GveDMd6NboMb9uBMvA; "Gong-Beating Woman Ends Quarantine on April 10, and Then Attacks Fang Fang" (敲锣女4月10日解除隔离, 发微博骂方方), May 14, 2020, https://news.163.com/20/0412/05/FA062JP400019B3E.html.

64. Second Uncle's Diary, May 16, 2020.

8. COVID NATIONALISM

1. Mark Juergensmeyer, "COVID-19 and Cultural Nationalism," *Global-e* 13, no. 41 (June 26, 2020), https://www.21global.ucsb.edu/global-e/june-2020/covid-19-and-cultural-nationalism.

2. Katie Benner and Michael D. Shear, "After Threats, Anthony Fauci to Receive Enhanced Personal Security," *New York Times*, April 1, 2020, https://www.nytimes.com/2020/04/01/us/politics/coronavirus-fauci-security.html

3. Mr. Song's Diary, March 13, 2020.

4. Sister Meng's Diary, March 1, 2020, quoting Yuval Harari, *21 Lessons for the 21st Century* (New York: Spiegel and Grau, 2018), chapter 13, "War: Never Underestimate Human Stupidity"; this book has a best-selling Chinese translation.

5. Sister Meng's Diary, April 22, 2020. On the policy of a new pension raise, see Ministry of Human Resources and Social Security of People's Republic of China 中国人力资源社会保障部, "The Ministry of Human Resources and Social Security and the Ministry of Finance Notice Concerning the Adjustment of Basic Retiree Pensions in 2020" (人力资源社会保障部 财政部关于2020年调整退休人员基本养老金的通知), April 10, 2020, http://www.gov.cn/zhengce/zhengceku/2020-04/19/content_5504190.htm.

6. Mr. Fei's Diary, April 21, 2020.

7. The phrase "add oil" appears under the entry *add* in *The Oxford English Dictionary*, which traces its origin to the Cantonese words *ga yau*, "with reference to petrol being

injected into an engine." The earliest example cited in the OED is from 1964. The Shanghai-based newspaper *Shen Bao* (申报, *Shanghai News*), however, contains many instances of the use of *jia you* going as far back as 1928. A sports story in the May 17, 1928, issue of *Shen Bao* reports the audiences cheering the teams by shouting, "Jiayou!" One of the two teams was from Nankai University in Tianjian, and those who rooted for it shouted, "Nankai, jia you!" The opponents of the Nankai team shouted back: "Nankai, jia you, and scramble an egg" (*Nankai jia you chao jizi'er* 南开加油炒鸡子儿). Based on this usage, some may think that the "oil" in "add oil" means cooking oil rather than petroleum, but that is a misreading of the original text in *Shen Bao*. In the original text, the audiences who shouted "Nankai, jia you, and scramble an egg" were not rooting for the Nankai team but for Nankai's opposing team. "Scramble an egg" is another way of saying "score 0" because an egg has the oval shape of the number 0. The audiences simply extended the meaning of *jia you* to mean cooking oil here in order to make their humorous point. See Hong Xiao 红绡, "Funny Stories About Ball Games in North China" (华北球战中之趣闻), *Shen Bao* (申报, *Shanghai News*), May 17, 1928. Also see the online article "Where Does 'Jiayou' Come From?" (加油是怎么来的?), February 25, 2020, https://kuaibao.qq.com/s /20200225AZPKXD00.

8. Axel Honneth, *The Struggle for Recognition: The Moral Grammar of Social Conflicts*, trans. Joel Anderson (Cambridge, MA: MIT Press, 1995), 137; Charles H. Cooley, *Human Nature and the Social Order* (New York: Scribner's, 1922), 184–85; Thomas J. Scheff, *Bloody Revenge: Emotions, Nationalism, and War* (Boulder, CO: Westview Press, 1994), 45–46.

9. Florian Schneider, *China's Digital Nationalism* (Oxford: Oxford University Press, 2018).

10. Foreign Ministry spokesperson Hua Chunying's daily briefing, February 4, 2020, https://www.fmprc.gov.cn/mfa_eng/xwfw_665399/s2510_665401/2511_665403 /t1740278.shtml.

11. Walter Russell Mead, "China Is the Real Sick Man of Asia," *Wall Street Journal*, February 3, 2020, https://www.wsj.com/articles/china-is-the-real-sick-man-of-asia-11580 773677.

12. Foreign Ministry spokesperson Zhao Lijian, regular press conference, February 24, 2020, https://www.fmprc.gov.cn/mfa_eng/xwfw_665399/s2510_665401/2511_665403 /t1748946.shtml.

13. Li Xiaoyan's Diary, February 25, 2020.

14. Mr. Yun's Diary, March 20, 2020.

15. "Chinese Students in Southampton Are Beaten Up, Chinese Embassy to the U.K. Issues Announcement" (南安普顿大学中国留学生被殴打, 中国驻英国使馆发布声明), *Beijing News* (新京报), March 25, 2020, http://www.bjnews.com.cn/news/2020/03/25/708529 .html.

16. Wang Ruochong's New York Pandemic Diary, May 30, 2020.

17. Panda Ponders Diary, March 31, 2020.

18. Vancouver Pandemic Diary, May 1, 2020.

19. Philadelphia Pandemic Diary, April 20, 2020.

20. Helier Cheung, Zhaoyin Feng, and Boer Deng, "Coronavirus: What Attacks on Asians Reveal About American Identity," *BBC News*, May 27, 2020, https://www.bbc.com/news/world-us-canada-52714804. Since March 2020, anti-Asian racism and violence have only gotten worse in the United States. See Weiyi Cai, Audra D. S. Burch, and Jugal K. Patel, "Swelling Anti-Asian Violence: Who Is Being Attacked Where," *New York Times*, April 3, 2021, https://www.nytimes.com/interactive/2021/04/03/us/anti-asian-attacks.html.

21. For one such story, see "Please Distribute Urgently! Some Chinese Students Had Their Electronics Confiscated at U.S. Customs on Route Back to China" (紧急扩散! 部分留学生回国时被美国海关强行没收所有电子设备!), *Insights* (视界), July 20, 2020, https://mp.weixin.qq.com/s/gjVgpWayc_Q8FI68j-v4MA.

22. Little Mao's Diary, March 26, 2020.

23. Little Mao's Diary, March 31, 2020.

24. For lengthy and detailed descriptions of the ordeals Chinese students experienced in traveling back to China in the summer of 2020, see Er Lu 二璐, "Diary About Returning to China for Quarantine from New York" (纽约回国隔离日记), September 30, October 2, 3, 6, and 24, 2020, in the author's archive.

25. Sheridan Prasso, "Lawsuits Against China Escalate Covid-19 Blame Game with U.S.," *Bloomberg*, May 6, 2020, https://www.bloomberg.com/news/articles/2020-05-06/lawsuits-against-china-escalate-covid-19-blame-game-with-u-s.

26. Alex Isenstadt, "GOP Memo Urges Anti-China Assault Over Coronavirus," *Politico*, April 24, 2020, https://www.politico.com/news/2020/04/24/gop-memo-anti-china-coronavirus-207244.

27. Michael D. Shear et al., "Inside Trump's Failure: The Rush to Abandon Leadership Role on the Virus," *New York Times*, July 18, 2020, https://www.nytimes.com/2020/07/18/us/politics/trump-coronavirus-response-failure-leadership.html.

28. Joseph W. Esherick, *The Origins of the Boxer Uprising* (Berkeley: University of California Press, 1987); Paul A. Cohen, *History in Three Keys: The Boxers as Event, Experience, and Myth* (New York: Columbia University Press, 1997); Jonathan D. Spence, *The Search for Modern China*, 3rd ed. (New York: Norton, 2012).

29. Esherick, *The Origins of the Boxer Uprising*, 311. On contemporary memories of the historical events in China's "Century of Humiliation," see Peter Gries, *China's New Nationalism: Pride, Politics, and Diplomacy* (Berkeley: University of California Press, 2004); Zheng Wang, *Never Forget National Humiliation: Historical Memory in Chinese Politics and Foreign Relations* (New York: Columbia University Press, 2012).

30. Mr. Wen's Diary, April 8, 2020.

31. "The U.S. Must Answer These Ten Questions" (这10个追问, 美国必须回答), *People's Daily* (人民日报), May 1, 2020, http://world.people.com.cn/n1/2020/0501/c1002–31695371.html.

32. Zhao Lijian, tweet, March 12, 2020, Twitter, https://twitter.com/zlj517/status/1238111898828066823.

33. Derek Wallbank and *Bloomberg*, "Twitter Applies Another Fact Check—This Time to China Spokesman's Tweets About Virus Origins," *Fortune*, May 28, 2020, https://fortune.com/2020/05/28/twitter-fact-check-zhao-lijian-coronavirus-origin/.

34. Jonathan Swan and Bethany Allen-Ebrahimian, "Top Chinese Official Disowns U.S. Military Lab Coronavirus Conspiracy," *Axios*, March 22, 2020, https://www.axios.com /china-coronavirus-ambassador-cui-tiankai-1b0404e8-026d-4b7d-8290 -98076f95df14.html.

35. The Twitbase.com research is discussed in Guobin Yang, "Power and Transgression in the Global Media Age: The Strange Case of Twitter in China," in *Communication and Power in the Global Era: Orders and Borders*, ed. Marwan M. Kraidy (London: Routledge, 2013), 166–83.

36. For example, Chinese Storytellers (@CNStorytellers) defines itself as "a community serving and elevating Chinese professionals in the global media industry." NüVoices (@NuVoices) is an "international editorial collective celebrating the creative, interdisciplinary work of women on the broad subject of China."

37. See chapters in Alexander C. Cook, ed., *Mao's Little Red Book: A Global History* (New York: Cambridge University Press, 2014).

38. See chapters in Monroe Price and Daniel Dayan, eds., *Owning the Olympics: Narratives of the New China* (Ann Arbor: University of Michigan Press, 2009).

39. "Beijing in 45b Yuan Global Media Drive," *South China Morning Post*, January 13, 2009, https://www.scmp.com/article/666847/beijing-45b-yuan-global-media-drive.

40. Zhao Alexandre Huang and Rui Wang, "'Panda Engagement' in China's Digital Public Diplomacy," *Asian Journal of Communication* 30, no. 2 (March 3, 2020): 118–40.

41. Manya Koetse, "The PRC Twitter List: The Rise of China on Twitter," *What's on Weibo* (blog), July 21, 2020, https://www.whatsonweibo.com/the-prc-twitter-list-the-rise-of -china-on-twitter/.

42. For example, in "The PRC Twitter List" Koetse notes that the account of the China State Council Information Office (@chinascio) used slang terms such as *dude* and *bro* in its tweets, "causing hilarity among Twitter users."

43. Foreign Ministry spokesperson Hua Chunying's regular press conference, July 29, 2019, https://www.fmprc.gov.cn/mfa_eng/xwfw_665399/s2510_665401/2511_665403 /t1684227.shtml.

44. White House guidelines quoted in Erin Banco, "White House Pushes U.S. Officials to Criticize China for Coronavirus 'Cover-Up,'" *Daily Beast*, March 21, 2020, https://www .thedailybeast.com/white-house-pushes-us-officials-to-criticize-china-for -coronavirus-cover-up.

45. Hua Chunying, tweets, March 22, 2020, Twitter, https://twitter.com/SpokespersonCHN /status/1241741098055135234.

46. Foreign Ministry spokesperson Geng Shuang's regular press conference, March 12, 2020, https://www.fmprc.gov.cn/mfa_eng/xwfw_665399/s2510_665401/2511_665403 /t1755093.shtml.

47. "Foreign Ministry's Geng Shuang Shows You the Power of the Chinese Language" (外交部耿爽让你看到语文的力量), *Luqi Online* (鲁齐在线), June 6, 2020, https://mp .weixin.qq.com/s/N4sLTER6kYNi6TNSf4IiyA.

48. "Foreign Ministry's Geng Shuang Shows You the Power of the Chinese Language."

49. Ms. Spring's Diary, March 12, 2020.

50. Melon Mass's Diary, March 14, 2020.

51. A *bei* is a mythical wolflike animal that is smarter than a wolf but cannot run on its own because its two front legs are very short. A *bei* would often walk with a wolf by putting its front legs on the body of the wolf and would offer advice to the wolf.

52. For an excellent interpretation of Cui Jian's songs, see W. L. Chong, "Young China's Voice of the 1980s: Rock Star Cui Jian," *China Information* 6, no. 1 (June 1, 1991): 55–74.

53. Sheng-mei Ma, *Sinophone–Anglophone Cultural Duet* (London: Palgrave MacMillan, 2017), 10.

54. Justin Hill, "Jiang Rong: The Hour of the Wolf," *Independent*, March 21, 2008, https://www.independent.co.uk/arts-entertainment/books/features/jiang-rong-the-hour-of-the-wolf-798697.html.

55. Hill, "Jiang Rong."

56. For a recent study of the sent-down movement, see Emily Honig and Xiaojian Zhao, *Across the Great Divide: The Sent-Down Youth Movement in Mao's China, 1968–1980* (Cambridge: Cambridge University Press, 2019).

57. Jiang Rong, *Wolf Totem*, trans. Howard Goldblatt (New York: Penguin, 2008), 377.

58. "The 2015 Second WiseLink Reading Festival Launched in Fanfare: Read *Wolf Totem* and Create a Wolfish Work Team" (2015年第二届智联读书节火热启动: 读《狼图腾》, 打造狼性执行团队), WiseLink Real Estate 智联商业, May 27, 2015, http://www.hzzldc.com/wap/newdetails.aspx?id=1345&tid=646.

59. Scott Mendelson, "'Wolf Warrior 2' Cracks 100 All-Time Biggest Grossers List," *Forbes*, August 14, 2017, https://www.forbes.com/sites/scottmendelson/2017/08/14/box-office-wolf-warrior-2-cracks-100-all-time-biggest-grossers-list/.

60. Ministry of Foreign Affairs of the People's Republic of China, "State Councilor and Foreign Minister Wang Yi Meets the Press," May 24, 2020, https://www.fmprc.gov.cn/mfa_eng/wjb_663304/wjbz_663308/2461_663310/t1782262.shtml.

61. "Ambassador to U.K. Liu Xiaoming: 'It's Because There Are "Wolves" in This World That There Are "Wolf Warriors"'" (驻英大使刘晓明: "之所以有 '战狼' 是因为这个世界有 '狼'"), CCTV.com, May 25, 2020, http://m.news.cctv.com/2020/05/24/ARTI8BYmADeqivsgNvMiMRF4200524.shtml.

62. Jeffrey M. Berry and Sarah Sobieraj, *The Outrage Industry: Political Opinion Media and the New Incivility* (Oxford: Oxford University Press, 2013), 6–7.

63. Berry and Sobieraj, *The Outrage Industry*, 36.

64. Benjamin Moffitt, *The Global Rise of Populism: Performance, Political Style, and Representation* (Stanford, CA: Stanford University Press, 2016), 45.

65. "After Geng Shuang, 'Wolf-Warrior Spokesperson' Zhao Lijian Is Trending: How Tough Is This 48-Year-Old Guy?" (继耿爽后, "战狼发言人" 赵立坚再上热搜, 48岁的他到底多厉害?), On Finance and Market (论经说市), July 8, 2020, in the author's archive.

66. "The East Is Pink," *Economist*, August 13, 2016, https://www.economist.com/china/2016/08/13/the-east-is-pink.

67. Another reason why the new patriots are called "Little Pinks" is that one of the main websites of mobilization, an internet literature website, has pink as its background color.

68. Berry and Sobieraj, *The Outrage Industry*, 127.

69. Benedict Anderson, *Imagined Communities: Reflections on the Origin and Spread of Nationalism* (New York: Verso, 1983), 4. For a complication of Anderson's use of emotions, see Barbara H. Rosenwein, "Afterword: Imagined Emotions for Imagined Communities," in *Imagined Communities on the Baltic Rim*, ed. Wojtek Jezierski and Lars Hermanson (Amsterdam: Amsterdam University Press, 2016), 381–88.

70. Sister Meng's Diary, April 22, 2020.

9. MOURNING AND REMEMBERING

1. Chu Ma 楚马 and Xuan Yue 炫悦, "Diary of Two Walking Trees" (两颗行走的树), April 8, 2020.

2. Chen Weihua, "China's Effort in Virus Fight Lauded as Individuals Honored," *China Daily*, September 8, 2020, https://www.chinadaily.com.cn/a/202009/08/WS5f569 8dba310675eafc580a1.html.

3. Oscar Holland and Shanshan Wang, "Beijing Art Exhibition Glorifies China's Covid-19 Response," CNN, August 16, 2020, https://www.cnn.com/style/article/beijing-covid -art-exhibition/index.html.

4. For example, on February 5, 2020, Zhang Meiling 张美玲, a nurse in a Wuhan hospital, fainted, fell, and suffered from several bone fractures on her way back to her hotel dorm after working for twelve hours of a night shift. See "Nurse Falls and Fractures Nose Bones, Surgery Continues After Delay" (护士累倒鼻骨骨折, 延后手术继续战斗), February 12, 2020, https://www.sohu.com/a/372578892_100159953?spm=smpc.author.fd-d .20.1581638400050Zw5NOp7&_trans_=000019_ha0123_pc.

5. China Artists Association 中国美术家协会, "Unity Is Power: Anti-Coronavirus Art Exhibition Opens in China National Museum" (众志成城——抗疫主题美术作品展在中国国家博物馆开幕), August 3, 2020, https://www.caanet.org.cn/newsdetail.mx?id=7740.

6. Arlie's Diary, February 7, 2020.

7. *Global Times* (@globaltimesnews), Twitter post, February 7, 2020, https://twitter.com /globaltimesnews/status/1225463707255242752.

8. Fang Fang's Diary, February 7, 2020.

9. Guo Jing's Diary, February 7, 2020.

10. Guo Jing's diary, February 7, 2020, emphasis in original.

11. Fang Fang's Diary, February 7, 2020.

12. Mark Oliver, "China Sacks Health Minister Over SARS," *Guardian*, April 20, 2003, https://www.theguardian.com/world/2003/apr/20/sars.markoliver; Philip P. Pan, "Chinese Pressure Dissident: Physician Hero of SARS Crisis Detained Since June 1," *Washington Post*, July 5, 2004.

13. Lan Xi's Diary, February 7, 2020.

14. Lan Xi's Diary, February 7, 2020, quoting Stefan Zweig, *Decisive Moments in History: Twelve Historical Miniatures* (Riverside, CA: Ariadne Press, 1999), 184.

15. "Fifty Small Things About Li Wenliang" (关于李文亮的50件小事), LateBus, February 8, 2020, no longer available online, in the author's archive.

16. I watched and tweeted this video on Twitter at 9:26 a.m., February 7, 2020, EST.

17. Sophie Wu, "Snow on Tonghui River: How Do People Mourn Dr. Li Wenliang in Beijing" (通惠河畔的雪: 在北京, 人們如何纪念医生李文亮), Initium Media, February 20, 2020, https://theinitium.com/article/20200210-notes-beijing-li-wenliang/.

18. Original document in the author's archive.

19. Guo Jing's Diary, February 8, 2020.

20. Tan Jianxing 覃建行, "'Whistleblower' of Novel Coronavirus Li Wenliang: Truth Is More Important Than Rehabilitation" (新冠肺炎 "吹哨人" 李文亮: 真相比平反更重要), *Caixin* (财新), January 31, 2020; the original web link has been removed, but the article is archived at https://project-gutenberg.github.io/nCovMemory-Web/post/59185d4162 7a723c19bae95bab17dafe/.

21. Charlotte Bruckermann, "Rumours as Moral Action: Contesting the Local State Through Housing in China," *Critique of Anthropology* 38, no. 2 (2018): 190.

22. Xiao Yin's Diary, February 7, 2020.

23. Xiao Yin's Diary, February 7, 2020.

24. Xiao Yin's Diary, February 7, 2020. The "height" of a particular block refers to the number of blocks preceding it in the blockchain. On its website, IBM defines a blockchain as "a shared, immutable ledger that facilitates the process of recording transactions and tracking assets in a business network" (https://www.ibm.com/topics/what-is -blockchain, n.d.).

25. Readers' comments on Li Wenliang's Weibo account, February 6, 2020, in the author's archive.

26. Also see Li Yuan and Rumsey Taylor, "How Thousands in China Gently Mourn a Coronavirus Whistle-Blower," *New York Times*, April 13, 2020, https://www.nytimes.com /interactive/2020/04/13/technology/coronavirus-doctor-whistleblower-weibo.html. The Chinese version of this story was published as Li Yuan 袁莉, "When Li Wenliang's Weibo Becomes China's Wailing Wall" (当李文亮的微博成为中国的哭墙), *New York Times* (Chinese), April 14, 2020, https://cn.nytimes.com/china/20200414/coronavirus -doctor-whistleblower-weibo/.

27. Yuanban Shidalin 院办屎大淋, "Everyday, Tens of Thousands of People Write Diaries on Li Wenliang's Weibo Timeline" (每天都有成千上万人在李文亮微博下写日记), March 10, 2020, https://mp.weixin.qq.com/s/frdiMgiKYjvvo1vVArazmQ.

28. Reader's comment on Li Wenliang's Weibo account, March 18, 2020.

29. For "affective publics," see Zizi Papacharissi, *Affective Publics: Sentiment, Technology, and Politics* (New York: Oxford University Press, 2014).

30. Using computational methods, Zhou Baohua and Zhong Yuan collected and analyzed all the user comments from February 6, 2020, to February 7, 2021, on Li Wenliang's last Weibo posting. Out of the total number of 1,343,192 comments in their data set, 38 percent are messages of mourning, 20 percent are everyday greetings, and 16 percent are expressions of personal feelings and even personal secrets. See Zhou Baohua

周葆华 and Zhong Yuan 钟媛, "Social Media, Collective Mourning, and Extended Affective Space: A Computational Communication Analysis of Li Wenliang's Weibo Comments(2020–2021)"(春天的花开秋天的风:社交媒体、集体悼念与延展性情感空间—以李文亮微博2020–2021 为例的算传播分析), *Chinese Journal of Journalism and Communication* (国际新闻界) 3 (2021): 90–91.

31. Reader's comment on Li Wenliang's Weibo account, February 11, 2020.

32. Readers' comments on Li Wenliang's Weibo account, March 19, 2020.

33. Reader's comment on Li Wenliang's Weibo account, March 19, 2020, in the author's archive. On the investigation, see Investigative Team of the National Supervisory Commission 国家监委调查组, "Public Announcement Concerning the Investigation of Certain Issues Reported by the Masses About Dr. Li Wenliang" (国家监委调查组发布《关于群众反映的涉及李文亮医生有关情况调查的通报》), March 19, 2020, http://m.news.cctv.com/2020/03/19/ARTIrEO6nz5wKzeVnNlyBgTM200319.shtml.

34. Readers' comments on Li Wenliang's Weibo account, March 20, 2020.

35. Readers' comments on Li Wenliang's Weibo account, February 7 and March 19, 2020.

36. Andrew J. Nathan, *Chinese Democracy* (Berkeley: University of California Press, 1986).

37. Steven Pfaff and Guobin Yang, "Double-Edged Rituals and the Symbolic Resources of Collective Action: Political Commemorations and the Mobilization of Protest in 1989," *Theory and Society* 30, no. 4 (2001): 539–89.

38. Louisa Lim, *The People's Republic of Amnesia: Tiananmen Revisited*, illus. ed. (New York: Oxford University Press, 2014).

39. Guobin Yang, *The Red Guard Generation and Political Activism in China* (New York: Columbia University Press, 2016), 80–83.

40. Fang Fang's Diary, March 5, 2020.

41. "National Supervisory Commission Responsible Person Says Li Wenliang Is Communist Party Member, Not an Anti-establishment Person" (国家监委调查组负责人: 李文亮是共产党员, 不是所谓的'反体制'人物), *Chinanews* (中国新闻网), March 19, 2020, http://www.chinanews.com/gn/2020/03-19/9131330.shtml.

42. "14 Individuals in Hubei Who Died on the Frontline Are Conferred Martyr Status" (湖北14名防疫一线牺牲人员被评为首批烈士), *Beijing New* (新京报), April 2, 2020, https://news.sina.com.cn/c/2020-04-02/doc-iimxyqwa4752641.shtml.

43. Xiao Nian is a traditional Chinese festival that falls a week before the Lunar New Year and marks the beginning of the celebrations. Hence, its name literally means "Small Year."

44. Xiao Yin 小引, "In Memory of Li Wenliang" (纪念李文亮), WeChat, February 7, 2021, https://mp.weixin.qq.com/s/8BDYsnmr2W3LzFGeW5gTtA.

45. Xiao Yin's Diary, February 7, 2020.

46. Guobin Yang and Shiwen Wu, "Remembering Disappeared Websites in China: Passion, Community, and Youth," *New Media & Society* 20, no. 6 (June 1, 2018): 2107–124.

47. Wendy Hui Kyong Chun, "The Enduring Ephemeral, or the Future Is a Memory," *Critical Inquiry* 35, no. 1 (2008): 171.

48. Kirsten Foot, Barbara Warnick, and Steven M. Schneider, "Web-Based Memorializing After September 11: Toward a Conceptual Framework," *Journal of Computer-Mediated Communication* 11, no. 1 (2005): 78.

49. Foot, Warnick, and Schneider, "Web-Based Memorializing After September 11."

50. Guobin Yang, "'A Portrait of Martyr Jiang Qing': The Chinese Cultural Revolution on the Internet," in *Re-envisioning the Chinese Revolution: The Politics and Poetics of Collective Memories in Reform China*, ed. Ching Kwan Lee and Guobin Yang (Washington, DC: Woodrow Wilson Press; Stanford, CA: Stanford University Press, 2007), 287–316.

51. The original URL of the website, now long gone, was http://china1966.vip.sina.com/index.html. On these Cultural Revolution Memorial websites, see Yang, "'A Portrait of Martyr Jiang Qing.'"

52. Chun, "The Enduring Ephemeral," 154.

53. Yang and Wu, "Remembering Disappeared Websites in China."

54. Amanda Lagerkvist, "The Netlore of the Infinite: Death (and Beyond) in the Digital Memory Ecology," *New Review of Hypermedia and Multimedia* 21, nos. 1–2 (2015): 185–95.

CONCLUSION

1. For an insightful study of the Tiananmen protest that illuminates the meaning of the tank man, see Craig Calhoun, *Neither Gods nor Emperors: Students and the Struggle for Democracy in China* (Berkeley: University of California Press, 1994).

2. Kenneth Burke, *A Grammar of Motives* (Berkeley: University of California Press, 1969), 3.

3. Daniel Silver, Terry Nichols Clark, and Clemente Jesus Navarro Yanez, "Scenes: Social Context in an Age of Contingency," *Social Forces* 88, no. 5 (July 1, 2010): 2297.

4. Barry Shank, *Dissonant Identities: The Rock 'n' Roll Scene in Austin, Texas* (Hanover, CT: Wesleyan University Press, 1994), 122.

5. Kimberly Creasap, "Social Movement Scenes: Place-Based Politics and Everyday Resistance," *Sociology Compass* 6, no. 2 (2012): 183.

6. Gong Jingqi 龚菁琦, "The Whistle-Giver" (发哨子的人), *People* (人物), March 10, 2020, currently available at https://medium.com/coronavirus19/%E4%BA%BA%E7%89%A9-%E5%8F%91%E5%93%A8%E5%AD%90%E7%9A%84%E4%BA%BA-26e2c5b64394.

7. Political scientists call the overconcern for appearance "'image-building' irresponsible behavior" or "performative governance." See Yongshun Cai, "Irresponsible State: Local Cadres and Image-Building in China," *Journal of Communist Studies and Transition Politics* 20, no. 4 (2004): 20–41; Iza Ding, "Performative Governance," *World Politics* 72, no. 4 (October 2020): 525–56; Alex L. Wang, "Symbolic Legitimacy and Chinese Environmental Reform," *Environmental Law* 48, no. 4 (2018): 699–760.

8. Mao Zedong, quoted in Christian P. Sorace, *Shaken Authority: China's Communist Party and the 2008 Sichuan Earthquake* (Ithaca, NY: Cornell University Press, 2017), 31.

9. Daniel Leese, *Mao Cult: Rhetoric and Ritual in China's Cultural Revolution* (Cambridge: Cambridge University Press, 2011).

10. Sorace, *Shaken Authority*, 31.

11. Margaret E. Roberts, *Censored: Distraction and Diversion Inside China's Great Firewall* (Princeton, NJ: Princeton University Press, 2018).

12. Li Zhang, *Anxious China: Inner Revolution and Politics of Psychotherapy* (Oakland: University of California Press, 2020).

13. World Health Organization, "Press Conference of WHO–China Joint Mission on COVID-19," February 24, 2020, https://www.who.int/docs/default-source/coronaviruse /transcripts/joint-mission-press-conference-script-english-final.pdf?sfvrsn=51c90b 9e_2.

14. Joseph Fewsmith and Andrew J. Nathan, "Authoritarian Resilience Revisited: Joseph Fewsmith with Response from Andrew J. Nathan," *Journal of Contemporary China* 28, no. 116 (March 4, 2019): 167–79.

15. Andrew J. Nathan, "China's Changing of the Guard: Authoritarian Resilience," *Journal of Democracy* 14, no. 1 (February 5, 2003): 6–17.

16. Kellee Tsai calls it "authoritarianism with adjectives" ("Evolutionary Governance in China: State–Society Interactions Under Authoritarianism," in *Evolutionary Governance in China: State–Society Relations Under Authoritarianism*, ed. Szu-chien Hsu, Kellee S. Tsai, and Chun-chih Chang [Cambridge, MA: Harvard University Asia Center, 2021], 3–37). For some of the studies of "authoritarianism with adjectives," see Christopher Marquis and Yanhua Bird, "The Paradox of Responsive Authoritarianism: How Civic Activism Spurs Environmental Penalties in China," *Organization Science* 29, no. 5 (June 8, 2018): 948–68; Robert Weller, "Responsive Authoritarianism and Blind-Eye Governance in China," in *Socialism Vanquished, Socialism Challenged: Eastern Europe and China, 1989–2009*, ed. Nina Bandelj and Dorothy J. Solinger (New York: Oxford University Press, 2012), 3–99; Rory Truex, "Consultative Authoritarianism and Its Limits," *Comparative Political Studies* 50, no. 3 (March 1, 2017): 329–61; William Hurst, "Chinese Law and Governance: Moving Beyond Responsive Authoritarianism and the Rule of Law," *Journal of Chinese Governance* 1, no. 3 (July 2, 2016): 457–69; Jidong Chen, Jennifer Pan, and Yiqing Xu, "Sources of Authoritarian Responsiveness: A Field Experiment in China," *American Journal of Political Science* 60, no. 2 (2016): 383–400; Jessica C. Teets, "Let Many Civil Societies Bloom: The Rise of Consultative Authoritarianism in China," *China Quarterly* 213 (2013): 19–38; Ching Kwan Lee and Yonghong Zhang, "The Power of Instability: Unraveling the Microfoundations of Bargained Authoritarianism in China," *American Journal of Sociology* 118, no. 6 (2013): 1475–508; Catherine Owen, "Participatory Authoritarianism: From Bureaucratic Transformation to Civic Participation in Russia and China," *Review of International Studies* 46, no. 4 (October 2020): 415–34.

17. Christopher Heurlin, *Responsive Authoritarianism in China: Land, Protests, and Policy Making* (Cambridge: Cambridge University Press, 2016).

18. You-tien Hsing and Ching Kwan Lee, eds., *Reclaiming Chinese Society: The New Social Activism* (London: Routledge, 2009); Fengshi Wu and Shen Yang, "Web 2.0 and Political Engagement in China," *VOLUNTAS* 27, no. 5 (October 1, 2016): 2055–76; Wei Lit Yew, "Matrix of Free Spaces in China: Mobilizing Citizens and the Law Through Digital and Organizational Spaces," *International Journal of Communication* 13 (July 22, 2019): 3341–360; Guobin Yang, *The Power of the Internet in China: Citizen Activism Online* (New York: Columbia University Press, 2009).

19. Yew, "Matrix of Free Spaces in China," 3342.

20. Engin F. Isin, "Theorizing Acts of Citizenship," in *Acts of Citizenship*, ed. Engin F. Isin and Greg M. Nielsen (London: Zed, 2008), 38.

21. I thank Elizabeth Perry for highlighting for me the significance of inaction as a form of action.

22. Elizabeth J. Perry, "Chinese Conceptions of 'Rights': From Mencius to Mao—and Now," *Perspectives on Politics* 6, no. 1 (March 2008): 37, 45–47; Elizabeth J. Perry, "A New Rights Consciousness?," *Journal of Democracy* 20, no. 3 (July 1, 2009): 17–20; Peter Lorentzen and Suzanne Scoggins, "Understanding China's Rising Rights Consciousness," *China Quarterly* 223 (2015): 638–57; Lianjiang Li, "Rights Consciousness and Rules Consciousness in Contemporary China," *China Journal* 64 (2010): 47–68.

23. Kevin J. O'Brien and Lianjiang Li, *Rightful Resistance in Rural China* (Cambridge: Cambridge University Press, 2006), 26.

24. Harold Garfinkel, quoted in James M. Jasper, *The Art of Moral Protest: Culture, Biography, and Creativity in Social Movements* (Chicago: University of Chicago Press, 1997), 135.

25. Brian Hook, ed., *The Individual and the State in China* (New York: Oxford University Press, 1996); Merle Goldman, Timothy Cheek, and Carol Lee Hamrin, eds., *China's Intellectuals and the State: In Search of a New Relationship* (Cambridge, MA: Harvard University Asia Center, 1987); Lucian W. Pye, "The State and the Individual: An Overview Interpretation," *China Quarterly* 127 (1991): 443–66.

26. On the social origins of these ethical principles of human relationship, see Xiaotong Fei, *From the Soil: The Foundations of Chinese Society*, a translation of Fei Xiaotong, *Xiangtu Zhongguo*, with an introduction and epilogue by Gary G. Hamilton and Wang Zheng (Berkeley: University of California Press, 1993), 76. For studies of moral discourses in contemporary China, see Ellen Oxfeld, *Drink Water, but Remember the Source: Moral Discourse in a Chinese Village* (Berkeley: University of California Press, 2010); Yunxiang Yan, *The Flow of Gifts: Reciprocity and Social Networks in a Chinese Village* (Stanford, CA: Stanford University Press, 1996); Mayfair Mei-Hui Yang, *Gifts, Favors, and Banquets: The Art of Social Relationships in China* (Ithaca, NY: Cornell University Press, 1994).

27. Moral persuasion is a form of relational persuasion similar to relational repression. See Yanhua Deng and Kevin J. O'Brien, "Relational Repression in China: Using Social Ties to Demobilize Protesters," *China Quarterly* 215 (2013): 533–52.

28. Wu Shangzhe 吴尚哲 [Ah-Nian 阿念], *Wuhan Girl An-Nian's Diary* (武汉女孩阿念日记) (Beijing: Beijing Lianhe, 2020), entry for February 10, 2020.

29. Early mobile phones were also seen as magical. See James E. Katz, *Magic in the Air: Mobile Communication and the Transformation of Social Life* (London: Routledge, 2006).

30. Yang, *The Power of the Internet in China*, chap. 7.

31. In early April 2020, Tencent issued an internal report summarizing its contributions to the fight against COVID-19. Besides its popular health-code app on WeChat, Tencent developed apps for virtual education, virtual office, virtual medicine, virtual retail, and even virtual tourism, thus providing digital infrastructures for both fighting COVID-19 and returning to work. See "Tencent's Main Achievements in the Fight Against COVID-19" (腾讯抗击疫情的主要工作), April 5, 2020, unpublished document in the author's archive.

32. David K. Herold and Peter Marolt, eds., *Online Society in China: Creating, Celebrating, and Instrumentalising the Online Carnival* (London: Routledge, 2011).

33. Robert D. Putnam, *Bowling Alone: The Collapse and Revival of American Community* (New York: Simon and Schuster, 2001).

34. Lü Ping 吕频, "Witnessing Twenty Years of Chinese Feminism" (见证中国女权二十年), Initium Media, August 4, 2020, https://theinitium.com/article/20200814-opinion -china-feminist-movement-20-years/.

35. Shaohua Guo, "'Occupying' the Internet: State Media and the Reinvention of Official Culture Online," *Communication and the Public* 3, no. 1 (2018): 19–33.

BIBLIOGRAPHY

Adami, Elisabetta. "Retwitting, Reposting, Repinning; Reshaping Identities Online: Towards a Social Semiotic Multimodal Analysis of Digital Remediation." *LEA—Lingue e letteratura d'Oriente e d'Occidente* 3 (2014): 223–43.

Agence France-Presse. "China Orders Square Dancing 'Aunties' to Avoid Dancing in Cemeteries, Spreading Superstitious Beliefs." November 15, 2017. https://hongkongfp.com/2017/11/15/china-orders-square-dancing-aunties-avoid-dancing-cemeteries-spreading-superstitious-beliefs/.

Althusser, Louis. "Ideology and Ideological State Apparatuses (Notes Towards an Investigation)." 1971. In Louis Althusser, *Lenin and Philosophy and Other Essays*, trans. Ben Brewster, 121–76. New York: Monthly Review Press, 2001.

Amnesty International. "Laws Designed to Silence: The Global Crackdown on Civil Society Organizations." February 21, 2019. https://www.amnesty.org/en/documents/act30/9647/2019/en/.

Anderson, Benedict. *Imagined Communities: Reflections on the Origin and Spread of Nationalism*. New York: Verso, 1983.

Banco, Erin. "White House Pushes U.S. Officials to Criticize China for Coronavirus 'Cover-Up.'" *Daily Beast*, March 21, 2020. https://www.thedailybeast.com/white-house-pushes-us-officials-to-criticize-china-for-coronavirus-cover-up.

Banet-Weiser, Sarah. *Empowered: Popular Feminism and Popular Misogyny*. Durham, NC: Duke University Press, 2018.

Bao, Hongwei. "'Anti–Domestic Violence Little Vaccine': A Wuhan-Based Feminist Activist Campaign During COVID-19." *Interface* 12, no. 1 (July 2020): 53–63.

——. "Diary Writing as Feminist Activism: Guo Jing's Wuhan Lockdown Diary." Modern Chinese Literature and Culture Resource Center, April 27, 2020. https://u.osu.edu/mclc/2020/04/27/guo-jings-wuhan-lockdown-diary/.

——. "Three Women and Their Wuhan Diaries: Women's Writing in a Quarantined Chinese City." *Cha*, October 17, 2020. https://chajournal.blog/2020/10/17/wuhan-diaries/.

Beijing News (新京报). "14 Individuals in Hubei Who Died on the Frontline Are Conferred Martyr Status" (湖北14名防疫一线牺牲人员被评为首批烈士). April 2, 2020. https://news.sina.com.cn/c/2020-04-02/doc-iimxyqwa4752641.shtml.

——. "Chinese Students in Southampton Are Beaten Up, Chinese Embassy to the U.K. Issues Announcement" (南安普顿大学中国留学生被殴打, 中国驻英国使馆发布声明). March 25, 2020. http://www.bjnews.com.cn/news/2020/03/25/708529.html.

——. "Woman Who Beats Gong to Cry Out for Help for Her Mom Recovers and Returns Home" (敲锣救母女子痊愈归家). April 12, 2020. https://news.163.com/20/0412/05/FA062JP400019B3E.html.

Ben-Amos, Batsheva, and Dan Ben-Amos, eds. *The Diary: The Epic of Everyday Life*. 2nd rev. ed. Bloomington: Indiana University Press, 2020.

Benner, Katie, and Michael D. Shear. "After Threats, Anthony Fauci to Receive Enhanced Personal Security." *New York Times*, April 1, 2020. https://www.nytimes.com/2020/04/01/us/politics/coronavirus-fauci-security.html.

Bennett, W. Lance, and Alexandra Segerberg. *The Logic of Connective Action*. Cambridge: Cambridge University Press, 2013.

Berry, Jeffrey M., and Sarah Sobieraj. *The Outrage Industry: Political Opinion Media and the New Incivility*. Oxford: Oxford University Press, 2013.

Berry, Michael. "Translator's Afterword." In Fang Fang, *Wuhan Diary: Dispatches from a Quarantined City*, trans. Michael Berry, 305–313. New York: HarperCollins, 2020.

Blecher, Marc. "The Mass Line and Leader–Mass Relations and Communication in Basic-Level Rural Communities." In *China's New Social Fabric*, edited by Godwin C. Chu and Francis L. K. Hsu, 63–86. London: Kegan Paul International, 1983.

Bloomberg. "Chinese DAMA, the World's Top Investment Group Will Be Certified with a Gold Seal from Alibaba." August 23, 2019. https://www.bloomberg.com/press-releases/2019-08-23/chinese-dama-the-world-s-top-investment-group-will-be-certified-with-a-gold-seal-from-alibaba.

Bräuer, Stephanie. "Becoming Public: Anti–Domestic Violence (ADV) Activism as a Public Event." *China Development Brief*, August 29, 2014. https://chinadevelopmentbrief.cn/reports/becoming-public-anti-domestic-violence-adv-activism-public-event/.

Bruckermann, Charlotte. "Rumours as Moral Action: Contesting the Local State Through Housing in China." *Critique of Anthropology* 38, no. 2 (2018): 188–203.

Buckley, Chris. "Wuhan Dispatch: Losing Track of Time in the Epicenter of China's Coronavirus Outbreak." *New York Times*, February 5, 2020.

Buford, Lena. "A Journey Through Two Decades of Online Diary Community." In *The Diary: The Epic of Everyday Life*, ed. Batsheva Ben-Amos and Dan Ben-Amos, 425–40. Bloomington: Indiana University Press, 2020.

Burke, Kenneth. *A Grammar of Motives*. Berkeley: University of California Press, 1969.

Cai, Weiyi, Audra D. S. Burch, and Jugal K. Patel. "Swelling Anti-Asian Violence: Who Is Being Attacked Where." *New York Times*, April 3, 2021. https://www.nytimes.com/interactive/2021/04/03/us/anti-asian-attacks.html.

Cai, Yongshun. "Irresponsible State: Local Cadres and Image-Building in China." *Journal of Communist Studies and Transition Politics* 20, no. 4 (2004): 20–41.

Caixin (财新). "Chronicle of Wuhan COVID-19 (December 2019–January 20, 2020)" (武汉新型冠状病毒肺炎大事记 [2019年12月–2020年1月20日]). January 20, 2020. http://www.caixin .com/2020-01-20/101506242.html.

——. "Why Does the Hospital Where Li Wenliang Worked Have Such Heavy Casualties?" (李文亮所在医院为何医护人员伤亡惨重?). March 10, 2020. http://china.caixin.com/2020 -03-10/101526309.html.

Calhoun, Craig. *Neither Gods nor Emperors: Students and the Struggle for Democracy in China.* Berkeley: University of California Press, 1994.

Campanelli, Vito. "Toward a Remix Culture: An Existential Perspective." In *The Routledge Companion to Remix Studies*, ed. Eduardo Navas, Owen Gallagher, and xtine burrough, 68–82. New York: Routledge, 2014.

Chamberlain, Heath B. "On the Search for Civil Society in China." *Modern China* 19, no. 2 (1993): 199–215.

Chang Jian 常健 and Xu Qian 徐倩. "A Study of the Role of Various Stakeholders in Doctor-Patient Conflicts—Based on an Analysis of 150 Cases" (医患冲突升级中各类主体作用研究—基于对150个案例的分析). *Journal of the Shanghai Administration Institute* (上海行政学院学报) 18, no. 4 (July 2017): 4–12.

Changjiang Daily (长江日报). "All Residential Communities to Be Under Closed Management" (住宅小区一律实行封闭管理). May 15, 2020.

Cheek, Timothy, David Ownby, and Joshua A. Fogel. "Introduction: Thinking China in the Age of Xi Jinping." In *Voices from the Chinese Century*, ed. Timothy Cheek, David Ownby, and Joshua A. Fogel, 1–26. New York: Columbia University Press, 2019.

——, eds. *Voices from the Chinese Century: Public Intellectual Debate from Contemporary China.* New York: Columbia University Press, 2019.

Chen Chaoyang 陈朝阳 and Tian Dongliang 田栋梁. "Details of Dr. Yang Wen's Murder Revealed" (杨文医生被害细节曝光). *Medical Field* (医学界), December 28, 2019. https://new .qq.com/omn/20191227/20191227A0OZ6O00.html.

Chen, Jidong, Jennifer Pan, and Yiqing Xu. "Sources of Authoritarian Responsiveness: A Field Experiment in China." *American Journal of Political Science* 60, no. 2 (2016): 383–400.

Chen, Simiao, Zongjiu Zhang, Juntao Yang, Jian Wang, Xiaohui Zhai, Till Bärnighausen, and Chen Wang. "Fangcang Shelter Hospitals: A Novel Concept for Responding to Public Health Emergencies." *The Lancet* 395, no. 10232 (April 18, 2020): 1305–14.

Chen, Thomas. "Ai Xiaoming and the Quarantine Counter-Diary." *Los Angeles Review of Books*, March 12, 2021. https://lareviewofbooks.org/article/ai-xiaoming-and-the -quarantine-counter-diary/.

Chen Weihua. "China's Effort in Virus Fight Lauded as Individuals Honored." *China Daily*, September 8, 2020. https://www.chinadaily.com.cn/a/202009/08/WS5f5698dba310675ea fc580a1.html.

Chen, Yujie, Zhifei Mao, and Jack Linchuan Qiu. *Super-Sticky WeChat and Chinese Society.* Bingley, U.K.: Emerald, 2018.

Chen, Zifeng, and Clyde Yicheng Wang. "The Discipline of Happiness: The Foucauldian Use of the 'Positive Energy' Discourse in China's Ideological Works." *Journal of Current Chinese Affairs*, February 23, 2020. https://doi.org/10.1177/1868102619899409.

Cheung, Helier, Zhaoyin Feng, and Boer Deng. "Coronavirus: What Attacks on Asians Reveal About American Identity." *BBC News*, May 27, 2020. https://www.bbc.com/news/world-us-canada-52714804.

China Central Television Station 中国中央电视台. *Fighting Covid in Unity* (同心战疫). Documentary film, episode 1. Beijing, September 2, 2020.

China Development Brief. "The New Draft on the Registration of Social Organisations: 15 Points of Note." August 15, 2018. https://chinadevelopmentbrief.cn/reports/the-new-draft-on-the-registration-of-social-organisations-15-points-of-note/.

China Economic Weekly (中国经济周刊). "Parading in the Street, Slapping the Face, Smashing Mahjong Table—Prevention and Control of COVID Should Follow the Law" (游街、抽耳光、砸麻将桌 . . . 疫情防控也要依法). February 17, 2020. https://mp.weixin.qq.com/s/lrs2TkTtFBTvJ68PUvh5Zw.

ChinaFile. "Document 9: A ChinaFile Translation: How Much Is a Hardline Party Directive Shaping China's Current Political Climate?" November 8, 2013. https://www.chinafile.com/document-9-chinafile-translation.

China Internet Network Information Center. "The 45th China Statistical Report on Internet Development." April 2020. http://www.cnnic.net/.

China Medical Doctors Association 中国医师协会. "White Paper on the Professional Conditions of Medical Practitioners" (中国医师执业状况白皮书). 2015. http://www.cmda.net/zlwqgzdt/596.jhtml.

——. "White Paper on the Professional Conditions of Medical Practitioners in China" (中国医师职业状况白皮书). December 2017. http://www.cmda.net/u/cms/www/201807/06181247ffex.pdf.

Chinanews (中国新闻网). "National Supervisory Commission Responsible Person Says Li Wenliang Is Communist Party Member, Not an Anti-establishment Person" (国家监委调查组负责人：李文亮是共产党员，不是所谓的'反体制人物), March 19, 2020. http://www.chinanews.com/gn/2020/03-19/9131330.shtml.

China Watch Institute, China Daily Institute of Contemporary China Studies, Tsinghua University School of Health Policy and Management, and Peking Union Medical College. *China's Fight Against COVID-19.* April 21, 2020. https://enapp.chinadaily.com.cn/a/202004/21/AP5e9e2c60a3100bb08af0898c.html?from=timeline&isappinstalled=0.

China Youth Daily (中国青年报). "Institutional Reform of the Salary and Compensation System in Public Hospitals Is the Main Trend" (公立医院医生薪酬制度改革是大势所趋). May 25, 2017. http://www.xinhuanet.com//politics/2017-05/25/c_1121031738.htm.

Chong, W. L. "Young China's Voice of the 1980s: Rock Star Cui Jian." *China Information* 6, no. 1 (June 1, 1991): 55–74.

Chun, Wendy Hui Kyong. "The Enduring Ephemeral, or the Future Is a Memory." *Critical Inquiry* 35, no. 1 (2008): 148–71.

Clark, Rosemary. "'Hope in a Hashtag': The Discursive Activism of #WhyIStayed." *Feminist Media Studies* 16, no. 5 (September 2, 2016): 788–804.

Clark-Parsons, Rosemary. "'I SEE YOU, I BELIEVE YOU, I STAND WITH YOU': #MeToo and the Performance of Networked Feminist Visibility." *Feminist Media Studies*, first view, June 24, 2019. https://doi:10.1080/14680777.2019.1628797.

Cohen, Paul A. *History in Three Keys: The Boxers as Event, Experience, and Myth*. New York: Columbia University Press, 1997.

Cook, Alexander C. *Mao's Little Red Book: A Global History*. Cambridge: Cambridge University Press, 2014.

Cooley, Charles H. *Human Nature and the Social Order*. New York: Scribner's, 1922.

Creasap, Kimberly. "Social Movement Scenes: Place-Based Politics and Everyday Resistance." *Sociology Compass* 6, no. 2 (2012): 182–91.

Creemers, Rogier. "Cyber China: Upgrading Propaganda, Public Opinion Work, and Social Management for the Twenty-First Century." *Journal of Contemporary China* 26, no. 103 (January 2, 2017): 85–100.

Davidson, Helen. "Chinese Writer Faces Online Backlash over Wuhan Lockdown Diary." *Guardian*, April 10, 2020. https://www.theguardian.com/world/2020/apr/10/chinese-writer-fang-fang-faces-online-backlash-wuhan-lockdown-diary.

Davis, Deborah S. "Urban Chinese Homeowners as Citizen-Consumers." In *The Ambivalent Consumer: Questioning Consumption in East Asia and the West*, edited by Sheldon Garon and Patricia L. Maclachlan, 281–99. Ithaca, NY: Cornell University Press, 2006.

Davis, Deborah S., and Helen F. Siu, eds. *SARS: Reception and Interpretation in Three Chinese Cities*. London: Routledge, 2006.

De Kloet, Jeroen, Thomas Poell, Zeng Guohua, and Chow Yiu Fai. "The Platformization of Chinese Society: Infrastructure, Governance, and Practice." *Chinese Journal of Communication* 12, no. 3 (July 3, 2019): 249–56.

Demick, Barbara. "Chinese Toddler's Death Evokes Outpouring of Grief and Guilt." *Los Angeles Times*, October 21, 2011. https://www.latimes.com/archives/la-xpm-2011-oct-21-la-mobile-china-toddler-death-story.html.

Deng Xiaoping 邓小平. *Selected Works of Deng Xiaoping* (邓小平文选). Vol. 2. Beijing: Renmin chubanshe, 1994.

Deng, Yanhua, and Kevin J. O'Brien. "Relational Repression in China: Using Social Ties to Demobilize Protesters." *China Quarterly* 215 (2013): 533–52.

Ding, Iza. "Performative Governance." *World Politics* 72, no. 4 (October 2020): 525–56.

Dodge, Patrick Shaou-Whea. "Imagining Dissent: Contesting the Facade of Harmony Through Art and the Internet in China." In *Imagining China: Rhetorics of Nationalism in an Age of Globalization*, ed. Stephen John Hartnett, Lisa B. Keränen, and Donovan Conley, 311–38. East Lansing: Michigan State University Press, 2017.

Douglas, Mary. *Risk and Blame: Essays in Cultural Theory*. London: Routledge, 1994.

Duara, Prasenjit. "The Discourse of Civilization and Pan-Asianism." *Journal of World History* 12, no. 1 (2001): 99–130.

Dynon, Nicholas. "'Four Civilizations' and the Evolution of Post-Mao Chinese Socialist Ideology." *China Journal* 60 (2008): 83–109.

Economic Observer (经济观察报). "Wuhan Time: The Puzzle of the Twenty Days from the Arrival of Experts Team to the Lockdown" (武汉时间: 从专家组抵达到封城的谜之20天). February 7, 2020. http://www.eeo.com.cn/2020/0207/375826.shtml.

Economist. "The East Is Pink." August 13, 2016. https://www.economist.com/china/2016/08/13/the-east-is-pink.

Economy, Elizabeth. *The Third Revolution: Xi Jinping and the New Chinese State.* Oxford: Oxford University Press, 2018.

Edwards, Michael, and John Gaventa, eds. *Global Citizen Action.* Boulder, CO: Lynne Rienner, 2001.

Elias, Norbert. *The Civilizing Process: Sociogenetic and Psychogenetic Investigations.* Rev. ed. Oxford: Blackwell, 2000.

Ellingson, Laura L., and Patricia J. Sotirin. *Aunting: Cultural Practices That Sustain Family and Community Life.* Waco, TX: Baylor University Press, 2010.

——. *Where the Aunts Are: Family, Feminism, and Kinship in Popular Culture.* Waco, TX: Baylor University Press, 2013.

Eltantawy, Nahed. "Pots, Pans, & Protests: Women's Strategies for Resisting Globalization in Argentina." *Communication and Critical/Cultural Studies* 5, no. 1 (2008): 46–63.

Engels, Jeremy David. *The Art of Gratitude.* Albany: State University of New York Press, 2018.

Esherick, Joseph W. *The Origins of the Boxer Uprising.* Berkeley: University of California Press, 1987.

——. *Reform and Revolution in China: The 1911 Revolution in Hunan and Hubei.* Berkeley: University of California Press, 1976.

Fan Wei 樊巍. "Wuhan Central Hospital Medical Staff Reveal the Truth: Epidemic Is a Magic Mirror for Exposing Demons" (武汉市中心医院医护人员吐真情: 疫情是面照妖镜). *Global Times* (环球时报), March 16, 2020. https://k.sina.cn/article_1974576991_75b1a75f01900q3xg.html.

Farrer, James. "China's Women Sex Bloggers and Dialogic Sexual Politics on the Chinese Internet." *Journal of Current Chinese Affairs—China Aktuell* 36, no. 4 (2007): 10–44.

Fei, Xiaotong. *From the Soil: The Foundations of Chinese Society.* A translation of Fei Xiaotong, *Xiangtu Zhongguo.* With an introduction and epilogue by Gary G. Hamilton and Wang Zheng. Berkeley: University of California Press, 1993.

Feng Jianxia 冯剑侠. "#MakeFemaleWorkersVisible#: Women's Social Media and Discursive Action During COVID-19" (#看见女性劳动者#: 新冠疫情中的女性自媒体与话语行动主义). *Shanghai Journalism Review* (新闻记者), no. 10 (2020): 32–44.

——. "'Voice' as Contention: Emotional Labor in the #MeToo Movement" ("发声" 作为一种抗争: #MeToo 运动中的情感劳动). *Press Circles* (新闻界), no. 10 (2019): 61–71.

Fewsmith, Joseph, and Andrew J. Nathan. "Authoritarian Resilience Revisited: Joseph Fewsmith with Response from Andrew J. Nathan." *Journal of Contemporary China* 28, no. 116 (March 4, 2019): 167–79.

Fincher, Leta Hong. *Betraying Big Brother: The Feminist Awakening in China.* New York: Verso, 2018.

Fisher, Dana R. *American Resistance: From the Women's March to the Blue Wave.* New York: Columbia University Press, 2019.

Foot, Kirsten, Barbara Warnick, and Steven M. Schneider. "Web-Based Memorializing After September 11: Toward a Conceptual Framework." *Journal of Computer-Mediated Communication* 11, no. 1 (2005): 72–96.

Ford, Christopher A. "The Party and the Sage: Communist China's Use of Quasi-Confucian Rationalizations for One-Party Dictatorship and Imperial Ambition." *Journal of Contemporary China* 24, no. 96 (2015): 1032–47.

Gan, Nectar. "Why China Is Reviving Mao's Grandiose Title for Xi Jinping." *South China Morning Post*, October 28, 2017. https://www.scmp.com/news/china/policies-politics /article/2117421/xi-jinpings-latest-grandiose-title-aims-take.

Gao Bingzhong 高丙中 and Yuan Ruijun 袁瑞军. "Introduction: Stepping Into Civil Society" (导论: 迈进公民社会). In *Blue Book on Civil Society Development in China* (中国公民社会发展蓝皮书), ed. Gao Bingzhong and Yuan Ruijun, 1–14. Beijing: Peking University Press, 2008.

Gillespie, Tarleton. "The Politics of 'Platforms.'" *New Media and Society* 12, no. 3 (2010): 347–64.

Global Times (环球时报). "Hubei Truck Driver Trapped on Highway for 20 Days" (湖北货车司机被困高速近20天). February 8, 2020. http://news.sina.com.cn/o/2020-02-08/doc -iimxyqvz1241865.shtml.

Goldman, Merle, Timothy Cheek, and Carol Lee Hamrin, eds. *China's Intellectuals and the State: In Search of a New Relationship*. Cambridge, MA: Harvard University Asia Center, 1987.

Gong Jingqi 龚菁琦. "The Whistle-Giver" (发哨子的人). *People* (人物), March 10, 2020. https:// medium.com/coronavirus19/%E4%BA%BA%E7%89%A9-%E5%8F%91%E5%93%A8%E5 %AD%90%E7%9A%84%E4%BA%BA-26e2c5b64394.

Gong, Ting. *The Politics of Corruption in Contemporary China: An Analysis of Policy Outcomes*. Westport, CT: Praeger, 1994.

Gray, J. Glenn. *The Warriors: Reflections on Men in Battle*. Lincoln: University of Nebraska Press, 1959.

Gries, Peter Hayes. *China's New Nationalism: Pride, Politics, and Diplomacy*. Berkeley: University of California Press, 2004.

Guangming Daily (光明日报). "Wuhan Baibuting Community: Residents Cook Ten-Thousand-Family Meal to Cheer a Beautiful Life" (武汉百步亭社区: 居民烹制万家宴为美好生活加油). January 19, 2020. http://difang.gmw.cn/hb/2020-01/19/content_33495078.htm.

Guo Miao 郭淼 and Hao Jing 郝静. "Virtual Aggregation and Precision Decoding: The Political Functions of Rural Radio Speakers in the Communication of Information About an Epidemic Outbreak" (虚拟聚合与精准解码: 农村广播大喇叭在突发疫情传播中的政治功能). *Journalism and Communication Review* (新闻与传播评论) 74, no. 2 (2021): 98–105.

Guo, Shaohua. "'Occupying the Internet': State Media and the Reinvention of Official Culture Online." *Communication and the Public* 3, no. 1 (2018): 19–33.

Guo Yuhua 郭于华. *The Stories of the Sufferers* (受苦人的讲述). Hong Kong: Chinese University of Hong Kong Press, 2013.

Hall, Stuart. "Notes on Deconstructing the 'Popular.'" In *People's History and Socialist Theory*, ed. Raphael Samuel, 227–40. London: Routledge and Kegan Paul, 1981.

Han, Rongbin. *Contesting Cyberspace in China: Online Expression and Authoritarian Resilience*. New York: Columbia University Press, 2018.

——. "Withering Gongzhi: Cyber Criticism of Chinese Public Intellectuals." *International Journal of Communication* 12 (2018): 1966–987.

Harari, Yuval. *21 Lessons for the 21st Century*. New York: Spiegel and Grau, 2018.

Hartnett, Stephen J. "Google and the 'Twisted Cyber Spy' Affair: U.S.-China Communication in an Age of Globalization." *Quarterly Journal of Speech* 97 (2011): 411–34.

Harwit, Eric. "WeChat: Social and Political Development of China's Dominant Messaging App." *Chinese Journal of Communication* 10, no. 3 (July 3, 2017): 312–27.

Hernández, Javier C. "Professors, Beware: In China, Student Spies Might Be Watching." *New York Times*, November 1, 2019. https://www.nytimes.com/2019/11/01/world/asia/china-student-informers.html.

——. "What Happened to the Chinese Professor Who Was Reported by a Student?" (被学生举报的中国大学教授后来怎么). *New York Times* (Chinese), November 13, 2019. https://cn.nytimes.com/china/20191113/china-informer-professor/.

Herold, David K., and Peter Marolt, eds. *Online Society in China: Creating, Celebrating, and Instrumentalising the Online Carnival*. London: Routledge, 2011.

Hershatter, Gail. *The Gender of Memory: Rural Women and China's Collective Past*. Berkeley: University of California Press, 2011.

Hessler, Peter. "Letter from Chengdu: Life on Coronavirus Lockdown in China." *New Yorker*, March 23, 2020. https://www.newyorker.com/magazine/2020/03/30/life-on-lockdown-in-china.

——. "Nine Days in Wuhan, the Ground Zero of the Coronavirus Pandemic." *New Yorker*, October 12, 2020. https://www.newyorker.com/magazine/2020/10/12/nine-days-in-wuhan-the-ground-zero-of-the-coronavirus-pandemic.

Heurlin, Christopher. *Responsive Authoritarianism in China: Land, Protests, and Policy Making*. Cambridge: Cambridge University Press, 2016.

Hildebrandt, Timothy. *Social Organizations and the Authoritarian State in China*. Cambridge: Cambridge University Press, 2013.

Hill, Justin. "Jiang Rong: The Hour of the Wolf." *Independent*, March 21, 2008. http://www.independent.co.uk/arts-entertainment/books/features/jiang-rong-the-hour-of-the-wolf-798697.html.

Hird, Derek. "Smile Yourself Happy: Zheng Nengliang and the Discursive Construction of Happy Subjects." In *Chinese Discourses on Happiness*, ed. Gerda Wielander and Derek Hird, 106–28. Hong Kong: University of Hong Kong Press, 2018.

Ho, Peter, and Richard Edmonds, eds. *China's Embedded Activism: Opportunities and Constraints of a Social Movement*. London: Routledge, 2012.

Hockx, Michel. *Internet Literature in China*. New York: Columbia University Press, 2015.

Holland, Oscar, and Shanshan Wang. "Beijing Art Exhibition Glorifies China's Covid-19 Response." CNN, August 16, 2020. https://www.cnn.com/style/article/beijing-covid-art-exhibition/index.html.

Hong Xiao 红绡. "Funny Stories About Ball Games in North China" (华北球战中之趣闻). *Shen Bao* (申报, *Shanghai News*), May 17, 1928.

Hong, Yu, and G. Thomas Goodnight. "How to Think About Cyber Sovereignty: The Case of China." *Chinese Journal of Communication* OnlineFirst (2019). https://doi.org/10.1080/17544750.2019.1687536.

Honig, Emily, and Xiaojian Zhao. *Across the Great Divide: The Sent-Down Youth Movement in Mao's China, 1968–1980*. Cambridge: Cambridge University Press, 2019.

Honneth, Axel. *The Struggle for Recognition: The Moral Grammar of Social Conflicts.* Trans. Joel Anderson. Cambridge, MA: MIT Press, 1995.

Hook, Brian, ed. *The Individual and the State in China.* New York: Oxford University Press, 1996.

Horvath, John. "Death of a Netizen." *Telepolis,* July 27, 2001. https://www.heise.de/tp/features /Death-of-a-Netizen-3451797.html.

Hou, Rui. "The Commercialisation of Internet-Opinion Management: How the Market Is Engaged in State Control in China." *New Media and Society,* November 27, 2019. https:// doi.org/10.1177/1461444819889959.

Hsing, You-tien, and Ching Kwan Lee, eds. *Reclaiming Chinese Society: The New Social Activism.* London: Routledge, 2009.

Hsu, Szu-chien, Kellee S. Tsai, and Chun-chih Chang, eds. *Evolutionary Governance in China: State–Society Relations Under Authoritarianism.* Cambridge, MA: Harvard University Asia Center, 2021.

Hu, Ming. "Making the State's Volunteers in Contemporary China." *VOLUNTAS,* January 2, 2020. https://doi.org/10.1007/s11266-019-00190-9.

Huang, Philip C. C. "'Public Sphere'/'Civil Society' in China? The Third Realm Between State and Society." *Modern China* 19, no. 2 (1993): 216–40.

Huang, Xian. "Peace in the Shadow of Unrest: Yinao and the State Response in China." *China Quarterly,* first view (2020). https://doi.org/10.1017/S0305741020001010.

Huang, Zhao Alexandre, and Rui Wang. "'Panda Engagement' in China's Digital Public Diplomacy." *Asian Journal of Communication* 30, no. 2 (March 3, 2020): 118–40.

Hubei Daily (湖北日报). "*Hubei Daily* Reporter Visits 13 'Temporary Hospitals' in the Three Towns of Wuhan" (湖北日报全媒记者多路探访武汉三镇13处 "方舱医院"). February 6, 2020. https://www.hubei.gov.cn/zhuanti/2020/gzxxgzbd/qfqk/202002/t20200206_2019958.shtml.

Hurst, William. "Chinese Law and Governance: Moving Beyond Responsive Authoritarianism and the Rule of Law." *Journal of Chinese Governance* 1, no. 3 (July 2, 2016): 457–69.

Isenstadt, Alex. "GOP Memo Urges Anti-China Assault Over Coronavirus." *Politico,* April 24, 2020. https://www.politico.com/news/2020/04/24/gop-memo-anti-china-coronavirus -207244.

Isin, Engin F. "Theorizing Acts of Citizenship." In *Acts of Citizenship,* ed. Engin F. Isin and Greg M. Nielsen, 15–43. London: Zed, 2008.

Jackson, Sarah J., Moya Bailey, and Brooke Foucault Welles. *#HashtagActivism: Networks of Race and Gender Justice.* Cambridge, MA: MIT Press, 2020.

Jacobs, Andrew. "Village Revolts Over Inequities of Chinese Life." *New York Times,* December 14, 2011. https://www.nytimes.com/2011/12/15/world/asia/chinese-village-locked-in -rebellion-against-authorities.html.

Jasper, James M. *The Art of Moral Protest: Culture, Biography, and Creativity in Social Movements.* Chicago: University of Chicago Press, 1997.

Jia, Xijin. "China's Implementation of the Overseas NGO Management Law." Trans. Cameron Carlson and Gabriel Corsetti. *China Development Brief,* March 6, 2017. https:// chinadevelopmentbrief.cn/reports/chinas-implementation-of-the-overseas-ngo -management-law/.

Jiang, Min. "Authoritarian Informationalism: China's Approach to Internet Sovereignty." *SAIS Review of International Affairs* 30, no. 2 (2010): 71–89.

——. "Internet Companies in China: Dancing Between the Party Line and the Bottom Line." *Asie Visions* 47 (2012). https://ssrn.com/abstract=1998976.

Jiang, Rong. *Wolf Totem*. Trans. Howard Goldblatt. New York: Penguin, 2008.

J. M. "Tilting Backwards: Whoever Wrote It, a New Policy Paper Is Making Xi Jinping's Government Look Chillingly Retrograde." *Economist*, June 24, 2013. https://www.economist.com/analects/2013/06/24/tilting-backwards.

Johnson, Ian. "Calls for a 'Jasmine Revolution' in China Persist." *New York Times*, February 23, 2011. https://www.nytimes.com/2011/02/24/world/asia/24china.html.

——. "How Did China Beat Its Covid Crisis?" *New York Review of Books*, November 5, 2020. https://www.nybooks.com/articles/2020/11/05/how-did-china-beat-its-covid-crisis/.

Jones, Rodney H. "The Problem of Context in Computer-Mediated Communication." In *Discourse and Technology: Multinodal Discourse Analysis*, ed. Philip Levine and Ron Scollon, 20–33. Washington, DC: Georgetown University Press, 2004.

Joseph, William A., ed. *Politics in China: An Introduction*. 3rd ed. Oxford: Oxford University Press, 2019.

Juergensmeyer, Mark. "COVID-19 and Cultural Nationalism." *Global-e* 13, no. 41 (June 26, 2020). https://www.21global.ucsb.edu/global-e/june-2020/covid-19-and-cultural-nationalism.

Katz, James E. *Magic in the Air: Mobile Communication and the Transformation of Social Life*. London: Routledge, 2017.

Koetse, Manya. "The PRC Twitter List: The Rise of China on Twitter." *What's on Weibo* (blog), July 21, 2020. https://www.whatsonweibo.com/the-prc-twitter-list-the-rise-of-china-on-twitter/.

Lagerkvist, Amanda. "The Netlore of the Infinite: Death (and Beyond) in the Digital Memory Ecology." *New Review of Hypermedia and Multimedia* 21, nos. 1–2 (2015): 185–95.

Lai, Weijun, Jiangang Zhu, Lin Tao, and Anthony J. Spires. "Bounded by the State: Government Priorities and the Development of Private Philanthropic Foundations in China." *China Quarterly* 224 (2015): 1083–92.

Lai Youxuan 赖祐萱. "Delivery Drivers Stuck in Algorithms" (外卖骑手，困在系统里). *People* (人物), September 9, 2020. https://mp.weixin.qq.com/s/Mes1RqIOdp48CMw4pXTwXw.

——. "A 'War' on Behalf of Women" (一场为女性发起的'战疫'). *People* (人物), February 22, 2020. https://www.weibo.com/ttarticle/p/show?id=2309404474700771229735#_0.

Lancet. "Chinese Doctors Are Under Threat." 376, no. 9742 (August 28, 2010): 657.

Lee, Chin-Chuan, Zhou He, and Yu Huang. "Party–Market Corporatism, Clientelism, and Media in Shanghai." *International Journal of Press/Politics* 12, no. 3 (2007): 21–42.

Lee, Ching Kwan, and Yonghong Zhang. "The Power of Instability: Unraveling the Microfoundations of Bargained Authoritarianism in China." *American Journal of Sociology* 118, no. 6 (2013): 1475–508.

Lee, Siu-yau. "Surviving Online Censorship in China: Three Satirical Tactics and Their Impact." *China Quarterly* 228 (2016): 1061–80.

Leese, Daniel. *Mao Cult: Rhetoric and Ritual in China's Cultural Revolution*. Cambridge: Cambridge University Press, 2011.

Lei Feng 雷锋. *Lei Feng's Diary: 1959–1962* (雷锋日记: 1959–1962). Beijing: Jiefangjun Wenyi chubanshe, 1963.

Lei, Ya-Wen. *The Contentious Public Sphere: Law, Media, and Authoritarian Rule in China.* Princeton, NJ: Princeton University Press, 2017.

Leong, Susan. "Sinophone, Chinese, and PRC Internet: Chinese Overseas in Australia and the PRC Internet." *Digital Asia* 3 (2016): 117–37.

Lessig, Lawrence. *Remix: Making Art and Commerce Thrive in the Hybrid Economy.* New York: Penguin, 2008.

Li Chunchang 李春昌 and Zhang Chong 张崇. "No Matter Whether Foreign or Chinese, They Are Good Methods as Long as They Are Useful: Reflections on the Practices of Loudspeakers in the Rural Areas of Cangzhou City" (洋办法, 土办法, 管用就是好办法-沧州市农村大喇叭广播的实践与思考). *Hebei Communist* (河北共产党员), no. 4 (2020): 8–10.

Li, Jie. "Revolutionary Echoes: Radios and Loudspeakers in the Mao Era." *Twentieth-Century China* 45, no. 1 (January 11, 2020): 25–45.

Li, Jun. "Social Movement, Media, and the State: The New Feminist Movement with Communication as Core in Contemporary China (2003–2016)." PhD diss., University of Macau, 2017.

Li, Lianjiang. "Rights Consciousness and Rules Consciousness in Contemporary China." *China Journal* 64 (2010): 47–68.

Li, Ling. "Politics of Anticorruption in China: Paradigm Change of the Party's Disciplinary Regime 2012–2017." *Journal of Contemporary China* 28, no. 115 (January 2, 2019): 47–63.

Lim, Louisa. *The People's Republic of Amnesia: Tiananmen Revisited.* Illus. ed. New York: Oxford University Press, 2014.

Lin Biao. *Long Live the Victory of People's War! In Commemoration of the 20th Anniversary of Victory in the Chinese People's War of Resistance Against Japan.* Beijing: Foreign Language Press, 1965. https://www.marxists.org/reference/archive/lin-biao/1965/09/peoples_war/index.htm.

Ling, Qi, and Sara Liao. "Intellectuals Debate #MeToo in China: Legitimizing Feminist Activism, Challenging Gendered Myths, and Reclaiming Feminism." *Journal of Communication* 70, no. 6 (2020): 895–916.

Ling, Rich. *Taken for Grantedness: The Embedding of Mobile Communication Into Society.* Cambridge, MA: MIT Press, 2012.

Litzinger, Ralph A. *Other Chinas: The Yao and the Politics of National Belonging.* Durham, NC: Duke University Press, 2000.

Liu, Hailong, ed. *From Cyber-nationalism to Fandom Nationalism: The Case of Diba Expedition.* London: Routledge, 2019.

Liu Heng 刘衡. *An Ordinary Official's Ordinary Words* (庸吏庸言). In *An Anthology of Readings for Officials* (官箴书集成), 10 vols., ed. Liu Junwen 刘俊文, 6:173–226. Hefei: Huangshan Shushe, 1997.

Liu, Jun. "From 'Moments of Madness' to 'the Politics of Mundanity'—Researching Digital Media and Contentious Collective Actions in China." *Social Movement Studies* 16, no. 4 (2017): 418–32.

Liu, Yu. "Maoist Discourse and the Mobilization of Emotions in Revolutionary China." *Modern China* 36, no. 3 (2010): 329–62.

Lorentzen, Peter, and Suzanne Scoggins. "Understanding China's Rising Rights Consciousness." *China Quarterly* 223 (2015): 638–57.

Lovell, Joseph. "The Party and the People: Shifting Sonic Politics in Post-1949 Tiananmen Square." In *Sound Communities in the Asia Pacific: Music, Media, and Technology*, ed. Lonán Ó Briain and Min Yen Ong, 151–70. New York: Bloomsbury.

Lu, Shen, and Mengwen Cao. "Thwarted at Home, Can China's Feminists Rebuild a Movement Abroad?" ChinaFile, August 28, 2019. https://www.chinafile.com/reporting-opinion /postcard/thwarted-home-can-chinas-feminists-rebuild-movement-abroad.

Ma, Sheng-mei. *Sinophone–Anglophone Cultural Duet*. London: Palgrave MacMillan, 2017.

MacFarquhar, Roderick, and Michael Schoenhals. *Mao's Last Revolution*. Cambridge, MA: Belknap Press of Harvard University Press, 2006.

MacKinnon, Rebecca. "Liberation Technology: China's 'Networked Authoritarianism.'" *Journal of Democracy* 22, no. 2 (2011): 32–46.

MacKinnon, Stephen R. *Wuhan, 1938: War, Refugees, and the Making of Modern China*. Berkeley: University of California Press, 2008.

Madsen, Richard. "The Public Sphere, Civil Society, and Moral Community: A Research Agenda for Contemporary China Studies." *Modern China* 19, no. 2 (1993): 183–98.

Manion, Melanie. *Corruption by Design: Building Clean Government in Mainland China and Hong Kong*. Cambridge, MA: Harvard University Press, 2004.

Marquis, Christopher, and Yanhua Bird. "The Paradox of Responsive Authoritarianism: How Civic Activism Spurs Environmental Penalties in China." *Organization Science* 29, no. 5 (June 8, 2018): 948–68.

Marwick, Alice E. *Status Update: Celebrity, Publicity, and Branding in the Social Media Age*. New Haven, CT: Yale University Press, 2013.

Mead, Walter Russell. "China Is the Real Sick Man of Asia." *Wall Street Journal*, February 3, 2020. https://www.wsj.com/articles/china-is-the-real-sick-man-of-asia-11580773677.

Mei, Ciqi. "Policy Style, Consistency, and the Effectiveness of the Policy Mix in China's Fight Against COVID-19." *Policy and Society* 39, no. 3 (July 2, 2020): 309–25.

Mellen, Ruby. "How Pots and Pans Became Tools of Protests, from Chile to Myanmar." *Washington Post*, February 4, 2021. http://www.washingtonpost.com/world/2021/02/04/pots -pans-protests-myanmar-coup/.

Mendelson, Scott. "Box Office: 'Wolf Warrior 2' Cracks 100 All-Time Biggest Grossers List." *Forbes*, August 14, 2017. https://www.forbes.com/sites/scottmendelson/2017/08/14/box -office-wolf-warrior-2-cracks-100-all-time-biggest-grossers-list/.

Meng, Bingchun. "From Steamed Bun to Grass Mud Horse: E Gao as Alternative Political Discourse on the Chinese Internet." *Global Media and Communication* 7, no. 1 (April 1, 2011): 33–51.

Mitchell, Lincoln A. *The Color Revolutions*. Philadelphia: University of Pennsylvania Press, 2012.

Moffitt, Benjamin. *The Global Rise of Populism: Performance, Political Style, and Representation*. Stanford, CA: Stanford University Press, 2016.

Moore, Aaron William. "Talk About Heroes: Expressions of Self-Mobilization and Despair in Chinese War Diaries, 1911–1938." *Twentieth-Century China* 34, no. 2 (2009): 30–54.

Mozur, Paul, Raymond Zhong, and Aaron Krolik. "In Coronavirus Fight, China Gives Citizens a Color Code, with Red Flags." *New York Times*, March 2, 2020. https://www.nytimes.com/2020/03/01/business/china-coronavirus-surveillance.html.

Nathan, Andrew J. "China's Changing of the Guard: Authoritarian Resilience." *Journal of Democracy* 14, no. 1 (February 5, 2003): 6–17.

——. *Chinese Democracy*. Berkeley: University of California Press, 1986.

Navas, Eduardo. *Remix Theory: The Aesthetics of Sampling*. New York: Springer-Verlag/Wien, 2012.

Newton, Casey. "Half of All Facebook Moderators May Develop Mental Health Issues." *Verge*, May 13, 2020. https://www.theverge.com/interface/2020/5/13/21255994/facebook-content-moderator-lawsuit-settlement-mental-health-issues.

Nieborg, David B., and Thomas Poell. "The Platformization of Cultural Production: Theorizing the Contingent Cultural Commodity." *New Media & Society* 20, no. 11 (2018): 4275–292.

O'Brien, Kevin J., and Lianjiang Li. *Rightful Resistance in Rural China*. Cambridge: Cambridge University Press, 2006.

Oliver, Mark. "China Sacks Minister Over Sars." *Guardian*, April 20, 2003. https://www.theguardian.com/world/2003/apr/20/sars.markoliver.

Owen, Catherine. "Participatory Authoritarianism: From Bureaucratic Transformation to Civic Participation in Russia and China." *Review of International Studies* 46, no. 4 (October 2020): 415–34.

Oxfeld, Ellen. *Drink Water, but Remember the Source: Moral Discourse in a Chinese Village*. Berkeley: University of California Press, 2010.

Pan, Phillip P. "Chinese Pressure Dissident: Physician Hero of SARS Crisis Detained Since June 1." *Washington Post*, July 5, 2004.

Papacharissi, Zizi. *Affective Publics: Sentiment, Technology, and Politics*. New York: Oxford University Press, 2014.

Paper, The (澎湃). "At Wuhan Baibuting Community, a Social Worker's Unsuccessful Request to Neighborhood Committee Leaders to Cancel the Ten-Thousand-Family Meal" (武汉百步亭社工: 曾和居委会领导反映取消万家宴, 但没成功). February 12, 2020. https://news.sina.com.cn/o/2020-02-12/doc-iimxxstfo816064.shtml.

——. "Cai Li Is No Longer Party Secretary of the Wuhan Central Hospital. Wang Weihua Is the Replacement" (蔡莉不再担任武汉市中心医院党委书记, 王卫华接任). August 28, 2020, http://www.chinanews.com/gn/2020/08-28/9276230.shtml.

——. "During the Pandemic, They Rescue Small Animals Stuck at Home in Wuhan" (疫情之下, 他们救助那些滞留在家的武汉小动物们). February 4, 2020. https://m.sohu.com/a/370483916_260616/?pvid=000115_3w_a.

——. "When Fan Club Girls Join the Anti-coronavirus War" (当饭圈女孩冲上抗疫战场). March 23, 2020. https://m.thepaper.cn/wap/v3/jsp/newsDetail_forward_6646110.

——. "Wuhan Builds 3 Temporary Hospitals Overnight to Provide 3,400 Beds" (武汉连夜建三所 "方舱医院" 将提供3,400张床位). February 4, 2020. https://www.thepaper.cn/news Detail_forward_5776218.

Peng Lan 彭兰. "Short Videos: The 'Genetic Modification' and Re-cultivation of Video Productivity" (短视频: 视频生产力的 '转基因'与再培育). *Journalism and Mass Communication Monthly* (新闻界), no. 1 (2019): 34–43.

People's Daily Online (人民网). "Public Opinion Office of People's Net Issues June Report on the Degree of Consensus in Online Opinion" (人民网舆情监测室发布6月网络舆论共识度报告). July 10, 2015. http://yuqing.people.com.cn/n/2015/0710/c210107-27283825.html.

——. "The U.S. Must Answer These Ten Questions" (这10个追问, 美国必须回答). May 1, 2020. http://world.people.com.cn/n1/2020/0501/c1002-31695371.html.

Perry, Elizabeth J. "Chinese Conceptions of 'Rights': From Mencius to Mao—and Now." *Perspectives on Politics* 6, no. 1 (March 2008): 37–50.

——. "Epilogue: China's (R)evolutionary Governance and the COVID-19 Crisis." In *Evolutionary Governance in China: State–Society Relations Under Authoritarianism*, ed. Szuchien Hsu, Kellee S. Tsai, and Chun-chih Chang, 387–96. Cambridge, MA: Harvard University Asia Center, 2021.

——. "Moving the Masses: Emotion Work in the Chinese Revolution." *Mobilization* 7, no. 2 (2002): 111–28.

——. "A New Rights Consciousness?" *Journal of Democracy* 20, no. 3 (July 1, 2009): 17–20.

Perry, Elizabeth J., and Li Xun. "Revolutionary Rudeness: The Language of Red Guard and Rebel Worker in China's Cultural Revolution." In *Twentieth-Century China: New Approaches*, ed. Jeffrey N. Wasserstrom, 221–36. New York: Routledge, 2002.

Pfaff, Steven, and Guobin Yang. "Double-Edged Rituals and the Symbolic Resources of Collective Action: Political Commemorations and the Mobilization of Protest in 1989." *Theory and Society* 30, no. 4 (2001): 539–89.

Pieke, Frank N. "The Communist Party and Social Management in China." *China Information* 26, no. 2 (June 17, 2012): 149–65.

Plummer, Ken. *Documents of Life 2: An Invitation to a Critical Humanism.* London: Sage, 2001.

Prasso, Sheridan. "Lawsuits Against China Escalate Covid-19 Blame Game with U.S." *Bloomberg*, May 6, 2020. https://www.bloomberg.com/news/articles/2020-05-06/lawsuits-against-china-escalate-covid-19-blame-game-with-u-s.

Price, Monroe, and Daniel Dayan, eds. *Owning the Olympics: Narratives of the New China.* Ann Arbor: University of Michigan Press, 2009.

Putnam, Robert D. *Bowling Alone: The Collapse and Revival of American Community.* New York: Simon and Schuster, 2001.

Pye, Lucian W. "The State and the Individual: An Overview Interpretation." *China Quarterly* 127 (1991): 443–66.

Qian, Gang. "As An Epidemic Raged, What Kept Party Media Busy?" *China Media Project* (blog), January 30, 2020. https://chinamediaproject.org/2020/01/30/too-busy-for-an-epidemic/.

Rankin, Mary Backus. "Some Observations on a Chinese Public Sphere." *Modern China* 19, no. 2 (1993): 158–82.

Ratcliffe, Rebecca, and Michael Standaert. "China Coronavirus: Mayor of Wuhan Admits Mistakes." *Guardian*, January 27, 2020. https://www.theguardian.com/science/2020/jan /27/china-coronavirus-who-to-hold-special-meeting-in-beijing-as-death-toll-jumps.

Read, Benjamin L. *Roots of the State: Neighborhood Organization and Social Networks in Beijing and Taipei*. Stanford, CA: Stanford University Press, 2012.

Repnikova, Maria. *Media Politics in China: Improvising Power Under Authoritarianism*. Cambridge: Cambridge University Press, 2017.

Repnikova, Maria, and Kecheng Fang. "Authoritarian Participatory Persuasion 2.0: Netizens as Thought Work Collaborators in China." *Journal of Contemporary China* 27, no. 113 (2018): 763–79.

Rettberg, Jill Walker. "Online Diaries and Blogs." In *The Diary: The Epic of Everyday Life*, ed. Batsheva Ben-Amos and Dan Ben-Amos, 410–23. Bloomington: Indiana University Press, 2020.

Roberts, Margaret E. *Censored: Distraction and Diversion Inside China's Great Firewall*. Princeton, NJ: Princeton University Press, 2018.

Rosenwein, Barbara H. "Afterword: Imagined Emotions for Imagined Communities." In *Imagined Communities on the Baltic Rim*, ed. Wojtek Jezierski and Lars Hermanson, 381–88. Amsterdam: Amsterdam University Press, 2016.

Rowe, William T. *Hankow: Conflict and Community in a Chinese City, 1796–1895*. Stanford, CA: Stanford University Press, 1989.

——. "The Problem of 'Civil Society' in Late Imperial China." *Modern China* 19, no. 2 (April 1, 1993): 139–57.

Sang Ye. "Memories for the Future." In *Yang Zhichao: Chinese Bible*, ed. Claire Roberts, 27–31. Sydney, Australia: Sherman Contemporary Art Foundation, 2015.

Scheff, Thomas J. *Bloody Revenge: Emotions, Nationalism, and War*. Boulder, CO: Westview Press, 1994.

Schneider, Florian. *China's Digital Nationalism*. New York: Oxford University Press, 2018.

Schwarz, Ori. "Facebook Rules: Structures of Governance in Digital Capitalism and the Control of Generalized Social Capital." *Theory, Culture, and Society* 36, no. 4 (2019): 117–41.

Selden, Mark. *The Yenan Way in Revolutionary China*. Cambridge, MA: Harvard University Press, 1971.

Shalson, Lara. *Performing Endurance: Art and Politics Since 1960*. Cambridge: Cambridge University Press, 2018.

Shank, Barry. *Dissonant Identities: The Rock 'n' Roll Scene in Austin, Texas*. Hanover, CT: Wesleyan University Press, 1994.

Shear, Michael D., Noah Weiland, Eric Lipton, Maggie Haberman, and David E. Sanger. "Inside Trump's Failure: The Rush to Abandon Leadership Role on the Virus." *New York Times*, July 18, 2020. https://www.nytimes.com/2020/07/18/us/politics/trump-coronavirus -response-failure-leadership.html.

Sheridan, Mary. "The Emulation of Heroes." *China Quarterly* 33 (1968): 47–72.

Shieh, Shawn, and Guosheng Deng. "An Emerging Civil Society: The Impact of the 2008 Sichuan Earthquake on Grassroots Associations in China." *China Journal* 65 (2011): 181–94.

Shirk, Susan L. "China in Xi's 'New Era': The Return to Personalistic Rule." *Journal of Democracy* 29, no. 2 (April 2018): 22–36.

Silver, Daniel, Terry Nichols Clark, and Clemente Jesus Navarro Yanez. "Scenes: Social Context in an Age of Contingency." *Social Forces* 88, no. 5 (July 1, 2010): 2293–324.

Simmel, Georg. "Faithfulness and Gratitude." In *The Sociology of Georg Simmel*, trans., ed., and with an introduction by Kurt H. Wolff, 379–95. New York: Free Press, 1950.

Sorace, Christian P. "Gratitude: The Ideology of Sovereignty in Crisis." *Made in China Journal*, May 18, 2020. https://madeinchinajournal.com/2020/05/18/gratitude-the-ideology-of-sovereignty-in-crisis/.

——. *Shaken Authority: China's Communist Party and the 2008 Sichuan Earthquake*. Ithaca, NY: Cornell University Press, 2017.

South China Morning Post. "Beijing in 45b Yuan Global Media Drive." January 13, 2009. https://www.scmp.com/article/666847/beijing-45b-yuan-global-media-drive.

Spence, Jonathan D. *The Search for Modern China*. 3rd ed. New York: Norton, 2012.

Spires, Anthony J. "Chinese Youth and Alternative Narratives of Volunteering." *China Information* 32, no. 2 (July 2018): 203–23.

Swan, Jonathan, and Bethany Allen-Ebrahimian. "Top Chinese Official Disowns U.S. Military Lab Coronavirus Conspiracy." *Axios*, March 22, 2020. https://www.axios.com/china-coronavirus-ambassador-cui-tiankai-1b0404e8-026d-4b7d-8290-98076f95df14.html.

Tan Jianxing 覃建行. "'Whistleblower' of Novel Coronavirus Li Wenliang Says Truth Is More Important Than His Rehabilitation" (新冠肺炎 "吹哨人" 李文亮: 真相比平反更重要). *Caixin* (财新), January 31, 2020. Archived at https://project-gutenberg.github.io/nCovMemory-Web/post/59185d41627a723c19bae95bab17dafe/.

Tan Jianxing 覃建行 and Wang Yanyu 王颜玉. "Another COVID-19 'Whistleblower' Goes Public" (新冠肺炎 又一 "吹哨人" 现身). *Caixin* (财新), February 1, 2020. http://china.caixin.com/2020-02-01/101510173.html.

Tang, Beibei. "Grid Governance in China's Urban Middle-Class Neighbourhoods." *China Quarterly* 241 (2020): 43–61.

Tatlow, Didi Kirsten. "A Merry Band of Rights Pranksters." *New York Times*, December 4, 2012. https://www.nytimes.com/2012/12/05/world/asia/05iht-letter05.html.

Tausig, Benjamin. *Bangkok Is Ringing: Sound, Protest, and Constraint*. New York: Oxford University Press, 2019.

Teets, Jessica C. "Let Many Civil Societies Bloom: The Rise of Consultative Authoritarianism in China." *China Quarterly* 213 (2013): 19–38.

Thiers, Paul. "Risk Society Comes to China: SARS, Transparency, and Public Accountability." *Asian Perspective* 27, no. 2 (2003): 241–51.

Thomas, William Isaac, and Florian Znaniecki. *The Polish Peasant in Europe and America*. Vol. 1. Boston: Gorham Press, 1918.

Thornton, Patricia M. "Crisis and Governance: SARS and the Resilience of the Chinese Body Politic." *China Journal* 61 (2009): 23–48.

Tomba, Luigi. *The Government Next Door: Neighborhood Politics in Urban China*. Ithaca, NY: Cornell University Press, 2014.

Tong, Jingrong. "The Taming of Critical Journalism in China." *Journalism Studies* 20, no. 1 (January 2, 2019): 79–96.

Tong Qi 童祁. "Fandom Girls' Battle for Online Traffic: Data Labor, Affective Consumption, and Neoliberalism" (饭圈女孩的流量战争: 数据劳动、情感消费与新自由主义). *Journal of Guangzhou University* (广州大学学报) (Social Sciences Edition), no. 5 (2020): 72–79.

Truex, Rory. "Consultative Authoritarianism and Its Limits." *Comparative Political Studies* 50, no. 3 (2017): 329–61.

Tsai, Kellee S. "Evolutionary Governance in China: State–Society Interactions Under Authoritarianism." In *Evolutionary Governance in China: State–Society Relations Under Authoritarianism*, ed. Szu-chien Hsu, Kellee S. Tsai, and Chun-chih Chang, 3–37. Cambridge, MA: Harvard University Asia Center, 2021.

Van der Kamp, Denise S. "Blunt Force Regulation and Bureaucratic Control: Understanding China's War on Pollution." *Governance*, March 4, 2020. https://doi.org/10.1111/gove.12485.

Van Dijck, José. *The Culture of Connectivity: A Critical History of Social Media*. New York: Oxford University Press, 2013.

Van Dijck, José, Thomas Poell, and Martijn De Waal. *The Platform Society: Public Values in a Connective World*. New York: Oxford University Press, 2018.

Veg, Sebastian. *Minjian: The Rise of China's Grassroots Intellectuals*. New York: Columbia University Press, 2019.

Vogel, Ezra F. *Deng Xiaoping and the Transformation of China*. Cambridge, MA: Belknap Press of Harvard University Press, 2013.

Wakeman, Frederic, Jr. "The Civil Society and Public Sphere Debate: Western Reflections on Chinese Political Culture." *Modern China* 19, no. 2 (1993): 108–38.

Wallace-Wells, David. "How the West Lost COVID." *New York*, March 15, 2021. https://nymag.com/intelligencer/2021/03/how-the-west-lost-covid-19.html.

Wallbank, Derek, and *Bloomberg*. "Twitter Applies Fact Check—This Time to China Spokesman's Tweets About Virus Origins." *Fortune*, May 28, 2020. https://fortune.com/2020/05/28/twitter-fact-check-zhao-lijian-coronavirus-origin/.

Wang, Alex L. "Symbolic Legitimacy and Chinese Environmental Reform." *Environmental Law* 48, no. 4 (2018): 699–760.

Wang Hongchun 王洪春, Wang Feixiang 王飞翔, and Sun Zhao 孙朝. "Zhong Nanshan Says Novel Coronavirus Transmits from Human to Human" (钟南山: 新型冠状病毒存在人传人现象). *Beijing News* (新京报), January 21, 2020. http://www.bjnews.com.cn/news/2020/01/21/677199.html.

Wang, Jing. *The Other Digital China: Nonconfrontational Activism on the Social Web*. Cambridge, MA: Harvard University Press, 2019.

Wang Ming 王名, ed. *Report on Civil Society Action in the Wenchuan Earthquake* (汶川地震公民行动报告). Beijing: Social Science Academic Press, 2008.

Wang, Qi. "Young Feminist Activists in Present-Day China: A New Feminist Generation?" *China Perspectives*, no. 3 (March 2018): 59–68.

Wang, Shaoguang. *Failure of Charisma: The Cultural Revolution in Wuhan*. Hong Kong: Oxford University Press, 1995.

Wang Xue 王雪 and Gao Meng 高萌. "Start a Gratitude Education in the Whole City, Form Strong Positive Energy" (在全市开展感恩教育 形成强大正能量). *Changjiang Daily* (长江日报), March 7, 2020. http://cjrb.cnhan.com/cjrb/20200307/8127.htm.

Wang, Zheng. *Never Forget National Humiliation: Historical Memory in Chinese Politics and Foreign Relations*. New York: Columbia University Press, 2012.

Wedeman, Andrew. "The Intensification of Corruption in China." *China Quarterly* 180 (2004): 895–921.

Weedon, Chris, Andrew Tolson, and Frank Mort. "Introduction to Language Studies at the Centre." In *Culture, Media, Language*, ed. Stuart Hall, Dorothy Hobson, Andrew Lowe, and Paul Willis, 177–85. London: Routledge, 1980.

Weller, Robert P. "Responsive Authoritarianism and Blind-Eye Governance in China." In *Socialism Vanquished, Socialism Challenged: Eastern Europe and China, 1989–2009*, ed. Nina Bandelj and Dorothy J. Solinger, 3–99. New York: Oxford University Press, 2012.

White, Melanie. "Can an Act of Citizenship Be Creative?" In *Acts of Citizenship*, ed. Engin F. Isin and Greg M. Nielsen, 44–56. London: Zed, 2008.

Wilson, Jason. "The Rightwing Groups Behind Wave of Protests Against Covid-19 Restrictions." *Guardian*, April 17, 2020.https://www.theguardian.com/world/2020/apr/17/far-right-coronavirus-protests-restrictions.

Wong, Edward. "Clampdown in China Restricts 7,000 Foreign Organizations." *New York Times*, April 28, 2016. https://www.nytimes.com/2016/04/29/world/asia/china-foreign-ngo-law.html.

Wong, Edward, Julian E. Barnes, and Zolan Kanno-Youngs. "Local Officials in China Hid Coronavirus Dangers from Beijing, U.S. Agencies Find." *New York Times*, August 19, 2020. https://www.nytimes.com/2020/08/19/world/asia/china-coronavirus-beijing-trump.html.

Wong, Edward, and Austin Ramzy. "China Keeps Lid on Information, as Hopes Dim in Yangtze Ship Disaster." *New York Times*, June 3, 2015. https://www.nytimes.com/2015/06/04/world/asia/hopes-dim-for-survivors-of-yangtze-cruise-ship-media-control.html.

World Health Organization. "Novel Coronavirus (2019-NCoV) Situation Report—22." February 11, 2020. https://www.who.int/docs/default-source/coronaviruse/situation-reports/20200211-sitrep-22-ncov.pdf.

——. "Novel Coronavirus (2019-NCoV) Situation Report—51." March 11, 2020. https://www.who.int/docs/default-source/coronaviruse/situation-reports/20200311-sitrep-51-covid-19.pdf.

——. "Timeline of WHO's Response to COVID-19." June 29, 2020. https://www.who.int/news-room/detail/29-06-2020-covidtimeline.

Wu, Fengshi, and Shen Yang. "Web 2.0 and Political Engagement in China." *VOLUNTAS* 27, no. 5 (October 1, 2016): 2055–76.

Wu Mi 吴宓. *Supplements to Wu Mi's Diaries: 1967–1968* (吴宓日记续编: 1967–1968). Vol. 8. Beijing: Sanlian shudian, 2006.

Wu Shangzhe 吴尚哲 [Ah-Nian 阿念]. *Wuhan Girl Ah-Nian's Diary* (武汉女孩阿念日记). Beijing: Beijing Lianhe, 2020.

Xi Jinping 习近平. "Speech at the 12th Study Session of the CCP Politburo" (在中国中央政治局第12 次学习会议上的讲话). January 25, 2019. http://www.wenming.cn/specials/zxdj /xzsjhwm_43255/201905/t20190524_5126562.shtml.

——. "Speech at the Meeting About Balancing COVID-19 Prevention and Control with Economic and Social Development" (在统筹推进新冠肺炎疫情防控和经济社会发展工作部署会议上的讲话). February 23, 2020. http://www.wenming.cn/specials/zxdj/xzsjhwm_43255 /202003/t20200304_5454781.shtml.

Xiao Gongqin. "From Authoritarian Government to Constitutional Democracy." In *Voices from the Chinese Century*, ed. Timothy Cheek, David Ownby, and Joshua A. Fogel, 198–208. New York: Columbia University Press, 2019.

Xiao, Meili. "China's Feminist Awakening." *New York Times*, May 13, 2015. https://www .nytimes.com/2015/05/14/opinion/xiao-meili-chinas-feminist-awakening.html.

Xu, Bin. *The Politics of Compassion: The Sichuan Earthquake and Civic Engagement in China*. Stanford, CA: Stanford University Press, 2017.

Xu, Jian. *Media Events in Web 2.0 China: Interventions of Online Activism*. Brighton, U.K.: Sussex Academic Press, 2016.

Xu, Yizhou (Joe). "Programmatic Dreams: Technographic Inquiry Into Censorship of Chinese Chatbots." *Social Media + Society* 4, no. 4 (November 11, 2018). https://doi.org/10.1177 /2056305118808780.

Xu Yongguang 徐永光. "2008: Year One of China's Civil Society" (中国公民社会元年). *NPO Surveys* (NPO 纵横), no. 4 (2008): 105.

Yan, Yunxiang. *The Flow of Gifts: Reciprocity and Social Networks in a Chinese Village*. Stanford, CA: Stanford University Press, 1996.

Yang, Guobin. "Achieving Emotions in Collective Action: Emotional Processes and Movement Mobilization in the 1989 Chinese Student Movement." *Sociological Quarterly* 41, no. 4 (2000): 593–614.

——, ed. *China's Contested Internet*. Copenhagen, Denmark: NIAS Press, 2015.

——. "A Chinese Internet? History, Practice, and Globalization." *Chinese Journal of Communication* 5 (2012): 49–54.

——. "Civil Society in China: A Dynamic Field of Study." *China Review International* 9, no. 1 (2002): 1–16.

——. "Contesting Food Safety in the Chinese Media: Between Hegemony and Counter-Hegemony." *China Quarterly* 214 (2013): 337–55.

——. "Demobilizing the Emotions of Online Activism in China: A Civilizing Process." *International Journal of Communication* 11 (2017): 1945–965.

——. "The Digital Radicals of Wuhan." Center on Digital Culture and Society, February 3, 2020. https://cdcs.asc.upenn.edu/guobin-yang-2/.

——. "The Dramatic Form of Online Collective Action in China." In *Methodological and Conceptual Issues in Cyber Activism Research*, ed. Asia Research Institute, 137–57. Singapore: National University of Singapore, 2012.

——. "Introduction: Social Media and State-Sponsored Platformization in China." In *Engaging Social Media in China: Platforms, Publics, and Production*, ed. Guobin Yang and Wei Wang, xi–xxxi. East Lansing: Michigan State University Press, 2021.

——. "Of Sympathy and Play: Emotional Mobilization in Online Collective Action." *Chinese Journal of Communication and Society* (Hong Kong) 9 (2009): 39–66.

——. " 'A Portrait of Martyr Jiang Qing': The Chinese Cultural Revolution on the Internet." In *Re-envisioning the Chinese Revolution: The Politics and Poetics of Collective Memories in Reform China*, ed. Ching Kwan Lee and Guobin Yang, 287–316. Washington, DC: Woodrow Wilson Press; Stanford, CA: Stanford University Press, 2007.

——. "Power and Transgression in the Global Media Age: The Strange Case of Twitter in China." In *Communication and Power in the Global Era: Orders and Borders*, ed. Marwan M. Kraidy, 166–83. London: Routledge, 2013.

——. *The Power of the Internet in China: Citizen Activism Online*. New York: Columbia University Press, 2009.

——. *The Red Guard Generation and Political Activism in China*. New York: Columbia University Press, 2016.

Yang, Guobin, and Shiwen Wu. "Remembering Disappeared Websites in China: Passion, Community, and Youth." *New Media & Society* 20, no. 6 (June 1, 2016): 2107–124.

Yang Hai 杨海. "Why Is Reporting of the Epidemic Situation in the Early Period in Wuhan Suspended at One Point?" (武汉早期疫情上报为何一度中断). *China Youth Daily* (中国青年报), March 5, 2020. https://new.qq.com/omn/20200305/20200305A0O3MV00.html.

Yang Jinzhi 杨金志. "Daring to Speak Up Is a Precious Attribute!" (敢言, 是一种宝贵的品格!). *China Comment* (半月谈), February 20, 2020. http://www.xinhuanet.com/politics/2020-02/20/c_1125603673.htm.

Yang Lin 杨琳. "Gong-Beating Workers Demand Pay at the Door" (工人上门敲锣讨薪). *China Economic Weekly* (中国经济周刊), October 30, 2020.

Yang, Mayfair Mei-Hui. *Gifts, Favors, and Banquets: The Art of Social Relationships in China*. Ithaca, NY: Cornell University Press, 1994.

Yang, Peidong, and Tang Lijun. " 'Positive Energy': Hegemonic Intervention and Online Media Discourse in China's Xi Jinping Era." *China: An International Journal* 16, no. 1 (March 15, 2018): 1–22.

Yap, Chuin-Wei. "China's Consumers Show Growing Influence in Gold Market." *Wall Street Journal*, August 12, 2013. https://www.wsj.com/articles/SB10001424127887323446404579008372464837550.

Yew, Wei Lit. "Matrix of Free Spaces in China: Mobilizing Citizens and the Law Through Digital and Organizational Spaces." *International Journal of Communication* 13 (July 22, 2019): 3341–360.

Yip, Ngai-ming, and Yihong Jiang. "Homeowners United: The Attempt to Create Lateral Networks of Homeowners' Associations in Urban China." *Journal of Contemporary China* 20, no. 72 (November 1, 2011): 735–50.

Yip, Winnie, Hongqiao Fu, Angela T. Chen, Tiemin Zhai, Weiyan Jian, Roman Xu, Jay Pan, Min Hu, Zhongliang Zhou, Qiulin Chen, Wenhui Mao, Qiang Sun, and Wen Chen. "10 Years of Health-Care Reform in China: Progress and Gaps in Universal Health Coverage." *The Lancet* 394, no. 10204 (September 21, 2019): 979–1112.

Yu, Hua. *China in Ten Words.* Trans. Allan H. Barr. New York: Anchor, 2011.

Yu, Jinli, Fei Zou, and Yirui Sun. "Job Satisfaction, Engagement, and Burnout in the Population of Orthopedic Surgeon and Neurosurgeon Trainees in Mainland China." *Neurosurgical Focus* 48, no. 3 (March 1, 2020): 1–8.

Yuan, Li 袁莉. "When Li Wenliang's Weibo Becomes China's Wailing Wall" (当李文亮的微博成为中国的哭墙). *New York Times* (Chinese), April 14, 2020. https://cn.nytimes.com/china/20200414/coronavirus-doctor-whistleblower-weibo/.

Yuan, Li, and Rumsey Taylor. "How Thousands in China Gently Mourn a Coronavirus Whistle-Blower." *New York Times*, April 13, 2020. https://www.nytimes.com/interactive/2020/04/13/technology/coronavirus-doctor-whistleblower-weibo.html.

Yuan Ruting 袁汝婷. "Shaving the Heads of Female Health Workers?" (给女性医护人员集体剃光头?). *China Comment* (半月谈), February 18, 2020. https://www.sohu.com/a/373898748_118900.

Zeng, Jing. "#MeToo as Connective Action: A Study of the Anti–Sexual Violence and Anti–Sexual Harassment Campaign on Chinese Social Media in 2018." *Journalism Practice* 14, no. 2 (February 7, 2020): 171–90.

Zeng, Jinghan, Tim Stevens, and Yaru Chen. "China's Solution to Global Cyber Governance: Unpacking the Domestic Discourse of 'Internet Sovereignty.'" *Politics and Policy* 45, no. 3 (2017): 432–64.

Zeng, Jinyan. "The Politics of Emotion in Grassroots Feminist Protests: A Case Study of Xiaoming Ai's Nude Breasts Photography Protest Online." *Georgetown Journal of International Affairs* 15, no. 1 (2004): 41–52.

Zhang, Honglong, Liping Wang, Shengjie Lai, Zhongjie Li, Qiao Sun, and Peng Zhang. "Surveillance and Early Warning Systems of Infectious Disease in China: From 2012 to 2014." *International Journal of Health Planning and Management* 32, no. 3 (July 2017): 329–38.

Zhang Kangkang 张抗抗. "Lost Diaries" (遗失的日记). In *When We Were in That Age* (那个年代中的 我们), ed. Zhe Yongping 者永平, 628–34. Beijing: Yuanfang chubanshe, 1998.

Zhang, Li. *Anxious China: Inner Revolution and Politics of Psychotherapy.* Oakland: University of California Press, 2020.

Zhang Shancun 张善存. "An Analysis of the Naming of 'Fire God Mountain' and 'Thunder God Mountain'" ("火神山" "雷神山" 命名探析). *Speech and Writing* (语言文字报), March 11, 2020.

Zhang, Weiyu. *The Internet and New Social Formation in China: Fandom Publics in the Making.* London: Routledge, 2016.

Zhang Xuelin 张雪霖. "A Study of the Reconstruction Mechanisms of Loudspeaker Systems in Rural Areas Against the Background of Media Convergence" (媒介融合背景下乡村'大喇叭'的重建及其机制研究). *Journalism and Communication Review* (新闻与传播评论) 74, no. 2 (2021): 87–97.

Zhang, Yu. "Chinese NGOs Receive Less from Overseas Backers as New Law Stresses National Security." *Global Times*, May 26, 2016. https://www.globaltimes.cn/content/985341.shtml.

Zhang, Ziyi, and Jia Zhang. "The Logic and Regulations of China's Medical Malpractice." *Chinese Public Administration* 1, no. 335 (2015): 137–41.

Zhao, Mengyang. "Solidarity Stalled: When Chinese Activists Meet Social Movements in Democracies." *Critical Sociology* 47, no. 2 (March 2021): 281–97.

Zhao, Yuezhi. *Media, Market, and Democracy in China: Between the Party Line and the Bottom Line*. Urbana: University of Illinois Press, 1998.

Zhong, Yong. "The Chinese Internet: A Separate Closed Monopoly Board." *Journal of International Communication* 18, no. 1 (2012): 19–31.

Zhou Baohua 周葆华 and Zhong Yuan 钟媛. "Social Media, Collective Mourning, and Extended Affective Space: A Computational Communication Analysis of Li Wenliang's Weibo Comments (2020–2021)" (春天的花开秋天的风: 社交媒体、集体悼念与延展性情感空间—以李文亮微博2020–2021 为例的算传播分析). *Chinese Journal of Journalism and Communication* (国际新闻界) 3 (2021): 79–106.

Zhou Yi 周仪, ed. *#MeToo in China Archives, 2018.1–2019.7* (中国米兔志, 2018.1–2019.7). https://www.equalityrights.hku.hk/post/%E4%B8%AD%E5%9C%8B%E7%B1%B3%E5%85%94%E5%BF%97%EF%BC%8820181-2019-7%EF%BC%89.

Zhu Jiangang 朱建刚 and Kin-man Chan 陈健民. "Post-earthquake Disaster Relief: An Opportunity for the Rise of Chinese Civil Society" (抗震救灾: 中国公民社会崛起的契机). *Twenty-First Century* (二十一世纪) 114 (2009): 4–13.

Zhu, Jiangnan, Huang Huang, and Dong Zhang. " 'Big Tigers, Big Data': Learning Social Reactions to China's Anticorruption Campaign Through Online Feedback." *Public Administration Review* 79, no. 4 (2019): 500–513.

Zhu Juanjuan 朱娟娟 and Lei Yu 雷宇. "Eight People Investigated and Dealt with for Spreading Untruthful Information About Wuhan Pneumonia" (8人散布武汉肺炎不实信息被查处). *China Youth Daily* (中国青年报), January 2, 2020. http://www.xinhuanet.com/2020-01/01/c_1125412773.htm.

Zhuangzi. *The Complete Works of Zhuangzi*. Illus. ed. Trans. Burton Watson. New York: Columbia University Press, 2013.

Zweig, Stefan. *Decisive Moments in History: Twelve Historical Miniatures*. Riverside, CA: Ariadne Press, 1999.

INDEX

CPSIA information can be obtained
at www.ICGtesting.com
Printed in the USA
JSHW021437170123
36378JS00001B/72